Jungle Warfare

An Ultimate Handbook

Attention Authors

'We Convert Fighters into Writers.' That's the motto of Manas Publications since more than four decades. Our message to the world is that India can win the battle not only by the bullet but also by the pen. There is no dearth of intellectuals in our country, but their knowledge is confined to them only. No sincere effort has been made by any other publisher to channelise their knowledge in national interest. That is why the talent of a large number of intellectuals remains latent. An author transforms his knowledge into a manuscript, and it is our job to spread his/her knowledge by converting it into a beautiful book. For over four decades, Manas has been motivating the intellectuals by publishing their manuscripts and would like to publish your manuscript too. So if you or your colleagues have any manuscript ready for publication or are working on it, kindly contact us with detailed synopsis and list of contents. We will transform your work into a valuable publication. If you wish, we can also suggest you the suitable subjects for writing the books related to your area of expertise. Manas is known for its publishing quality and commitments. We take utmost care in production and give wide publicity to the book as well as its author through our national and international distribution network.

Jungle Warfare

An Ultimate Handbook

Dr NC Asthana, IPS

Manas Publications
(We Convert Fighters into Writers)
New Delhi-110002 (INDIA)

MANAS PUBLICATIONS

(We Convert Fighters into Writers)
(Publishers, Library Suppliers, Importers & Exporters)
4402/5-A, Ansari Road (Opp. HDFC Bank)
Darya Ganj, New Delhi-110 002 (India)
Off. ✆ 23260783, 23265523, Fax: 011-23272766
E-mail: manaspublications@gmail.com
manaspublications@yahoo.com

2nd Impression 2016

ISBN 978-81-7049-443-0

Rs. 995/-

Designed at
Manas Publications

Printed in India at
RK Print Services, Delhi
and published by Mrs Suman Lata for
Manas Publications, 4402/5-A, Ansari Road
(Opp. HDFC Bank), Darya Ganj,
New Delhi-110 002 (INDIA)

Contents

"If it was risky,
it worked and no one got hurt: you were brilliant.

If it was risky,
it worked and someone got hurt; you were courageous.

If it was risky,
it didn't work and no one got hurt; you were lucky.

If it was risky,
it didn't work and someone got hurt; you were stupid
(and probably dead)".

Acknowledgements

An unprecedented work of this sort could be accomplished only by the grace of the Almighty God and nothing else. Man can only aspire and strive to acquire knowledge; the intellect to comprehend it is given by Him. Equally important is the capability to present knowledge in such a form so that it becomes comprehensible to others also—that's how knowledge is preserved and perpetuated; one of the sacred duties that have been cast upon the human race. This capability too is given by Him. I thank God that in my life, He gave me the opportunities and the resources to acquire knowledge and also the intelligence to comprehend it. I have made an all-out effort to present the subject in such a way that it becomes a source of knowledge and inspiration for posterity. If this work reflects genius and scholarship, the source is none but Him; if some mistakes are left, they are entirely mine. I humbly offer this treatise at His feet for all the kindness He has bestowed upon me.

Preface

No poor bastard ever won a war by making 'Power Point Presentations'; you win a war by blood and guts, and above all, by mastering the art of warfare, the real McCoy. When it comes to the crunch, if you have to fight and fight damned well to survive and win, you got to know the nitty-gritty for yourself. Hence this book.

This treatise is the hitherto most comprehensive exposition of the subject of jungle warfare anywhere in the world. Jungle warfare can take place in two situations. The book has been written to address the requirements of both. The first is jungle warfare in a counter-insurgency situation; the second is jungle warfare in a situation where regular armies are obliged to fight an unconventional war in a forest environment for long. The second type of jungle warfare occurs when armies have to fight with other armies, insurgents or armies fighting in the fashion of insurgents—the only difference is that the scene of action happens to be a jungle. In a warfare involving regular armies fighting in a jungle, all other wings of the armed forces, such as the artillery, armour, and air force etc are actively involved. Such a situation is usually transitory. Some army could be advancing. It might be obliged to negotiate a jungle. The enemy could offer some resistance there. So they fight there. The war takes place in exactly the same manner as it would have taken place in plains—only the terrain differs. The situation becomes different if the enemy refuses to fight on your terms. He may refuse to fight like regular armies do and might start fighting guerrilla fashion or could indulge in irregular warfare of any other kind. The jungle could be vast, or the jungle could be the only battlefield. Vietnam was a classic example—the Americans brought in conventional forces but the enemy refused to fight on their terms. Had they fought conventionally on the terms of the Americans, they would have been easily beaten because they simply could not match the American firepower. Rather, they chose to fight unconventionally. Even though they had large forces that could fight conventionally and had artillery as well as some air power too, they thought it fit to fight guerrilla warfare in their jungles because the Americans were unfamiliar with both. That way they could drag the war to nearly two decades which could have been otherwise over in a few weeks and eventually made it untenable for the Americans. Vietnam had utterly flummoxed the Americans. Even as I hate American ideology, I have the greatest admiration for the tremendous courage with which the Americans fought in Vietnam—I would stand up any day and salute the men who fought there. Still, the fact remains that whatever prestige they could salvage in the jungles of Vietnam was largely due to the great firepower unleashed by the artillery and from the air. The infantry would have been swallowed up in Vietnam had it not been for the napalm and the machine guns from the air and the artillery which very quickly brought in the heavies to land right where they were needed—the Casevac was also as excellent as it could be. Byron Hill, the Forward Observer of the 3rd battalion, 5th Marines recalls about the blood bath at Operation Swift (September 4-15, 1967): "I saw one 155 howitzer which had been fired so long in support of 'Operation Swift' that the tube had actually overheated and warped. The howitzer had to be scrapped"! The morning after the fight an officer walking among the survivors and chatting with them asked one of the young soldiers: "What did you think of the artillery and the air strikes—were they coming in a little close"? The soldier turned on a big grin and replied: "Sir, I was getting sprayed all over. But God, it felt good"!

The first thing the officers did after coming under fire was to radio for help. Before Vietnam, jungle warfare was experienced in the Pacific Theater and in Burma in the Second World War. There is a myth very carefully cultivated by the American propaganda machine that the mighty American military was invincible and that it was due to poor strategic and political handling of the war that they suffered so much—amounting almost to stabbing in the back. This is far from truth. Dispassionate and unbiased analysis is rare. But when it is done, startling truths come tumbling out. As America's most decorated officer of that war, Col David Hackworth, states in his book 'About Face', the myth is now dead. The US military had every advantage, yet mistakes were made and battles lost—from the attack on Camp Holloway in 1965 to the Battle of Koh Tang in 1975, they have made a list of at least 50 battles which the American military had lost in Vietnam. Given their tremendous advantage in artillery and airpower, battles with large American casualties have to be treated as nothing but losses, which led to the decision to eventually withdraw from Vietnam. This is precisely what the Viet Cong always intended to do. They never said that their objective was to seize ground or avoid casualties themselves—all they wanted was to inflict casualties and material losses on the American forces so as to make the war untenable for them. Precisely that's what every insurgent ought to aim for—precisely that's what may be the nemesis of the Indians—counter-insurgencies are wars of attrition, but more of nerves than of resources. Then counter-insurgency war was fought for long in Malaysia, Borneo etc places. But other armies or paramilitary forces fighting in their own counter-insurgency operations may not have the luxury of calling in the artillery and the air support the moment the going got tough. Hence, regular armies must also learn the art and science of jungle warfare sans artillery and air support. I could have used the words 'jungle operations' also. However, that is rather uncommon and most target readership would not have been able to relate to it instantly.

There is no treatise in the whole world, not to speak of India which so comprehensively discusses the art and science of jungle warfare—this is the Bible of jungle warfare. Though there have been numerous books on the subject, they are mostly anecdotal in character. Most of them have been written with an eye on the sensational. That's how you get books which only highlight the exploits of individual soldiers, leaders or elite forces like the British SAS. They might be interesting but they do not, cannot deal with the science of jungle warfare. This leads to the propagation of myths which nobody questions critically. Myths are anathema to science. One of the basic objectives of any science is to bust myths. It is necessary to learn the science because a foolish attitude of claiming to know without knowing always leads to miscalculations and more losses. Army officers are historically known to be dumb and they have a bad habit of thinking that they are invincible and their 'boys' will finish off those 'jokers' in no time—it is all the more true for the Indians. The 'boys' go by their commonsense bereft of any knowledge; and the officers refuse to acquire knowledge. Thus the crisis of knowledge perpetuates. Those in the American establishment who refused to learn from the lessons of Vietnam, paid the price for it in Iraq and Afghanistan. In Vietnam, they had to fall back on artillery and airpower to salvage the men on the ground; in Afghanistan they fell back on the drones. The Indians have nothing on which they may fall back on.

The book hits hard, extremely hard at all the nonsense that has pervaded this field. This book discusses a lot many things about which nothing has ever been published in India or abroad. Though I am known for and excel at making things as simple as possible, this is not a book for dummies. I write only for the sake of posterity. This is a serious reference work and has to have world-class material in it. The knowledge contained within the pages of this book is universal and would be of great use to forces anywhere in the world. However, since I hold a senior position in the Indian forces, it was expected of me to make it of particular relevance to the Indian context. Do not expect stuff that you are used to seeing in training manuals of Indian forces prepared by the intellectually bankrupt for the dumbest of the dumb.

This book is about the art of fighting; not about the morality of war or counter-insurgency operations. I often find myself in the position of several warriors of the epic war of *Mahabharata*. Many of them, including the greatest of them all, Bheeshma, did know where the '*dharma*' (righteous path) or '*adharma*' (deviation from the righteous path) in the war lay and whose side they happened to be. But they also knew where their '*kartavya*' (duty) lay. As warriors, it was their duty, their '*kartavya*', to fight. I too am a warrior by profession. Moreover, I love fighting as an art and I have had occasions to observe first hand that there is hell of a lot that could be done to improve the standards of fighting. Hence this book. According to the Hindu '*shaastra*', one of the duties cast upon mankind is to disseminate knowledge to the deserving so that knowledge is perpetuated. Knowing more than others, it was incumbent upon me to disseminate the knowledge and I have discharged that duty in writing this book.

Dr NC Asthana, IPS

PS: The views expressed in the book are my own and have nothing to do with the Government of India or my official capacity.

1

The Doyens of Guerrilla Warfare and their Theories

A leader is a man, who has the ability to get other people to do what they don't want to do in the first place, and yet come to like it too when they eventually do it.

(1.1) Lenin's Spirited Defence of Guerrilla Warfare

Commenting on the inevitability of revolution, Lenin observed in his work '*People and Revolution*': "A people's insurrection and a people's revolution are not only natural but inevitable". A natural question would be as to how the revolution would take place? Lenin answered the question at length in his '*Collected Works*' '(Vol. 11, 1906): "The question of guerrilla action is one that greatly interests our Party and the mass of the workers. What is its significance in the general course of the revolution"?

The phenomenon in which we are interested is the armed struggle. It is conducted by individuals and by small groups. Some belong to revolutionary organisations, while others (the majority in certain parts of Russia) do not belong to any revolutionary organisation. Armed struggle pursues two different aims, which must be strictly distinguished: in the first place, this struggle aims at assassinating individuals, chiefs and subordinates in the army and police; in the second place, it aims at the confiscation of monetary funds both from the government and from private persons. The confiscated funds go partly into the treasury of the Party, partly for the special purpose of arming and preparing for an uprising, and partly for the maintenance of persons engaged in the struggle.

This form of struggle was adopted as the preferable and even exclusive form of social struggle by the vagabond elements of the population, the lumpen proletariat and anarchist groups. On the other hand, declaration of martial law, mobilisation of fresh troops, Black-hundred pogroms (Sedlets), and military courts must be regarded as the "retaliatory" form of struggle adopted by the autocracy.

The usual appraisal of the struggle we are describing is that it is anarchism, Blanquism, the old terrorism, the acts of individuals isolated from the masses, which demoralise the workers, repel wide strata of the population, disorganise the movement and injure the revolution. Examples in support of this appraisal can easily be found in the events reported every day in the newspapers. But are such examples convincing? The Lettish Social-Democratic Labour Party (a section of the Russian Social-Democratic Labour Party) regularly issues its paper in 30,000 copies. The announcement columns publish lists of spies whom it is the duty of every decent person to exterminate. People who assist the police are proclaimed "enemies of the revolution", liable to execution and, moreover, to confiscation of property. Nobody will be so bold as to call these activities of the Lettish Social-Democrats anarchism, Blanquism or terrorism. But why? Because here we have a clear connection between the new form of struggle and the uprising which is again brewing. The old Russian terrorism was an affair of the intellectual conspirator; today as a general rule guerrilla warfare is waged by the worker combatant, or simply by the unemployed worker. The example of the Letts clearly demonstrates how incorrect, unscientific and unhistorical is the practice so very common among us of analysing guerrilla warfare without reference to the circumstances of an uprising.

Guerrilla warfare is an inevitable form of struggle at a time when the mass movement has actually reached the point of an uprising and when fairly large intervals occur between the "big engagements" in the civil war. A Marxist cannot regard civil war, or guerrilla warfare, which is one of its forms, as abnormal and demoralising in general. A Marxist bases himself on the class struggle, and not social peace. In certain periods of acute economic and political crises the class struggle ripens into a direct civil war, i.e., into an armed struggle between two sections of the people. In such periods, a Marxist is obliged to take the stand of civil war. Any moral condemnation of civil war would be absolutely impermissible from the standpoint of Marxism.

(1.2) Chairman Mao Tse-Tung's Consummate Exposition of Guerrilla Warfare

Never forget that no military leader has ever become great without audacity. If the leader is filled with high ambition, and if he pursues his aims with audacity and strength of will, he will reach them in spite of all obstacles.

Based on more than a decade of his personal experience, and the basic strategy and tactics of warfare as propounded by Sun-tzu, Mao placed great value on guerrilla warfare tactics in a revolutionary war ('Selected Works of Mao Tse-Tung, Vol IX). Written by Chairman Mao in 1937, when Japanese imperialists occupied all of China, this book served as an instruction manual for guerrilla fighting and has become the Bible of red revolutionaries all over the world since then.

(1.2.1) What is Guerrilla Warfare?

In a war of revolutionary character, guerrilla operations are a necessary part. This is particularly true in war waged for the emancipation of a people who inhabit a vast nation. They are the inevitable result of the clash between oppressor and oppressed when the latter reach the limits of their endurance. These guerrilla operations must not be considered as an independent form of warfare. They are but one step in the total war, one aspect of the revolutionary struggle. This warfare must be developed to an unprecedented degree and it must coordinate with the operations of our regular armies. If we fail to do this, we will find it difficult to defeat the enemy.

What is the relationship of guerrilla warfare to the people? Without a political goal, guerrilla warfare must fail, as it must, if its political objectives do not coincide with the aspirations of the people and their sympathy, cooperation, and assistance cannot be gained. The essence of guerrilla warfare is thus revolutionary in character.

What is the organisation for guerrilla warfare? Though all guerrilla bands that spring from the masses of the people suffer from lack of organisation at the time of their formation, they all have in common a basic quality that makes organisation possible. All guerrilla units must have political and military leadership. These men must be well-educated in revolutionary technique, self-confident, able to establish severe discipline, and able to cope with counter-propaganda. This is true regardless of the source or size of such units. Such units may originate locally, in the masses of the people; they may be formed from an admixture of regular troops with groups of the people, or they may consist of regular army units intact.

Unorganised guerrilla warfare cannot contribute to victory and those who attack the movement as a combination of banditry and anarchism do not understand the nature of guerrilla action. We should study the corrupt phenomena and attempt to eradicate them in order to encourage guerrilla warfare, and to increase its military efficiency. The whole people must try to reform themselves during the course of the war.

(1.2.2) *What is Basic Guerrilla Strategy?*

As to the matter of military responsibilities, those of the guerrillas are to exterminate small forces of the enemy; to harass and weaken large forces; to attack enemy lines of communications; to establish bases capable of supporting independent operations in the enemy's rear, to force the enemy to disperse his strength; and to coordinate all these activities with those of the regular armies on distant battle fronts.

The strategy of guerrilla warfare is manifestly unlike that employed in orthodox operations, as the basic tactic of the former is constant activity and movement. There is in guerrilla warfare no such thing as a decisive battle; there is nothing comparable to the fixed, passive defense that characterises orthodox war. In guerrilla warfare, the transformation of a moving situation into a positional defensive situation never arises. The general features of reconnaissance, partial deployment, general deployment, and development of the attack that are usual in mobile warfare are not common in guerrilla war.

Guerrilla strategy must be based primarily on alertness, mobility, and attack. It must be adjusted to the enemy situation, the terrain, the existing lines of communication, the relative strengths, the weather and the situation of the people.

In guerrilla warfare, select the tactic of seeming to come from the east and attacking from the west; avoid the solid, attack the hollow; attack; withdraw; deliver a lightning blow, seek a lightning decision. When guerrillas engage a stronger enemy, they withdraw when he advances; harass him when he stops; strike him when he is weary; pursue him when he withdraws. In guerrilla strategy, the enemy's rear, flanks, and other vulnerable spots are his vital points, and there the enemy must be harassed, attacked, dispersed, exhausted and annihilated.

We must unite the strength of the army with that of the people; we must strike the weak spots in the enemy's flanks, in his front, in his rear. We must make war everywhere and cause dispersal of his forces and dissipation of his strength.

(1.2.3) *The Relation of Guerrilla Hostilities to Regular Operations*

The general features of orthodox hostilities, that is, the war of position and the war of movement, differ fundamentally from guerrilla warfare. There are other readily apparent differences such as those in organisation, armament, equipment supply, tactics, command; in conception of the terms 'front' and 'rear'; in the matter of military responsibilities.

When considered from the point of view of total numbers, guerrilla units are many. As individual combat units, they may vary in size from the smallest, of several score or several hundred men, to the battalion or the regiment, of several thousand. This is not the case in regularly organised units. A primary feature of guerrilla operations is their dependence upon the people themselves to organise battalions and other units. As a result of this, organisation depends largely upon local circumstances. In the case of guerrilla groups, the standard of equipment is of a low order and they must depend for their sustenance primarily upon what the locality affords.

There are differences also in the matter of leadership and command. In guerrilla warfare, small units acting independently play the principal role and there must be no excessive interference with their activities. In orthodox warfare particularly in a moving situation, a certain degree of initiative is accorded to the subordinates, but in principle, command is centralised. This is done because all units and all supporting arms in all districts must coordinate to the highest degree. In the case of guerrilla warfare, this is not only undesirable but impossible. Only adjacent guerrilla units can coordinate their activities to any degree. Strategically, their activities can be roughly correlated with those of the regular forces, and tactically, they must cooperate with adjacent units of the regular army. But there are no strictures on the extent of guerrilla activity nor is it primarily characterised by the quality of cooperation of many units.

When we discuss the terms 'front' and 'rear' it must be remembered that while guerrillas do have bases, their primary field of activity is in the enemy's rear areas. They themselves have no rear. Because an orthodox army has rear installations, it cannot operate as guerrillas can. Orthodox armies may, due to changes in the situation, temporarily function as guerrillas. Likewise, guerrilla units formed from the people may gradually develop into regular units and, when operating as such, employ the tactics of orthodox mobile war. While these units function as guerrillas, they may be compared to innumerable gnats, which, by biting a giant both in front and in rear, ultimately exhaust him. They make themselves as unendurable as a group of cruel and hateful devils, and as they grow and attain gigantic proportions, they will find that their victim is not only exhausted but practically perishing.

The concept that guerrilla warfare is an end in itself and that guerrilla activities can be divorced from those of the regular forces is incorrect. If we do not fit guerrilla operations into their proper niche, we cannot promote them realistically. Guerrillas would be led to assume responsibilities they could not successfully discharge. While we must promote guerrilla warfare as a necessary strategic auxiliary to orthodox operations, we must neither assign it the primary position in our war strategy nor substitute it for mobile and positional warfare as conducted by orthodox forces.

From 1927 to 1936, the Chinese Red Army fought almost continually and employed guerrilla tactics contently. At the very beginning, a positive policy was adopted. Many bases were established and from guerrilla bands, the Reds were able to develop into regular armies. As these armies fought, new guerrilla regimes were developed over a wide area. These regimes coordinated their efforts with those of the regular forces. The leaders of that period properly combined guerrilla operations with a war of movement both strategically and tactically.

(1.2.4) *Organisation for Guerrilla Warfare*

Four points must be considered under this subject. These are:

- How are guerrilla bands formed?
- How are guerrilla bands organised?
- What are the methods of arming guerrilla bands?
- What elements constitute a guerrilla band?

The unit may originate in any one of the following ways:

a) From the masses of the people.

b) From regular army units temporarily detailed for the purpose.

c) From regular army units permanently detailed.

d) From the combination of a regular army unit and a unit recruited from the people.

e) From the local militia.

f) From deserters from the ranks of the enemy.

g) From former bandits and bandit groups.

In spite of inescapable differences in the fundamental types of guerrilla bands, it is possible to unite them to form a vast sea of guerrillas. The ancients said, "Tai Shan is a great mountain because it does not scorn the merest handful of dirt; the rivers and seas are deep because they absorb the waters of small streams".

Without question, the fountainhead of guerrilla warfare is in the masses of the people, who organise guerrilla units directly from themselves. There are those who say: 'I am a farmer', or, 'I am a student'; "I can discuss literature but not military arts". This is incorrect. There is no profound difference between the farmer and the soldier. You must have courage. You simply leave your farms and become soldiers. That you are farmers is of no difference, and if you have education, that is so much the better. When you take your arms in hand, you become soldiers; when you are organised, you become military units. Guerrilla hostilities are the University of War, and after you have fought several times valiantly and aggressively, you may become a leader of troops and there will be many well-known regular soldiers who will not be your peers.

(1.2.5) Organisation of Guerrilla Units

Since Chairman Mao was not short of willing men, he took the liberty of organising his guerrilla squads, platoons, companies, battalions, regiments, divisions on standard military pattern, though he allowed considerable flexibility in weapons because they were not as abundant. "Each combatant soldier should be armed with the rifle. If there are not enough rifles, each squad should have two or three. Shotguns, lances, and big swords can also be furnished. The distribution of rifles does not have to be equalised in platoons. As different missions are assigned to platoons, it may be necessary to give one platoon more rifles than the others. Each company must have at least 25 rifles. The remaining weapons may be fowling pieces, etc., big swords, or locally made shotguns".

Mao was very keen on intelligence. In company strength of 122 men, he provided 10 men for intelligence alone. He was flexible about some other duties. For example: "If there are insufficient personnel, the medical section is not separately organised. If there are only two or three medical personnel, they may be attached to the administrative section". "If there is no barber, it is unimportant. If there is an insufficient number of cooks, any member of the company may be designated to prepare food". "If no men are available for stretcher-bearers, omit them and use the cooks or ask aid from the people".

The equipment of guerrillas cannot be based on what the guerrillas want, to even what they need, but must be based on what is available for their use. Equipment cannot be furnished immediately but must be acquired gradually. After a period of resistance, it is possible to increase the supply of equipment by capturing it from the enemy. The enemy is the principal source of their supply.

For destruction of railway tracks, bridges, and stations in enemy-controlled territory, it is necessary to gather together demolition materials. Troops must be trained in the preparation and use of demolitions, and a demolition unit must be organised in each regiment.

In the guerrilla army in general, and at bases in particular, there must be a high standard of medical equipment. Besides the services of the doctors, medicines must be procured. Although guerrillas can depend on the enemy for some portion of their medical supplies, they must, in general, depend upon contributions. Mao had no aversion to western medicine and he says: "If Western medicines are not available, local medicines must be made to suffice".

Propaganda materials are very important. Every large guerrilla unit should have a printing press and a mimeograph stone. They must also have paper on which to print propaganda leaflets and notices. They must be supplied with large brushes. In guerrilla areas, there should be a printing press or a lead-type press.

(1.2.6) The Method of Organising Guerrilla Regimes

The subject of the organisation of such regimes is not confined to the organisation of specific units but includes all guerrilla activities within the area where the regime functions. As an example of such organisation, we may take a geographical area in the enemy's rear. To this 'military area', a military commander and political commissioners are appointed. In the military headquarters, there will be the staff, the aides, the supply officers, and the medical personnel. They are controlled by the chief of staff, who acts in accordance with orders from the commander. In the political headquarters, there are bureaus of propaganda organisation, people's mass movements, and miscellaneous affairs. Control of these is vested in the political chairman.

Under these, the necessary officers both military and political, are appointed. The military areas are sub-divided into smaller districts in accordance with local geography, the enemy situation locally, and the state of guerrilla development. Each of these smaller divisions within the area is a district, each of which may consist of from two to six counties. To each district, a military commander and several political commissioners are appointed. Under their direction,. military and political headquarters are organised. Tasks are assigned in accordance with the number of guerrilla troops available.

All the people in an area should arm themselves and be organised into two groups. One of these groups is a combat group, the other a self-defence unit with but limited military quality. All the people of both sexes from the ages of sixteen to forty-five must be organised into self-defence units, the basis of which is voluntary service. As a first step, they must procure arms, and then they must be given both military and political training. Their responsibilities are: local sentry duties, securing information of the enemy, arresting traitors, and preventing the dissemination of enemy propaganda. When the enemy launches a guerrilla-suppression drive, these units, armed with what weapons there are, are assigned to certain areas to deceive, hinder, and harass him. Thus, the defence units assist the combatant guerrillas. If a locality can organise such a self-defence unit as we have described, the traitors cannot hide nor can bandits and robbers disturb the peace of the people. Thus the people will continue to assist the guerrilla and supply manpower to our regular armies. 'The organisation of self-defence units is a transitional step in the development of universal conscription. Such units are reservoirs of manpower for the orthodox forces'.

Regular combatant guerrillas are organised into one of three general types of units. The first of these is the small unit, the platoon or company. In each county, three to six units may be organised. The second type is the battalion of from two to four companies. One such unit should be organised in each county. While the unit fundamentally belongs to the county where it was organised, it may operate in other counties. While in areas other than its own, it must operate in conjunction with local units in order to take advantage of their manpower, their knowledge of local terrain and local customs, and their information of the enemy. The third type is the guerrilla regiment, which consists of from two to four of the above-mentioned battalion units. If sufficient manpower is available, a guerrilla brigade of from two to four regiments may be formed.

(1.2.7) Elements of the Guerrilla Army

The term 'element' as used in the title to this section refers to the personnel, both officers and men, of the guerrilla army. A guerrilla group ought to operate on the principle that only volunteers are acceptable for service. It is a mistake to impress people into service. As long as a person is willing to fight, his social condition or position is no consideration, but only men who are courageous and determined can bear the hardships of guerrilla campaigning in a protracted war. Since each guerrilla group fights in a protracted war, its officers must be brave and positive men. The most important natural quality is that of complete loyalty to the idea of people's emancipation. If this is present, the others will develop; if it is not present, nothing can be done. An officer should have the following qualities: great powers of endurance so that in spite of any hardship he sets an example to his men and be a model for them; he must be able to mix easily with the people; his spirit and that of the men must be one in strengthening the policy of resistance. If in any locality there are not enough men of sufficiently high qualifications to become officers, an effort must be made to train and educate the people so these qualities may be developed and the potential officer material increased. There can be no disagreements between officers native to one place and those from other localities.

A soldier who habitually breaks regulations must be dismissed from the army. Vagabonds and vicious people must not be accepted for service. Victory in guerrilla war is conditioned upon keeping the membership pure and clean. The traitors who are in the ranks must be discovered and expelled, and punishment and expulsion meted out to those who have been influenced by them. In all such cases, the officers should summon the soldiers and relate the facts to them, thus arousing their hatred and detestation for traitors. This procedure will serve as well as a warning to the other soldiers. A revolutionary army must have discipline that is established on a limited democratic basis. In all armies, obedience of the subordinates to their superiors must be exacted. This is true in the case of guerrilla discipline, but the basis for guerrilla discipline must be the individual conscience. With guerrillas, a discipline of compulsion is ineffective. Discipline must be self-imposed, because only when it is, is the soldier able to understand completely, why he fights and why he must obey. The idea that officers can physically beat or severely tongue-lash their men is a feudal one and is not in accord with the conception of self-imposed discipline. Discipline of the feudal type will destroy internal unity and fighting strength.

Further, in such an army, the mode of living of the officers and the soldiers must not differ too much, and this is particularly true in the case of guerrilla troops. Officers should live under the same conditions as their men, for that is the only way in which they can gain from their men the admiration and confidence so vital in war. It is incorrect to hold to a theory of equality in all things but there must be equality of existence in accepting the hardships and dangers of war.

(1.2.8) *The Political Problems of Guerrilla Warfare*

There are some militarists who say: "We are not interested in politics but only in the profession of arms". It is vital that these simple-minded militarists be made to realise the relationship that exists between politics and military affairs. Military action is a method used to attain a political goal. While military affairs and political affairs are not identical, it is impossible to isolate one from the other. Political activities are the life of both the guerrilla armies and of revolutionary warfare. In a war of long duration, those whose conviction that the people must be emancipated is not deep-rooted are likely to become shaken in their faith or actually revolt. Hence, a concrete explanation of the political systems used is important not only to guerrilla troops but to all those who are concerned with the realisation of our political goal.

The Eighth Route Army put into practice a code known as "Three Rules and the Eight Remarks", which we list here. The Red Army adhered to this code for ten years.

Rules:

- All actions are subject to command.
- Do not steal from the people.
- Be neither selfish nor unjust.

Remarks:

- Replace the door when you leave the house.
- Roll up the bedding on which you have slept.
- Be courteous.
- Be honest in your transactions.
- Return what you borrow.
- Replace what you break.
- Do not bathe in the presence of women.
- Do not without authority search those you arrest.

Many people think it impossible for guerrillas to exist for long in the enemy's rear. Such a belief reveals lack of comprehension of the relationship that should exist between the people and the troops. The former may be likened to water and the latter to the fish who inhabit it. How may it be said that these two cannot exist together? It is only undisciplined troops, who make the people their enemies and who, like the fish out of its native element cannot live.

(1.3) Ernesto 'Che' Guevara Hones the Concepts Further

(1.3.1) Essence of Guerrilla Warfare

Guerrilla warfare, the basis of the struggle of a people to redeem itself, has diverse characteristics, different facets, even though the essential will for liberation remains the same. Though geographical and social conditions in each country determine the mode and particular forms that guerrilla warfare will take, there are general laws that hold for all fighting of this type. The armed victory of the Cuban people over the Batista dictatorship was not only the triumph of heroism as reported by the newspapers of the world; it also forced a change in the old dogmas concerning the conduct of the popular masses of Latin America. It showed plainly the capacity of the people to free themselves by means of guerrilla warfare from a government that oppressed them. It proved that popular forces could win a war against the army. It also showed that it is not necessary to wait until all conditions for making revolution exist; the insurrection can create them. It contradicted the defeatist attitude of revolutionaries or pseudo-revolutionaries, who remain inactive and take refuge in the pretext that against a professional army nothing can be done; who sit down to wait until in some mechanical way all necessary objective and subjective conditions are given without working to accelerate them.

Who are the combatants in guerrilla warfare? Guerrilla warfare is used by the side which is supported by a majority but which possesses a much smaller number of arms for use in defense against oppression. The guerrilla band is not to be considered inferior to the army against which it fights simply because it is inferior in firepower. It is important to emphasise that guerrilla warfare is a war of the masses, a war of the people. The guerrilla band is an armed nucleus, the fighting vanguard of the people. The guerrilla fighter needs full help from the people of the area. This is an indispensable condition. This is clearly seen by considering the case of bandit gangs that operate in a region. They have all the characteristics of a guerrilla army: homogeneity, respect for the leader, valour, knowledge of the ground, and, often, even good understanding of the tactics to be employed. The only thing missing is support of the people; and, inevitably, these gangs are captured and exterminated by the public force. Why does the guerrilla fighter fight? We must come to the inevitable conclusion that the guerrilla fighter is a social reformer, that he takes up arms responding to the angry protest of the people against their oppressors, and that he fights in order to change the social system that keeps all his unarmed brothers in ignominy and misery.

The struggles of the city masses of organised workers should not be underrated; but their real possibilities of engaging in armed struggle must be carefully analysed where the guarantees which customarily adorn our constitutions are suspended or ignored. In these conditions the illegal workers' movements face enormous dangers. They must function secretly without arms. The situation in the open country is not so difficult. There, in places beyond the reach of the repressive forces, the inhabitants can be supported by the armed guerrillas.

When we analyse more fully the tactic of guerrilla warfare, we will see that the guerrilla fighter needs to have a good knowledge of the surrounding countryside, the paths of entry and escape, the possibilities of speedy manoeuvre, good hiding places; naturally, also, he must count on the support of the people. All this indicates that the guerrilla fighter will carry out his action in wild places of small population. The fundamental principle is that no battle, combat, or skirmish is to be fought unless it will be won. There is a malevolent definition that says: "The guerrilla fighter is the Jesuit of warfare". By this is indicated a quality of secretiveness, of treachery, of surprise that is obviously an essential element of guerrilla warfare. It is a special kind of Jesuitism, naturally prompted by circumstances, which necessitates acting at certain moments in ways different from the romantic and sporting conceptions with which we are taught to believe war is fought.

Besides using force, they will have recourse to all possible tricks and stratagems in order to achieve the goal. These means contemplate taking advantage of all the weak points of the enemy. "Hit and run", some call this scornfully, and this is accurate. Hit and run, wait, lie in ambush, again hit and run, and thus repeatedly, without giving any rest to the enemy. There is in all this, it would appear, a negative quality, an attitude of retreat, of avoiding frontal fights. Just as the general of a division in a modern war does not have to die in front of his soldiers, the guerrilla fighter, who is general of himself, need not die in every battle. He is ready to give his life, but the positive quality of this guerrilla warfare is precisely that each one of the guerrilla fighters is ready to die, not to defend an ideal, but rather to convert it into reality. This is the basis, the essence of guerrilla fighting. Thus, it is clear that guerrilla warfare is a phase that does not afford in itself opportunities to arrive at complete victory. It is one of the initial phases of warfare and will develop continuously until the guerrilla army in its steady growth acquires the characteristics of a regular army. At that moment it will be ready to deal final blows to the enemy and to achieve victory. Triumph will always be the product of a regular army, even though its origins are in a guerrilla army.

(1.3.2) Guerrilla Strategy

The guerrilla fighter, on the other hand, must analyse the resources which the enemy has for trying to achieve that outcome: the means in men, in mobility, in popular support, in armaments, in capacity of leadership on which he can count. The essential task of the guerrilla fighter is to keep himself from being destroyed. Little by little it will be easier for the members of the guerrilla band or bands to adapt themselves to their form of life and to make flight and escape from the forces that are on the offensive an easy task, because it is performed daily. When this condition is reached, the guerrilla, having taken up inaccessible positions out of reach of the enemy, or having assembled forces that deter the enemy from attacking, ought to proceed to the gradual weakening of the enemy. This will be carried out at first at those points nearest to the points of active warfare against the guerrilla band and later will be taken deeper into enemy territory, attacking his communications, later attacking or harassing his bases of operations and his central bases, tormenting him on all sides to the full extent of the capabilities of the guerrilla forces.

The blows should be continuous. The enemy soldier in a zone of operations ought not to be allowed to sleep. At every moment the impression ought to be created that he is surrounded by a complete circle. In wooded and broken areas this effort should be maintained both day and night; in open zones that are easily penetrated by enemy patrols, at night only. In order to do all this absolute cooperation of the people and a perfect knowledge of the ground are necessary. These two necessities affect every minute of the life of the guerrilla fighter. Therefore, along with centers for study of present and future zones of operations, intensive popular work must be undertaken to explain the motives of the revolution, its ends, and to spread the incontrovertible truth that victory of the enemy against the people is finally impossible. Whoever does not feel this undoubted truth cannot be a guerrilla fighter.

This popular work should at first be aimed at securing secrecy; that is, each peasant, each member of the society in which action is taking place, will be asked not to mention what he sees and hears; later, help will be sought from inhabitants whose loyalty to the revolution offers greater guarantees; still later, use will be made of these persons in missions of contact, for transporting goods or arms, as guides in the zones familiar to them; still later, it is possible to arrive at organised mass action in the centers of work, of which the final result will be a very important factor in civil war, namely, the general strike.

Another of the terrible arms of the guerrilla band is sabotage. With sabotage, it is possible to paralyse entire armies, to suspend the industrial life of a zone, leaving the inhabitants of a city without factories, without light, without water, without communications of any kind, without being able to risk travel by highway except at certain hours. If all this is achieved, the morale of the enemy falls, the morale of his combatant units weakens, and the fruit ripens for plucking at a precise moment. It is ridiculous to carry out sabotage against a soft-drink factory, but it is absolutely correct and advisable to carry out sabotage against a power plant. In the first case, a certain number of workers are put out of a job but nothing is done to modify the rhythm of industrial life; in the second case, there will again be displaced workers, but this is entirely justified by the paralysis of the life of the region.

All this presupposes an increase in the territory included within the guerrilla action, but an excessive increase of this territory is to be avoided. When the guerrilla band has reached a respectable power in arms and in number of combatants, it ought to proceed to the formation of new columns. This is an act similar to that of the beehive when at a given moment it releases a new queen, who goes to another region with a part of the swarm. The mother hive with the most notable guerrilla chief will stay in the less dangerous places, while the new columns will penetrate other enemy territories. A moment will arrive in which the territory occupied by the columns is too small for them; and in the advance toward regions solidly defended by the enemy, it will be necessary to confront powerful forces. At that instant the columns join, they offer a compact fighting front, and a war of positions is reached, a war carried on by regular armies. However, the former guerrilla army cannot cut itself off from its base, and it should create new guerrilla bands behind the enemy acting in the same way as the original bands operated earlier, proceeding thus to penetrate enemy territory until it is dominated.

It is thus that guerrillas reach the stage of attack, of the encirclement of fortified bases, of the defeat of reinforcements, of mass action, ever more ardent, in the whole national territory, arriving finally at the objective of the war: victory.

(1.3.3) Guerrilla Tactics

The numerical inferiority of the guerrilla makes it necessary that attacks always be carried out by surprise; this great advantage is what permits the guerrilla fighter to inflict losses on the enemy without suffering losses. A dead soldier of the guerrillas ought never to be left with his arms and his ammunition. The fundamental characteristic of a guerrilla band is mobility. This permits it in a few minutes to move far from a specific theatre and in a few hours far even from the region, if that becomes necessary; permits it constantly to change front and avoid any type of encirclement. As the circumstances of the war require, the guerrilla band can dedicate itself exclusively to fleeing from an encirclement which is the enemy's only way of forcing the band into a decisive fight that could be unfavourable; it can also change the battle into a counter-encirclement (small bands of men are presumably surrounded by the enemy when suddenly the enemy is surrounded by stronger contingents; or men located in a safe place serve as a lure, leading to the encirclement and annihilation of the entire troops and supply of an attacking force).

Characteristic of this war of mobility is the so-called minuet, named from the analogy with the dance: the guerrilla bands encircle an enemy position, an advancing column, for example; they encircle it completely from the four points of the compass, with five or six men in each place, far enough away to avoid being encircled themselves; the fight is started at any one of the points, and the army moves toward it; the guerrilla band then retreats, always maintaining visual contact, and initiates its attack from another point. The army will repeat its action and the guerrilla band, the same. Thus, successively, it is possible to keep an enemy column immobilised, forcing it to expend large quantities of ammunition and weakening the morale of its troops without incurring great dangers.

Another fundamental characteristic of the guerrilla soldier is his flexibility. Against the rigidity of classical methods of fighting, the guerrilla fighter invents his own tactics at every minute of the fight and constantly surprises the enemy. In the first place, there are only elastic positions, specific places that the enemy cannot pass, and places of diverting him. The form of attack of a guerrilla army is also different; starting with surprise and fury, irresistible, it suddenly converts itself into total passivity. The surviving enemy, resting, believes that the attacker has departed; he begins to relax, to return to the routine life of the camp or of the fortress, when suddenly a new attack bursts forth in another place, with the same characteristics, while the main body of the guerrilla band lies in wait to intercept reinforcements. At other times an outpost defending the camp will be suddenly attacked by the guerrilla, dominated, and captured. The fundamental thing is surprise and rapidity of attack.

Terrorism, a measure that is generally ineffective and indiscriminate in its results, since it often makes victims of innocent people and destroys a large number of lives that would be valuable to the revolution. Terrorism should be considered a valuable tactic when it is used to put to death some noted leader of the oppressing forces well known for his cruelty, his efficiency in repression, or other quality that makes his elimination useful. But the killing of persons of small importance is never advisable, since it brings on an increase of reprisals, including deaths.

One of the weakest points of the enemy is transportation by road and railroad. It is virtually impossible to maintain a vigil yard by yard over a transport line, a road, or a railroad. At any point a considerable amount of explosive charge can be planted that will make the road impassable; or by exploding it at the moment that a vehicle passes, a considerable loss in lives and materiel to the enemy is caused at the same time that the road is cut.

The technique of lying in ambush along roads in order to explode mines and annihilate survivors is one of the most remunerative in point of ammunition and arms. The surprised enemy does not use his ammunition and has no time to flee, so with a small expenditure of ammunition large results are achieved. As blows are dealt, the enemy also changes his tactics, and in place of isolated trucks, veritable motorised columns move. However, by choosing the ground well, the same result can be produced by breaking the column and concentrating forces on one vehicle. In these cases the essential elements of guerrilla tactics must always be kept in mind. These are: perfect knowledge of the ground; surveillance and foresight as to the lines of escape; vigilance over all the secondary roads that can bring support to the point of attack; intimacy with people in the zone so as to have sure help from them in respect to supplies, transport, and temporary or permanent hiding places if it becomes necessary to leave wounded companions behind; numerical superiority at a chosen point of action; total mobility; and the possibility of counting on reserves.

(1.3.4) Warfare on Favourable Ground

When the guerrilla band is located in zones difficult to reach, either because of dense forests, steep mountains, impassable deserts or marshes, the guerrilla band should advance to the regions where the army can arrive and where there will be a possibility of combat. As soon as the survival of the guerrilla band has been assured, it should fight; it must constantly go out from its refuge to fight. Nocturnal character of warfare in this situation is not so important; it will be possible in many cases to carry out daytime operations. The mobility of the band does not have to be as great as in those cases where the ground is unfavourable; because the band must adjust itself to the capabilities of the enemy to engage it. It is also possible to persist in a military action for a much longer time. His aggressiveness (on account of the difficulties that the enemy faces in bringing up reinforcements) can be greater, he can approach the enemy more closely, fight much more directly, more frontally, and for a longer time, though these rules may be qualified by various circumstances, such, for example, as the amount of ammunition.

(1.3.5) *Warfare on Unfavourable Ground*

All favourable conditions, all facilities of life normally induce men to settle; but for the guerrilla band the opposite is the case. The more facilities there are for social life, the more nomadic, the more uncertain the life of the guerrilla fighter. Hiding and taking refuge amongst the people does become a problem. The reprisals of the enemy are so violent, usually so brutal, inflicted not only on the head of the family but frequently on the women and children as well, that pressure on individuals lacking firmness may result at any moment in their giving way and revealing information as to where the guerrilla band is located and how it is operating. This would immediately produce encirclement. The guerrilla bands on the plain suffer the enormous inconvenience of being subject to a rapid encirclement and of not having sure places where they can set up a firm resistance; therefore, they must live in conditions of absolute secrecy for a long time, since it would be dangerous to trust any neighbour whose fidelity is not perfectly established. In order to carry on warfare in country that is not very hilly, lacks forests, and has many roads, the mobility of this type of guerrilla should be extraordinary; strikes should be made preferably at night; they should be extremely rapid, but the guerrilla should move to places different from the starting point, the farthest possible from the scene of action, assuming that there is no place secure from the repressive forces that the guerrilla can use as its garrison. A man can walk between 30 and 50 kilometers during the night hours. Action cannot endure for long, but must be rapid; it must be of a high degree of effectiveness, last a few minutes, and be followed by an immediate withdrawal.

The number of men that a guerrilla band of this type should include does not exceed ten to fifteen. In forming a single combat unit it is of great importance always to consider the limitations on numbers: ten, twelve, fifteen men can hide anywhere and at the same time can help each other in putting up a powerful resistance to the enemy. Four or five would perhaps be too small a number, but when the number exceeds ten, the possibility that the enemy will discover them in their camp or on the march is much greater.

(1.3.6) *Suburban Warfare*

The importance of a suburban struggle has usually been underestimated; it is really very great. A good operation of this type extended over a wide area paralyses almost completely the commercial and industrial life of the sector and places the entire population in a situation of unrest, of anguish, almost of impatience for the development of violent events that will relieve the period of suspense. However, it is fundamental to recognise that a suburban guerrilla band can never spring up of its own accord. It will be born only after certain conditions necessary for its survival have been created. It ought not to number more than four or five men. The limitation on numbers is important, because the suburban guerrilla must be considered as situated in exceptionally unfavourable ground, where the vigilance of the enemy will be much greater and the possibilities of reprisals as well as of betrayal are increased enormously. The essential qualities of the guerrilla fighter in this situation are discipline (perhaps in the highest degree of all) and discretion. He cannot count on more than two or three friendly houses that will provide food; it is almost certain that encirclement in these conditions will be equivalent to death. Another aggravating circumstance is that the suburban guerrilla band cannot depart far from the places where it is going to operate. To speed of action and withdrawal there must be added a limitation on the distance of withdrawal from the scene of action and the need to remain totally hidden during the daytime. This is a nocturnal guerrilla band in the extreme, without possibilities of changing its manner of operating until the insurrection is so far advanced that it can take part as an active combatant in the siege of the city.

The suburban guerrilla will always be under the direct orders of chiefs located in another zone. The function of this guerrilla band will not be to carry out independent actions but to coordinate its activities with overall strategic plans in such a way as to support the action of larger groups situated in another area, contributing specifically to the success of a fixed tactical objective, without the operational freedom of guerrilla bands of the other types. If its function is to cut down telephone poles or electric wires, to destroy sewers, railroads, or water mains, it will limit itself to carrying out these tasks efficiently. They will concentrate their action on prescribed sabotage and never carry out armed attacks, except by surprising one or two members or agents of the enemy troops.

2

What the Jungle means to a Warrior?

There is no job in the jungle for the weak, the timid or the indecisive.

(2.1) Myths and Folklore about Jungle Warfare

Most people have highly exotic notions about the jungles and jungle warfare—shaped largely by Hollywood films—and they are highly reluctant to question them because they do not question anything anyway. Think of jungle warfare and the first thing that comes to mind is 'Rambo; First Blood Part II'. That Rambo is perfectly adept at using a variety of weapons ranging from his iconic survival knife and Torque Bow shooting explosive-tipped arrows to the legendary M60 machinegun can perhaps be understood as cinematic license. That he displays an incredibly varied and one might dare say, perversely imaginative prowess at killing people—shooting, strangling, and stabbing with grace that could put a ballerina to shame can be pardoned as the result of the supposedly great training the Americans imparted to their Green Berets. That a very large number of AK-47 bullets fired at him by Viet Cong and Russian soldiers refuse to touch his lovely, heavily-muscled and chiseled body can be passed off as examples of American jingoism. That he stoically endures tortures of massive electric shocks and some surgically precise cuttings by a white-hot knife blade are copybook examples of tough American guys. Yes, we all love hardcore machismo, don't we? If you were not fascinated by Rambo, you were not man enough. But one thing puzzles me and it should puzzle you also if you have any mind. Did you ever see Rambo eat anything, drink anything, sleep a moment or, God forbid, take a leak or shit? Looks like, Rambo does not have such mundane human necessities. And this cannot be pardoned or passed off as a cinematic license. Why did we not raise this question? By the time dear John Rambo left Vietnam, there was hardly any tree, hut or stupid villager left standing in half of Vietnam, and yet Rambo had no occasion to eat a bite! The myths were carried further in other blockbusters like 'Predator' starring Arnold Schwarzenegger. Gentlemen, real life is different. More than half the stuff real soldiers are obliged to haul over their straining backs consists of food, water, shelter, change of clothes, medicines—essentials that they need to survive.

Jungle warfare is not about bare-bodied Rambos blazing away non-stop with everything ranging from torque bows to machineguns

Some other notions make the jungle appear a place where venomous snakes crawl everywhere—and you are not a true-blooded jungle warrior unless you catch them by the tail, dangle them upside down for your buddies to see, roast them over open fire and eat them regularly! If you are more macho or belong to one of those Mongoloid races, you must cut off the cobra's head and drink his blood straight from the body—they actually do that in the exercise Cobra Gold in Thailand before the US Marines. Remember, how a bamboo viper slithers out of a tree to attack Rambo; one swift move and he chokes it with his bare hand. Now that's macho—but Rambo did not stop to eat him because he did not need to! If at all some guy in a Hollywood movie needed food, one could fish trout in the streams—his survival knife would have a fishing line and hook inside its handle!

Jungle warfare is not about drinking blood of cobras either

Life was certainly more difficult before Hollywood films provided solutions to every problem. "To our men the jungle was a strange, fearsome place; moving and fighting in it were a nightmare. We were too ready to classify jungle as 'impenetratable'. To us it appeared only as an obstacle to movement; to the Japanese it was a welcome means of concealed manoeuvre and surprise. The Japanese reaped the deserved reward; we paid the penalty". Field Marshal William Slim's words, commenting on the dark, early days of the Burma campaign during the Second World War, reflect the image of the jungle most armies carry into jungle warfare. In a country like India where you have many insurgencies and where a large number of insurgents like the naxals (professedly ultra-leftists) and secessionists in the north-eastern states are mostly tribal people and operate from dense jungles, people keep on wondering as to what is keeping the government from eliminating them? A popular refrain is that the Indian troops are not well-versed in the art of jungle warfare or operating in the jungles—clearly implying, if not insinuating outright that fighting in the jungles is a secret art in which only Rambo or those tribal people excel—Rambo, because of his out-of-the-world training and the tribal people because they have been born and brought up there. Well, that should lead to a natural question as to what is so mysterious or difficult about jungle operations. This book shall demystify the business of jungle warfare.

The entire business of jungle warfare or operations in jungles is laced liberally with folklore and myths. One of the most prevalent myths is that those who are born near jungles or in deep rural areas are intrinsically better suited for fighting there in the sense that they are tougher people; they may not be able to bench press as much weight as a soldier can do but they can survive on far lesser food, can drink even contaminated water and can walk tirelessly for an unlimited length of time. From this derives the myth that the tribal people and the guerrillas who live in rural areas and jungles are intrinsically superior fighters when it comes to fighting in jungles in comparison to those soldiers who do not come from such backgrounds and who have been raised in an urban setting. Another myth is about 'living off the land'. Most people imagine that the insurgents live off the land—either hunting game in the jungles or eating whatever that comes their way—whereas the soldiers have to carry huge loads of provisions which make them ponderous and less mobile—a clear disadvantage in combat. Leave that to the Hollywood films and the dumb Indians, dear. Living off the land is a full-time occupation. Soldiers are supposed to fight; that's their primary task—not to waste their time in ensnaring a solitary bird by an improvised snare. Even if you catch a bird, it would not suffice for even two guys—you are many times that!

(2.2) Scientific Scrutiny Busts the Myths

Such myths and notions have no scientific basis. Granted that people who are born in or near certain rural/jungle areas do know them better than any outsider but it does not mean that they have been blessed with a constitution that would defy the basic biological limitations of the human body. Granted that a rustic tribal (or a self-trained man like Cody Lundin you see on the Discovery Channel programme 'Dual Survival') who hasn't worn a shoe in 20 years, can walk barefoot in jungles for 40 km. It, however, does not mean that soldiers wearing proper jungle boots cannot walk 40 km. And why should the soldiers not be found wearing jungle boots? The chances that they would ever land in a situation where they would not have even boots on their feet are hopelessly low. In all other situations, if reflects badly on armies in general and the concerned commanders in particular if the soldiers do not have proper jungle boots. You must understand that the environment affects everyone. The degree to which soldiers are trained to live and fight in harsh environments will determine their unit's success or failure. It is all about adaptation and a basically fit man will adapt in due course.

The enemy or the insurgents do not have a monopoly on jungle know-how. The US army had discovered that US units adapted quickly and well to jungle fighting, and when they operated against the North Vietnamese along the Cambodian border they found that the VC (Viet Cong) had as much difficulty operating in the area as they had. The 25th Infantry Division has had reported on record that the prisoners they had captured were, as a rule, undernourished, emaciated, and sick with malaria. They stated that almost everyone in their unit had malaria, and many had even died from it. That's correct and commonsense too. Science does not know of any resistance or immunity to malaria that could be built up naturally. The fact is that at first, the jungle seems to be very hostile, but the hostility wanes as troops learn more about the jungle environment.

Another jungle myth that was popular both during World War II and the Vietnam War was that "the night belongs to the enemy". The simple scientific fact is that the enemy has no better night vision or stealth than do trained soldiers. Biologically, he is also a homo sapiens and cannot have night vision like some animals. The only advantage the enemy has is that of the element of surprise. If he is hiding in the jungles, he could be waiting for you—if he sees you first, he can fire first. The point being made is that except the fact that, barring the advantage of surprise at times, he has no other intrinsic advantage. On the contrary, you have the advantage of more extensive and more systematic training—he is certainly not as skilled a fighter as you are. Remember, millions of men have fought in the jungles since Burma, Philippines, the Pacific Islands, Malaysia and Vietnam. With the experience of millions of men having fought in the jungles behind you, there is no excuse for not fighting well. You can; you must; and by Jove, you will fight well.

Bereft of this belief, most troops are actually likely to literally blunder in the jungle. The US army has had very succinctly described that too. During the fog of war and the confusion of the night LGOPs (Little Groups of Paratroopers) rule. These are best described as handfuls of lost, heavily armed, seriously scared, 18-19-year-old kids wandering around in the dark lacking any serious, experienced, adult supervision. They've received a detailed operations order and have promptly forgotten most of it. But they vaguely remember their commander's intent as being something like, "Move toward the sound of the shooting and kill anybody who is not dressed like you"!

(2.3) Romanticised Notions of the Jungle

Never attribute to malice that can be ascribed to sheer stupidity.

Till a good part of the 20th century western armed forces had heard only stories about jungles. Their notions stemmed from the accounts of intrepid civilian travellers and explorers like Dr Livingstone or hunters like Frederick Selous who had been wandering in the jungles of Africa in a show of academic curiosity, missionary zeal or simply macho bravado. Nobody in the armed forces had any direct idea of the jungle. As a result, the jungle was considered both exotic and fascinating. It continued to fascinate them even as they were obliged to be in it and fight there. The following is an account from 'Jungle Survival: A Personal Narrative' by Major Frank Clark of the British army which very typically illustrates how they viewed the jungle and all that it entailed. Back home they had the woods and the deep woods; here they had something which was both creepy and dangerous – the very strangeness of the jungle became more important than the art of war there; a reaction very typical of the English pubic school boys who were fascinated and intrigued by all things Oriental!

"We were picking our way through the jungle. I was an untrained soldier in jungle warfare and was being indoctrinated into the green hell. The jungle training course was for several weeks and I will never forget the humidity, the stench of rotting vegetation, the deprivation of daylight by the greatness of the dark canopy above and its eerie feeling of being enveloped by the gloom. This was my first introduction to the jungle although I was not a raw National Serviceman, just out from UK, poor buggers. I had lived rough on the battlefield and did consider myself a trained solider. In 1944, I had landed in Normandy and had fought throughout the war. Later, posted to Korea theatre where I spent a year of my three years in the Far East before being sent to Malaya for the last two years. Afterwards, I served a further three years tour this time in North Malaya Sub-district based originally at Taiping, Perak and later at Prai near RAAF Butterworth and Penang, thus making a total of five years service in the peninsular but this was in the future. Right now I was as inexperienced as the young National Service lads in my squad. We had all just arrived in Malaya and were all greener than the tropical rain forest about us. The terrorist war in Malaya was the National Service Army's longest and most successful campaign that would leave real life memories of savage victorious jungle fighting for these young conscript soldiers. They earned mine and other regular soldiers respect.

Dark emerald green rain forests covered a great part of the Malayan peninsula. The coastal strip in mainly mangrove swamp which grows on the alluvial soil bought down and silted up by the many rivers and streams. Behind this line rise ranges of heavily forested plains and mountains. This vast mass of vegetation was the tropical rain forest, dark and humid and a place for terrorists to hide. As I travelled north from Johore Bahru by rail along the forest edge, it was just jungle scenery broken by small towns, small holdings, rubber plantations and paddy fields. There were vast areas of land, stripped by Chinese coolies searching for tin, only to be reclaimed by scrubby secondary jungle, then came more rain forest. Now I detrained and as part of a group of squadies, we travelled by truck part of the way and then marched to a jungle camp in the rain forest. Here we were to be taught how to survive in the vastness of the jungle. At first there was deep apprehension about this prospect but later in some of us at least, in inner aboriginal soul of some distant ancestor emerged and it was possible to feel at one with natures wonder.

"Right then, minute's break", roared the instructor and I slumped down against a massive tree after an hour's slog into the enveloping vegetation. Salty rivulets of sweat were running down my face stringing my eyes after a gruelling climb up a slippery jungle track. As I sat on the moist jungle floor I felt a strange itching around my ankles. I unlaced my jungle boot and my grey woolen sock was bright red with blood. To my revulsion I had my first sight of leeches at work. "Gather round", called the instructor to the rest of the patrol as he used me to demonstrate how to deal with leeches. "Never pull them off, he told the course, as their jaws will remain in the bite and it will become infected and become a jungle sore. These are blood sucking little predators and they have a thirst for mammalian blood. That is what you lot are, after the odd wild pig that passes this way you're the next meal. Now how to get them off? You know you can't smoke in the jungle, a good tracker can smell it a mile off but a bit of cigarette ash, or even raw nicotine juice from a damp fag, salt or lime juice will do the trick. It is important that they drop off, so if nothing else is to hand let 'em drip off when they are full". The course let out a gasp of despair when they all discovered a few leeches on somewhere themselves.

A base camp had been established deep in the jungle and that night we sat round a camp fire and swapped yarns. We listened to the voice of the rain forest after dark. Cicadas were singing, a remarkable laud noise for an insect. Most insects make a noise by stridulating that is rubbing one surface of the body against another but the cicada has a built-in drum set in its body cavity which acts as a sound box. As we sat one of the Malays who was guiding our party told us "Happy is the cicada – he has a voiceless wife", only the males can sing. Crickets, tree frogs and geekos calling chi cha, joined the chorus making the night air full or an eerie sound, or added to chock, chock, chock of the nightjar nocturnally hunting for food. At night the tropical rain forest is alive with reverberations. No wonder the local people believe that it is the home of ghosts and spirits.

Lying in my hammock under my mosquito net the following morning, I was awoken by the sound of the Wak-wak swinging through the trees. These were the White-handed Gibbons that we heard every morning loudly and musically shouting at each other as they swung in groups through the high canopy of the forest trees. The gnarled faced instructor told us from personal experience, "the CTs (communist terrorists) have been in the jungle a long time. You have to learn to see him before he sees you. Don't shoot from the shoulder, shoot low at the undergrowth and shoot at every blade of grass that moves". This was an intense jungle training course where the term shoot to kill had to be learnt, along with how to fight the terrorists; we had to survive in the jungle.

So I learnt jungle survival, how to adjust to the tropical rain forest environment, how to cook food over smoky fires, to find water inside bamboo, to use natures food such as ferns, tor or tapioca. To make sure that the jungle fruit was safe to eat. I learnt to watch monkeys and birds for if they did not try them, better leave them alone. So I was trained to know the friendlier side of the rain forest. I learnt to live in the jungle for weeks without being able to wash properly; to only cross a river or stream above any human settlement, because of the risk of leptospirosia carried by rats. And I knew what to do when it pelted down with monsoon rain. When one talked about movement through the rainforest it was by yards not miles. We as a squad leant not to consider movement in a straight line. All sorts of obstacles needed to be circumnavigated; Bamboo clumps sometimes miles deep, rivers and streams, boulder, fallen trees. Movement was generally at a snails pace and yet the training school was easier than the real jungle patrols performed afterwards. The jungle can be a hard taskmaster but there are also striking moments of beauty watching butterflies congregating around a moist spot or round some special tree or bush. Then at the end of the day there were exquisite sunsets like nowhere else on earth, even if over in a few minutes.

When a man lives in the rain forest it steals a small part of his soul. It is cruelty and natural wonder, its mysteries, vastness, wild creatures and its supernatural spirits, will remain in my psyche for ever more. Putting aside the hardship of the arduous jungle patrol searching for CTs, my modest understanding of its enormity and secrets the jungle held will always strengthen my affection and reverence for this place. I therefore hope that this glimpse of the jungle may show others some of the experience which enlightened me. Even with the often harsh, gruelling and horrendous conditions of living in the jungle, yet the rain forest of Malaysia was the most enchanting fascinating phenomenon of my military service".

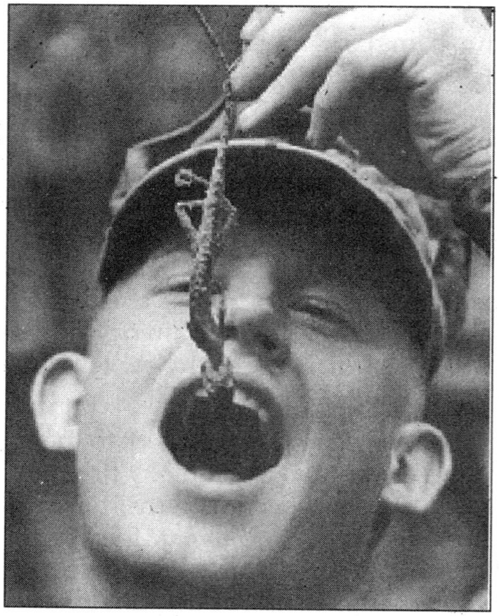

Jungle warfare does not mean that you are obliged to survive by eating lizards or chameleons

(2.4) Special Features of Fighting in the Jungles

The difficult we do immediately; the impossible takes a little longer.

There can be but a few types of jungles. Hence, the basic concepts of fighting in jungles will remain common to all forces and jungles. You will have to evolve your own specific systems for various situations, however. This book will teach you both. Then you will also have to keep in mind as to what are the overall objectives and how far your government is prepared to commit itself in jungle warfare? The Americans are known for the thoroughness with which they do any work; still, you must keep in mind that the concepts of operations in jungles which the Americans have evolved are largely dictated by their own experience in Vietnam. They are not uniformly applicable to all other places. Air and artillery support was central to the American war-fighting doctrine in Vietnam. One of the great pleasures of the Vietnam War for the Americans was to bomb villages and drop napalms in jungles and villages. The Americans had no qualms about clearing jungles to create helicopter landing strips. Naval artillery shells (weighing typically a ton) of 16-inch guns were regularly fired form battleships to create landing zones. They also liberally used herbicides and defoliants like the notorious Agent Orange. One of the most enduring images of the Vietnam War is that of the great B-52 strategic bomber unleashing its 60,000 lbs load of bombs to carpet bomb all that lay beneath. God, how much I miss that wonderful era! Fighting in jungles is admittedly much more difficult than fighting in open. Life of soldiers fighting in the plains of Europe was infinitely better than the horrors which the poor GI Joes underwent in Vietnam. Other countries facing insurgencies in their own territory may find it difficult to use them. You may not have that luxury.

The first thing about jungle is dense vegetation and foliage. This means that it would restrict visibility in the first place—you cannot see far. Remember, dense foliage offers cover to the adversary also. This means he could hide easily and lie in ambush for you. Foliage has an adverse effect on mobility and manoeuvrability. The jungle could also have hilly features. Hilly features mean that the enemy could already be on commanding heights having vantage points for observation and fire. Also, this could pose problems in LOS (line-of-sight) communication using VHF. The following are the major operational concerns in fighting in jungles:

- The vegetation limits the distance of clear line of sight on the ground.
- This has a bearing on the use of LOS (line-of-sight) weapons. Range automatically gets limited by what you cannot see beyond.
- If you try to shoot through the vegetation cover, bullets tend to get deflected in bushes, thereby limiting their effectiveness.
- Even NLOS (non-line-of-sight) weapons run into problems when mortar shells might strike tree branches both while going up and while coming down and get deflected.
- The tree cover greatly reduces the effectivity of airborne observation platforms like UAVs.
- The natural camouflage works to the advantage of the adversary as well.
- Problems pertaining to operations and shelter arise during rains when the ground is muddy all around and it is difficult to find dry ground.
- Command and control are difficult in the jungle. The thick foliage allows commanders to see and control only a small part of their units. You cannot control what you cannot see.
- The thick foliage and rugged terrain of most jungles limit fields of fire and speed of movement.

- Lack of line-of-sight and clearance is detrimental to visual contact between units and inter-locking fires.
- Machineguns are not able to attain grazing fire.
- Sound in the jungle could be confusing. Noises often turn out to be closer than believed.
- It becomes difficult to locate source of fire by reports of the guns.
- The enemy who has seen you first is obviously having some concealment and also a clear line of sight to you. On other hand, since you are not able to locate him, it becomes difficult for you to decide where exactly you should be shooting.
- Thick jungle foliage and heavy rains considerably weaken radio signals, making communications difficult. To reduce the effects of the problem, use of the helicopter as a command and control vehicle is recommended. But heavy monsoon rains may not allow helicopters to fly when you need them; hence an alternate means of command and control must be planned for. Helicopter pilots in places like India are a shit-scared lot anyway and produce ten thousand excuses as to why they cannot fly to a certain place. The helicopters may be shot at.
- Ground surveillance radars can be employed basically in those jungle areas only where vegetation and terrain do not restrict line of sight.
- Unattended ground sensors, which are not affected by poor line of sight, are affected by poor weather and are difficult to move in thickly forested areas.
- In aerial surveillance, side-looking airborne radar (SLAR) is not very effective in thick foliage, but can be used for surveillance along roads, trails, or streams.
- Infrared detection devices are limited by fog, clouds, rain, and vegetation.
- The jungle also increases the difficulty of efforts to provide continuous support.
- And finally, there are nasty surprises in store.

Michael A Snider, American soldier of the Alpha Company, 4th/47th, 2nd Brigade, 9th Infantry Division recalls of the 'nasty surprises' in his 'Walking Into A Trap': "June 19, 1967 while on a battalion size operation near Ap Bac Village, we had moved across several rice paddies and were nearing a tree line in front and to the right of our unit. To our left was the river we landed on. Our company commander radioed and asked for artillery into the tree line because it looked suspicious, but the request was denied because no enemy had been sighted and there were civilians in the area. So at this point we moved on, the lead squad was almost to the tree line and the rest of us were in open rice paddies spread out across two or three rice paddies. All at once all hell broke loose. The NVA and VC had permanent bunkers set up made of cement. The tree line was in an L shape covering the front and right side of us. They had 50 calibers and AK-47s shooting at us in crossfire; our men in the middle of the rice paddies didn't have a chance and 75 per cent of Alpha Company was wiped out in the first five minutes of the battle. The ones who were not hit initially were trying to find cover but couldn't. We started crawling when it got dark. We were able to crawl to the river where the Navy was waiting. A Navy corpsman put us on boats and took us to Nha Be".

The outcome of an action in the jungle is largely decided by the ability of individuals to:

- live and move silently;
- detect and locate the enemy before he detects you;
- make full use of concealment; and
- shoot quickly and accurately at partially concealed or fleeting targets.

Since the enemy can employ similar skills, it is essential to use special techniques to:

- reduce the possibility of being surprised;
- react swiftly and sensibly to sudden contacts; and
- locate, ambush or attack the enemy with complete surprise, to prevent him escaping or
- counter-attacking effectively when you are caught anyway.

(2.5) How Everything can go wrong in the Jungle?

Failure of Plan A will directly affect your ability to carry out Plan B.

In early March 1969, the US Army's Fourth Infantry Division launched Operation Wayne Grey. Its mission was to engage the 66th North Vietnamese Army Regiment and prevent its movements against the vulnerable mid-section of South Vietnam anchored by the cities of Kontum and Pleiku. The lead element for the operation was the third battalion, 8th Infantry, comprised of Companies A, B, C, and D. They were deployed by helicopter assault into the Plei Trap Valley, an area northwest of Pleiku and Kontum. John F Bauer has compiled the accounts of the survivors of the A company in his 'Ambushed and Overrun: Survivors of Company A Tell their Stories'. These accounts provided the basis for a feature story in VFW Magazine's February 2008 edition, titled 'Ambush in the Plei Trap Valley'. Remember that official military histories are notorious for both glossing over and presenting a particularly desiccated and highly impersonal version of what had really happened. Truth is revealed only through such personalised accounts.

It shows how practically everything could go wrong in the jungle. In this case, things went wrong from the beginning. The insertion of the troops by helicopters betrayed the very operation to the waiting Vietnamese. Contrary to sound infantry tactics, the four companies of the battalion were deployed in such a way as to be non-supporting of each other. Quite expectedly, they ran into a terrible ambush. The Americans had become so used to artillery support that they were utterly at sea when they discovered that, in this operation, some elements were out of the supporting range of friendly artillery. Their next hope was air support but to their horror, they discovered that when limited air support could be provided with great difficulty during daylight engagements, it was of little use in the thick jungle canopy of the Central. Helicopter gunships support was often requested but not provided. In short, they were simply screwed. Company A fared the worst. Undermanned at the outset, in just 24 hours of fighting the company had ceased to exist as a fighting unit. It was forced from its fighting position after three hours of fierce combat when a far superior NVA element broke through its perimeter defense. A hasty withdrawal to an extraction point led by Lt Buddy Williams was all that saved the rest of the company. It was not sound military strategy to send such a small company in search of a vastly superior force, the 66th NVA. The following are the words of Lt Buddy Williams.

"Alpha Company was dropped into an Area of Operation (AO), on the morning of 3rd March. Our sister company, Delta, landed in the same zone, but it went elsewhere. It was the usual hump through the forest with one exception. We had a helicopter drop of supplies of radio equipment; signal SQIs and SSIs I think they are called. I didn't think about it at the time, but it must have tripped our location and would account for what happened a little later. Anyway, by 1540 we began setting up our night location after gaining some high ground on a fairly high-speed trail up a ridgeline. We weren't too far along when my point man surprised an enemy soldier who dashed up the hill. What we then found was an NVA observation post (OP) with a cooking pot and a sleeping site prepared in the vegetation. Capt Isom was notified of the events and made the decision to dispatch my platoon, 23 of us, in pursuit. The artillery Forward Observer (FO), Lt Flannigan, advised that the area to our front be prepped with an artillery barrage first. The CO declined and we went ahead. What we did not know then was that we were out of artillery range. Maybe the CO knew that.

Having seen one enemy soldier, we inched carefully up the trail and soon made contact. We came upon two NVA and quickly took them out. Then it started. A machinegun and other small arms opened fire at close range on our left, nailing one soldier, and wounding another. We took cover as best we could and returned fire. This included our own M 60 machinegun. At this point, another NVA machinegun and B-40 rocket fire came from our right. We were smack in a deadly crossfire, and guys began to drop all over. I radioed Isom that we were in major contact, and I began trying to urge the platoon out of the killing zone. My third platoon was up against what I figure was at least a platoon or company size force of NVA regulars. Isom said he would proceed to my location.

About this time, Capt Isom had arrived with his lead headquarters element but stopped right in the middle of the killing zone. Within moments his RTO, Robbie something, was hit and his left arm and hand were almost blown off. As he screamed, I'll never forget his cries for God and his mother. Isom himself was killed trying to help Robbie. The second platoon arrived next in the hot zone, but its platoon leader, Lt Griffith, was killed right away.

Darkness was setting in and we had dead and wounded and were disorganised to the point of being critical. There was no first sergeant, no senior NCOs to help organise a defensive position. We needed ammo, a medevac, reinforcements, anything. I made the call to pull back to the night location. High-tail it was more like it. We managed to take the walking wounded but had to leave others in the fight zone.

The battalion CO flew overhead in an effort to direct action on the ground. This was not going to work. We were in triple canopy jungle, and they could hardly make us out. He said ammo was on the way, but by the time it was dropped the choppers had pretty much lost our location. We ended up with about 20 per cent of the ammunition re-supply. Guess who got most of it.

Our orders were to search there for dead and wounded at first light. That's right! Ordered to go back up with the NVA consolidating heir position the whole night.

Well, we gave it a shot. I asked for volunteers to recover our people. Sgt. Sam Jones came forth and recruited about half of our remaining strength, about 25 men, to probe the area and make the recoveries. Jones' patrol did not get a hundred meters before they got hit by a wall of fire. They bolted back into the perimeter after just minutes. Then we just waited. We had no more options.

I met with key troops and we all agreed that we had to make a run for it. If we didn't, we'd all be killed, an entire company up in smoke. I gave the word to pull back down the finger of the hill toward a dry creek bed. A gunship was dispatched to cover us and kept the NVA at bay. The pilot said he could see "about 100 gooks" following us as we stumbled along the creek bed. The chopper located a clearing. If we could get to it, there was a chance for an extraction. The rescue helos were on their way. But we had to fight a delaying action until they got there. As it happened, the pilot that spotted us was in a red-bird armed with miniguns. We popped smoke at our rear, and between the rear-guard action that we set up and his firepower, we blew a big hole in the enemy ranks. It stopped their advance. The pilot then led us to the clearing and continued to cover us until the Hueys arrived to get us out".

(2.6) A Critical Evaluation of the Jungle Training Regimens of various Elite Forces

Come on you sons of bitches! Do you want to live forever?

Many countries have institutions imparting training in jungle warfare and related subjects. Jungle warfare, by itself, is a vast subject. Hence, the priorities of different countries vary depending on their own history, racial characteristics, traditions and notions of what constitutes jungle warfare. For some forces survival a la the Discovery Channel programme Man vs. Wild is important; some focus on all sorts of rope bridges; the Far Eastern guys focus on eating reptiles and insects, something that comes to them naturally anyway; the SAS and the Royal Marine commandos emphasise sheer physical endurance and load carrying capacity; and the Americans try a mix of everything.

The Americans faced the jungle for the first time in the Second World War in the Far Eastern theater. In that war, they were facing conventional army units against conventional army units—mostly infantry and amphibious troops, but very solidly supported by artillery and, at times, even armour. There was little secretive about enemy positions or his method of fighting. It was a no-holds-barred affair and they felt free to bombard enemy positions with artillery and flame-throwers. The objective was simple. Here was an enemy position and you had to take it—the only difference from the European theater

The US Marines place a lot of emphasis on water obstacles

was that the enemy position happened to be in jungles. By and large, a similar experience continued in both Korea and Vietnam. It was, however, for the first time in Vietnam that they encountered irregular warfare too—that is, ambushes, punji stakes, booby-trapped bombs, and other dishonourable tricks of war. That changed the perspective of the Americans somewhat. They also realised that though at times, such situations demanded rather small units, there was a good chance that they would be lost. They were also greatly worried about aircraft crew having to bail out in enemy-held areas. Hence, the focus shifted to the issue of 'survival' in the jungles. You may not face that sort of situation if you are operating in your own country.

US Marines' training in booby-traps and punji stakes—a reminder of Vietnam

The British also faced the jungle in the Second World War only. Until the Second World War, many military experts believed that jungles were impenetrable for the Whiteman and unsuitable for modern military operations of their style. The successful Japanese attack on the British in Singapore through the Malaysian jungles in 1942 changed conventional thinking. Faced with an awkward situation, a knee-jerk response was the creation of the Chindits of Brig Wingate. Wingate trained this force as Long-range Penetration units that were to be supplied by stores parachuted or dropped from transport aircraft, and use close air support as a substitute for heavy artillery. I am very well aware of how they have been eulogised in popular folklore and fiction. The reality is, however, very much to the contrary. Without going into the debate, I would just like to quote Field Marshal Slim himself: "The Chindits gave a splendid examples of courage and hardihood. Yet I came firmly to the conclusion that such formations, trained equipped and mentally adjusted for one kind of operation were wasteful. They did not give, militarily, a worth-while return for the resources in men, material and time that they absorbed".

Then came the British experience of counter-insurgency in Malaysia and the SAS. Here also, we have more legends woven around the SAS than proven or verifiable facts. When the Communists surrendered in Malay, a total of 6,400 of them had been killed at the hands of the British—of these only 108 had been tracked and killed by the SAS. I am of the confirmed opinion that the achievement of the SAS was not really significant in terms of overall military objective—it, however, served greatly to bolster the morale of the British that they could live and fight in the jungles as good as any native and the myths about the problems of the Whiteman in jungles were busted.

In the beginning of the Malay affair no institutionalised thought went into the whole thing. It was highly personalised affair. One Brig Mike Calvert was given the job. He was a drunkard, and a former boxer. There was no selection process for recruits at that time apart from just a verbal interview. Many of the recruits were national servicemen, keen young officers and a wild bunch of deserters. As a result, although there were many good volunteers, there were also many who were deemed not up to scratch. I am very much against that sort of thing. Institutions must be built upon scientific knowledge, not on idiosyncrasies even if they are of the greatest man on earth.

The SAS had been sent in to the jungle on a secret mission, but found themselves more like on a safari. The men endured encounters with tigers, monkeys, porcupines and very painful and annoying leeches. They had to learn about the jungle the hard way and were failing to even find the guerrillas, let alone kill them. Fed up with unproductive patrols the SAS looked for another way in, they decided on surprise attacks by parachuting in directly on top of the Communist terrorists. This outlandish idea was known as 'tree jumping'. If all went to plan, each man would be successfully entangled in the top of a tree, whereupon, he would simply absail (rappel) down to the ground. However, many of the men, on collision with the tree-tops, broke arms and legs and thus became sitting targets to the terrorists. Due to the serious injuries and in some cases death due to 'tree jumping', it was considered far too impractical, so it was back to walking for the men. Things started changing only when Calvert died following some strange diseases caught in the jungles. In his place came John Woodhouse, ordered with the task of devising a far stricter selection process for the SAS.

Cobra Gold is a coalition of multi-national military exercises, which are held annually in Thailand. They are attended by six countries—Thailand, US, South Korea, Japan, Indonesia and Singapore. It is singularly ridiculous. I don't think that anything is to be gained by making a man drink a little blood of cobras or making them eat fried scorpions. This is no different from primitive tribal rites of initiation—it has no combat value at all. Normally, in India we do not envisage a situation where soldiers would get almost drowned in mud or morass; we may never encounter a situation where we actually have to construct all sorts of rope bridges in the jungle; or where we have to eat snakes and scorpions to survive. Though snakes are there in the jungles and in some places they find about two scorpions every day, they are not seen in enough numbers to enable even a man to survive, not to speak of several of them together.

Mud obstacle at US Marines' Camp Gonsalves

It also needs to be kept in mind that the objective of the SAS was fundamentally different from the objective of the counter-insurgency operations that the Indians have to undertake now. Their basic job was to undertake border patrolling to detect Indonesian military or communist incursions. Yes, it is true that they developed their own intelligence system. By gaining an understanding of their lifestyle and language, by living with them and dispensing medical aid when needed, the SAS gained important allies in intelligence gathering. The local people, who still crossed the border freely into Kalimantan to trade their goods, often brought back valuable information on Indonesian troop movements. A stupid concept called 'winning the hearts and minds of the people' has become rather popular with the dumb Indians. By the Mother of God, if 65 years after independence you are still trying to win the hearts and minds of the people, what the heck did you do all these years? It was a concept that was applicable in that scenario only—it does not apply to troops operating in their own country—it is yet another example of how the idiots mindlessly copy Western phrases. And if you admit that you have to do that, it means that you also admit that there is something very fundamentally wrong that those people (insurgents and non-combatant civilians sympathetic to them) are, for some reason, alienated with the nation state of India. Do not be stupid and do not expect the security forces to do what the nation has not been able to do in 65 years.

The SAS methods are simply not applicable in India. It is very much open to doubt whether the tribes they encountered had enough intellectual capacity for the Communist propaganda to be understood by them. Quite possibly, and it has been argued by many, that their cooperation was secured by coercion and even then it was essentially limited to a part of logistics such as foraging food etc. I maintain so because had it not been so, the British would not have been able to make any inroads amongst them. Quite surprisingly, this could be done with things as simple as medicines and trinkets. In this connection, it must be kept in mind that they were indeed very primitive people who may not be rightly compared with the tribes in India in 2012.

None of these Special Forces have ever demonstrated the actual benefits that have accrued from their idiosyncratic jungle trainings or other fancy training that they undergo. If we leave Malaysia behind, the current generation of the Royal Marine commandos or the US Marines has not been able to translate their training into any great success story in any conflict they have been in since then. Both have been deployed in Afghanistan and they do not have any illustrious record there.

(2.7) Fighting in Jungle is Different from Survival in the Jungle

Eat when you can. Sleep when you can. Visit the head when you can. The next opportunity may not come around for a long time. If ever.

There are a lot of misconceptions and romantic notions about survival and fighting in the jungles, usually gathered from TV programmes and books indulging in some hyperbolic praise for forces like the SAS, basically as a marketing gimmick and to perpetuate myths about that Special Force. That nobody questions them critically would not help you. Forget them; it still remains bullshit. Leave it to the morons who derive their knowledge from TV programmes. You are a soldier on a mission. You are there in the jungle to fight and you have gone there on purpose—you have not landed there by accident. You are not a camper; and you are not on a mission to prove that you can survive eating three earthworms or four locusts a day. By God, dear, we all know that many insects and worms can be eaten. People have eaten them for centuries; the practice is called entomophagy. But those people had all the time in the world. A soldier does not have time. He has to attend to many other tasks and above all, save his ass from getting shot off to pieces. He can't waste hours foraging insects!

You should never lose sight of your primary objective. Your primary objective is to fight in the jungles, not to survive in the jungles. You would find many fools who have acquired their notions from films and folklore. They would like the jungle warrior to be some sort of superman who does not need to eat, drink or sleep—who can chew a couple of leaves, take a swig, and catch a few winks while perched on a treetop—sorry, gentlemen, it does not happen that way. Your men need proper food to enable them to have strength in the body so that they can carry the loads, are alert and are able to fight any moment. Bear Grylls of the 'Man vs. Wild' programme may be an individual with an exceptionally tough constitution; he is not a soldier. He travels very light with practically nothing on him by way of tools except a knife and a flint. I have doubts whether he can even carry the load which soldiers carry—not to speak of fighting. Hence, there is little to be gained in increasing the combat effectiveness of soldiers even if Bear Grylls in person were to teach them the secrets of survival in the jungles. Bear Grylls has demonstrated eating raw snakes without even disemboweling them (that is, with all the sickening stuff in its gut), raw earthworms, insects of all types, carrion (rotting corpses of animals), and has drunk his own urine besides drinking the blood of a reindeer from its slit throat while it was still alive. That's all bullshit and absolutely unscientific. You do that and you will end up with a battery of such diseases that you will croak. He has to make a show. Soldiers need not do such stunts. They have to remain healthy to fight. Remember one thing—yes, there are many things in the jungle which are edible—that may include many plants and insects. They may help somebody who is really lost in the wilderness and has absolutely nothing on him. They are not for soldiers. The soldier may not have enough of these larvae, insects and plants to get the necessary strength. We all know that cacti and other succulent plants have some water in their pulp. But you cannot use it directly, nor is it in enough amounts to meet your requirements. The moisture is acidic and many cacti have toxic alkaloids too. The pulp would require a solar still to take out potable water. A soldier on a fighting mission is not supposed to waste time or energy carrying a solar still or improvising one. The Seri Red Indians sometimes used the Fishhook barrel cactus (Ferocactus wislizeni) for emergency water. However, drinking the juice on an empty stomach often caused diarrhea, and some Seri report pain in their bones if they walk a long distance after drinking the juice. The Seri called the Coville barrel (Ferocactus emoryi), "barrel that kills" because eating the flesh of the cactus caused nausea, diarrhoea, and temporary paralysis. Think you can tell the two apart in a crisis? The bottom line is you really cannot get a drink from a cactus in spite of what you may have seen in old cowboy movies or what some stupid survival experts might be showing on TV.

There is another guy called Cody Lundin in the show 'Dual Survival', also on the Discovery Channel. This man is built like a bull. He is a minimalist and expert in primitive (or aboriginal, as he calls them) survival skills. That's all very fine. He has not worn shoes for the past 20 years. Well, let him be happy with that. Do you want to do that? Soldiers need shoes. Don't wear them and you will end up with very sore feet that will leave you stranded.

You are a soldier. It is very unlikely that you will ever land up in a situation where you will have nothing on you and you will have to light a fire by grinding wood on wood. Leave that bullshit to aborigines, campers and boy scouts. It may be fascinating to watch someone start a fire with nothing but two pieces of wood, but you do not have to waste a minute learning a skill that has only one-in-a-billion chance of being used. Even if you are lost in the wilderness, you are not likely to remain lost for long. You are a soldier and someone will trace you. For heating your food, carry a proper butane lighter and hexamine tablets, waxed solid fuel, gelled alcohol, or similar things with you to start a fire. Matches get wet—don't waste time with them. The gas in a

A soldier is not obliged to light fires the primitive way – leave the survivalist's stuff for TV programmes and boy scouts

butane lighter will be enough for the length of your operation. You do not have to bother even with steel and flint! You shall not waste your time in foraging for and collecting tinder.

3

Security and Movement in Jungles: Basic Principles and Techniques

If you find yourself in front of your platoon they know something you don't.

(3.1) The Significance of Security and Defence in Jungle

From the moment you enter the jungle or are dropped in the midst of it by helicopter, you are exposed to a new environment altogether. And remember, the bad bandit or his spotters may be watching you. You may have to build a base. The base may be strictly temporary, but still it is imperative that you protect your ass well. While camp defence is a separate subject in itself and has been discussed at length later in the book, there are certain things that must be kept in mind in the special context of jungles. Then you are going to sit there tight and do nothing. Unless you are large in number and go about building a permanent camp in the jungle where a party always mans the base, it is presumed that you would be in the strength of a company or two, and you would have to move out for operation after the planning. Hence, the next thing that you must learn about jungle warfare is movement in the jungles.

Compared with operations in other types of terrain, security measures in the jungle must be intensified because of the poor observation and difficulties of control and movement. Operations must be slower than normal, and security forces must be closer to the units secured in order to provide adequate security in the jungle. Because it provides all-round security, the perimeter defense will be the defensive technique used most often by units operating independently in the jungle. The "stand-to" is an important security technique in jungle fighting. When a unit stand-to, all of its soldiers don their fighting loads and occupy their fighting positions. The unit is 100 per cent alert and ready to fight an attacking enemy. Common stand-to times are before first light, before last light, before helicopter re-supply, and before movement.

Units should plan halts on terrain which lends itself to all-round defence. During short halts, soldiers must drop to one knee and face outward, their weapons at the ready. If the halt occurs at a trail crossing, security elements are sent out along the trail. The security element remains in place until the unit clears the crossing. During longer halts, units must establish a perimeter defence. They run security patrols around their positions, and employ Claymore mines and early warning devices. Before an overnight halt, units should stop while there is still enough daylight to establish a secure perimeter defence, prepare ambushes, and dispatch patrols as necessary. If halted units are separated, connecting patrols should be run periodically to detect enemy infiltration.

Command and control are extremely difficult in jungle defence. Decentralised control is important to insure that subordinate units can react to multiple threats. Aggressive leadership at the small unit level is necessary in fighting off isolated assaults at close range. Alternate communications means must be established wherever possible. An example might be a communications system using wire as the primary means, radio as the secondary means, and pyrotechnics for certain prearranged signals.

(3.2) Planning for Defence in Jungle

The only thing more accurate than incoming enemy fire is incoming friendly fire.

Planning for jungle defence requires some special considerations. Nights, especially under jungle canopies, are extremely dark. Defensive preparations should therefore begin at least two hours before nightfall. It may also be kept in mind that the heat and humidity will fatigue troops rapidly. Tropical rain will flood positions unless they are adequately drained. During the rainy season, defensive positions should be dug on high ground, if possible. Because jungle terrain favours infiltration of the enemy into your area, the use of starlight scopes, OPs, and early warning devices is very important. Leaders must insure that troops do not cut too much vegetation. Mines and obstacles should be emplaced where they are covered by friendly fires. These should be located beyond hand grenade throwing range of the defensive positions. In order to ensure that they are mutually supporting, positions must be closer together than on other types of terrain. In addition to attaining mutual support, this reduces the possibility of enemy infiltration too.

There are occasions when a unit will have to establish a defence with minimum planning time. The normal course of action in these cases is to establish a perimeter defence. Machineguns are employed singly in order to cover as many enemy approaches as possible. As soon as possible; OPs (observation posts) and other local security measures are established. Frontages are smaller than in other types of terrain, especially at night, to guard against enemy infiltration. Indirect fires are registered and fighting positions are dug as soon as possible. An alert system must be established, so that a portion of the defensive force is always awake. Although the poor observation in jungles favours the enemy's attack at any time, the early hours of the morning afford him the greatest chance of surprise unless positive alert measures are taken. All troops should therefore stand-to before dawn.

Another basic fact that must be kept in mind is that the jungle enemy will try to probe a position to locate the flanks of positions and key weapons. Soldiers must not give away their positions by premature firing. Claymores and hand grenades should be used to engage these probes. When probed, riflemen near machineguns should fire, and not the machine gunners so that their position is not disclosed. The importance of machinegun nets cannot be overemphasised. The universal rule is that the machinegun would be firing from some solid cover. Hence, it becomes difficult to take it out with direct fire. The only possible way is to lob or fire grenades on to the position—you never know, someone courageous may crawl close also! Now grenades can be defeated only by a net. Hence, never forget the net for the machinegun position.

Whenever you get time, dig in defensive firing positions. This is what the US army lovingly calls 'foxhole'; the Marines call the 'fighting hole'; and the Brits call a 'slit trench'. A man in a foxhole presents a very small target and is difficult to hit—however, since he is standing he has great flexibility of delivering fire in many directions and thereby engage fleeting targets. They can be made very elaborate also that would permit you to withstand even artillery fire and tank treads. But in the jungle you have only to make a hole that is no deeper than your armpits. That would serve your purpose. Having done that, you must put any rocks, boulders, logs, or even packed earth that you can get in front of you for frontal protection of your head. That would enable you to move a little sideways and continue delivering oblique fire even as fire is coming on you from the front. They can be made to accommodate two men also—they can be made curved for that purpose or in an L-shape. Make little pits in earth to plant your elbows so that they remain steady—they are called elbow holes.

A simple fox-hole

(3.3) Point, Flank, and Rear Security

The thick foliage makes ambush a constant danger. Point, flank, and rear security teams will help keep a force from being ambushed. These teams must be far enough away from the main body that if they make contact the whole force will not be engaged. They should not be so far away, however, that they cannot be supported. If contact is broken between elements or individuals, the rear element should remain in position. Those in front should return to establish contact. These security elements must be alert to signs of the enemy, and should carry as light a load as possible so they are able to manoeuvre. Security duties should be rotated often to avoid fatigue. In planning to concentrate combat power at critical times and places, the defender must first plan the massing of small-arms fire. Since fields-of-fire will be limited, positions must be placed close together for mutual support. In order to move troops and weapons rapidly to supplementary positions or alternate positions; it may be necessary to cut paths through the bush. Units should rehearse these manoeuvres.

Perimeter Defence: in this, all elements are generally configured in a circular formation. The advantages of this formation are that it is mutually supported by observation/communication; offers 360-degree security; patrols are easily coordinated; is quick in emplacement, and it can be executed by unit of any size. The disadvantages are that any penetration creates problems of enfilade, masking, and/or cross fires.

Triangle Defence: This formation is a modification of the perimeter. The advantages are that it provides 360-degree security;

is quick in emplacement; and it can be executed by any size unit. A target approaching perpendicular to any side of the triangle becomes vulnerable to at least one-third of the fighting force and at least two automatic weapons. It is a dual purpose formation in that it may be used as either a defensive or offensive ambush formation. The disadvantages are that one or more legs of the triangle may be subjected to enfilade fire. Soldiers located at the corners are bunched, thus increasing the danger from indirect fire.

"Y" Defence: This formation, like the triangle, may also be utilised as an offensive formation, usually in an ambush. Since all legs of the "Y" are mutually supporting, the commander has the option of having all soldiers on each leg face the same direction, or he may alternate fire teams. Once the decision is made regarding which method is to be used, subsequent legs of the "Y" must conform to the initial one. The great advantage of this formation is that each penetration by the enemy places him in a new kill zone. The disadvantages are that it must be emplaced during daylight to ensure that aiming stakes are accurately emplaced, to preclude firing into adjacent positions; and the central point of the "Y" creates bunching, thereby increasing the danger from indirect fire.

(3.4) Movement in Jungle

The easy way is always mined.

(3.4.1) Planning the Route and avoiding Trails

Keep the following in mind when planning the route:

- Avoid roads and trails. Unless you are absolutely dumb, you must know that they are most likely to be under enemy observation—very likely to be ambushed, mined or booby-trapped.
- Lines of drift, such as ridgelines, are easy to guide on because they avoid streams and gullies and because they are usually less vegetated.
- Danger areas, such as streambeds and draws, are usually more thickly vegetated. They offer excellent concealment, but travel along them is slow and difficult.

General Wesley K Clark, the Supreme Allied Commander, NATO, Europe had fought in Vietnam as a young officer. He has recounted his experiences in his book 'A Time to Lead'. Here is what he recalls about the consequences of following a trail in War Zone D—they got ambushed and he himself was shot and injured.

"We would have had to move cross-country through the jungle, and that would have been not only slow, but also very difficult and noisy. In order to move effectively, therefore, we had to walk staggered out single file on one of the many trails made by the woodcutters in the area. We moved down a wide, hard-packed trail, sunlight splashing green all around us. I had told the point man to stay on a main trail headed generally to the north, and we passed intersections with other wide trails. Was it only woodcutting in this area, I wondered? We moved patiently, slowly, everyone on high alert, stopping every few hundred meters to send riflemen off to either side and check for enemy presence in the jungle around us. But there was nothing.

Then the point man halted and turned back toward me, beckoning with his hand. I moved up the column, and was standing next to him as he turned and pointed forward.

"Sir, the trail just ends right there".

He was right. Suddenly, the big broad trail vanished. There was thick jungle all around us.

Okay, I thought, we'd just stay on course. We were bound to pick up a trail somewhere up ahead if we kept moving in the same direction. I didn't want to backtrack, and the jungle floor was flat. It wasn't going to be hard to simply move forward. I turned around toward my left to get the rest of the column moving, but as I turned a spray of bullets ripped the air above us. "I've been shot!" I shouted as bullets were zinging overhead and ricocheting off the hard-packed earth".

The watchword in the jungle is: move cautiously; expect the unexpected

Jungle tends to confine movement and channel it into potential ambush killing areas, and it is, therefore, essential that all moves are conducted tactically. Points deserving special attention are as follows:

- In jungle operations, silence must be maintained and signals given by hand until surprise is lost. The skill and alertness of each individual is especially important; a single human error can have far greater repercussions than in more open warfare. It is essential that every man understands exactly what he is expected to do.
- Silent movement is of course very slow and only the commander on the ground can dictate the speed. It is unwise to try and force the pace, as troops who are tired or exhausted will not be fully alert: this is particularly important when returning from an operation.
- In a column, control must be from the front to the rear and everyone must continually check that the man behind is following and halt if he is not. If the column splits, the rear portion must remain where it is while the front elements retrace their steps to find it. Commanders must be well forward behind the leading group or subunit, and seconds-in-command should be between the rear groups or subunits from where they can exercise command if the forward subunit is ambushed or if action originates from the rear.

(3.4.2) Night Movement

Silent movement at night requires careful planning and the selection of the most suitable route. Exact bearings and distances must be followed between check points, which must themselves be unmistakable. Leading scouts must have assistance from night vision devices, GPS or patrol dogs. Providing tracks and defiles are avoided meticulously, the chances of a patrol walking into an ambush at night are greatly reduced.

Unless you have a clear advantage in having night vision devices (and the enemy not having them) for each one of you, fighting in the night is not a very advisable thing. The simple reason is that neither the enemy nor you can see each other. If each one of you do not have the NVDs, those without the NVDs will be shooting in the dark only. An action fought at night in thick jungle is generally confused and seldom profitable. You have, however, no option but to fight if it is forced upon you. If a patrol is surprised, troops should drop flat on the ground and crawl back the way they have come, freezing whenever the enemy uses lights. If they are taking casualties, they should disperse at the run, lie up, and rendezvous (RV) at first light. Remember, shooting back is usually pointless as it will be of more advantage to the enemy. The exact position will seldom be known accurately enough to call down immediate fire support although smoke may, at times, be useful. Once clear of the enemy or regrouped at an RV, the patrol commander must appreciate the situation, report to his higher command and take the appropriate action.

(3.5) Combat Patrolling in Jungles

We, the willing, led by the unknowing, are doing the impossible for the ungrateful. We have now done so much for so long with so little, we are now capable of doing anything with nothing.

(3.5.1) *Basics of Patrolling*

Patrolling is the means by which a force dominates the jungle and as such it is the basis of jungle warfare. The reconnaissance and fighting patrols common to other theatres are all used in the jungle. However, a patrol which is of greater than platoon strength becomes unwieldy and difficult to control in jungle conditions. Should a larger force be needed, it should generally be broken down into smaller mutually supporting patrols each no larger than a platoon. A patrol is a mission. The requirements of the mission determine the size, organisation, and equipment of a patrol—always remember the *mantra* of METT-C (mission, enemy, terrain, troops available, and civil considerations). There should always be an overall patrol plan within which patrol tasks, boundaries, timings, and routes out and back should be carefully coordinated with flanking units to avoid any possibility of a clash. Some missions may require only two or three men, lightly armed with no special equipment; some missions may require a squad or platoon, specially armed and equipped. A unit is always tailored for the mission it is to execute. The effectiveness of a patrol is limited only by the ingenuity of the planner and the skill and aggressiveness of the unit leader. For this reason, they are one of the commander's most valued tools. Patrols are especially valuable in counter-guerrilla operations. Aggressive patrolling in an area greatly reduces the guerrillas' freedom of movement, hampers their operations, and weakens their influence on the local population. Patrols may be inserted by parachute, helicopter, surface or sub-surface watercraft, or ground methods. The conduct of the patrol itself remains unchanged, even though the method of insertion changes.

There are some special considerations for jungle patrols that must always be kept in mind. These include the following.

- Requiring all troops to wear boots that have the same pattern on their soles.
- Requiring troops to carry only the mission essentials, and do not let them litter.
- During rainy periods, the sound of movement is less obvious. Wet ground and wet vegetation also muffle noise. This must be kept in mind.
- Silence, in both voice and movement, is essential at all times during a jungle patrol. Troops should avoid walking on dry leaves, sticks, rotten wood, or anything that would make noise.
- Talking should be done in a whisper, and arm-and-hand signals should be used whenever possible.
- Machetes should be used to cut trails only as a last resort. With practice, it is possible to move steadily, deliberately, and carefully through the jungle, parting the undergrowth instead of crashing through it or cutting through it with machetes as you often see in Hollywood films.
- Cautioning troops to avoid small saplings, when going uphill. The shaking of overhead branches can be seen and heard at a distance.
- Requiring troops to keep off trails. If necessary to monitor or guide on a trail, patrols should move parallel to the trail and not on it.
- Patrols should make every effort to hide signs of movement, especially when moving through un-travelled territory or near enemy positions.
- Native scouts are valuable in patrolling because they are often very familiar with the terrain. Patrol leaders must realise, however, that a scout's function is only to show direction and provide information. He should never start leading the patrol. He is not a professional soldier and, even with good intent, can at times give such advice that would land you in serious trouble. The correct position of a scout is with the patrol leader, so that the leader can make decisions based on the scout's advice.
- Patrolling a jungle along a river: Rivers often have heavy vegetation and dense undergrowth along the banks which provide excellent hiding places for the enemy. To afford better

observation of vegetated riverbanks, employ a team of riflemen in a 15-feet multipurpose barge with a 15 hp outboard motor to sweep the riverbanks while ground forces conduct sweep operations parallel to the river. By viewing the bank from two different angles, the chances of the enemy to successfully hide are greatly reduced.

(3.5.2) Reconnaissance Patrols

They collect information and confirm or disprove the accuracy of information previously received. Area reconnaissance patrols have a specific location to be observed for intelligence. Reconnaissance patrols provide the commander with timely, accurate information of guerrillas and the terrain they control. In addition to reaching the objective without discovery, if possible, a reconnaissance patrol also tries to conduct its reconnaissance or surveillance without being discovered. Stealth, patience, and maximum use of concealment are mandatory. A reconnaissance patrol fights only to protect itself or, when authorised, to accomplish its mission. A reconnaissance patrol should be able to draw an accurate sketch map of enemy positions and obtain information in enough detail to enable a sound appreciation and plan to be made from it. If an attack or ambush is contemplated, the commander may decide to take part personally in the close reconnaissance or send his subordinate commanders. In any case, those who have done the close reconnaissance should play a major part in guiding the assault or ambush elements into position.

Reconnaissance patrols of up to four men are required:

- To observe enemy or local habits and traffic.
- To collect topographical information on tracks, rivers, obstacles, etc.
- To select sites for bases, LSs, ambushes, RVs, assembly areas, etc.
- To check that areas remain clear of the enemy and that minefields or other defense are intact.

Reconnaissance patrols should be lightly equipped and should avoid contact with the enemy. Each patrol should carry a lightweight radio and possibly an optical or electronic aid to vision. The patrol should move slowly and silently through the jungle in two groups, each leapfrogging past the other to the limit of visibility. Every 10 minutes or 100 yards, whichever is less, they should stop and listen for about 5 minutes, sensing the atmosphere of the jungle, searching for unusual sounds and scents, and observing and interpreting the reactions of wild life. Traces of enemy movement must be reported with details, where these can be recognised, of:

- the position;
- enemy strength;
- direction of movement;
- and time since enemy appears to have been present.

Once the patrol has located the enemy position, the patrol commander should select an RV where the remainder of his patrol can remain silent in all round defense. They must be briefed on exactly what he intends to do and the action to be taken should be either not return by a stated time or the RV be compromised. The commander should then take one man as an escort and circle the enemy position at 100 to 200 m distance to locate sentries and outposts. All movement must be extremely slow and cautious, with the commander and escort leapfrogging past each other to the limit of visibility. After each five minutes (or even less) they should stop and listen for about 10 minutes.

On the first circuit, sentries should be pinpointed and the best covered approaches noted; these approaches can then be used to crawl close to the enemy without being detected. It will probably be necessary to crawl in on several of these approaches before the necessary information has been gained. After each approach up to the enemy position the patrol commander must crawl back at least 100 m before moving round to make a fresh approach. Infinite patience and extreme caution must be exercised throughout the reconnaissance with frequent halts to listen; all tracks must be concealed. It is always easier to get close to the enemy under the cover of heavy rain.

If there is the slightest suspicion that they may have been seen or heard, the commander and his escort must freeze. If detected, whichever one has been seen should fire and throw a smoke grenade while the other runs past him to a second cover position and repeats the process until both are out of contact, when they should take a circuitous route to the emergency RV. If certain that they are undetected, the commander and his escort should continue with the reconnaissance. When it is complete, they should withdraw with great care, leapfrogging past each other until well clear of the enemy. Compass bearings must be checked continually, not only to determine their exact position, but also to ensure they run in the right direction if detected. This type of reconnaissance of an enemy position is an exacting task and it will often be essential for both commander and escort to withdraw to a safe distance between approaches to the enemy position to snatch a short rest and make a sketch map and notes.

When this stage of the reconnaissance is complete, the commander and his escort should move to the RV by a circuitous route and brief the rest of the patrol so that each man has as much information as possible in case all do not return. The final withdrawal should be by a different route to that taken on the outward journey. During this move, each man must study the route to ensure that he can confidently guide a force back at any time in the future. On their return, the patrol should be debriefed on a large scale model of the area.

If detected by the enemy, the patrol should withdraw quickly under cover of smoke from a smoke grenade and fire from alternate groups as the others run past them for cover: the process being repeated until they are out of contact. Once clear, the patrol leader should report the contact by radio. The commander must then clearly decide, keeping the enemy strength in mind, whether the patrol is to follow up, return to base, or continue with the patrol. Other patrols hearing firing should report:

- their own position;
- the time firing was heard;
- the bearing to the firing;
- the estimated distance; and
- the number and type of shots or explosions.

(3.5.3) Combat or Fighting Patrols

A combat or fighting patrol has the general mission of seeking out and attacking targets of opportunity within its capability. An ambush is thus a combat patrol. Engagement is by raid, ambush, or any form of attack suitable to the situation. They provide security and harass, destroy, or capture enemy personnel, equipment, and installations. Combat patrols also collect and report information whether it is related to the assigned mission or not. A fighting patrol should be large enough and have the fire power to destroy any group of enemy it is likely to meet. They are required:

- To prevent enemy patrols gaining information or the initiative by aggressive patrolling and ambushing.
- To harass the enemy and lower his morale.
- To follow up the enemy after contacts.
- To carry out raids and capture prisoners.

- To maintain contact with flanking units and provide flank protection, and
- To escort reconnaissance, supply, casualty evacuation, and working parties

The combat patrol is one of the commander's most flexible weapons. Uses vary from a two-man patrol executing a harassing ambush of opportunity to a reinforced platoon conducting raids, ambushes, and target-of-opportunity operations. In some instances, a patrol encountering a superior force may maintain contact with the force until reinforcements permit decisive engagement. Effectiveness of the patrol depends, not on size, but on the suitability to a given situation. The use of combat patrols forces guerrillas to engage in decisive combat at unfavourable times and places. They can be used to locate and destroy enemy camps, elements, and supply points. Saturation of an area with patrols forces the guerrillas to either curtail operations or consolidate in larger groups, which are favourable targets for air, artillery, and large-scale attack.

(3.5.4) Motorised Patrols

Patrols may be motorised (usually as an economy-of-force measure) to allow them to cover greater distances in less time than dismounted patrols; operate in contaminated areas too dangerous for dismounted patrols; and carry more or heavier equipment, weapons, and ammunition. Motorising enables a patrol to carry heavy and bulky equipment such as anti-tank weapons and ammunition; surveillance equipment; and additional automatic weapons and ammunition. A motorised patrol is organised into elements and teams in the same manner as a dismounted patrol. When soldiers are assigned to vehicles, squad or fire team integrity is maintained as far as possible. One soldier is designated commander of each vehicle. In all cases, the unit moves from a Start Point (SP) to an Objective Rally Point (ORP) and then on to its objective (OBJ) area. The unit may then return to the ORP upon mission accomplishment, or it may proceed through the objective area and onto a linkup point. From there the unit continues with a follow-on mission, or returns to base.

A motorised patrol must move by one of three methods: continuous movement, successive bounds, and alternate bounds. In continuous movement, all vehicles travel at a moderate rate of speed, with all personnel alert. The lead vehicle stops to investigate only those areas that appear dangerous. This is the fastest, but least secure, method of movement. In successive bounds, vehicles keep their relative positions in the column. The first and second vehicles operate as a team in moving from one observation point to another. The second vehicle is placed in a concealed position, occupants dismounting if necessary, to cover movement of the first vehicle to an observation point. On reaching this point, occupants of the first vehicle observe and reconnoiter, dismounting if necessary. When the area is determined to be clear, the second vehicle is signalled forward to join the first vehicle. The commander of the first vehicle carefully observes the terrain to the front for signs of guerrillas and selects the next stopping point. The first vehicle then moves out and the process is repeated. Movement distance of the lead vehicle does not exceed the limit of observation or the range of effective fire support from the second vehicle. The lead vehicle and personnel are replaced frequently to ensure constant alertness. The other vehicles in the column move by bounds from one concealed position to the next. Each vehicle maintains visual contact with the vehicle ahead but avoids closing up. In alternate bounds, all except the first two vehicles keep their relative places in the column. The first two vehicles alternate as lead vehicles on each bound. Each covers the bound of the other. This method provides more rapid advance than movement by successive bounds but is less secure; it does not allow soldiers in the second vehicle enough time to thoroughly observe the terrain to the front before passing the first vehicle. Security is obtained by the vehicle commander who assigns each soldier a direction of observation: to the front, flank(s), or rear. This provides each vehicle with some security against surprise fire from every direction and provides visual contact with vehicles to the front and rear. For maximum observation, all canvas is removed from the vehicles.

The commander of the leading vehicle immediately notifies the unit leader when he encounters an obstacle or other danger area. Designated soldiers reconnoiter these places under cover of the weapons in the vehicle. Obstacles are bypassed, if possible. When they cannot be bypassed, they are cautiously removed. Side roads intersecting the route of advance are investigated. Soldiers from one vehicle secure the road junction; one or two vehicles investigate the side road. The amount of reconnaissance of side roads is determined by the patrol leader's knowledge of the situation. Men investigating side roads do not, however, move past supporting distance of the main body of the patrol. Bridges, road junctions, defiles, and curves (that deny observation beyond the turn) are danger areas. Soldiers dismount and take advantage of available cover and concealment to investigate these areas. The vehicle is moved off the road into a covered or concealed position; weapons from the vehicle cover the advance of the investigating personnel. When approaching a village, two or three soldiers may go forward on foot to reconnoiter. Other soldiers cover their movement from covered or concealed positions. Actions on contacting guerrillas depend on whether the mission permits or prohibits engaging in combat. For example, if the mission permits or requires the exploitation of opportunities for combat and the lead vehicle detects, or is attacked by, an ambush, then soldiers in the lead vehicle move to positions from which the guerrillas can be brought under fire. The soldiers dismount and manoeuvre to destroy the ambush. In any situation where the soldiers dismount, drivers remain with and protect their vehicles. The vehicles are moved off the road, after ensuring that the shoulders of the road are not mined. If possible, they are positioned so that the drivers can support the attack. At least one automatic weapon remains with the vehicles.

(3.5.5) Patrol Bases

Three types of bases are generally used in a counter-insurgency situation: patrol bases, operational support bases, and support bases. Patrol bases are used by a company or smaller units. Operational support bases are used by battalions, and support bases are used by brigades and larger units. The length of time a patrol base is occupied depends on the need for secrecy. A patrol base is occupied the minimum time necessary to accomplish the mission. In most situations, occupation should not exceed 24 hours except in an emergency. The same base is not (usually) used again. In counter-guerrilla operations, patrol base secrecy is required; and evacuation (if discovered) depends on the degree of control the guerrilla force has in the base area, their ability to react to the discovery of a base, and their ability to affect the unit's mission. When a guerrilla force is relatively small and weak, patrol base secrecy may not be an overriding consideration; and if the base is discovered, evacuation may not be required. In an area controlled by a large guerrilla force with a high degree of combat capability, patrol base secrecy is mandatory; and if discovered, evacuation is required.

Plans to establish a patrol base include consideration of: alternate location, linkup point and rallying point. Alternate location is used if the initial location proves unsuitable or if the unit is required to evacuate the initial location prematurely. In counter-guerrilla operations, reconnaissance and surveillance of an alternate location, until occupied or no longer needed, are desirable. Linkup point is used if the unit evacuates the patrol base by exfiltration in groups. The linkup point does not have to be reconnoitered. Rallying point is used if the unit is dispersed from the patrol base. It is a point over which the unit has previously passed, and it is known to all. Needless to say, when planning for a patrol base, passive and active security measures must be accorded the priority they deserve.

With regard to passive security measures, base selection must select places that are located in difficult terrain; have dense vegetation; are far from human habitation; are near a water source; and are away from known or suspected enemy positions, built-up areas, ridgelines, topographic crests (except as necessary for maintaining adequate communications), roads or trails and natural lines of drift and wet areas, steep slopes, and small valleys that may be lines of drift. With regard to active security measures, base selection must include: outpost and listening post systems covering avenues of approach into the area; communications with outposts and listening posts; defence of the patrol base (if required); withdrawal, to include multiple withdrawal routes (if required); an alert plan; enforcement of camouflage, noise, and light discipline; and conduct of necessary activities with minimum movement and noise. A patrol base maybe occupied in two ways: by moving to a selected site and organising the area in the same manner as an on-the-spot establishment; or by halting near the selected site and sending forward reconnaissance forces.

(3.5.6) Operation Security in Patrol Bases

Only one point of base entry and exit is used. It is camouflaged and guarded at all times. Fires are built only when necessary and, as a rule, only in daylight. Where terrain permits, fires are built in pits and, if built at night, are carefully covered and shielded. The driest and hardest wood available is used (to reduce smoke). In most areas, the best time for building fires is when the air is thin and smoke dissipates quickly (usually around noon); early morning may be appropriate, however, in areas where there is ground fog. The risk of detection, because of lingering odour, must be weighed against the risk of detection due to visible smoke. With regard to sanitation and personal hygiene, in daylight, cat holes outside the perimeter must be used. The user must be guarded. At night, cat holes are used inside the perimeter. Similarly, guarded water parties must provide water. Lone individuals must not visit the water source. When possible, noisy tasks must be performed when other sounds could cover them. Movement, both inside and outside the patrol base, is restricted to the minimum. Civilians who discover the location of the patrol base must be detained until the base is moved. If necessary, they may be blindfolded and their ears covered so that they do not learn anything about us. A 1-hour stand-to must be observed morning and evening: 30 minutes before and 30 minutes after light in the morning, and 30 minutes before and 30 minutes after dark in the evening. This ensures that every man is acclimated to changing light conditions, and is dressed, equipped, and ready for action. Defensive measures are planned, but a patrol base is usually defended only when evacuation is not possible. Elaborate firing positions are not constructed; nonetheless, camouflage and concealment are stressed. An alert plan includes evacuation and defence. All members must know the plans and the signals or orders for their implementation. Plans cover pursuit and destruction of the attacking force. For departure, all signs of the unit's presence must be removed or concealed to the extent possible. This is intended to prevent the enemy from learning that the unit is in the area, prevent pursuit, or prevent the enemy from learning how the patrol base is operated.

(3.5.7) Coping with IEDs

Admittedly, a most difficult job—the only limitation to IEDs is set by the ingenuity of the enemy. A clever enemy may hide his IEDs even in mud cakes. The notorious mud ball mine used in Vietnam consists of a hand grenade encased in sun-baked mud or clay. The safety pin (pull ring) is removed, and mud is moulded around the grenade. After the mud dries, it holds the lever of the grenade in the safe position. The mud ball is placed on trails or anywhere troops may walk. Stepping on the mud ball breaks the dried mud apart and releases the lever, detonating the grenade. A hollow bamboo mine is made from a large piece of bamboo. It is hollowed out and filled with plastic explosive or even black powder, together with improvised shrapnel like nuts and bolts, and scrap metal. This mine may be command detonated with an electrical firing system. Command-detonated mines and explosive devices can theoretically be detected by the wires leading away from the shoulders of the road. Quite often it is very difficult because if at all there are wires, the enemy would know to bury them deeper than the depth at which they may be detected by a mine detector. Then there may be no wire at all—the enemy could have used detonating cord instead. Theoretically, you may use a pole-hook for scraping the sides of a road where you have a doubt. But it is impractical to expect that a pole with a hook at the end would be pulled through the edges of the road as you walk, and hope that it would entangle any wires which might not be buried deep there.

(3.6) Basic Techniques of Patrolling

There is always a way, and it usually doesn't work.

(3.6.1) *Base Line Patrols*

This method ensures an even coverage across the grain of the area to be searched. Small patrols, usually of four men each, start at 200 m intervals along a base line which can be a ridge, stream, or track. Each patrol searches on a given bearing at right angles to the general direction of the base line for about 1000 yards, turns right for 100 yards and returns to the base line on a back-bearing. In very close jungle or swamp, these distances should be halved, while in open jungle, although the interval between patrols should remain the same, they can normally cover 2000 yards out and 2000 yards back if required. This method gives even coverage of the ground but suffers from the disadvantage that some patrols have much further to go along the base line than others.

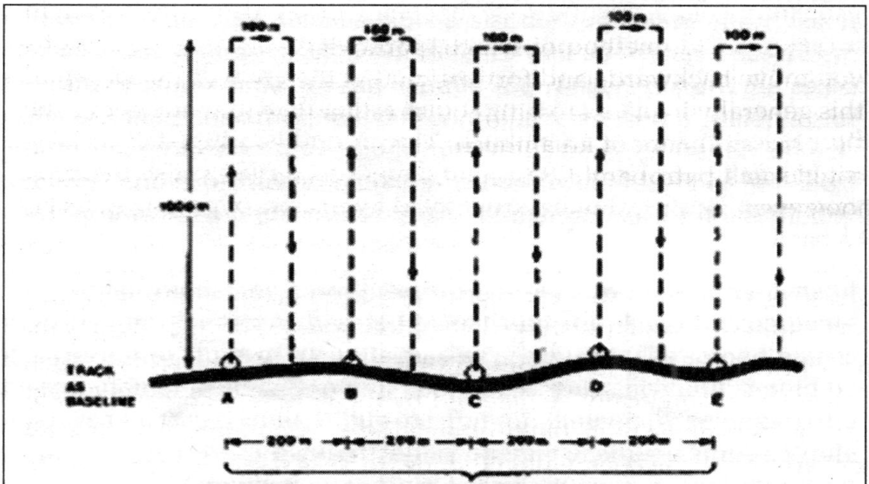

Base line patrol

(3.6.2) *Fan Patrols*

In the fan patrolling techniques, the requisite numbers of patrols leave the same start point on bearings at intervals of 200 mils, search for 1000 yards, turn right 100 yards and return on a backbearing plus 100 mils. Fan patrolling is easy to control at the start as all patrols leave from the same point; however, it does not cover the ground evenly and there is a considerable danger of patrols clashing as they return on converging bearings.

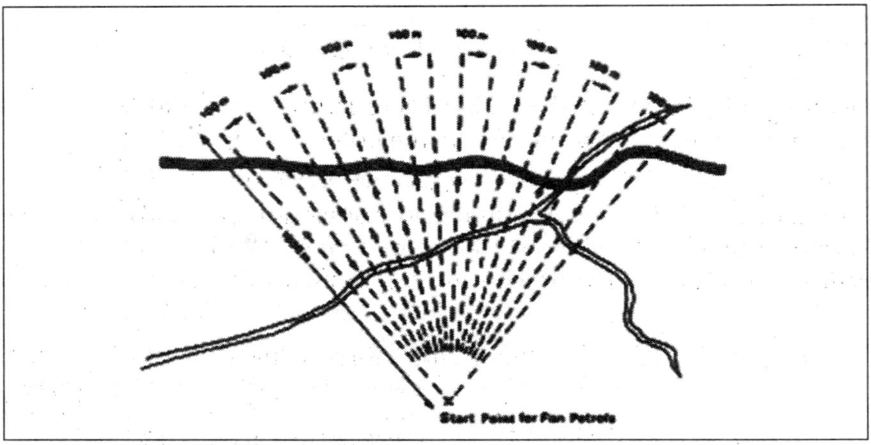

11 Fan patrol

(3.6.3) *Cross Grain Patrol*

This is a useful method of search, particularly in a large area. In this you move backwards and forwards across the grain of the terrain. As this generally involves crossing routes rather than moving along them, there is less chance of an ambush. The ground is covered evenly by a single small patrol and there is no danger of clashing. The method is however, slow as it cannot be operated by a series of patrols except off a base line.

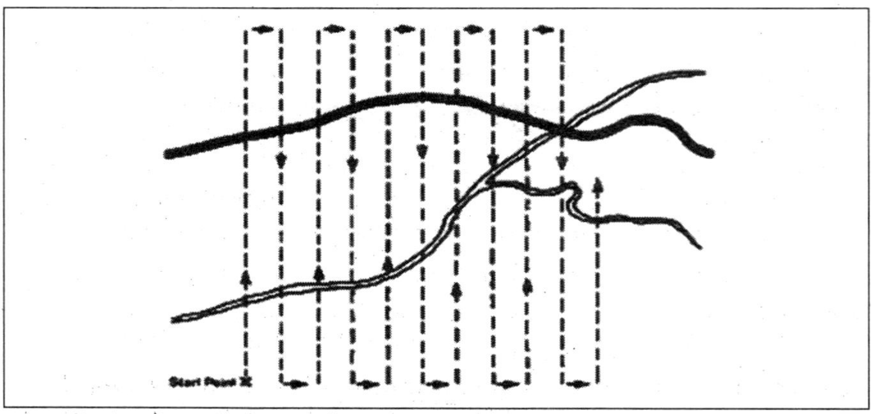

12 Cross grain patrol

(3.7) Scout or Patrol Dogs: Myths and Reality

Scout or patrol dogs may also be used with the security element. These dogs may detect the enemy before he is detected by humans. If a dog picks up an unfamiliar scent while on patrol, he will give an alert, which the handler will pass on to the others. There is no special method by which all dogs alert. Each dog is an individual in his manner of alerting. Therefore, the handler must observe the dog's behaviour carefully so he does not miss its signal of alert. Dogs can give early silent warning of enemy hiding in caves, canal banks, foxholes, trees, and rice paddies, etc. They accomplish this through their superior sense of smell, sight, and hearing, by detecting sounds too faint for human ears, for example, the scraping of clothing against brush, harsh breathing, the rasp of a sandal against a rock, and the accidental clicking of a bolt, etc. At times they were able to detect the presence of a trip wire in total darkness by the faintest of all sounds—sound waves by the vibration of the wire, plus its ability to scent the booby-trap and associated human odour. The best scout dogs are described as having a disposition intermediate to docile tracking dogs and aggressive attack dogs. Scout dogs were used in World War II, Korea, and Vietnam by the United States to detect ambushes, weapon caches, or enemy fighters hiding underwater, with only reed breathing straws showing above the waterline. However, quite often the capacities of the dog are exaggerated by sentimental dog lovers.

The US operated a number of scout dog platoons (assigned on a handler-and-dog team basis to individual patrols) and had a dedicated dog training school in Fort Benning, Georgia. The mission of a scout dog platoon is to support infantry, airborne and other type units in tactical operations against hostile forces by detecting and giving silent warning of any foreign presence outside the main body. Scout dog teams have been utilised for specific missions:

- Detection of ambush sites
- Detection of snipers close-in
- Detection of enemy hideouts or stay-behind groups
- Detection of enemy caches of weapons, food, and ammunition
- Detection of mines or booby-traps during road-clearing operations
- Assist in village block and search or block and sweep operations
- Accompany ambush patrols and/or listening posts to give early warning of enemy approach
- Work with combat tracker teams in special situations requiring both teams' capabilities.

But it is not wise to depend too much on them. Even though a dog hears 40 times better than a man, smells with an ability 20 times greater, and sees 10 times better, do not think that a dog team is infallible, incapable of errors or devoid of limitations. The poor dog was not designed by Mother Nature to fight your anti-terrorist operations for you. To a dog, duty and instinct are inextricably intermingled and as a dog lover, I would be very unhappy if a poor dog were to get killed in fighting a war between those people none of whom could rightly lay a claim to '*dharma*'. Remember that the enemy could easily kill the dog from a distance noiselessly using bows and arrows also—many tribal people are naturally adept at that.

Americans are good at exploiting the emotions of dog lovers and write very lovingly, very touchingly about the exploits of their dogs and how they remember them. Many army units of the US still have websites devoted to their dogs and have erected memorials too. Americans also make deeply stirring films about dogs—haven't we cried seeing films like *Marley and Me, Lassie Come Home, Yellow, and White Fang*? But as a scientist and as a professional warrior, it is my duty to lay bare the truth. The poor dog, for example, cannot distinguish between an armed hostile and an unarmed villager in the jungle. And mind it; this is not Vietnam where you were at liberty to shoot at anything that was not like you. In fact, this is a classic example of how the intellectually bankrupt Indians plagiarise foreign concepts and seek to introduce them in India. In a counter-insurgency situation, there is a very good chance that there would be unarmed non-combatants or villagers in the jungles. Terrorists or insurgents, who know that patrols have dogs, could deliberately mislead the dog and create difficult situations for the forces. An unarmed villager could be deliberately planted to be detected by the dog. They could also be listening to the dog's growl or even watching him. As the dog alerts the patrol, some shots could be fired just like that, and not necessarily aiming at the patrol. The patrol would react, and in the process could kill the unarmed 'bait'. This could be used in mounting a propaganda offensive against the forces for human rights violations. Further, quite often the nearest armed hostile will be way beyond the dog's limit of sensing him. In situations where vegetation is extremely thick, such as dense jungle, the travel of scent will be considerably restricted; causing it to drift aimlessly because of the lack of circulation in such areas. An alert range of 10-15 yards is considered good under such conditions. But the enemy could very well be much beyond that. In many ambushes or in cases of purely harassing fire, the fire is often delivered from 100-200 yards. There is little which the poor dog can do in such conditions. In jungle-covered mountains, experience has shown that what little wind is available usually is headed directly up the slope. In such a situation, careful consideration should be given to the placement of the team so as to afford maximum use of the wind. There may be many other diversions present in the jungle, such as carrion, etc. Further, the jungle heat is hard on the dogs, and they need to be rested frequently.

4

Basic Concepts and Skills of Combat in Jungles

In ten years nobody will remember the details of caliber, stance, or tactics. They will only remember who lived.

(4.1) Cover and Concealment

Natural cover includes such things as logs, trees, stumps, ravines, and hollows. Man-made cover includes such things as fighting positions, trenches, walls, rubble, and craters. Even the smallest depression or fold in the ground can give some cover. Look for and use every bit of cover the terrain offers. To get protection from enemy fire in the offense or when moving, use routes that put cover between you and the places where the enemy is known or thought to be. Use ravines, gullies, hills, wooded areas, walls, and other cover to keep the enemy from seeing and firing at you. Avoid open areas, and do not skyline yourself on hilltops and ridges.

Concealment is anything that hides you from enemy observation. Concealment does not protect you from enemy fire. Do not think that you are protected from the enemy's fire just because you are concealed. Concealment, like cover, can also be natural or man-made. Natural concealment includes such things as bushes, grass, trees, and shadows. If possible, natural concealment should not be disturbed. Man-made concealment includes such things as battle-dress uniforms, camouflage nets, face paint, and natural material that has been moved from its original location. Man-made concealment must blend into the natural concealment provided by the terrain.

Light discipline, noise discipline, movement discipline, and the use of camouflage contribute tc concealment. Light discipline is controlling the use of lights at night by such things as not smoking in the open, not walking around with a flashlight on, and not using vehicle headlights. Noise discipline is taking action to deflect sounds generated by your unit (such as operating equipment) away from the enemy and, when possible, using methods to communicate that do not generate sounds (arm-and-hand signals). Movement discipline is such things as not moving about fighting positions unless necessary, and not moving on routes that lack cover and concealment. In the defence, build a well-camouflaged fighting position and avoid moving about. In the offence, conceal yourself and your equipment with camouflage and move in woods or on terrain that gives concealment. Darkness cannot hide you from enemy observation in either offence or defence. The enemy's night vision devices and other means of detection let them find you in both daylight and darkness.

(4.2) Camouflage

Thou shalt blend with thy surroundings, for trees groweth not in yon desert.

Camouflage is anything you use to keep yourself, your equipment, and your position from looking like what they are. Both natural and man-made material can be used for camouflage. Change and improve your camouflage often. The time between changes and improvements depends on the weather and on the material used. Natural camouflage will often die, fade, or otherwise lose its effectiveness. Likewise, man-made camouflage may wear off or fade. When those things happen, you and your equipment or position may not blend with the surroundings. That may make it easy for the enemy to spot you.

Movement draws attention. When you give arm-and-hand signals or walk about your position, your movement can be seen by the naked eye at long ranges. In the defence, stay low and move only when necessary. In the offence, move only on covered and concealed routes.

Positions must not be where the enemy expects to find them. Build positions on the side of a hill, away from road junctions or lone buildings, and in covered and concealed places. Avoid open areas.

Outlines and shadows may reveal your position or equipment to air or ground observers. Outlines and shadows can be broken up with camouflage. When moving, stay in the shadows when possible.

Shine may also attract the enemy's attention. In the dark, it may be a light such as a burning cigarette or flashlight. In daylight, it can be reflected light from polished surfaces such as shiny mess gear, a worn helmet, a windshield, a watch crystal and band, or exposed skin. A light, or its reflection, from a position may help the enemy detect the position. To reduce shine, cover your skin with clothing and face paint. Also, dull the surfaces of equipment and vehicles with paint, mud, or some type of camouflage material.

Shape is outline or form. The shape of a helmet is easily recognised. A human body is also easily recognised. Use camouflage and concealment to breakup shapes and blend them with their surroundings. Be careful not to overdo it.

The colours of your skin, uniform, and equipment may help the enemy detect you if the colours contrast with the background. For example, a green uniform will contrast with snow-covered terrain. Camouflage yourself and your equipment to help blend with the surroundings.

Dispersion is the spreading of men, vehicles, and equipment over a wide area. It is usually easier for the enemy to detect soldiers when they are bunched. So, spread out. The distance between you and your fellow soldier will vary with the terrain, degree of visibility, and enemy situation.

Exposed skin reflects light and may draw the enemy's attention. Even very dark skin, because of its natural oil, will reflect light. Use the following methods when applying camouflage face paint to camouflage the skin. When applying camouflage stick to your skin, work with a buddy (in pairs) and help each other. Apply a two-colour combination of camouflage stick in an irregular pattern. Paint shiny areas (forehead, cheekbones, nose, ears, and chin) with a dark colour. Paint shadow areas (around the eyes, under the nose, and under the chin) with a light colour. In addition to the face, paint the exposed skin on the back of the neck, arms, and hands. Palms of hands are not normally camouflaged if arm-and-hand signals are to be used. Remove all jewellery to further reduce shine or reflection. When camouflage sticks are not issued, use burnt cork, bark, charcoal, lamp black, or light-coloured mud.

(4.3) Moving Stealthily

You're only better than your enemy if you kill him first.

Your unit's ability to move stealthily depends on your movement skills and those of your fellow soldiers. Use the following techniques to avoid being seen or heard by the enemy: Camouflage yourself and your equipment. Tape or pad the parts of your weapon and equipment that rattle or are so loose that they may snag (the tape or padding must not interfere with the operation of the weapon or equipment). Jump up and down and listen for rattles. Wear soft, well-fitting clothes. Do not carry unnecessary equipment. Move from covered position to covered position (taking no longer than 3 to 5 seconds between positions). Stop, look, and listen before moving. Look for your next position before leaving a position. Look for covered and concealed routes on which to move. Change direction slightly from time to time when moving through tall grass. Stop, look, and listen when birds or animals are alarmed (the enemy may be nearby). Use battlefield noises, such as weapon noises, to conceal movement noises. Cross roads and trails at places that have the most cover and concealment (large culverts, low spots, curves, or bridges). Avoid steep slopes and places with loose dirt or stones. Avoid cleared, open areas and tops of hills and ridges.

In addition to walking, you may move in one of three other methods — low crawl, high crawl, or rush.

The low crawl gives you the lowest silhouette. Use it to cross places where the concealment is very low and enemy fire or observation prevents you from getting up. Keep your body flat against the ground. With your firing hand, grasp your weapon sling at the upper sling—swivel. Let the front hand guard rest on your forearm (keeping the muzzle off the ground), and let the weapon butt drag on the ground. To move, push your arms forward and pull your firing side leg forward. Then pull with your arms and push with your leg. Continue this throughout the move.

The high crawl lets you move faster than the low crawl and still gives you a low silhouette. Use this crawl when there is good concealment but enemy fire prevents you from getting up. Keep your body off the ground and resting on your forearms and lower legs. Cradle your weapon in your arms and keep its muzzle off the ground. Keep your knees well behind your buttocks so your body will stay low. To move, alternately advance your right elbow and left knee, then your left elbow and right knee.

The rush is the fastest way to move from one position to another. Each rush should last from 3 to 5 seconds. The rushes are kept short to keep enemy machine gunners or riflemen from tracking you. However, do not stop and hit the ground in the open just because 5 seconds have passed. Always try to hit the ground behind some cover. Before moving, pick out your next covered and concealed position and the best route to it. Make your move from the prone position as follows: Slowly raise your head and pick your next position and the route to it. Slowly lower your head. Draw your arms into your body (keeping your elbows in). Pull your right leg forward. Raise your body by straightening your arms. Get up quickly. Run to the next position.

When you are ready to stop moving, do the following: Plant both of your feet. Drop to your knees (at the same time slide a hand to the butt of your rifle). Fall forward, breaking the fall with the butt of the rifle. Go to a prone firing position. If you have been firing from one position for some time, the enemy may have spotted you and may be waiting for you to come up from behind cover. Hence, before rushing forward, roll or crawl a short distance from your position. By coming up from another spot, you may fool an enemy who is aiming at one spot, waiting for you to rise. When the route to your next position is through an open area, rush by zig-zagging. If necessary, hit the ground, roll right or left, then rush again.

Moving with stealth means that you must move quietly, slowly and carefully. This requires great patience. To move with stealth, use the following techniques: Hold your rifle at port arms (ready position). Make your footing sure and solid by keeping your body's weight on the foot on the ground while stepping. Raise the moving leg high to clear brush or grass. Gently let the moving foot down toe first, with your body's weight on the rear leg. Lower the heel of the moving foot after the toe is in a solid place. Shift your body's weight and balance to the forward foot before moving the rear foot. Take short steps to help maintain balance. At night and when moving through dense vegetation; avoid making noise. Hold your weapon with one hand, and keep the other hand forward, feeling for obstructions.

When going into a prone position, use the following techniques: Hold your rifle with one hand and crouch slowly. Feel for the ground with your free hand to make sure it is clear of mines, tripwires, and other hazards. Lower your knees, one at a time, until your body's weight is on both knees and your free hand. Shift your weight to your free hand and opposite knee. Raise your free leg up and back, and lower it gently to that side. Move the other leg into position the same way. Roll quietly into a prone position.

Use the following techniques when crawling: Crawl on your hands and knees. Hold your rifle in your firing hand. Use your non-firing hand to feel for and make clear spots for your hands and knees to move to.

(4.4) Negotiating Dense Terrain

You will usually move as a member of a team. Small teams, such as infantry fire teams, normally move in a wedge formation that has been discussed later in detail. Each soldier in the team has a set position in the wedge, determined by the type weapon he carries. That position, however, may be changed by the team leader to meet the situation. The normal distance between soldiers is 10 yards. You may have to make a temporary change in the wedge formation when moving through close terrain. The soldiers in the sides of the wedge close into a single file when moving in thick brush or through a narrow pass. After passing through such an area, they should spread out, again forming the wedge. You should not wait for orders to change the formation or the interval. You should change automatically and stay in visual contact with the other team members and the team leader. The team leader leads by setting the example. His standing order is, 'follow me and do as I do'. When he moves to the left, you should move to the left. When he gets down, you should get down. When he fires, you should fire.

When visibility is limited, control during movement may become difficult. Two l-inch horizontal strips of luminous tape, sewn directly on the rear of the helmet camouflage band with a l-inch space between them, are a device for night identification. Night identification for your patrol cap could be two l-inch by 1/2-inch strips of luminous tape sewn vertically, directly on the rear of the cap. They should be centered, with the bottom edge of each tape even with the bottom edge of the cap and with a l-inch space between two tapes.

(4.5) Fire and Movement

The buddy system is essential to your survival; it gives the enemy somebody else to shoot at.

When a unit makes contact with the enemy, it normally starts firing at and moving towards the enemy. Sometimes the unit may move away from the enemy. That technique is called fire and movement. It is conducted either to close with and destroy the enemy, or to move away from the enemy so as to break contact with him. Firing and moving take place at the same time. There is a fire element and a movement element. These elements may be single soldiers, buddy teams, fire teams, or squads. Regardless of the size of the elements, the action is still fire and movement. The fire element covers the move of the movement element by firing at the enemy. This helps keep the enemy from firing back at the movement element. The movement element moves either to close with the enemy or to reach a better position from which to fire at him. The movement element should not move until the fire element is firing.

Depending on the distance to the enemy position and on the available cover, the fire element and the movement element switch roles as needed to keep moving. Before the movement element moves beyond the supporting range of the fire element (the distance within which the weapons of the fire element can fire and support the movement element), it should take a position from which it can fire at the enemy. The movement element then becomes the next fire element and the fire element becomes the next movement element. If your team makes contact, your team leader should tell you to fire or to move. He should also tell you where to fire from, what to fire at, or where to move to. When moving, use the low crawl, high crawl, or rush.

(4.6) Observation during Day and Night

If the enemy is in range, so are you.

In daylight, use the visual search technique to search terrain. Do this in two steps:

Step 1: Make a quick, overall search of the entire sector for obvious targets and unnatural colours, outlines, or movements. Look first at the area just in front of your position, and then quickly scan the entire area out to the maximum range you want to observe. If the sector is wide, divide it and search each sub-sector as in Step 2.

Step 2: Observe overlapping, 50-meterwide strips, alternating from left to right and right to left, until you have searched the entire sector. When you see a suspicious spot, search it well.

At night, use anyone of three night observation techniques to search terrain.

Dark Adaptation Technique: First, let your eyes become adjusted to the darkness. Do so by staying either in a dark area for about 30 minutes, or in a red-lighted area for about 20 minutes followed by about 10 minutes in a dark area. The red-lighted method may save time by allowing you to get orders, check equipment, or do some other job before moving into darkness.

Off-center Vision Technique: Focus your attention on an object but look slightly away from it. The object will be more visible this way than when you look straight at it.

Scanning Technique: Again focus your attention on an object, but do not look directly at it. Now move your eyes in short, abrupt, and irregular movements around it, pausing a few seconds after each move.

In trying to find the enemy in a sector of observation, look and listen for these signs of his presence:

Sounds: Listen for such things as footsteps, limbs or sticks breaking, leaves rustling, men coughing, and equipment or vehicle sounds. Remember that these may be hard to distinguish from other battlefield and animal sounds. Sounds can alert you to the direction or general location of the enemy. They may not pinpoint his exact location.

However, if a sound alerts you, you are more apt to spot the enemy. Moving foot soldiers or vehicles often raise dust. Vehicle exhaust smoke also rises. You can spot dust and vehicle smoke at long ranges.

Movement: Look for movement in your visual search technique.

Positions: Look for enemy positions in obvious places, such as road junctions, hilltops, and lone buildings. Also look at areas with cover and concealment, such as woods and draws.

Outlines or Shadows: Look for outlines or shadows of enemy soldiers, equipment, vehicles, or guns. The enemy may use the shadows of trees or buildings to hide himself and his equipment. Look for him in shaded areas.

Shine or Glare: In darkness, look for light sources such as burning cigarettes, illuminated screens of mobile phones, iPods, headlights, or flashlights. In daylight, look for reflected light or glare from smooth, polished surfaces such as windshields, headlights, mess gear, watch crystals, or un-camouflaged skin.

Contrasting Colours: Look for contrasts between background colour and the colours of uniforms, equipment, and skin. For example, a soldier's T-shirt or towel may contrast with its background.

(4.7) Range Estimation

You must often estimate ranges. Your estimates will be easier to make and more accurate if you use the 100-meter unit-of-measure method, the appearance-of-objects method, or the flash-and-sound method. This section discusses the use of these methods.

(4.7.1) 100-Meter Unit-of-Measure Method (Daytime)

Picture a distance of 100 meters on the ground. For ranges up to 500 meters, count the number of 100-meter lengths between the two points you want to measure. Beyond 500 meters, pick a point halfway to the target, count the number of 100-meter lengths to the halfway point, and then double that number to get the range to the target. Sloping ground changes the appearance of 100-meter lengths. Ground that slopes upward makes them look longer than 100 meters, and ground that slopes downward makes them look shorter than 100 meters. Thus, the tendency is to underestimate 100-meter lengths on upslopes and overestimate them on downslopes. The accuracy of the 100-meter method depends on how much ground is visible. This is most true at long ranges. If a target is at a range of 500 meters or more, and you can only see part of the ground between yourself and the target, it is hard to use this method with accuracy.

(4.7.2) *Appearance-of-Objects Method (Daytime)*

This method is a way to estimate range by the apparent size and detail of an object. It is a common method that is used in everyday life. For example, a motorist trying to pass another car judges the distance of oncoming cars based on their apparent size. He is not interested in exact distances, but only in having enough room to safely pass the car in front of him. Suppose he knows that at a distance of 1 mile an oncoming car appears to be 1 inch wide and 2 inches high, with a half inch between the headlights. Then, any time he sees an oncoming car that fits those dimensions, he knows it is about 1 mile away. The same technique can be used to estimate ranges on the battlefield. If you know the apparent size and detail of troops and equipment at known ranges, then you can compare those characteristics to similar objects at unknown ranges. When the characteristics match, the range does also. To use the appearance-of-objects method, you must be familiar with characteristic details of objects as they appear at various ranges. As you must be able to see those details to make the method work, anything that limits visibility (such as weather, smoke, or darkness) will limit the effectiveness of this method.

(4.7.3) *Combination of Methods*

Battlefield conditions are not always ideal for estimating ranges. If the terrain limits the use of the 100-meter unit-of-measure method, and poor visibility limits the use of the appearance-of-objects method, you may have to use a combination of methods. For example, if you cannot see all of the terrain out to the target, you can still estimate distance from the apparent size and detail of the target itself. A haze may obscure the target details, but you may still be able to judge its size or use the 100-meter method. By using either one or both of the methods, you should arrive at a figure close to the true range.

(4.7.4) *Flash-and-Sound Method (Best at Night)*

Sound travels through air roughly at 300 meters (1,100 feet) per second. That makes it possible to estimate distance if you can both see and hear a sound-producing action. When you see the flash or smoke of a weapon, or the dust it raises, immediately start counting. Stop counting when you hear the sound associated with the action seen. The number at which you stop should be multiplied by three. This gives you the approximate distance to the weapon in hundreds of meters. If you stop at one, the distance is about 300 meters. If you stop at three, the distance is about 900 meters. If you are obliged to count higher than nine, start over again after counting nine (counting higher numbers throws the timing off).

(4.8) Combat in the Night

Never get into a fight with any guy having more ammunition than you.

(4.8.1) Problems Unique to Fighting in the Night

Night fighting is indispensable in counter-insurgency operations. Combat at night may also be an extension of combat actions begun during the day. The battle may be carried on into the night to retain the initiative with a high offensive tempo. Soldiers are generally apprehensive of night combat. Forces need to be specially trained and conditioned to fight successfully in the night. It is worthwhile to learn what the Soviets thought of this. In the Soviet view, however, night cannot be a reason for decreasing activity. On the contrary, they use the dark of night to achieve surprise, to increase the rate of advance, and to win time. The Soviets considered darkness to be more of an advantage and an opportunity than a reason for interruption of combat. The Soviets recognised that darkness favoured the performance of marches and manoeuvre; made it easier to concentrate men and materiel in a decisive direction; hampered enemy use of most weapons, airborne troops, and aviation; and provided favourable conditions for achieving surprise. By skillfully employing the advantages of night conditions, attacking units can fulfill their mission with smaller losses in personnel and equipment.

Night fighting does present problems beyond the most obvious. It is more difficult to orient oneself at night and to maintain direction of movement. Night combat is affected significantly by the physical and psychological conditions of the troops. Darkness stimulates the imagination and a feeling of insecurity that might eventually lead to panic. Nights are normally reserved for rest. The biological clock or circadian rhythm of the men gets naturally adjusted that way. Unless conscious attempts have been made during the training to change the circadian rhythm, fatigue and symptoms of exhaustion may affect those who have to stay awake—even when they are doing so by rotation.

Darkness modifies the outline, shape, and colouring of local objects and distorts separation distances. Dark objects seem farther away than they really are, while lighter ones appear to be closer. According to the

Soviets, on a clear night one can recognise land relief and colouration up to 400 meters with the naked eye. Under a high moon, one can spot a moving man at 240 meters, and using binoculars, at 700 meters. Sound is another factor that changes at night and leads to both physical and psychological distortion. At night, sounds seem louder and carry farther. Directions from which sounds originate cannot always be determined. Weather conditions such as rain can affect both audibility and visibility and serve as a definite advantage for the attacker. The lack of convection (vertical streams of air) also affects night combat, since the persistence of gas, fog, or smoke is considerably increased in the absence of vertical air streams. Effectiveness of aimed fire is reduced considerably by darkness, and reconnaissance and selection of targets become more difficult. Effective fires are almost impossible without night-vision equipment or illumination.

The Soviets maintained, however, that all these negative factors could be successfully overcome through frequent and careful training. Soviet doctrine stated that the difficulty inherent in a night attack aided the soldier in the defence and that the defender was more confident. However, they also recognised that a well-organised surprise attack had a strong negative psychological effect on the defender.

(4.8.2) Distances at which Light Sources can be observed at night with the Naked Eye

This is highly instructive and would be of great help to soldiers both in offence and defence. These facts have been discovered both by the Soviets and the Americans after a great deal of research and experimentation in the field and hence need to be valued.

Vehicle headlights	4-8 km
Muzzle flashes from single cannons	4-5 km
Muzzle flashes from small arms	1.5-2 km
Bonfire	6-8 km
Flashlight up to	1.5-2 km
Lighted match up to	1.5 km
Lighted cigarette	0.5-0.8 km

Note that for observation from the air, these distances are increased 2 to 3 times.

(4.8.3) *Distances at which Sounds are Audible to Man at Night in Open Areas*

This is also highly instructive and would be of great help to soldiers both in offence and defence. They also have been discovered both by the Soviets and the Americans after a great deal of research and experimentation in the field and hence need to be valued.

Cannon shot up to	15 km
Single shot from a rifle	2-3 km
Automatic weapons fire	3-4 km
Tank movement on a dirt road up to	1.2 km
- on a highway	3-4 km
Motor vehicle movement - on a dirt road up to	500 m
- on a highway up to	1 km
Movement of troops on foot- on a dirt road up to	300 m
- on a highway up to	600 m
Loading/Cocking of small arms up to	500 m
Metal on metal sound up to	300 m
Conversation of a few men up to	300 m
Steps of a single man up to	40 m
Axe blow, sound of a saw up to	500 m
Blows of shovels and pickaxes up to	1,000 m
Screams up to	1,500 m
Oars on water up to	2,000 m

(4.9) Engagement with the Enemy

Always cheat; always win. The only unfair fight is the one you lose.

(4.9.1) *The Importance of Supporting the Element that is Engaged*

In the jungle firefight, the side which initiates contact and gains fire superiority in the first few seconds will normally have a decisive advantage. Successful jungle attacks usually combine dispersion and concentration. For example, a rifle company may move out in a dispersed formation so that it can find the enemy. Once contact is made, its platoons close on the enemy from all directions. In this way, they move to support each other and destroy the enemy. To concentrate overwhelming combat power against enemy weakness in jungle operations, the attacker must be able to bring up other elements quickly to support an element that is engaged. In determining how far he can separate his subordinate units, the commander must consider the factors of mission, enemy, terrain and weather, troops available, time available, and civil considerations (METT-TC). The separation may be expressed in time or in distance but the prime concern must be the ability to provide mutual support. The importance of supporting the element that is engaged should never be underestimated. The US army combat historian SLA Marshall had noted: "It is a situation that too frequently occurs in the Vietnam fighting. The forward element, losing men and becoming pinned down, compromises the position of all others. What has started out as an attack loses all form and deteriorates into a costly rescue act".

(4.9.2) *Movement to contact and hasty Attack*

You, you, and you ... panic. The rest of you, come with me.

The successful follow-on action to movement to contact is a violently executed hasty attack. This action capitalises on the advantage of surprise and the confusion prevalent in the jungle for companies and higher strengths, multiple columns are a sound movement practice because this formation provides more firepower to the front and because it is easier to deploy troops from two or three columns than from one file. In order to speed up deployment, units should develop and rehearse SOPs and immediate action drills. Troops should try to maintain a distance of five to seven paces between men, but must maintain visual contact. All-round defense and security measures must be maintained throughout movement. Some Indian forces disperse the men greatly under a mistaken notion that it would reduce casualties in an ambush. This is sheer imbecility. It only helps you when they deliver the first volley. After that, the fact is that dispersed men are not at all able to deliver effective fire, are picked up one-by-one and eliminated. Once contact with the enemy is made, the unit's first action must be to build up a large volume of fire. The commander must then assess the situation and deploy his unit to overrun the enemy's positions while they are still suppressed. In this way, he seizes the initiative. There should be no delay in the troops' movement from the march formation into assault formation. Security elements protect the rear and prevent the enemy's counter-attack. These forces may be used later to exploit a success, but should not be committed until the commander understands the situation.

Example of a violently executed hasty attack immediately on contact

As the situation is developed and an enemy position is located, a violent assault should be made over the enemy's position. Soldiers must stay on the alert for hidden enemy positions, snipers in the trees, and tunnels or concealed pits through which the enemy might emerge to attack the attacker's rear. The assault should be made using fire and manoeuvre. Soldiers should cover each other, moving by crawls and short rushes. Fire should be well-aimed shots and short bursts of automatic fire. The standard American practice which they developed since Korea and Vietnam was that they immediately made a request for supporting indirect fire. To receive effective and timely fire support, accurate and continuous land navigation was necessary. This is not really possible in anti-terrorist operations by other forces—particularly that are operating in their own country.

(4.9.3) The Deliberate Attack

If you have specific intelligence, you may formulate a plan to attack a larger objective using a deliberate attack. This, in effect, becomes like a regular infantry assault on an enemy position and hence does not warrant a detailed discussion here because it is well-known.

(4.9.4) Exploitation and Pursuit

Local successes should be exploited as soon as possible to cut off the retreat of isolated enemy forces. During exploitations, rear areas must be secured against the actions of bypassed or infiltrating enemy.

(4.9.5) Raids

Jungles favour raid operations. The excellent concealment enables skilled raiding patrols to operate deep in enemy territory. Platoon-sized units are best suited to jungle raids. Raids in the jungle environment must be keyed to reliable intelligence. The actions of the raiding unit must be decisive and rapid in order to catch an elusive jungle enemy. A raid's success depends on good intelligence and a sound plan.

(4.9.6) Encirclement and various Techniques of Destruction

Encirclement is designed to cut off all ground routes for escape and reinforcement of the encircled guerrilla force. It does not mean that you make a circle around him. Should you do that, you would also be shooting at some of your guys. Encirclement offers the best possibility for fixing guerrilla forces in position and achieving decisive results. Obviously, you can do it best only under the cover of darkness. The problem is that only battalion and larger units may conduct encirclements. The company and smaller units normally lack enough men and command and control capability to conduct encirclements (except against small, concentrated guerrilla forces). Encircling movements must be executed rapidly. Positions must be occupied simultaneously in order to block escape. If simultaneous occupation is not possible, escape routes most likely to be used are covered first. Initial occupation is the most critical period of encirclement. If large guerrilla formations realise that they are being encircled, they can be expected to react immediately to probe for gaps or attack weak points to force a gap. Mobile reserves must be positioned for immediate movement to counter any threat of a breakout, and to reinforce difficult areas such as deep ravines or areas containing cave or tunnel complexes. Indirect fire support can cloak an impending encirclement by gaining and maintaining the guerrilla's attention while encircling units move into position.

Following the initial encirclement, the capture or destruction of the guerrilla force must be methodical and thorough. Fire and manoeuvre are used in a simultaneous, controlled contraction of the encirclement. One technique, employed after some degree of contraction, is to employ a blocking force on one or more sides of the perimeter while part of the encirclement forces the guerrillas against the blocking force by offensive action. In the so-called hammer and anvil method, one or more units in the encirclement remain stationary while the others drive the guerrilla unit against it. In the wedge method, a unit is used to divide the enemy while the encircling elements remain in place.

(4.10) Attacks during Limited Visibility

Attacks during limited visibility achieve surprise, avoid heavy losses, cause panic in a weak and disorganised enemy, exploit success and maintain momentum, and keep pressure on the enemy. Limited visibility operations are one of the main missions of ground forces. Whenever possible, commandos will use limited visibility to conduct attacks.

a. **Planning:** The planning considerations for daylight attacks are the same as for limited visibility attacks. However, limited visibility attacks require additional control measures to prevent fratricide and keep the attack focused on the objective. Leaders may use boundaries, restrictive fire lines, and limits of advance to assist in control.

b. **Reconnaissance:** Reconnaissance is key to successful night attacks. It should be conducted during daylight down to the lowest level possible. The platoon should reconnoiter the routes on which they will move, the positions that they will occupy, and the assigned objective. The need for detailed information about the enemy must be balanced against the risk of being detected and the loss of surprise.

   (1) The reconnaissance plan should also establish surveillance on the objective in case the enemy repositions units and weapons or prepares additional obstacles. Surveillance and security forces should also secure critical locations, such as assault and support positions, LD and PLD, routes, and RPs, to protect the platoon from enemy ambushes and spoiling attacks. These security forces may become part of the isolation element during the attack.

   (2) When reconnaissance does not succeed due to lack of time, the platoon leader requests a delay in the attack time to allow for further reconnaissance. If this is not possible, an illuminated and supported attack should be considered. A night attack with marginal information of the enemy's defense is risky and difficult to conduct.

c. **Use of Guides:** During limited visibility attacks, the platoon may use guides to provide better control while moving into the assault position and onto the probable line of deployment (PLD).

   (1) The company may organise a patrol to place platoon guides from the LD to subsequent RPs, at the entrance to the assault positions and at points along the PDL.

(2) Guides must be fully briefed on the plan and on their specific duties. They must rehearse their actions, to include—

- Reconnaissance of their assigned routes and release points.
- Pick-up and release of their assigned units. They must be able to identify the leader of the element they will guide (or the lead soldier of that element). They must also know and rehearse recognition signals.

(3) Platoons must rehearse their actions in the same order of march and sequence that they intend to use during the attack in order to make the pick-up and release of guides go smoothly.

d. **Fire Control Techniques:** Fire control techniques for limited visibility include the following.

(1) **Tracer fire:** Leaders in the assault element fire all tracers; their soldiers fire where the leader's tracers impact. The support element positions a machinegun on a tripod on the flank nearest the assault force. This weapon fires a burst of tracers every 15 seconds to indicate the near limit of the supporting fires. All other weapons in the support element keep their fires on the appropriate side of this tracer. The assault force signals to shift fires to the next position or to a set distance. If required, these rounds can be adjusted over the assault element to preclude fratricide.

(2) **Luminous tape or chemical lights:** Leaders must mark assault personnel with these to prevent fratricide. The enemy should, however, not be able to see the marking. The techniques are to place tape on the back of the helmet or to use small infrared chemical lights (if the enemy has no NVDs). The support element must know where the lead assault element is. If the individual soldier markings do not suffice, large chemical lights (infrared or visible) are used. These lights are placed on the ground or thrown in front of the assault element. When clearing a trench line, soldiers may put chemical lights on a stick and move them with the lead element to ensure the support element shifts fires.

(3) **Weapon control restrictions:** To reduce the risk to the assault element, the leader may assign weapon control restrictions.

(a) The squad on the right in the assault might be given weapons free to the right flank because no friendly soldiers are there.

However, weapons tight or hold on the left means that another friendly unit is located there.

(b) No automatic weapons will be fired by the assault force on the objective. This ensures that all automatic weapons are enemy.

(4) **Other techniques:** To increase control during the assault, the leader may use the following.

- No flares, grenades, or smoke used on the objective.
- Only certain personnel with NVDs can engage targets on the objective.
- A magnetic azimuth for maintaining direction.
- Mortar or artillery rounds to orient attacking units.
- Guides.
- A base squad or fire team to pace and guide others.
- Reduced intervals between soldiers and squads.
- Luminous tape on armbands or helmets.

(4.11) Waterborne Combat Operations in Jungles

The use of inland and coastal waterways can add flexibility, surprise, and speed to tactical operations in jungle areas. Use of these waterways will also increase the load-carrying capacity of units which normally operate dismounted. Thus, every combat leader should be familiar with the tactical and technical aspects of small boat handling.

Special considerations in the conduct of jungle waterborne operations include the following:

- The heavy vegetation along the banks of inland waterways offers excellent concealment and enhances the effectiveness of ambushes against watercraft. Therefore, counter-ambush measures must be planned in conjunction with all water movements.
- Steep, slippery river banks coupled with dense vegetation often make committing the waterborne force in a coordinated assault landing extremely difficult. This must be taken into account while planning.
- Fire support to include mortar, artillery, close air support, and available naval gunfire must be preplanned for all water movements.
- Actions taken on enemy contact resemble those taken ashore. The elements caught in the enemy's fire return fire, beach the boats,

seek cover, and continue to fire. Other elements beach their boats and manoeuvre ashore to destroy the enemy.

- When a patrol is inserted by boat, the landing site must be secured before all elements of the patrol disembark. A good technique is to have the lead boat unload its personnel at the landing site while the other boats cover them from a distance. After the site is secured, the other boats are landed on signal. After the boats have landed, the crews either hide the boats or have them removed from the area. In either case, the crews remove any signs of activity on the landing site.

(4.12) Searching Populated Areas

There are four fundamentals of searching a populated area.

Approach: On some operations, the situation may allow mounted movement directly into the area to be searched. On others, the situation may dictate dismounted movement into the area. What is important is that you must enter rapidly and in a coordinated manner into the area.

Surrounding the Area: Move to the area silently under the cover of darkness through as many different routes as possible. At first daylight, if it is a large area, it can be occupied by a chain of observation posts with gaps covered by patrols or barbed wire/concertina.

Reserves: If there is a chance that hostile elements from outside the area could interfere, measures are taken to prevent them from joining the inhabitants of the area under search.

Search Parties: Most forces are familiar with the drill; still for the sake of completeness, we must mention that when a decision is made to gather inhabitants at a central point, the head of the house should necessarily accompany the search party when his house is searched. Legal issues apart, the fact is that he would be obliged to reveal the presence of terrorists in his house, in case he does not want to get caught in the crossfire. Buildings must be searched from top to bottom, if possible. Mine detectors must be used to search for arms and ammunition. In areas where tunnels have been reported, it is imperative that the search unit have a tunnel reconnaissance team trained for this type of operation. They should have special equipment such as flashlights or miner helmets, protective masks, communication with the surface, and silencer-equipped pistols. They should know how to sketch a tunnel system.

(4.13) Field Expedient Communications

VHF communication, being a line-of-sight communication, has obvious limitations in a jungle where you cannot have the luxury of repeaters. Portable HF communication solves the problem to some extent. Field expedient antennas will enhance the communications capacity of a unit operating in the jungle if they are properly constructed. This is a fascinating subject in itself. The Americans have applied a great deal of mind to it and have even published literature as to how to construct it. They fought the whole Vietnam War with them. American radio communication was excellent. Any unit in distress could summon help through radio. Even if he could not get through to his own unit's net, somebody else came to his help. It would be instructive for anyone interested in communication to study the Vietnam era US military communication in detail. That's a classic example of how a given technology can be perfected and exploited to the maximum.

5

Fundamental Techniques of Movement in Jungles

It's not a lot of work unless you have to do it.

(5.1) Travelling, Travelling Overwatch and Bounding Overwatch

A movement technique is the manner a unit uses to traverse terrain. There are three fundamental movement techniques: travelling, travelling overwatch, and bounding overwatch. The selection of a movement technique is based on the likelihood of enemy contact and the need for speed. Factors to consider for each technique are control, dispersion, speed, and security.

Movement techniques refer to the distances between soldiers, teams, and squads that vary based on mission, enemy, terrain, visibility, and any other factor that affects control. Soldiers must be able to see their fire team leader. The distances mentioned above are purely indicative and refer to daytime movement—you can vary them greatly depending on the thickness of the vegetation, terrain contours, and visibility. As a rule of thumb, formations in night will be much tighter—to the extent of men within touching distance of each other. The squad leader must be able to see his fire team leaders. The platoon leader should be able to see his lead squad leader, and the like. Leaders control movement with arm-and-hand signals during daytime. They use radios only when needed, such as in the night. Any of the three movement techniques (travelling, travelling overwatch, bounding overwatch) can be used with any formation.

(5.1.1) *Techniques of Squad/Section Movement*

(1) **Travelling:** Travelling is used when contact with the enemy is not likely and speed is needed. You can think of it as roughly three file formations in parallel which support each other. The

distance between the head and the tail of the section could be up to 80 yards.

(2) **Travelling overwatch:** Travelling overwatch is used when contact is possible. You still maintain the three supporting files structure but the distance between the head and the tail is increased up to 150 yards.

(3) **Bounding overwatch:** Bounding overwatch is used when contact is expected, when the squad leader feels the enemy is near (movement, noise, reflection, trash, fresh tracks, or even a hunch), or when a large open danger area must be crossed.

(a) The lead fire team overwatches first. Soldiers scan for enemy positions. The squad leader usually stays with the overwatch team.

(b) The trail fire team bounds and signals the squad leader when his team completes its bound and is prepared to overwatch the movement of the other team.

(c) Both team leaders must know if successive or alternate bounds will be used and which team the squad leader will be with. The overwatching team leader must know the route and destination of the bounding team. The bounding team leader must know his team's destination and route, possible enemy locations, and actions to take when he arrives there. He must also know where the overwatching team will be, and how he will receive his instructions. The cover and concealment on the bounding team's route dictates how its soldiers move.

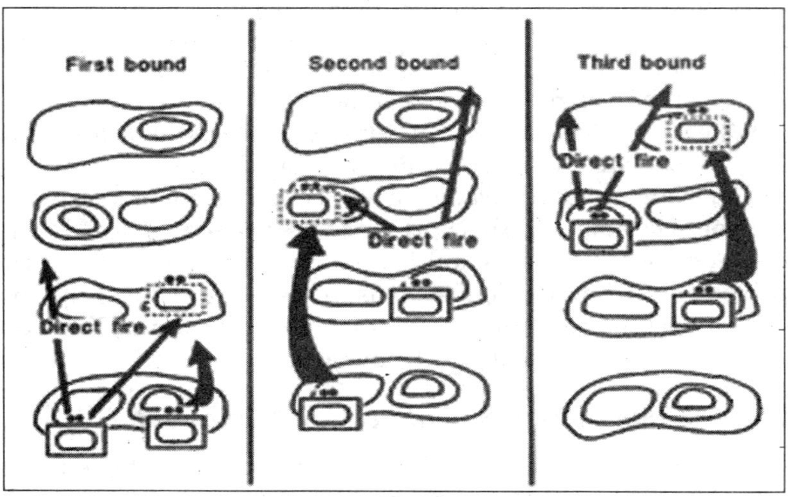

Movement by alternating bounds

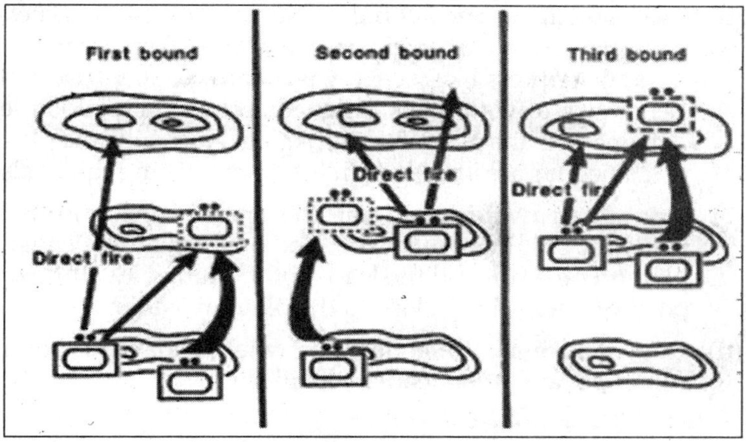

Movement by successive bounds

(d) Teams can bound successively or alternately. Successive bounds are easier to control; alternate bounds can be faster.

(5.1.2) Techniques of Platoon Movement

(1) **Travelling:** Travelling is used when enemy contact is not likely and speed is needed. The basic structure is as follows. The lead squad is in travelling overwatch formation. It is followed by the platoon HQ weapons. That is followed by the second squad. It is followed by the platoon leader and his radio operator et al. They are followed by the last squad. Each element is separated from the other by about 20 yards.

(2) **Travelling overwatch:** Travelling overwatch is used when contact is possible but speed is needed. The lead squad uses travelling overwatch, and the trailing squads use travelling. The distance between the lead squad and the platoon HQ weapons is increased to 50-100 yards. Other elements retain the same relative positions.

(3) **Bounding overwatch:** Bounding overwatch is used when contact is expected. Platoons conduct bounding overwatch using successive or alternate bounds.

(a) **One squad bounding:** One squad bounds forward to a chosen position and then it becomes the overwatching element unless contact is made en route. The bounding squad can use either travelling overwatch, bounding overmatch, or individual movement techniques (low and high crawl, and short rushes by fire team or pairs).

(b) **One squad overwatching:** One squad overwatches the bounding squad from covered positions from which it can see and suppress likely enemy positions. Soldiers use sunning techniques to view their assigned sector. The platoon leader remains with the overmatching squad. Normally, the platoon's machineguns are located with the overwatching squad also.

(c) **One squad awaiting orders:** One squad is uncommitted and ready for employment as directed by the platoon leader. The platoon sergeant and the leader of the squad awaiting orders position themselves close to the platoon leader.

(d) **Considerations:** When deciding where to have his bounding squad go, a platoon leader considers—

- The requirements of the mission.
- Where the enemy is likely to be.
- The routes to the next overwatch position.
- The ability of an overwatching element's weapons to cover the bound.
- The responsiveness of the rest of the platoon.
- The fields of fire at the next overwatch position.

(e) **Instructions:** Before a bound, the platoon leader gives an order to his squad leaders from the overwatch position. He tells and shows them the following:

- The direction or location of the enemy (if known).
- The positions of the overwatching squad.
- The next overwatch position.
- The route of the bounding squad.
- What to do after the bounding squad reaches the next position.
- What signal the bounding squad will use to announce it is prepared to overwatch.
- How the squad will receive their next orders.

(f) **Machineguns:** The machineguns are normally employed in one of two ways:

- Attach both guns to the overwatch squad(s).
- One machinegun with the overwatch squad and the other with the bounding squad. This technique requires the guns to move between squads as they leave the overwatch to join the bounding squad.

(5.2) Movement during Limited Visibility Conditions

Don't ever be the first, don't ever be the last and don't ever volunteer to do anything.

Even at night or when visibility is poor, a unit must still be able to control, navigate, maintain security, move, and stalk.

(a) **Control:** When visibility is poor, the following methods aid in control:

- Selected personnel use of night vision devices.
- Leaders move closer to the front.
- The unit reduces speed.
- Each soldier uses two small strips of luminous tape on the rear of his helmet to allow the soldier behind him to see him. (Duffers need not worry—they will not be seen by the enemy unless he is very close. And if he is very close, he can detect you through other means also).
- Leaders reduce the interval between soldiers and between units to make sure they can see each other.
- Leaders conduct headcounts at regular intervals and after each halt to ensure personnel accountability.

(b) **Navigation:** To assist in navigation during limited visibility, leaders use:

- Terrain association (general direction of travel coupled with recognition of prominent map and ground features).
- Dead reckoning (compass direction and specific distances or legs). At the end of each leg, leaders should verify their location.
- Movement routes that parallel identifiable terrain features.
- Guides or marked routes.
- Position-location devices such as GPS. (But remember that the GPS is a blind navigator. It does not tell you much about the ground that is going to come under your feet—it may lead you to an area which is open, thereby constituting a kill zone where you have no cover. Moreover, it may have broken ground, like a field which has been ploughed and which has hardened after that. The result is that you cannot run on it in case you are fired upon. If you happen to chance upon such an area in the dark you may perhaps not take the risk of making a detour also for fear of unknown dangers

there. The GPS may lead you to a patch where a lot of noise is created by dry leaves or broken twigs; it may lead you to a place where the ground is unduly slippery, has numerous pits, boulders, or stumps. If it leads you to hilly features, you will have to reason and decide whether you would like to take a detour or climb them anyway).

- GSRs (Global Positioning System Software Radio) to vector units to the proper location.

(c) **Security:** For stealth and security in night moves, squads and platoons-:

- Designate a point man to maintain alertness, the lead team leader to navigate, and a pace man to count the distance travelled. Alternate compass and pace men are designated.
- Allow no smoking, no lights, and no noise.
- Use radio-listening silence.
- Camouflage soldiers and equipment.
- Use terrain to avoid detection by enemy surveillance or night vision devices.
- Make frequent listening halts.
- Mask the sounds of movement with artillery fires.

(d) **Night walking:** Proficiency in night walking is gained through practice. A soldier walking at night looks ahead, then slowly lifting his right foot, he eases it forward about 6 inches to the front of the left foot. While easing his foot forward and keeping his toes pointed downward, the soldier feels for twigs and trip wires. He slowly places his foot on the ground. Confident of solid, quiet footing, the soldier slowly moves his weight forward, hesitates, and then repeats the process with the other foot. This technique is slow and time-consuming.

(e) **Stalking:** Soldiers stalk to get as close as they can to an enemy sentry, patrol, or base. This is best described as a slow, crouching night walk. The soldier watches the enemy continuously. When close to the enemy, the soldier squints to help conceal light reflected by his eyes. He breathes slowly through his nose. If the enemy looks in his direction, the soldier freezes. He takes advantage of the background to blend with shadows and to prevent glare or contrast. Soldiers move during distractions such as gusts of wind, vehicle movement, loud talking, or nearby weapons fire.

(5.3) Movement by Water

Movement by water must be avoided as far as possible. Remember, you are very much exposed and vulnerable while you are on the water. There is a classic example in this regard. Indian readers may recall how in June 2008, the naxal insurgents had fired upon a boat of the Andhra Pradesh Special Force called Greyhounds crossing the Balimela reservoir in Malkangiri, Orissa from the shores. Many were shot and several of them drowned when the boat capsized, apparently as a result of frightened people running in it to take cover. There were 66 people in the boat—38 of them perished in the attack. After three days of combing in the forest the exhausted commandos had thought to take a short-cut to their base through the water route. The decision cut short their lives. As a rule of thumb, when platoons or squads must move into, through, or out of rivers, lakes, streams, or other bodies of water, they must treat the water obstacle as a danger area.

While on the water, the unit is exposed and vulnerable. To offset the disadvantages, the unit must try to:

- Move during limited visibility;
- Disperse;
- Cross load key soldiers and equipment.
- Make sure that the radio is with the leader.
- Camouflage thoroughly; and
- Move near the shore to reduce the chances of detection;
- If boats are not available, several other floating aids can be used such as poncho rafts; air mattresses; water-proof bags; and water wings (made from a set of trousers).
- A 7/16-inch rope can be used as a semi-submersible one-rope bridge or safety line.
- Leaders should identify weak or non-swimmers and pair them with a good swimmer in their squad.

(5.4) Actions at Danger Areas

The enemy diversion you've been ignoring is their main attack.

A danger area is any place on a route where the leader's estimate process tells him that his unit might be exposed to enemy observation, fire, or both. Units try to avoid danger areas. If a unit must cross a danger area, it does so with great caution and as quickly as possible.

a. **Types of Danger Areas:** The following are some examples of danger areas and crossing procedures.

(1) **Open areas:** Conceal the unit on the near side and observe the area. Post security to give early warning. Send an element across to clear the far side. When cleared, cross the remainder of the unit at the shortest exposed distance and as quickly as possible.

(2) **Roads and trails:** Cross roads or trails at or near a bend, a narrow spot, or on low ground.

(3) **Villages:** Pass villages on the downwind side and well away from them. Avoid animals, especially dogs, which might reveal the presence of the unit.

(4) **Enemy positions:** Pass on the downwind side (the enemy might have scout dogs). Be alert for trip wires and warning devices.

(5) **Minefields:** Bypass minefields if at all possible—even if it requires changing the route by a great distance. Bother to clear a path through minefields only if necessary.

(6) **Streams:** Select a narrow spot in the stream that offers concealment on both banks. Observe the far side carefully. Emplace near and far-side security for early warning. Clear the far side, and then cross rapidly but quietly.

(7) **Wire obstacles:** Avoid wire obstacles (the enemy covers obstacles with observation and fire).

b. **Crossing of Danger Areas:** When the unit crosses a danger area independently or as the lead element of a larger force, it must:

- Designate near- and far-side rally points.
- Secure the near side (right, left flanks, and rear security).
- Reconnoiter and secure the far side.
- Execute crossing the danger area.

(1) The platoon leader or squad leader decides how the unit will cross-based on the time he has, the size of the unit, the size of the danger area, the fields of fire into the area, and the amount of security he can post. A small unit may cross all at once, in buddy teams, or one soldier at a time. A large unit normally crosses its elements one at a time. As each element crosses, it moves to an overwatch position or to the far-side rally point until told to continue movement.

(2) To maintain momentum, leading platoons may cross the danger area without conducting their own reconnaissance or establishing far-side security. The lead platoon conducts reconnaissance and maintains far-side security for the whole force.

Note: The secured area must be large enough to allow the full deployment of the remainder of the unit.

c. **Crossing of Linear Danger Areas (Platoon):** The platoon crosses the danger area in the formation and location specified by the platoon leader. On the far side of the danger area, platoon personnel and equipment are accounted for. The platoon continues the mission.

(1) When the lead team signals "danger area" (relayed throughout the platoon), the platoon halts.

(2) The platoon leader moves forward, confirms the danger area, and determines what technique the platoon will use to cross.

(3) The platoon leader informs all squad leaders of the situation and the near-side and far-side rally points.

(4) This is followed by positioning of the near-side security (usually conducted by the trail squad). These two security teams may follow him forward when the platoon halts and a danger area signal is passed back.

(5) The platoon leader reconnoiters the danger area and selects the crossing point that provides the best cover and concealment.

(6) Near-side security observes to the flanks and overmatches the crossing.

(7) When the near-side security is in place, the platoon leader directs the far-side security team to cross the danger area.

(8) The far-side security team clears the far side.

(9) The far-side security team leader establishes an OP forward of the cleared area.

(10) The far-side security team signals to the squad leader that the area is clear. The squad leader relays the message to the platoon leader.

(11) The platoon leader selects the method the platoon will use to cross the danger area.

(12) The platoon quickly and quietly crosses the danger area.

(13) Once across the danger area, the main body begins moving slowly on the required azimuth.

(14) The near-side security element, controlled by the platoon sergeant, crosses the danger area where the platoon crossed. They may attempt to cover any tracks left by the platoon.

(15) The platoon sergeant ensures everyone crosses and sends up the report.

(16) The platoon leader ensures accountability and resumes movement at normal speed.

Note: The same principles stated above are used when crossing a smaller unit across a danger area.

d. **Crossing of large open areas:** This is an area so large that the platoon cannot bypass due to the time to accomplish the mission. A combination of travelling overwatch and bounding overwatch is used to cross the open area. The travelling overwatch technique is used to save time. At any point in the open area where contact may be expected or once the squad or platoon comes within range of small-arms fire of the far side (about 250 yards), the squad or platoon moves using the bounding overwatch technique. Once beyond the open area, the squad or platoon reforms and continues the mission.

e. **Crossing of small open areas:** This is an open area small enough so that it may be bypassed in the time allowed for the mission. Two techniques can be used:

(1) **Detour bypass method:** By the use of 90-degree turns to the right or left, the squad or platoon moves around the open area until the far side is reached, then continues the mission. The pace count of the offset and return legs is not added to the distance of the planned route.

(2) **Contouring around the open area:** The leader designates a rally point on the far side with the movement azimuth, decides which side of the open area to contour around (after considering the distance, terrain, cover and concealment), and moves around the open area. He uses the wood line and vegetation for cover and concealment. When the squad or platoon arrives at the rally point on the far side, the leader reassumes the azimuth to the objective area and continues the mission.

6

Combat Techniques of Fire and Fire Formations

The only time suppressive fire works, is when it is used on abandoned positions.

(6.1) The Secrets of Machinegun Fire

(6.1.1) Machinegun versus the Rifle

Infantrymen love their personal rifles; but they must learn to love their squad machineguns more. A rifle is a personal weapon—that's all; a personal weapon. It is given to you basically to relieve you of your fears and anxieties—to reassure you that if the enemy comes close, he won't get you cheap and that you shall have a respectable chance of threatening him seriously. Maybe he will be deterred to some extent; nothing more. The personal weapon also gives you some vim and vigour in combat and gives you a sense of involvement in battle. But for God's sake, do not nurse a fond misconception that rifles kill enemies or win battles. No my dears, rifles do not win battles—at least not in the modern era. You shall not be able to wipe out the ranks of the enemy with the rifle. Ever since the machinegun has been invented, the honours belong to the machinegun. Remember, the machinegun is the *carte blanche*—the decisive arm of infantry battles. The rifle is just a companion of the machinegun to assist it by its 'personal control'. You must value your rifle because it can save your ass; you are not going to whip the ass of the bad bandit by the poor rifle. Firing from the rifle is a pleasurable activity; but firing from the machinegun is orgasmic! Respect the firepower of the machinegun, and learn to use it properly.

It has been traditionally an area of great deficiency in countries like India where they have tended to use machineguns as simply heavy rifles which won't heat up quickly. The proper role of the machinegun in combat has never been appreciated by the dumb Indians. You would therefore better do to learn and appreciate the proper role of the machinegun in combat. It's a whole science in itself. Once you read the following, it will be clear to you that hitherto you knew practically nothing about machineguns, except the customary stripping and assembling it.

(6.1.2) *Basic Characteristics of Machinegun Fire*

Cone of Fire: When several rounds are fired in a burst from any machinegun, each round takes a slightly different trajectory. The pattern these rounds form on the way to the target is called a cone of fire. This pattern is caused primarily by vibration of the machinegun and variations in ammunition and atmospheric conditions

Beaten Zone: The beaten zone is the elliptical pattern formed by the rounds striking the ground or the target. The size and shape of the beaten zone changes when the range to the target changes or when the machinegun is fired on different types of terrain. On uniformly sloping or level terrain, the beaten zone is long and narrow. As the range to the target increases, the beaten zone becomes shorter and wider. When fire is delivered on terrain sloping down and away from the machinegun, the beaten zone becomes longer. When fire is delivered on rising terrain, the beaten zone becomes shorter. The terrain has little effect on the width of the beaten zone.

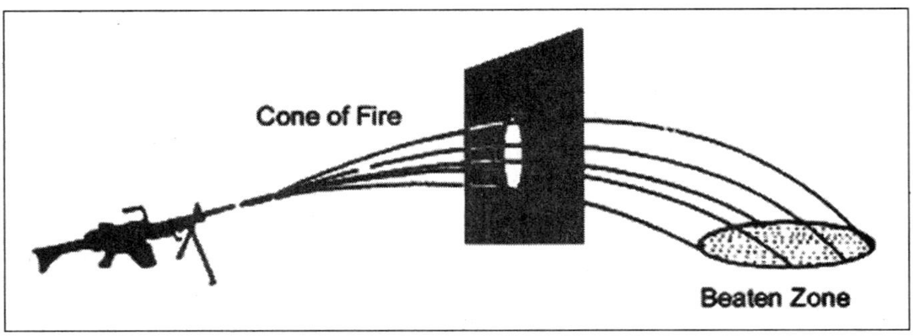

Cone of fire and beaten zone

Danger Space: The danger space is the space between the machinegun and the target where the trajectory does not rise above 1.8 meters (the average height of a standing soldier). This space includes the area of the beaten zone. When the machinegun is fired on level or uniformly sloping terrain at a target less than 700 meters away, the trajectory does not rise above the average height of a standing soldier. When targets are engaged on level or uniformly sloping terrain at ranges greater than 700 yards, the trajectory rises above the average height of a standing soldier, therefore, not all the distance between the machinegun and the target is danger space.

Defilade Positions: A machinegun is in defilade when the weapon and its crew are completely behind terrain that masks them from the enemy (usually on the reverse slope of a hill). Fire, from a defilade position, is controlled by an observer (the leader or a member of the crew who can see the target) that is in a position near the machinegun.

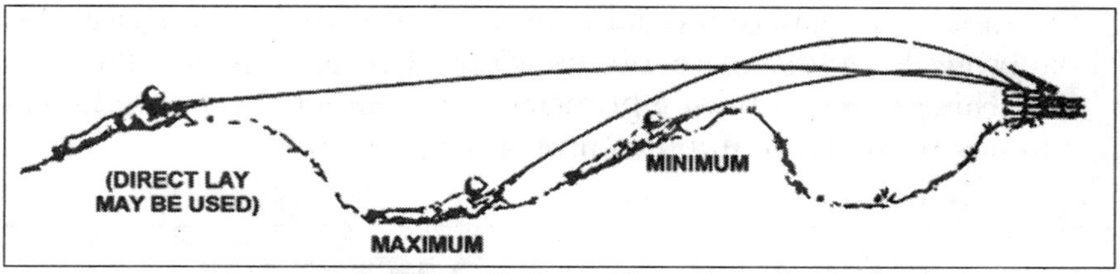

Defilade positions

(6.2) Classes of Fire

When in doubt, empty the magazine.

Machinegun fire is classified with respect to the ground, the target, and the weapon.

(6.2.1) With Respect to the Ground

a. **Grazing Fire:** Grazing fire occurs when the center of the cone of fire does not rise more than 1 meter above the ground. When firing on level or uniformly sloping terrain, the gunner can obtain a maximum of 600 meters of grazing fire.

b. **Plunging Fire:** Plunging fire occurs when the danger space is confined to the beaten zone. Plunging fire also occurs when firing at long ranges, from high ground to low ground, into abruptly rising ground, or across uneven terrain, resulting in a loss of grazing fire at any point along the trajectory.

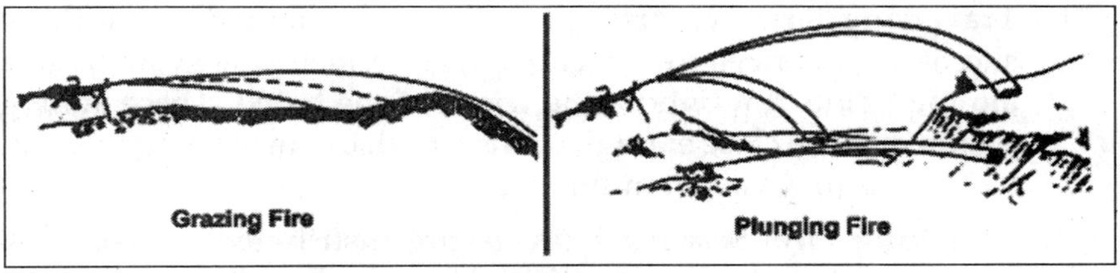

Classes of fire with respect to the ground

(6.2.2) *With Respect to Target*

a. **Frontal Fire:** Frontal fire is when the long axis of the beaten zone is at a right angle to the front of the target. An example is when firing at the front of a target.

b. **Flanking Fire:** Flanking fire is firing at the side of a target.

c. **Oblique Fire:** Oblique fire is when the long axis of the beaten zone is at an angle other than a right angle to the front of the target.

d. **Enfilade Fire:** Enfilade fire is when the long axis of the beaten zone coincides or nearly coincides with the long axis of the target. This type of fire is either frontal or flanking. It is the most desirable type of fire with respect to a target, because it makes maximum use of the beaten zone.

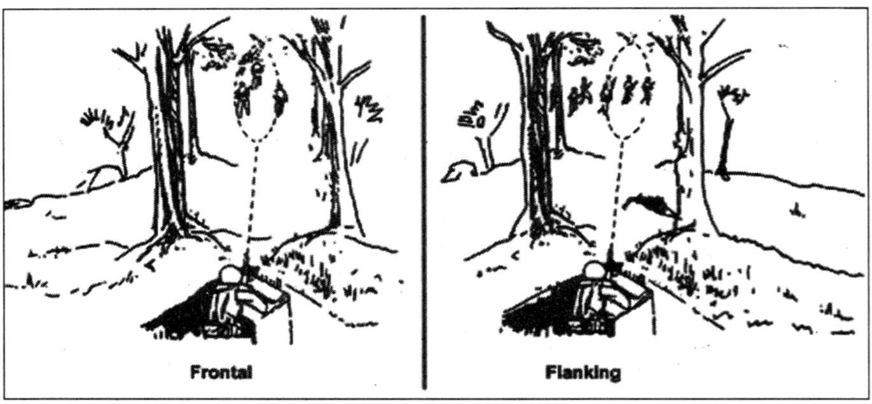

Classes of fire with respect to target

(6.2.3) *With Respect to Machinegun*

a. **Fixed Fire:** Fixed fire is fire delivered against a point target when the depth and width of the beaten zone covers the target. Fixed fire also means only one aiming point is necessary to provide coverage of the target.

b. **Traversing Fire:** Traversing fire is fire distributed in width by successive changes in direction. The gunner selects successive aiming points throughout the width of the target. These aiming points must be close enough to ensure adequate coverage but not so close as to waste ammunition.

c. **Searching Fire:** Searching fire is fire distributed in depth by successive changes in elevation. The gunner selects successive aiming points in depth. The changes made in each aiming point will depend on the range and slope of the ground.

d. **Traversing and Searching Fire:** Traversing and searching fire is fire distributed in width and depth by successive changes in direction and elevation. Combining traversing and searching provides good coverage of the target. Adjustments are made in the same manner as described for traversing and searching fire.

e. **Free-gun Fire:** Free-gun fire is fire delivered against targets requiring rapid major changes in direction and elevation that cannot be applied with the T&E mechanism. To deliver this type of fire, the gunner removes the T&E mechanism from the traversing bar on the tripod, allowing the weapon to be moved freely in any direction.

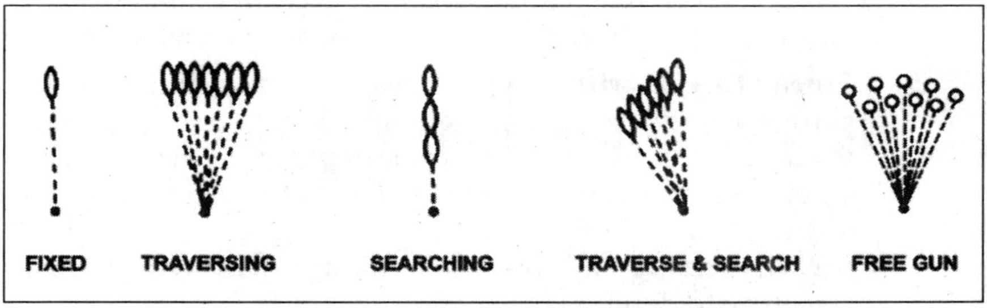

Classes of fire with respect to the machinegun

(6.3) Application of Fire

When in a fire fight, kill as many as you can,
the one you miss may not miss you tomorrow.

Application of fire consists of the methods the gunner uses to cover a target area. Training these methods of applying fire can be accomplished only after the soldiers have learned how to recognise the different types of targets they may find in combat, how to distribute and concentrate their fire, and how to maintain the proper rate of fire. Normally, the gunner is exposed to two types of targets in the squad or platoon sector: enemy soldiers and supporting automatic weapons. These targets have priority and should be engaged immediately.

(6.3.1) Types of Targets

Targets presented to the gunner in combat are usually enemy troops in various formations, which require distribution and concentration of fire. Targets with width and depth must be thoroughly covered by fire.

a. **Point Targets:** Point targets require the use of a single aiming point. Examples of point targets are enemy soldiers, bunkers, weapons emplacements, and lightly armoured vehicles. Fixed fire is delivered at point targets.

b. **Area Targets:** Area targets may have considerable width and depth and may require extensive traversing and searching fire. These include targets in which the exact location of the enemy is unknown. The following are varieties of area targets likely to be engaged.

i. **Linear Targets:** Linear targets have sufficient width to require successive aiming points (traversing fire). The beaten zone effectively covers the depth of the target area. Traversing fire is delivered at linear targets.

ii. **Deep Targets:** Deep targets require successive aiming points (searching fire). Searching fire is delivered at deep targets.

iii. **Linear Targets with Depth:** Linear targets with depth have sufficient width requiring successive aiming points in which the beaten zone does not cover the depth of the target area. A combined change in direction and elevation (traversing and searching) is necessary to effectively cover the target with fire. Traversing and searching fire are delivered at linear targets with depth.

Linear Target

Deep Target

Linear Targets with depth

(6.3.2) *Distribution, Concentration, and Rate of Fire*

The size and nature of the target determine how the gunner applies his fire. He must manipulate the machinegun to move the beaten zone throughout the target area. The rate of fire must be controlled to adequately cover the target but not waste ammunition or destroy the barrel.

a. Distributed fire is delivered in width and depth such as at an enemy formation.

b. Concentrated fire is delivered at a point target such as an automatic weapon or an enemy fighting position.

c. The rates of fire that can be used with the machinegun are sustained, rapid, and cyclic. These rates enable leaders to control and sustain fire and prevent the destruction of barrels. More than anything else, the size of the target and ammunition supply dictate the selection of the rate of fire.

1. **Sustained Fire:** Sustained fire for the M249 is 85 rounds per minute in bursts of 3 to 5 rounds. The M60 and M240B are 100 rounds per minute in bursts of 6 to 9 rounds. The gunner pauses 4 to 5 seconds between bursts. The barrel should be changed after firing at sustained rate for 10 minutes. This is the normal rate of fire for the gunner.
2. **Rapid Fire:** Rapid fire for the M249, M60, and M240B gunner is 200 rounds per minute in bursts of (6 to 8 M249) 10 to 12 rounds. The gunner pauses 2 to 3 seconds between bursts. The barrel should be changed after firing at a rapid rate for 2 minutes. This procedure provides for an exceptionally high volume of fire, but for only a short period.
3. **Cyclic Fire:** Cyclic fire uses the most ammunition that can be used in 1 minute. The cyclic rate of fire with the machinegun is achieved when the trigger is held to the rear and ammunition is fed into the weapon uninterrupted for one minute. Normal cyclic rate of fire for the M249 is 850 rounds, M60 is 550 rounds, and for the M240B it is 650 to 950 rounds. Always change the barrel after firing at cyclic rate for 1 minute. This procedure provides the highest volume of fire that the machinegun can fire, but this adversely affects the machinegun, and should only be fired in combat under emergency purposes only.

(6.3.3) Predetermined Fires

Predetermined fires organise the battlefield for the gunners. They allow the leader and gunner to select potential targets or target areas that will most likely be engaged or that have tactical significance. This includes dismounted enemy avenues of approach, likely positions for automatic weapons, and probable enemy assault positions. The gunners do this by using sectors of fire, final protective lines, or a principal direction of fire and selected target areas. This preparation maximises the effectiveness of the machinegun during good as well as limited visibility. It enhances fire control by reducing the time required to identify targets, determine range, and manipulate the weapon onto the target. Abbreviated fire commands and previously recorded data enable the gunner to aim or adjust fire on the target quickly and accurately. Selected targets should be fired on in daylight whenever practical to confirm data. The range card identifies the targets and provides a record of firing data.

Several terms are associated with predetermined fire that every gunner needs to know.

a. **Sector of Fire:** A sector of fire is an area to be covered by fire that is assigned to an individual, a weapon, or a unit. Gunners are normally assigned a primary and a secondary sector of fire.

b. **Final Protective Fire:** An FPF is an immediately available prearranged barrier of fire to stop enemy movement across defensive lines or areas.

c. **Final Protective Line:** An FPL is a predetermined line along which grazing fire is placed to stop an enemy assault. If an FPL is assigned, the machinegun is sighted along it except when other targets are being engaged. An FPL becomes the machinegun's part of the unit's final protective fires. An FPL is fixed in direction and elevation; however, a small shift for search must be employed to prevent the enemy from crawling under the FPL and to compensate for irregularities in the terrain or the sinking of the tripod legs into soft soil during firing. Fire must.be delivered during all conditions of visibility.

d. **Principal Direction of Fire:** A PDF is a direction of fire assigned priority to cover an area that has good fields of fire or has a likely dismounted avenue of approach. It also provides mutual support to an adjacent unit. Machineguns are sighted using the PDF if an FPL has not been assigned. If a PDF is assigned and other targets are not being engaged, machineguns remain on the PDF. A PDF has the following characteristics.

   i. It is used only if an FPL is not assigned; it then becomes the machinegun's part of the unit's final protective fires.

   ii. When the target has width, direction is determined by aiming on one edge of the target area and noting the amount of traverse necessary to cover the entire target.

   iii. The gunner is responsible for the entire wedge-shaped area from the muzzle of the weapon to the target, but elevation may be fixed for a priority portion of the target.

(6.4) Methods of Target Engagement

There is no such thing as an atheist under fire.

The gunner engages targets throughout his sector. He must know how to effectively engage all types of targets either by himself or in conjunction with another gunner. The concepts apply equally well to individual riflemen also.

(1) **Point Target:** When engaging a point target, the gunner uses fixed fire. If the target moves after the initial burst, the gunner adjusts fire onto the target by following its movement.

(2) **Area Target:** When engaging an area target, the gunner fires in the center of mass, then traverses and searches to either flank. Upon reaching the flank, he reverses direction and traverses and searches in the opposite direction. A leader may indicate the width and depth of the target.

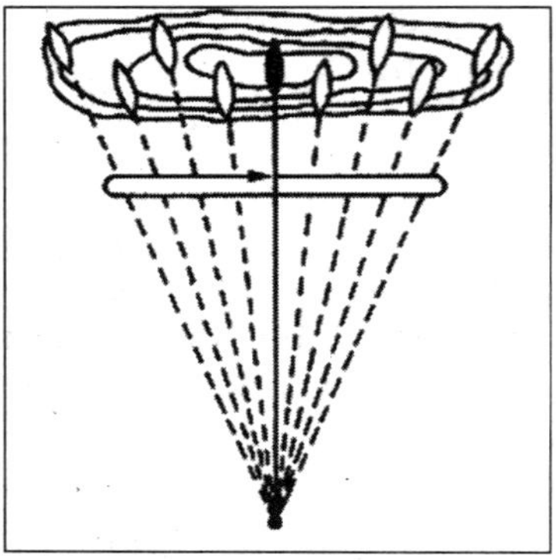

Engagement of area target

(3) **Linear Target:** When engaging a linear target, the gunner traverses the machinegun to distribute fire evenly onto the target. He must cover the entire width of a linear target. The initial point of aim is on the midpoint. The gunner then manipulates to cover the rest of the target. If a linear target is hard to identify, a leader may designate the target by using a reference point. When this method is used, the leader determines the center of mass of the target and announces the number of meters from the reference point that will cause the gunner to aim on the center of mass. The reference point may be within or adjacent to the target. However, the reference point should be on line with the target for the best effect. After the command to fire has been given, the leader maintains and controls the fire by subsequent fire commands.

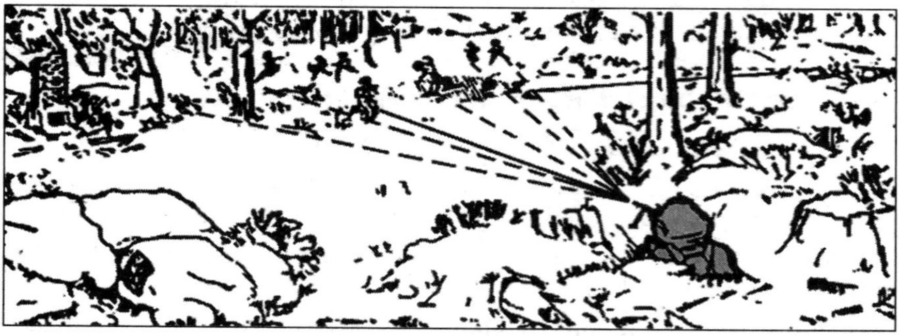

Engagement of hard-to-identify linear targets with a reference point outside the target area

(4) **Deep Target:** When engaging a deep target, the gunner must use searching fire. If the range is announced, he initially aims on the midpoint of a deep target unless another portion of the target is more critical or presents a greater threat. The gunner then searches down to one aiming point in front of the near end and back up to one aiming point beyond the far end. If a deep target is hard to identify, use the reference points to designate the center of mass. The extent (depth) of the target is always given in meters.

(5) **Linear Target with Depth:** When engaging a linear target with depth, the gunner uses traversing and searching fire. He begins engagement at the midpoint of the target unless another portion of the target is more critical or presents a greater threat. He traverses and searches to the near flank, then back to the far flank. When engaging hard-to-identify linear targets with depth, he designates the flanks and midpoint with rifle fire. The reference-point method is not used because at least two reference points are required to show the angle of the target.

Engagement of hard-to-identify targets with a reference point within the target area

(6.5) Using the Machinegun without the Bipod

All soldiers must master the bipod-supported prone firing fighting position, and tripod-supported prone firing position to be effective. But it is also equally important that they know other positions. Who said that only Rambo could fire without the bipod? I have done it to deliver aimed fire from the shoulder also and you too can do it. Each soldier must be trained to assume different positions quickly during various combat conditions. The situation determines the appropriate position. The soldier must establish his position so that he can effectively observe and engage the target yet minimise his exposure to enemy fire.

(1) **Underarm Firing Position:** This position is used almost exclusively when moving in and around the objective during the assault. To assume this position, the gunner-

(a) Puts the bipod legs and rear sight down for instant use in the prone position if necessary.

(b) Faces the target with his feet spread about shoulder width apart.

(c) Places his left foot in front of the right with most of his weight on his left foot.

(d) Bends both legs at the knees and leans forward at the waist.

(e) With his right hand, firmly grasps the pistol grip, and with his right forearm holds the stock firmly against the side of his body at a point between his armpit and waist.

(f) With his left hand, grasps the handguard firmly.

(g) Points his left foot in the direction of the target while his right foot provides stability.

(h) Depresses the muzzle of the machinegun slightly so the strike of rounds can be observed. (This reduces shooting high and takes advantage of ricochets).

(i) Leans toward the target before and during firing.

Underarm firing position

(2) **Hip Firing Position:** This position is used when closing with the enemy, when a heavy volume of fire in the target area is required, and when rapid movement is not necessary. The only differences between this position and the underarm position are that the gunner-

(a) Holds the rear of the stock firmly against the forward position of his right thigh.

(b) Extends his arms fully downward.

Hip firing position

(6.6) Fire Team Formations

Try to look unimportant, they may be low on ammo.

Formations are arrangements of elements and soldiers in relation to each other. Squads use formations for control flexibility and security. Leaders choose formations based on their analysis of the factors of METT-T. This allows the fire team leader to lead by example, "Follow me and do as I do". All soldiers in the team must be able to see their leader. The wedge is the basic formation for the fire team. The interval between soldiers in the wedge formation is normally 10 yards. The wedge expands and contracts depending on the terrain. When rough terrain, poor visibility, or other factors make control of the wedge difficult, fire teams modify the wedge. The normal interval is reduced so that all team members can still see their team leader and the team leaders can still their squad leader. The sides of the wedge can contract to the point where the wedge resembles a single file. When moving in less rugged terrain, where control is easier, soldiers expand or resume their original positions. When the terrain precludes use of the wedge, fire teams use the file formation.

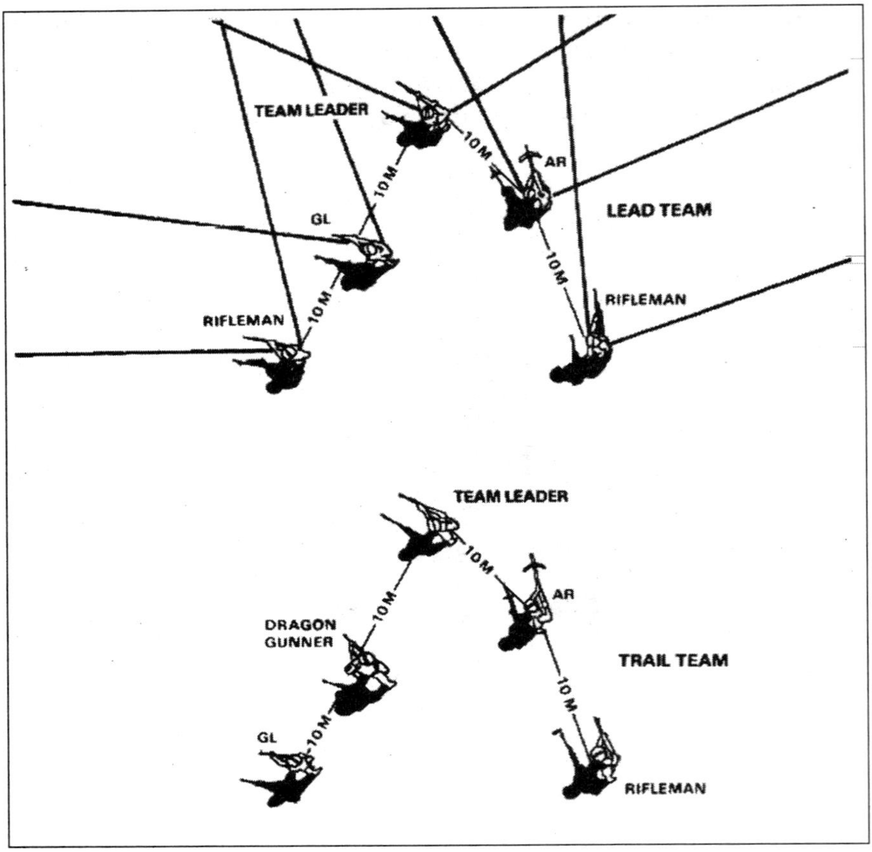

Basic wedge formation fire team

(6.6.1) Squad Formations

Squad formations describe the relationships between fire teams in the squad. They include the squad column and squad line.

a. **Squad Column:** The squad column is the squad's most common formation. It provides good dispersion both laterally and in depth without sacrificing control, and facilitates manoeuvre. The lead fire team is the base fire team. When the squad moves independently or as the rear element of the platoon, the rifleman in the (rail fire team provides rear security. You can think of it roughly as a three-column formation.

b. **Squad Line:** The squad line provides maximum firepower to the front. When a squad is acting as the base squad, the fire team on the right is the base fire team.

c. **Squad File:** When not travelling in a column or line, squads travel in file. The squad file has the same characteristics as the fire team file. If the squad leader desires to increase his control over the formation, exert greater morale presence by leading from the front, and be immediately available to make key decisions, he will move forward to the first or second position. Additional control over the rear of the formation can be provided by moving a team leader to the last position.

(6.6.2) Platoon Formations

Platoon formations include the platoon column, the platoon line (squads on line or in column), the platoon vee and the platoon wedge. The leader should weigh these carefully to select the best formation based on his mission and on METT-T analysis. METT-T will also determine where crew-served weapons move in the formation. They normally move with the platoon leader so he can quickly establish a base of fire. Establishing a base of fire was something that was deeply ingrained in American military tactics—it was highly reassuring to the troops. Usually, in the Vietnam era, they did it with the M60 machinegun, giving rise to the dictum "happiness is a belt-fed weapon". Others may do well to learn from it.

a. **Platoon Column:** This formation is the platoon's primary movement formation—lead squad, center squad, and trail squad. It provides good dispersion both laterally and in depth, and simplifies control. The lead squad is the base squad. Think of it roughly as a four-column formation.

b. **Platoon-Line, Squads-on-Line:** This is the basic platoon assault formation. This formation allows the delivery of maximum fire to the front but little fire to the flanks—left flank squad, center squad, and right flank squad. This formation is hard to control, and it does not lend itself well to rapid movement. When two or more platoons are attacking, the company commander chooses one of them as the base platoon. The base platoon's center squad is its base squad. When the platoon is not acting as the base platoon, its base squad is its flank squad nearest the base platoon. The machineguns can move with the platoon, or they can support by fire from a support position.

c. **Platoon-Line, Squads-in-Column:** The platoon leader can use this formation when he does not want to deploy all personnel on line, and when he wants the squads to react to unexpected contact. This formation is easier to control, and it lends itself better to rapid movement than the platoon-line or squads-online formation; however, it is harder to control than and does not facilitate rapid movement as well as a platoon column. When two or more platoons are moving, the company commander chooses one of them as the base platoon. The base platoon's center squad is its base squad. When the platoon is not the base platoon, its base squad is its flank squad nearest the base platoon.

d. **Platoon Vee:** This formation has two squads up front to provide a heavy volume of fire on contact. It also has one squad in the rear that can either overwatch or trail the other squads. This formation is hard to control; movement is slow. The platoon leader designates one of the front squads to be the platoon's base squad.

e. **Platoon Wedge:** This formation has two squads in the rear that can overwatch or trail the lead squad. Think of it as an inverted Vee. It provides a large volume of fire to the front or flanks. It allows the platoon leader to make contact with a squad and still have one or two squads to manoeuvre. The lead squad is the base squad.

f. **Platoon File:** This formation may be set up in several methods. One method is to have three-squad files follow one another using one of the movement techniques. Another method is to have a single platoon file with a front security element (point) and flank security elements. This formation is used when visibility is poor due to terrain, vegetation, or light conditions. The distance between soldiers is less than normal to allow communication by passing messages up and down the file. The platoon file has the same characteristics as the fire team and squad files.

(6.6.3) Selecting the Best Formations

The US Army in Vietnam found that the more complicated a formation and the more numerous its parts, the greater the danger that control would be lost in a moment of emergency, especially when moving over countryside which prohibited visual contact between the various elements of the formation.

The intrinsic problems of the popular wedge formation: The 'wedge', and its numerous variations, was the most widespread formation adopted by US rifle companies during advances into enemy territory, yet it was extremely difficult to control and possessed no inherent advantages in bringing fire power to bear quickly against any threatened quarter. In fact it had several built-in disadvantages. The forward platoon in the center and the two platoons, right and left, each used a point, with scouts out. So there were never less than seven elements to control, which was several too many should the body have to reform suddenly to meet an assault from an unexpected direction. Formed in this way, the company extended over a wider area than if the columns were more compact, though the advantage was marginal. The 'Wedge' neither strengthened security on the move nor favoured rapid and practical deployment for combat. If the formation should be hit from either flank, greater confusion would ensue than with a more simple formation. Should the enemy be set up and ready to fight on a broad front directly to the fore, all three columns were likely to become engaged before the commander had a chance to weigh-up whether full-scale involvement was desirable.

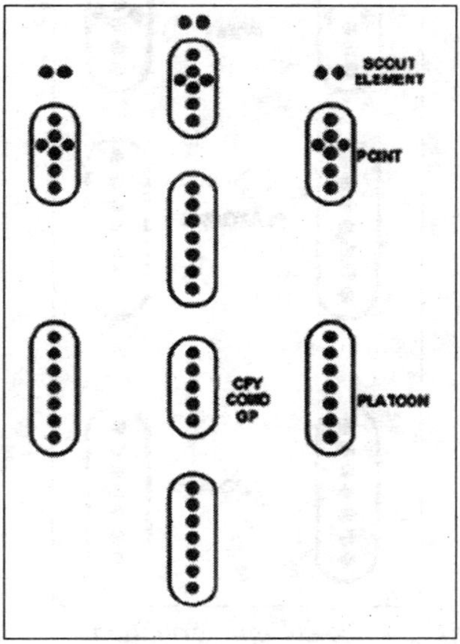

Conventional wedge formation

Two-or three-column Formation: However, the situation is very different when the company is making its approach march in two-column formation. The width between columns would be approximately equal to their length when the terrain permitted. If either column is hit from the flank and faced toward the fire, the other would automatically be in place to serve as a reserve and protect against a turning manoeuvre. Further, if the advance guard (scouts and point) draw fire in volume, signifying the enemy's determination to stand, the force would be in a position to be either commit whole at once, or to fight on a narrower front with half of its strength while retaining a 50 per cent reserve. When the enemy fire and the condition of the advance element permit it, the scouts and point would displace to rearward as the company shifts to a line of skirmishers. In this way the whole formation would not be drawn willy-nilly into a full-scale commitment, a disarrangement that occurs frequently in attacks upon fortified positions. In circumstances where the scouts or the men in the point become engaged and take casualties, the lead platoon would become scattered and disorganised in the effort to extricate them and the fire line thereafter would gradually find itself reformed on ground too far forward, greatly to its disadvantage and harshly limiting the supporting air and artillery fires.

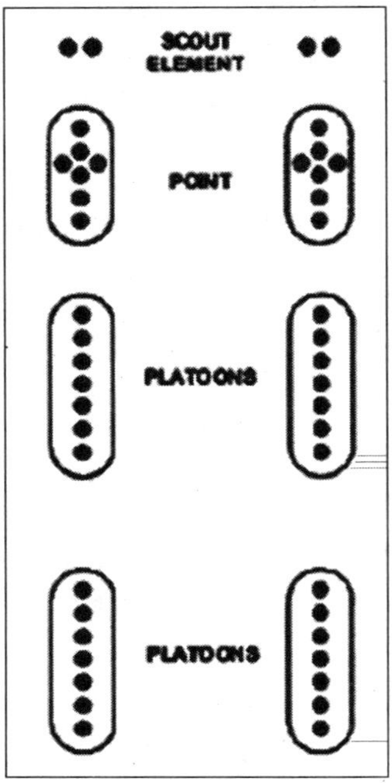

Two-column formation

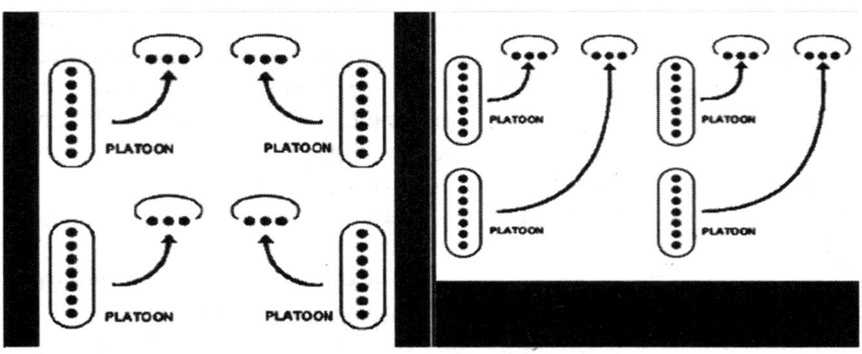

Columns partially committed (left) and columns fully committed (right)

7

The Helicopter in Jungle Operations

Give them hell:
"I love the smell of napalm in the morning.
You know, one time we had a hill bombed, for 12 hours.
When it was all over, I walked up.
We didn't find one of 'em, not one stinkin' dink body.
The smell, you know that gasoline smell, the
whole hill. Smelled like...victory".

(7.1) Effective uses of Helicopters

The helicopter is a combat system that can be used for delivering accurate fire in the aid of besieged troops or even in a purely attack mode as air assault, as well as reconnaissance. The US forces have made liberal use of helicopters in the jungle for command and control, resupply, and medical evacuation. Advantage was taken of the fact that it remains unaffected by the poor manoeuvrability of the jungle command and control systems on the ground. Command and Control (C&C) helicopters are specially outfitted with radios which allow communications with elements on the ground, supporting artillery, and other aircraft. The attack helicopter unit can perform three basic missions: over-watch and security; engagement of targets located by ground elements; and independent target engagements. Attack helicopters in an over-watch and security role protect other assets, such as other helicopters or convoys. Attack helicopters in the heliborne fire role can augment the fires of units fighting on the ground. In jungle operations, they may be the only additional means of fire available. Finally, attack helicopters may acquire and engage targets independent of any other operations. The 2.75-inch rocket, 7.62-mm "Flechette" minigun and 40-mm grenade launcher on the attack helicopter are extremely effective against dismounted troops.

To a soldier in peril there was no sight more reassuring than a Huey gunship blazing away at the enemy with its M60 Machinegun, M134 Minigun and the M158 Rocket launcher

Heliborne operations are offensive operations in which combat forces and their equipment move out in the battlefield aboard air vehicles under the control of the ground force commander to engage in ground combat. The heliteam consists of combat equipped troops lifted in a helicopter at one time. A helicopter wave consists of helicopters which arrive together and land approximately at the same landing zone. The landing zone is a specified ground area for landing assault helicopter to embark or disembark troops and cargo. The landing point is a point where one helicopter can land. It is often designated by two (2) digits number. Ready Circle are alert points from which the heli-teams are called to be enplaned.

The helicopter makes deep enemy territory accessible to combat units for conduct of offensive operations. Its versatility and unique capabilities makes it the most suited aircraft for vertical envelopment missions. The helicopter is also excellent for reconnaissance and security operations, and to block and screen enemy avenues of approach. Other uses of the helicopter include:

- Long-range combat patrols which would otherwise be very difficult;
- Seizure and retention of key terrain;

- Counter-attack of enemy penetrations;
- Short and sharp raids; and
- Diversionary actions.

(7.2) Limitations in the use of Helicopters

Whenever you have plenty of ammo, you never miss. Whenever you are low on ammo, you can't hit the broad side of a barn.

Do not be misled into believing that the helicopter is the panacea for all your problems in the battlefield. You are likely to get your ass whipped if you think so. Helicopters are glamourous. Hence, dumb armies tend to get unduly fascinated by them. For example, in India we often hear from uninformed media persons and even officers of the forces that the forces are faring badly against the naxal insurgents because enough helicopters are not being used. Helicopters have their uses provided the helicopter pilots are both skilful and courageous. You cannot even imagine casualty evacuation sans the helicopter in any battle scenario. The Huey helicopter was the signature flying machine of the Vietnam War—they were to be found anywhere and everywhere they were needed—amidst flak, gunfire, bursting shells and burning napalm—for casualty evacuation, dropping troops, supplies, and firing heavily on enemy positions with machineguns and automatic grenade launchers, much to the cheer of beleaguered troops. If the American infantrymen have to be grateful to one machine in Vietnam, it would be the Huey helicopter. If you have to use helicopters, use it like the Americans did

The cavalry arrives: the Hueys move into the battlefield in Vietnam

in Vietnam or forget about it. Use it any other way and you are not exploiting its full potential. It was so very useful in Vietnam because it fitted well into the type of war they were fighting. Similar situations may not be found in many counter-insurgency operations.

Remember, therefore, the helicopter is not the panacea to all ills; it has several limitations.

- The helicopter makes the forces lose all element of surprise in a jungle. The noise is a dead give-away. There is a small chance that Special Forces could be quietly inserted and even reach the insurgents unnoticed if they move stealthily on the ground. However, insertion of troops by helicopter is often impractical if you seek an element of surprise. The noise of the helicopter is heard miles away in a jungle. The Rhodesian Light Infantry tested it on themselves. In their so-called Fire Force, once the AB205A Cheetahs could be heard full eight minutes before they arrived.
- Further, the helicopter is such a rarity in many countries that even if a villager happens to notice a helicopter flying overhead, he would understand that some operation is underway—those sympathetic to the insurgents among the villagers would instantly inform them.
- Adverse weather conditions may curtail the use of helicopter—this becomes particularly acute if the helicopter has to do Casevac or extricate troops that have run into problems.
- Those who are inserted by the helicopter can, usually, come out by helicopter only. This limits their options severely—if the landing zone is compromised or is taken by the enemy, the troops get trapped or they have to create another landing zone for extraction which may be quite difficult.
- The helicopter is vulnerable to ground fire—particularly so during landing, assembly, and pick-up. Although the nature of the air defence threat will be different in every conflict, no helicopter should expect to survive if it maintains a stationary position anytime in the vicinity of ground contact or orbits at high altitudes. The helicopter is extremely vulnerable to heat-seeking missiles in particular.
- Small arms fire also could be dangerous to the chopper if it hits the rotors, particularly the tail rotor. The tail rotor of the helicopter is the Achilles Heel of the machine—hit it and the chopper will go down with the fuselage rotating uncontrollably. Otherwise, the fuselage itself will take a lot of flak and it will not explode the way you see the exploding in the films. The rotor blade is

not made of solid steel. They are honeycomb sandwich structure which is not designed to resist small arms fire.

- Small arms fire has been getting slow-moving aircrafts. In the Korean War, the US air force lost as many as 544 aircraft to combined small-arms and air defence fire. During the Middle East War in 1973, units on both sides used small-arms weapons to drive off, damage, or destroy attacking aircraft. During the Vietnam War, the Viet Cong claim that they shot down as many as 674 helicopters.
- In the recent past, we have an official admission by Brig Stephen Mundt of the US in this regard. Till 2010 in Iraq and Afghanistan, the American forces had lost as many as 43 helicopters to small arms fire from the ground and 83 to other reasons like crashes, accidents, collisions, etc all indirectly attributable to battle stress. Considering that the Americans have the best of everything and are perfectly willing to lay down the heaviest amount of firepower and explosives on anything that shoots at them, this is a sizeable number. The Indians could take note of this. But that should not become an excuse for not flying in the combat zone!
- The key to effective small-arms fire against aircraft is volume. Put up a large volume of fire with small calibre weapons. Accuracy is not important; volume is! If the insurgents have enough ammunition to waste, your choppers are likely to be hit. You must know this.
- Do not think that firing on aircrafts requires mounts for the machineguns. Who said it? Any tree or a large rock to help support the weapon and provide some protection would do. In fact a buddy can also act as a hasty firing support for the machineguns. The Americans prescribe this technique to their own soldiers for the eventuality of the convoy coming under fire from the air.
- The helicopter cannot become a substitute for command presence on the ground. A commander cannot merely fly over a unit and be satisfied that he knows its situation. The view from the air often gives a distorted picture of conditions on the ground.
- The helicopter should not interfere with ground operations. If a unit has to devote time to cutting and preparing a landing zone every day for a visit from the commander, it will get little else done.
- The helicopter must not violate a ground unit's security. A helicopter hovering overhead soon reveals the location of a unit on the ground.

- The helicopter must not intrude on a ground unit's internal radio nets. The helicopter's radios are more powerful, and will interfere with the ground commander's ability to control his own unit.
- Limited support weapons, heavy equipment and means of communications.
- Limited capability to engage in sustained combat.
- Lack of vehicular mobility.

(7.3) Vulnerability of the Helicopter in Combat

Fools would fire on the fuselage of the helicopter and shout in joy. Intelligent men know better. They know that hitting the fuselage by bullets, even though exciting and rather easy, would not produce spectacular results. The Achilles' Heel of a copter is the tail rotor and its drive shaft/tail boom. A helicopter hit in the fuselage, engine, fuel tank (which, against popular misconception, won't explode) or even the main rotors can still manage to land safely some distance away—but a damaged tail rotor would make it spin out of control. The reason is simple. All of you know Newton's Third Law of Motion. From this follow the laws of conservation of momentum and angular momentum. This can be understood very easily with the help of a spring driven toy car. You wind the spring and place the car on the ground. The wheels turn and the car moves. The rotating wheels are actually pushing the ground backwards but the ground is too heavy to move noticeably though in theory it does move a very very tiny wee bit. You can see the phenomenon more clearly if you jump out on the shore from a boat—the boat would move in an opposite direction in the water. Now suppose you take the car into your hand and hold just the wheels—hold them fast so that they are not able to rotate. Now leave the car free—as the boat is free in water. The spring will make the car rotate instead. A similar thing happens for the helicopter also. The engine rotates the main rotor. But this should result in an equal and opposite reaction on the fuselage also to which the engine is fixed. If the helicopter is resting on ground, the ground becomes too heavy to result in any observable movement. But when the chopper is in the air and the fuselage is free, the fuselage will rotate damn well. That becomes a problem. You cannot fly a helicopter the fuselage of which is rotating. To prevent this, most helicopters have a tail rotor. The tail rotor, quite like the propeller of an aircraft produces thrust on the tail, but in a direction opposite to the direction in which the reaction force on the fuselage would have made it rotate. The thrust produced by the tail rotor counters the tendency of the fuselage to rotate. For this the tail rotor must have a certain size and design of the propellers and rotate at a certain speed. This is critical. However, the same purpose can be achieved by another method. Instead of the tail rotor you can also have another main rotor which is made to rotate in another direction—that is contra-rotating rotors. Each one would tend to rotate the fuselage in opposite directions. Their reactions would exactly cancel out each other's tendency to rotate the fuselage as long as they are rotating at the same speed and have exactly the same weight etc; that is, no part of them is broken. The contra-rotating rotors can be on the same axis on top of each other, as in the Russian Kamov series helicopters; or in tandem (side-by-side) as in the American Chinook helicopter.

As stated above, the thrust produced by the tail rotor is very critical and it must have a critical value. Now thrust depends on the integrity of the propeller blades and their rotational speed. You damage one of them, and the critical balance goes. Suppose you damage the blades or one of them—it will result in the thrust getting affected even if the drive shaft is rotating as before. Suppose you damage the tail rotor drive shaft in the boom but the blades remain intact—still, the thrust will be affected because then they will be rotating slower. In essence it means that for tail rotor copters if you hit the tail rotor and do nothing else or are not able to damage any other part of the helicopter, it will serve your purpose. The delicate balance will be disturbed and the fuselage will start rotating. In case of twin-rotor choppers, you hit one of the rotors and the forces will become unbalanced—the result will be the same. It is very difficult to control and fly the chopper then. If at all it can manage to land by a remote chance, it will have to land right there provided it was already close to the ground. The ideal low-cost weapon to attack a helicopter is the RPG. This weapon, designed to attack tanks, is excellent against other vehicles and the explosive warhead increases the chances that something will be damaged. One can take his chances with bullets also. Bullets can hit the pilots. I will give two famous examples to illustrate the point.

In the 'Black Hawk Down' incident (called so after the name of the famous film made on the incident) of 1993, the Somalis had shot down a UH-60 Black Hawk helicopter by RPG fire. The Americans had planned to capture the Somali warlord Mohammed Aidid in Mogadishu in what they thought would be a very clever commando operation. Dumb and crooked as they are, the stupid idea was that the informer would give the correct location of the warlord in a building and then the Special Forces would go, rappel down into the building from the rooftop, capture the man and fly back before the Somalis woke up—as simple as that. The intelligence, as any intelligent man would know, turned out to be hopelessly wrong. The operation ran into serious resistance. And the poor buggers had not counted on some improvised use the RPG. The RPG was fired from a rooftop and the first UH-60 Cobra crashed. A rescue Cobra helicopter was also fired at and crippled though it did not crash. The Cobra is one of the most sophisticated and advanced helicopters of the US armed forces but there is no running away from the intrinsic vulnerability of the chopper. In this incident also, the rocket had struck the tail rotor and sent the chopper spinning to the ground into one of the houses. It then rolled over into an adjacent alleyway and crashed.

In August 2011, an American Chinook helicopter was shot down by the Taliban in Wardak, Afghanistan, killing 30 Americans SEALs and eight Afghan soldiers, making it the deadliest single loss of the US forces in their decade long war in Afghanistan. It was brought down by multiple shots fired from just about 150 yards. The Tangi Valley, dubbed 'Death Valley', is known for being one of the most hostile corridors in Afghanistan. The volatile Wardak province is an infamous insurgent stronghold. The Taliban lured US forces into an elaborate trap to shoot down their helicopter. The Taliban commander Qari Tahir lured US forces to the scene by tipping them off that a Taliban meeting was taking place. The Taliban knew which route the helicopter would take. That's the only route, so they took position on the either side of the valley on mountains and as the helicopter approached, they attacked it with RPGs.

Remember that insurgents can take the chance of shooting at rather close ranges—a risk certainly worth taking because if a chopper goes down, the attention of the forces on the ground, even if they happen to be present nearby, would most likely be diverted to that and it would provide the attacker a reasonably good chance of escape.

(7.4) Clever use of the Helicopter by the Rhodesians

Body count math on which medals are decided: "three guerrillas plus one probable plus two pigs equals 37 enemies killed in action".

The use of helicopters by the Americans is well-known. They had all the resources in the world and used a variety of great helicopters for various purposes. The Rhodesians, in their counter-insurgency drive during 1974-1980, suffered from a severe resource crunch. Yet, they made some very innovative use of their limited resources and used the helicopter very effectively. For that reason, it is worthwhile to learn about it. The Rhodesians were to produce a unique and deadly variant of the tactic of 'vertical envelopment' of a target by helicopter-borne infantry which they called 'Fire Force'. One of the great advantages of the Fire Force was its flexibility, as all that was needed was a reasonable airstrip. But you must remember that the Rhodesians could do so because their helicopters were not threatened seriously by the insurgents. The Fire Force was used most successfully in tandem with information on insurgent locations obtained from static observation posts, Selous Scouts "pseudo-operations", and other ground intelligence sources. As an immediate reaction force, it could be also scrambled whenever any ground forces required support. This was a great morale-builder for the average soldier, who knew that assistance was only 30 minutes away at the most. Demands on the Fire Force continued to increase during the closing years of the conflict, to the point where it was not unusual for it to be deployed as often as three times a day in certain heavily contested areas.

The standard troop carrying/utility version of the Alouette III in the Rhodesian Air Force were called 'G-Cars'. Three of the helicopters, referred to as 'G-cars,' were used to transport four fully-quipped troops, while a fourth helicopter, called the 'K (for kill)-car,' carried a pilot who was the senior Air Force officer, a gunner- technician, and the Army unit commander, who directed the operations below. The 'K-car' could also be used as a gunship when required (hence, its appellation). As with the 'K-Car', not only did the technician fly in combat and operate the aircraft's weapons, he was also responsible for all the maintenance of the helicopter too. One of the riflemen was a fully trained combat medic and carried a medical pack. Every man also carried a saline drip.

The Rhodesian practice was to operate the 'G-Car' with a gunner/ technician and to mount twin Mk 2 .303 Brownings machineguns, with about 400 rounds per gun. In the troop carrying role, a "Stick" of four soldiers was the standard load for the RhAF Alouette III. Experience in combat led the Rhodesians to remove all but the pilot's door on the 'G-Car' and to reverse the front passengers to widen the available floorspace and gain flexibility. With the doors removed, it was easier for the soldiers to leave the helicopter quickly. While carrying troops, casualties on a stretcher could be carried laterally across the rear of the cabin, one on the floor and another stretcher on a rack above it. For Fireforce missions a gunship version of the Alouette III was fitted with a Matra MG 151/20 20 mm cannon with about 400-440 rounds. The 'K-Car', as it was known, was operated usually with a crew of three, (pilot, gunner and fireforce commander). The 'K-Car' was used as a mobile command post to allow the army commander of the heliborne troops to direct their operations from the air above them.

The four helicopters were supported by a fixed-wing aircraft equipped with rockets and machineguns. In the early stages of the conflict, this was usually a single-engine Aermacchi-Lockheed AL-60 Trojan. A particularly noisy aircraft, the AL-60 generally preceded the helicopters, effectively blotting out the noise of their engines and helping to maintain at least a modicum of surprise about the impending ground attack. If Dakotas were available, paratroopers were also sent.

Any sighting of the enemy within the Fire Force zone was reported and a siren sounded in the base. The First Wave of troops went in the helicopters. They were followed by a Second Wave or Land Tail by road. The Land Tail was often an important factor in refuelling of helicopters and recovering of deceased persons (enemy and civilian), parachutes and enemy weapons and equipment. The K-car was always the first to arrive at the scene. The K-car Commander had to first attempt to confirm the precise area where the enemy had been spotted by the OP. Quite often the K-car occupants would see the enemy (or any perceived enemy), and then the Helicopter Gunner/ Technician would attack them with his 20 mm cannon. The accuracy of this firing was extraordinary, due to the machine flying in tight anti-clockwise circles just a few hundred feet above the ground. Usually the G-car sticks were positioned in areas where the enemy would most likely run through (often a riverbed or dry 'donga'), where there was more vegetation, therefore attempting to surround or cut off enemy movement. Sometimes, the G-Cars would make dummy landings to confuse the enemy, while placing men in cut-off or stop positions. When paratroopers were available, the para-sticks would form the main sweep, and the G-car sticks would carry out blocking actions.

Later in the conflict, a heliborne mortar unit could be deployed from the 'G-car,' which would then act as the unit's aerial spotter. Two Alouettes were deployed with a mortar team. One Alouette carried the tube and ammunition, and the other carried the crew. Once the mortar was in action, the second helicopter provided aerial spotting which produced hits on target often with third bomb fired. The Rhodesians also used a 1000 lbs bomb known as the Golf bomb. This was an interesting invention. Instead of a military high explosive like TNT, it used essentially ANFO type explosive. A regular bomb seeks to shatter its thick cast iron shell into fragments; this bomb had a double wall of rather thin sheets between which were loaded thousands of pieces of 10 mm steel bars. Thus fragments were already made and the bomb had only to propel them. This made it into a particularly effective anti-personnel bomb in the bushes.

How soon the enemy heard the approaching helicopters and his reaction to it was of course decisive. Wind direction and speed, the presence of a tree covered ridge line or a multitude of other factors would make the difference of life or death. Where he was caught in unfavourable terrain for him (like a village surrounded by open ground) he had no chance and normally none escaped (unless it was near nightfall). Noise, however, was a constant problem in giving away the approach of an attacking force. On 5 February 1979, during Operation Dabchick, a raid on Mucheneze Camp across Rhodesia's south eastern border in Mozambique, the SAS call-sign watching the camp heard the approaching AB205A Cheetahs eight minutes before they arrived. The Rhodesians also often flew the noisy Aermacchi AL60-B2L Trojans (The Aermacchi AL-60 was a light civil utility aircraft of the late 1950s and early 1960s Lockheed) ahead of the Fire Force to mask the whine of the helicopters.

(7.5) How does a modern Heliteam Enplane and Deplane?

In the US, the heliteam means combat equipped troops lifted in one helicopter at one time. The heliteam is composed of nine men—the heliteam commander and two fire teams (usually called A and B). In an operation, the troops first assemble in the assembly area where they are briefed. The heliteams are then moved to the control point and from the control point, the loading supervisor directs them to departure line or ready circle. The departure lines or read circle are alert points from which the heliteams are called to be enplaned. The basic safety procedures with respect to helicopters are as follows:

- Do not approach from or depart to the rear of the helicopter.
- Keep body low when approaching and departing a helicopter, especially on slopes.
- Keep safety belts fastened when airborne.
- Keep weapons unload and on safe.
- Keep radio antennas down and secured.
- Keep hand grenades secured.
- Do not jump from a hovering helicopter unless that's precisely what you are supposed to do in that operation.

In enplaning helicopters, the following procedure is adopted:

- On signal by the loading officer, the heliteam commander leads his team on the double from the ready circle to the aircraft.
- The dangerous rotor blades being in the left rear of the helicopter, the heliteam should always approach the aircraft in column 45

degrees from the left or right directly in front or 90 degrees from the right facing the aircraft.

- The heliteam should load the helicopter only upon the signal of the loading officer or signal man, and in their absence, the heliteam commander must wait until the aircraft had actually landed or stabilised itself before ordering his men to enplane.
- Heliteam should run to the helicopter at port arms keeping their head low.
- Upon reaching the aircraft, the heliteam commander takes position near the skid of the helicopter and assists team member to enplane.
- Personnel enter the helicopter carrying rifles in their hands and seat on proper position.
- When seated, each member places his rifle between his knees, fastens his seat belts and raises his right arm to signal the heliteam commander that he is ready for takeoff.
- When the heliteam commander sees that all members are strapped and ready to be airborne, he either gives the crew chief a thumbs-up signal or taps the pilot's shoulder and signals him to take off.

In deplaning from the helicopter, the following procedure is adopted:

- When approaching the landing zone, the pilot or crew chief will orient the heliteam commander as to the direction of north, south, east, and west. They must also try to establish for the heliteam commander his position in relation to an object that is well known to him on the ground.
- When the helicopter is about to land, the pilot signals the heliteam commander and he in turn orders his man to unfasten seat belts.
- As soon as the helicopter has landed or when it has stabilised into a hover about the ground, the pilot signals the heliteam commander to disembark.
- On the go signal of the heliteam commander, the members immediately exit from the side of the helicopter.
- They form a tactical formation in front of the helicopter, and assumed the prone-firing position until the aircraft had pulled out.
- The heliteam later regroups and proceed to its objective.

(7.6) Helicopter Rappelling

Rappelling increases the mobility and flexibility of forces and also permits maximum use to be made of helicopters. Helicopter rappelling can provide a means of quick insertion with or without a landing zone (LZ). The following are some applications of this technique:

- Insertion of personnel into a potential landing zone (LZ) to clear or improve a suitable landing site;
- Insertion of reconnaissance parties near a suitable LZ to confirm that it is clear of enemy and safe for a helicopter landing site;
- Clandestine insertion of patrols;
- Insertion of forward observation officer (FOO) parties or artillery reconnaissance parties;
- Positioning of radio rebroadcast personnel and equipment in otherwise inaccessible areas; and
- Insertion of medical rescue parties.

The personnel required for helicopter rappelling are the rappel master, the rappel safety officer (RSO), the pilot in command, the rappelers, and the belayers. Safety is the rappel master's number one priority. He also:

- Ensures internal communication between the pilot and rappel master, and external communication between the aircraft and the ground.
- Inspects all equipment and uses only authorised, serviceable equipment.
- Inspects and tests all anchor points and knots before the mission starts.
- Ensures that all rappellers receive a safety briefing and the pilots and aircrew receive an air mission brief.
- Ensures that the rappelers are rappel qualified before conducting helicopter rappelling to include tactical rappelling.
- Maintains communications with the pilot at all times.

The RSO has overall responsibility for the safety of all rappellers and ensures that all safety precautions are followed. He maintains communications at all times with the pilot and rappel master through FM radio. He alerts the rappel master and pilot of any unsafe acts. The pilot in command must, among other things, ensure that the donut ring anchoring device assembly and/or aircraft anchor points have been inspected for completeness and functionality, and that they are installed properly. If you are not going to botch up the operation then you must ensure that the soldiers, who are going to rappel, know their job. They must have satisfactorily completed three rappels from a helicopter from a height of 60 feet; out of which two rappels must be with combat equipment and weapon. A belayer is assigned to each rope. He is responsible for walking the rope beneath the helicopter during the descent. (Walking the rope is defined as removing the slack from underneath the helicopter by walking backwards with the rope as the helicopter descends to land). The belayer makes sure the ropes are not caught on the aircraft skids or tires to ensure a safe landing.

Quick insertion of troops by rappelling from helicopter

Rappel operations should not be conducted under the following conditions:

- Winds in excess of 30 knots.
- Lightning strikes within 1 nautical mile of rappelling operations.
- Blowing particles produced by rotor wash causes the aircrew or the rappel master to lose visual contact with the ground.
- Ambient temperature is 30 degrees Fahrenheit (that is, -1 degrees Celsius) or less.

- Wind chill factors caused by the helicopter's rotor wash or extraction cruise air speeds, which could cause cold weather injuries.
- Water or ice on the rope inhibiting the ability of the rappellers to control their descent.
- The rope is exposed to the elements for a sufficient length of time to freeze, thereby reducing its tensile strength.

The governing factor on whether or not helicopter rappelling at night is possible is the pilot's ability to see the ground or a reference point that will enable him to maintain a stationary hover. Under normal conditions, the aircrew uses night vision devices (NVDs) during night rappelling to aid in their ability to see adequate ground references. The following requirements are necessary for night rappelling operations.

- One chemlight will be attached to the end of the rope and one on each rappeller.
- One chemlight will be secured to the attachment point of the rope.
- Night vision goggles (NVG) will not be worn by rappellers during the descent.

(7.7) Deployment of Ropes and Rappelling Procedures

Deployment of the ropes from a helicopter is a critical task. It can cause a planned rappelling operation to fail, or it can increase the time required to conduct the operation. This is due to the likelihood of the ropes becoming entangled. To prevent this, ropes must be deployed using a positive control technique. Two of the techniques that may be used are the deployment bag technique (D-bag) and the log coil technique. In addition to the usual equipment requirements for rappelling operations, an anchor assembly is fabricated. This anchor assembly is commonly known as a donut ring. The secondary anchor point is a floating safety ring.

All rappellers must use safety belts. For safety emphasis during flight, each rappeller's brake hand must be in position with no slack in the rope between the brake hand and the donut ring. Rappellers ensure that their rappelling ropes are not tangled on any part of the interior of the helicopter or their equipment. They ensure that they can drop their D-bag or log coil using the guide hand. The D-bag or log coil is placed so it does not fall out of the aircraft. Once over the target area, the rappel master issues the rappel commands and ensures the rappel ropes are on the ground (about 20 feet of rope should be on the ground).

Due to the noise created by the helicopter, all rappel commands should be accompanied by arm-and-hand signals. All commands are issued by the rappel master and confirmed orally by the rappellers. On the command GO, the rappeller flexes at the knees and vigorously pushes away from the skid gear, allowing the rope to pass through his brake hand and guide hand. The descent is accomplished smoothly at a rate of about eight feet per second, avoiding jerky stops. The rappeller initiates his braking action slowly when he is about halfway to the ground. The rappel safety officer ensures that at least a five-second delay is maintained between each rappeller. Another technique used to deploy rappellers is to issue the command GO to the rappellers diagonally opposite each other. In the early phase of performance, the rappeller's feet are together (particularly if over woods or jungle) and his guide hand is used (not the brake hand) to remove any entanglements.

Upon reaching the ground, the rappeller clears the rappel rope through the snaplink (or rappel ring) until the rope is free. If other rappellers are to follow on the same rope, the rappeller on the ground separates or untwists the ropes and becomes the belayer for each subsequent rappeller. If ropes are to be released from the aircraft following the last rappeller, untwisting and separating the ropes is not necessary. A two-second interval is maintained between exit groups (two men exiting at the same time). The rappel master releases the rope from the donut ring after he confirms (by visual inspection) that the rappeller is off rappel. He then drops the rope away from the helicopter.

(7.8) Helicopter Casualty Evacuations

The evacuation of the wounded in jungle warfare presents numerous problems. Because of the prevalence of rapidly debilitating tropical diseases and the likelihood of quick infection of wounds in the jungle, speedy evacuation is vital. Units must use all available methods to augment means of organic medical evacuation. These may include tracked vehicles, pack animals, watercraft, helicopters, and litter bearers. Ground medical evacuation in the jungle will normally be along supply routes, as they are usually given all possible protection from the enemy. In air evacuation, the reduction of time between injury and treatment increases the chance of survival and raises morale. A helicopter equipped with a cable hoist system can easily evacuate casualties from thick jungle vegetation where no landing zones are available. This is old technology and innumerous heroic evacuations were done by the Americans in Vietnam. If your stupid country does not provide you with this simple stuff even half a century later then you must blame your '*karma*' for having been born in such a place! Nothing brings more solace and confidence to the soldier than the knowledge that in the eventuality if his getting seriously injured; he would be evacuated by a helicopter and would be saved from death or amputation. Talk of morale? The morale of the soldiers can never be high if they know that it may take even 24 hours for them to be evacuated because the helicopters of their country do not have the cable hoist system; they would not fly if the sun has set; they would not fly if there is some shooting going on at the place of evacuation; and they would not fly till they got clearance from every conceivable authority in the country.

An American HH-43 SAR Helicopter winches up a wounded American soldier from a place it cannot land during operation Silver City, March 1966, Vietnam

In some remote and densely foliaged jungles, the only means of evacuation may be by litter. This is a slow and exhausting task requiring well-conditioned soldiers to carry the litters. There are several types of litters. In very rugged terrain, the basket litter offers most security to the patient. However, it is bulky to carry even during normal operations. The standard folding litter or field expedient variations made of cloth and poles are less bulky and get the job done just as well if patients are moved with great care.

8

All about Laying Ambushes

In the battlefield, there is but one commandment: "Thou Shalt Kill".

(8.1) Ambushes and their Objectives

An ambush is a surprise attack upon a moving or temporarily halted enemy by a force lying in wait. It is usually a brief encounter and does not require the capture and holding of ground. The ambush is undoubtedly one of the oldest stratagems of battle. Even the invention and refinement of modern weapons, motor vehicles and aircraft have had little effect on the ambush pattern and techniques. The attack from ambush in ancient days was an action at close quarters, and it still is, despite the range of modern weapons. A series of successful ambushes make the enemy apprehensive and cautious in movement. Continued success with ambushes may finally inflict a virtual paralysis on the enemy. Ambushes are laid with the following objectives:

To kill the enemy: Well-laid ambushes are an effective way in which to kill the enemy. They offer the opportunity to inflict high casualties on the enemy with minimum resources.

To disrupt enemy movement: Ambushes may be used in front of and behind the forward edge of the battle area. A series of successful ambushes will disrupt the enemy's freedom of movement.

To gain information: Ambushes can be laid as a means of obtaining information about the enemy or to capture a prisoner.

To provide security: Continued success in ambushing restricts enemy movement and reduces his ability to obtain information.

(8.2) Different types of Ambushes

(8.2.1) *The Deliberate Ambush*

A deliberate ambush is one planned and executed as a separate operation. Generally, time allows for planning, preparation, and rehearsal in great detail. The deliberate ambush may vary in size from a small four-man ambush to a major operation using an infantry battalion. Many opportunities exist for small-scale ambushes; the ambush of up to platoon strength is, however, the normal size used. Successful large-scale ambushes are more difficult to achieve. As a rule of thumb, the smaller the force the easier it is to introduce it into the ambush area, to control the operation, and to extricate the force after contact. A deliberate ambush could be, for example, laid when information provides exact enemy locations, such as an assembly area, or the movement of large numbers of reinforcements.

(8.2.2) *The Immediate Ambush*

An immediate ambush is one set with a minimum of planning to anticipate imminent enemy action, or is a purely defensive technique by a force such as a patrol. In these circumstances, little or no time is available for reconnaissance before occupation of the site. The degree of success achieved depends upon the initiative of the commander concerned, prior rehearsal of proven drills and teamwork. It should normally be laid in areas where civilian movement by night is prohibited.

(8.2.3) *Ambush Sites*

Suitable places for ambush include known enemy routes in forward and rear areas; administrative areas and supply and water points; probable lines of enemy withdrawal after a successful attack by own forces; and in counter-insurgency operations, known or suspected food dumps and arms caches.

(8.3) Essentials of Laying a Successful Ambush

Anything worth shooting is worth shooting twice. Ammo is cheap. Life is expensive.

A successful ambush requires:

Sound intelligence: Sound intelligence is essential for the success of an ambush. A detailed knowledge of the enemy must be obtained from all available sources including patrol reports, recent contact incident reports, intelligence reports and summaries and information from local civilian inhabitants. The details should enable the ambush commander to plan the size of his ambush, the type of ambush he has to employ, the types of weapons that he requires and the ground best suited to catch the enemy by surprise. Of particular interest to the ambush commander during the planning period are the following: likely enemy strength, composition and method of movement; front and flank security, main body and rearguard elements; the means of identifying the enemy, particularly if operations are being conducted with allied troops; the pattern of enemy defensive fire that could include mortar and artillery fire in a war situation; enemy air activity, including the use of observation aircraft and the availability of tactical air support in a war situation; any recent enemy movement patterns, including their ability to concentrate; and known enemy counter-ambush techniques.

A high standard of battle discipline: Ambushing demands a high standard of battle discipline. Once in their fire positions, soldiers must remain motionless with safety catches off, refraining from scratching, slapping at insects, smoking, eating, drinking or relieving themselves. An ambush can be ruined by the accidental discharge of a weapon or by an excited soldier firing before the order is given. Unless this standard of battle discipline can be reached in all aspects, it is useless to embark on an ambush.

Thorough preparation: The preparation for an ambush includes planning, reconnaissance and rehearsals. These tasks must be undertaken with care so that all the factors which may influence the result of the ambush are taken into consideration and all possible eventualities are foreseen and rehearsed. Plans must be made to meet the unexpected. Alternative plans must be made, known and rehearsed.

A simple and clear plan: The plan for the ambush must be as simple as possible for the simple reason that in a complicated plan chances are higher that someone somewhere would commit a mistake. It should cover all possible contingencies and must include clear directions on how the ambush is to be initiated and terminated.

Overall plan and instructions to be clearly understood by everybody before the action: Because there is little opportunity for orders once the occupation of the ambush site is under way, the following must be planned and made known to all members of the ambush party before deployment into the ambush site begins: the sequence of occupation and deployment of groups within the ambush; and the signal for the initiation of the ambush including a secondary means in case of failure of the primary means. Both means of initiation should be colocated and controlled by the ambush commander. The support element commander should always be provided with back-up means of initiation because he has visual into the kill zone and can initiate the back up before the enemy passes through the kill zone. All members must also know: the location of the ambush commander; the means of communication between groups in the ambush; and the signal to be used to control stages of the ambush. The signals for ceasing fire and for each element's withdrawal, in accordance with the sequence in orders, to the rendezvous must also be known. Further, everybody should be aware of alternative arrangements to be used if the ambush is detected or otherwise compromised.

Administration: A large number of ambushes are sprung within a few hours of setting and require no administration other than rest within groups. These are called short term ambushes and are the normal ambush. Where ambushes are set for protracted periods it is necessary to make administrative arrangements for the relief of groups, feeding and rest. In protracted ambushes, a secure administrative area must be established. It should be sited far enough away so that noises and smells do not disclose the presence of troops. Although the whole party in the ambush will eventually be relieved, the whole group must not be changed at the one time. Reliefs should take place when enemy movement is more unlikely. Ideally, each group in the ambush should be divided into three parties: a resting group, a reserve group and an ambush group, who are rotated through the rest area as required. This leaves two-third of the group in the ambush site at any one time.

Surprise: The success of an ambush is dependent upon complete surprise being achieved. The means of achieving surprise include: attention to security; the selection of the ambush site; effective camouflage and concealment; the avoidance of a set pattern in layout and technique used in each ambush; good battle discipline; and radio discipline.

Proper selection of ambush site: While possible ambush sites may be identified by careful study of air photographs and recent patrol reports (routes to the sites and the rendezvous point are usually selected in this manner), a detailed ground reconnaissance is essential nevertheless to select: covered lines of approach and withdrawal; cover from view within the ambush area; suitable locations for observation posts (OPs); likely enemy escape routes; suitable fields of fire; detailed fire positions for fire support, assault and cut-offs; and an acceptable base area in case of a prolonged ambush.

Reconnaissance: If possible, the ambush commander should carry out a reconnaissance of the ambush site prior to the issue of preliminary orders. This is often impossible and initial reconnaissance is confined to a study of air photographs, maps and patrol reports. During his reconnaissance the ambush commander should not walk in the kill zone, as foot marks or disturbed earth may warn an alert enemy. Therefore reconnaissance must be done from the rear of the selected ambush site. Observing the ground from the enemy's point of view may be desirable, but prejudices security.

Camouflage and concealment: In the ambush, protection from observation and surveillance is essential. The members of the ambush must be hidden and vehicles and routes must be camouflaged. In a war situation, concealment from the air and from enemy night vision aids and/or electronic detection devices must be considered, as well as ensuring that there is an absence of light, noise, movement and abnormal smells. Careful selection of sentry positions covering enemy approaches is required to alert the ambush before the enemy reaches the kill zone. Each individual soldier in the ambush area must be responsible for: personal camouflage; taking up the best available firing position; and remaining still and silent for protracted periods.

Routes: The selection of routes into and from the ambush should be well clear of local inhabitants and provide cover from observation. Routes for the withdrawal should differ from those used on the way in. Information rarely gives the enemy's exact route. Irrespective of information gained, the enemy may still approach from an unexpected direction. The failure to consider this factor causes many ambushes to be unsuccessful. It is essential that all likely approaches be covered.

Obstacles: Maximum use should be made of both natural and artificial obstacles. The employment of artificial obstacles must, however, be given careful consideration as the use of wire in particular could compromise surprise. Natural obstacles should also be used with care as they could provide cover for the enemy to escape. Artificial obstacles are most useful on likely enemy withdrawal routes and in dead ground that is difficult to cover with fire from the ambush site.

Grouping: An ambush is made up of a number of groups. The size of a group is dictated by the task of that group. In planning, provision may be required for rest by relieving in location.

Communications: Communication requirements vary according to the size of the ambush. In a small ambush hand signals may suffice, whereas in a large ambush, line, radio, and light signals may have to be employed. As far as possible, signal systems should always be duplicated in case the primary means fails. Means of alerting individual members while in the ambush are also required. A length of vine or cord tied between members has proven successful but can also lead to the ambush being detected due to the noise and movement which might be generated.

Fire control: An ambush is not a place to fire like crazy. Fire must be delivered where it matters. The ambush commander must provide himself with the means to command the ambush and to direct and control his firepower resources even when direct communication is not possible. He must place himself in a position where he can receive early warning of the enemy's approach and where he can initiate the ambush. His plan must include details of which weapons will spring the ambush, as well as alternative plans in case the enemy approaches from an unexpected direction or if he does not receive sufficient warning.

Maximum use of firepower: All available firepower must be coordinated to achieve the best result. The maximum weight of fire must be brought to bear on the enemy immediately—the ambush is initiated so that the enemy does not have time to extricate himself from the kill zone. Cut-off groups should cover likely enemy escape routes.

Positions of support weapons: These must cover the kill zone with subsidiary roles of sealing each end of the ambush and covering likely enemy withdrawal routes. This can be achieved by dividing the kill zone into specific kill zones. Ground not covered by automatic weapons must be covered by riflemen or Claymores. Grenades and Claymores may also be sited to protect the flanks and rear of the ambush against quick enemy counter action. For the protection of the ambush party they should be sited in defiladed ground. Consideration must be made in regard to the danger of using grenades at night.

Planning for action after springing the ambush: The enemy might initially get confused due to the element of surprise; casualties among his ranks; the noise of the ambush; and possibly his inability to locate the source of fire. There will certainly be some loss of control. Panic may result, but with a well-trained enemy, counter-ambush drills or preparation for a more deliberate assault may be expected after the initial confusion. Hence, your assault must commence immediately after the initial firing which should be restricted to seconds. This speed of action is essential so that the initial period of shock created in the enemy is further intensified by the assault. The plan for an immediate assault from ambush may include passing directly through the enemy to a rendezvous (RV) on the far side. Limitations in employment of this technique are: the ambush layout must be single-sided and as close as possible to a straight line; the ground on the far side of the kill zone, as well as the approach to it, must be free of obstacles, both natural and artificial; and this technique is unsuitable if the aim of the ambush is the deliberate capture of a prisoner. An immediate assault not involving passing directly through the enemy is only suitable when the enemy force is small. It has the fundamental advantage of exploiting the surprise created, and providing an opportunity to search enemy dead. The problem of control is more difficult. This type of assault is aimed at complete destruction of a small force by closing with the enemy and mopping-up thoroughly. The deliberate capture of a prisoner by an ambush requires a detailed plan. The action after springing should provide for the following: isolating the prisoner by fire and by movement if necessary; seizing and securing the prisoner; and a sound plan for evacuation of the prisoner.

Withdrawal: The route and method of withdrawal have a bearing on the selection of the ambush site and frequently on the detailed layout. When an ambush is sprung and it is quite obvious that the aim of the ambush cannot be fully achieved, the ambush commander must make full use of the surprise and temporary confusion achieved. He must take the opportunity to inflict the maximum amount of damage on the enemy, and at the same time ensure a clean break. Under some circumstances, small parties may be left behind to cover the withdrawal and to ambush any enemy relief force moving into the area. The use of defensive fire (DF) targets to assist the ambush party in achieving a clean break should be considered. Detailed plans for the withdrawal must be made. This involves specifying the sequence of movement of groups. Plans for withdrawal must cover: action after springing; action when no enemy enters the ambush site and the ambush is not sprung; and action to be taken when too large an enemy force approaches or enters the ambush site.

Medical arrangements: This must include casualty evacuation plan and any hygiene arrangements. The evacuation plan depends on: the remaining active strength of the force; the nature of the casualty; if the casualties occur en route, at the objective or on return; the distance to the nearest friendly location; and available areas for possible helicopter evacuation.

Security: It is necessary to deny the enemy knowledge of the friendly force's intentions during the preparation and execution of the ambush.

Do not think that it is an easy thing to do. Mere intelligence is not enough. You have to wait and wait patiently. As dear Sun-Tzu said: "One who is prudent and lies in wait for an enemy, shall be victorious". General Wesley Clark of the US army recalls from his days as a young officer in Vietnam: "You just lay out flat, rifle at the ready, and tried to stay awake while staring at the dark and listening to the night. And if you weren't extremely tough on yourself—and everyone else—you fell asleep even when you thought you were awake. Most people would probably think that a soldier on an ambush in a real war would have trouble falling asleep. Wrong! it may be true on your first ambush but pretty soon you have the opposite problem. It is extremely difficult to stay awake after humping all day. The typical ambush might have 100 per cent alert until midnight, 2 people plus radio watch until stand to some ungodly hour in morning when you would go back to 100 per cent. It's pretty scary when you wake up to find everyone asleep".

(8.4) Ingredients of Proper Execution of Ambushes

Be polite. Be professional. But, have a plan to kill everyone you meet.

(8.4.1) Lying in Wait

(a) Every soldier must learn to select a comfortable position quickly, and must remain at that place without any movement or making any noise, as long as he has to be there. This may be some hours. Specific orders must be given concerning eating and drinking.

(b) Weapons must be cocked before moving into position and safety catches left off once the ambush has been set.

(c) If all members of the ambush observe continuously, no rest is possible and keenness will deteriorate. On the other hand, the kill zone must be under observation at all times. This is achieved by rostering observers within groups. The ambush commander and his second-in-command relieve each other. Other members relax but remain so that, without undue movement, they can fire on their arcs as soon as they are alerted. Furthermore, a 100 per cent stand-to should be initiated on initial occupation and at first and last light.

(8.4.2) Signals

Three signals, often four, are needed to execute the ambush. Audible and visual signals, such as whistles and pyrotechnics, must be changed often to avoid establishing patterns. Too frequently, use of the same signals may result in their becoming known to the enemy. A guerrilla might recognise a signal and be able to react in time to avoid the full effects of an ambush. For example, if white star cluster is habitually used to signal withdrawal in a night ambush, an alert guerrilla might fire one and cause premature withdrawal. A signal by the security force to alert the patrol leader to the guerrilla's approach may be given by: arm-and-hand signals; radio; as a quiet voice message; by transmitting a pre-arranged number of taps, by signalling with the push-to-talk switch; field telephone, when there is no danger that wire between positions will compromise the ambush. A signal to initiate the ambush, given by the patrol leader or a designated individual, may be a shot or the detonation of mines or explosives. A signal for lifting or shifting fires, if the guerrilla force is to be assaulted, may be given by voice command, whistles, or pyrotechnics. All fire stops immediately so that the assault can be made before the guerrilla can react.

(8.4.3) Springing the Ambush

When a sentry sights the enemy he communicates via tug line, radio or telephone and gives the signal for the direction of approach and size of the enemy party. When the enemy appears in the kill zone each man aims awaiting the order to fire. The ambush should be sprung when as many enemy as possible are in the kill zone and the range has been reduced to a minimum. There must be no half-heartedness or premature action. The ambush should be initiated with a mass casualty producing weapon (Claymore anti-personnel mine or machinegun). The drill for opening fire is as follows:

(a) A small-scale ambush is normally sprung by the commander, but should any enemy act as though he has seen the ambush, any man who sees this action should spring the ambush. Because of the risk of the ambush being prematurely sprung, only well-trained and experienced soldiers should be sited in those positions close to the kill zone where an alert enemy could discover the ambush.

(b) All shots must be aimed to kill. Once fire has been opened men often have to adjust their positions to fire at moving targets.

(c) Firers must fire only within their allocated arcs in order to stop any potential firing into friendly positions.

(d) The commander should be so placed that he has a good view of the enemy. The commander initiates the ambush by a pre-arranged signal which would normally be: an aimed burst of fire from an automatic weapon; the command detonation of Claymores, explosives or grenades; and the setting-off of a booby-trap or trip flare.

(e) The commander must always make alternative arrangements for springing the ambush in the event of something going wrong with the person or method nominated. A deputy commander should always be appointed and the chain of command in seniority must be known.

(8.4.4) *Subsequent Action*

Once the ambush is sprung, the subsequent action proceeds according to the plan, i.e., either an immediate assault or remain in the ambush positions. Normal action is to maintain a heavy volume of fire until the enemy has been destroyed. The fire fight should normally be of a short duration. The signal to stop fire can be given by the commander—voice or a flare is suggested—or, as it is difficult to hear over machinegun fire, the ceasefire could occur after a predetermined amount of ammunition has been fired, say for example, 60 rounds by each man firing from AK rifle. After the ceasefiring order is given the assault element moves in or the ambush party is withdrawn. If required, the assault element assaults the objective and checks the kill zone for enemy and secure any who are still living. The dead should also be searched. Needless to say, you also search for any equipment left behind at the ambush site and collect the enemy's arms, ammunition, equipment, and documents. Dead bodies may be photographed for identification.

Tracker Teams: Some enemy troops that have been wounded in the ambush may attempt to escape by rushing into the undergrowth and lying low until the ambush has withdrawn. If the operational situation permits the employment of trackers it quite often leads to their capture.

(8.4.5) *Withdrawal*

It is at this stage that the ambush is most vulnerable. If no assault is planned, a fast withdrawal should be made during the brief period of enemy confusion and before he has re-established control. A rendezvous is necessary for the ambush party as members may take some time to clear the site. If an assault is planned, a search of victims and collection of prisoners is required; planning must include arrangements for the withdrawal of these groups covered by the remainder of the party. The objective rallying point must be far enough from the ambush site so that it will not be overrun if the guerrilla force attacks the ambush. Routes of withdrawal to the objective rallying point must be reconnoitered. If possible, each person walks the route he is to use and picks out checkpoints. When the ambush is to be executed at night, each person must be able to follow his route in the dark. On signal, the unit quickly but quietly withdraws to the objective rallying point, reorganises, and begins its return march. If the ambush was not successful and the unit is pursued, withdrawal may be by bounds. The last group may arm mines, previously placed along the withdrawal route, to further delay pursuit. All men must know the signal and the sequence of withdrawal.

Withdrawal route must be known to all. A check point between the ambush site and the rendezvous may be required. For a small-scale ambush this is the Release Point. Troops make a clean break from the ambush site, and concentrate at the rendezvous quickly in an orderly manner. Time in the rendezvous must be short; the force must be checked, formed up and moved-off as quickly as possible. More than one route of withdrawal may be necessary. It may be desirable and practicable to set a further ambush along the withdrawal route.

(8.4.6) Casualties

Arrangements must be made before occupation for the evacuation of both our own and enemy casualties. Stretchers or material for improvising stretchers may be dumped at the rendezvous so that the minimum time is lost during withdrawal.

(8.5) Ambushes at Night

Your mortar fire will put exactly one round on the intended target. That round will be a dud.

Night ambushes are often the most successful because enemy movement generally increases during the hours of darkness. Night ambushes have similar characteristics to ambushes by day. However, you should be especially conscious of the following facts:

- Concealment is easy but shooting is much less accurate. Fire at night tends to be high and bayonets may be fixed in order to lower the barrels of weapons to prevent firing high.
- Automatic weapons become the essential fire elements—single shot weapons are too slow to produce the necessary volume of fire.
- All weapons, particularly machineguns firing down tracks, should have their left and right arcs of fire fixed by means of stakes, etc, to eliminate danger to own troops.
- The ambush party must never move about. Any movement is regarded as enemy.
- Men and groups must be sited closer together than by day.
- It is difficult to take up an ambush position at night. Where possible it should be occupied before last light.
- Consideration must be given to a method of illuminating the kill zone at the moment the commander wishes to spring the ambush. Illumination can be provided by means of trip flares set-off by

the ambush commander either electrically or by pulling a trip wire. Illumination rounds can also be used if vegetation permits. Flares may be set-off by animals, so it is generally better if they are command detonated. The flares should be sited so that they illuminate the enemy whilst at the same time; members of the ambush are shielded from the direct glare of the light. Trip flares can also be connected to Claymores to detonate simultaneously with the command detonation of the Claymore.

- The use of night vision goggles and other night viewing devices should also be considered.

(8.6) Various types of Ambushes distinguished on Layout

A retreating enemy is probably just falling back and regrouping.
Or else they're trying to suck you into a serious ambush!

Point ambush: A point ambush, whether independent or part of an area ambush, is positioned along the expected route of approach of the guerrilla force. Formation is important because, to a great extent, it determines whether a point ambush can deliver the heavy volume of highly concentrated fire necessary to isolate, trap, and destroy the guerrillas.

Near ambush: A near ambush is a point ambush with the assault element within reasonable assaulting distance of the kill zone (less than 50 meters). Close terrain, such as jungle and heavy woods, may require this positioning. It may also be appropriate in open terrain in a "rise from the ground" ambush.

Far ambush: A far ambush is a point ambush with the assault element beyond reasonable assaulting distance of the kill zone (beyond 50 meters). This location may be appropriate in open terrain offering good fields of fire or when attack is by fire for a harassing ambush.

Harassing ambush: A harassing ambush is an ambush in which attack is by fire only.

Destruction ambush: A destruction ambush is an ambush which includes assault to close with and decisively engage the guerrilla force.

Spider-hole ambush: This point ambush is designed for open areas that lack the cover and concealment and other features normally desirable in a "good" ambush site. The attack element is deployed in the formation best suited to the overall situation. The attack element is concealed in the "spider-hole" type of covered fox-hole. Soil is carefully removed and positions expertly camouflaged. When the ambush is initiated, the attack element members throw back the covers and literally "rise from the ground" to attack. This ambush takes advantage of the tendency of patrols, and other units, to relax in areas that do not appear to favour ambush. The chief disadvantage is that the ambush element is vulnerable if detected prematurely.

Area ambush: It consists of a series of small groups, each with its own commander, sited as part of an overall plan to encompass a particular enemy party which is expected. Groups are sited as part of an overall plan to ambush an enemy party whose exact direction of movement is unknown. The ambush party moves to a dispersal point from which groups move by selected routes to their positions. The ambush commander may be able to position only one group in detail, leaving the remainder to be positioned by the group commanders themselves. Where there is more than one approach, all approaches must be covered. Approaches should be covered in depth to catch enemy scattering from the position of the ambush.

Area ambush—Multiple point: Point ambushes are established along the trails or other escape routes leading away from the central kill zone. The site may be a water hole, guerrilla campsite, or known rendezvous point, or a frequently travelled trail. This site is the central kill zone. The guerrilla force, whether a single group or several parties approaching from different directions, is permitted to move to the

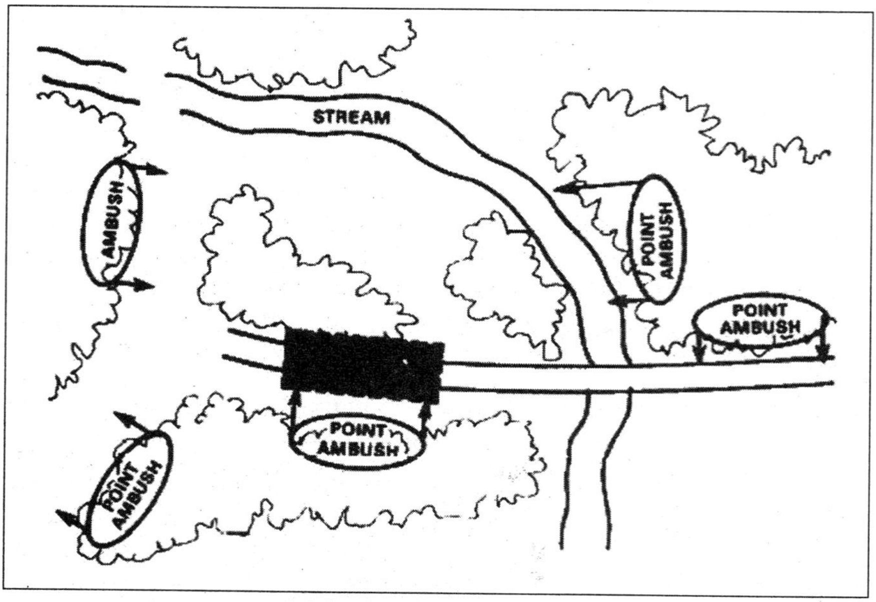

Multiple point area ambush

central kill zone. Outlying ambushes do not attack unless discovered. The ambush is initiated when the guerrillas move into the central kill zone. When the guerrillas break contact and attempt to disperse, escaping portions are intercepted and destroyed by the outlying ambushes. The multiple point ambush increases casualties and harassment and produces confusion. This version of the area ambush is best suited in terrain where movement is largely restricted to trails. It provides best results when established as a deliberate ambush. When there is not sufficient intelligence for a deliberate ambush, an area ambush of opportunity (hasty ambush) may be established. The outlying ambushes are permitted to attack guerrillas approaching the central kill zone, if the guerrilla force is small. If it is too large for the particular outlying ambush, the guerrillas are allowed to continue and they are attacked in the central kill zone.

Area ambush—Baited trap: A variation of the area ambush is the "baited trap" ambush. A central kill zone is established along the guerrilla's route of approach. Point ambushes are established along the routes over which units relieving or reinforcing the guerrilla will have to approach. The guerrilla force in the central kill zone serves as "bait" to lure relieving or reinforcing guerrilla units into the kill zones of the outlying ambushes. A friendly force can also be used as the "bait". The outlying point ambushes need not be strong enough to destroy their targets. They may be small harassing ambushes that delay, disorganise, and cause casualties by successive contacts. This version can be varied by using a fixed installation as "bait" to lure relieving or reinforcing guerrilla units into the kill zone of one or more of the outlying ambushes. The installation replaces the central kill zone and is attacked. The attack may intend to overcome the installation or may use it as a ruse. These variations are best suited for situations where routes of approach for relieving or reinforcing guerrilla units are limited to those favourable for ambush.

Demolition ambush: Dual primed, electrically detonated mines or demolition charges are planted in an area over which a guerrilla force is expected to pass. This may be a portion of a road or trail, an open field, or any area that can be observed from a distance. Activating wires are run to a concealed observation point sufficiently distant to ensure safety of the ambush element. As large a force as desired or necessary can be used to mine the area. The ambush element remains to fire the charges; other personnel return to the unit. When a guerrilla force enters the mined area (kill zone), the element on site detonates the explosives and withdraws immediately to avoid detection and pursuit.

(8.7) Different Formations in Limited Ambushes

No Operations Plan ever survives initial contact.

When, because of the ground, there is only one likely approach, a group or groups may be sited in depth with all-round defense at a place on that route which gives adequate concealment. This is a limited ambush. It is used when the area ambush is impossible or as part of an area ambush, along a very likely approach track. Basic forms of limited ambushes are discussed below.

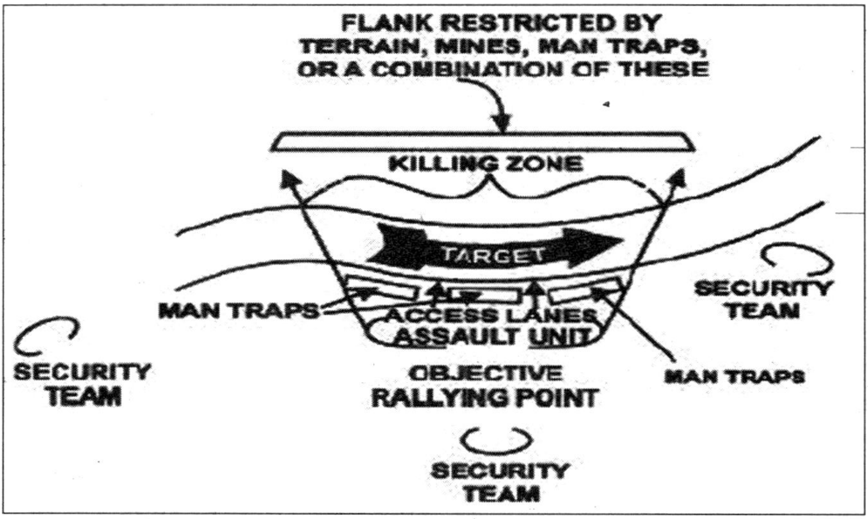

Line formation ambush with access lanes for assaulting the target

Line formation: The attack element is deployed generally parallel to the guerrilla force's route of movement (road, trail, stream, etc). This positions the attack element parallel to the long axis of the kill zone and subjects the guerrilla force to heavy flanking fire. The size of the force that can be trapped in the kill zone is limited by the area which the attack element can effectively cover with highly concentrated fire. The force is trapped in the kill zone by natural obstacles, mines (Claymore, anti-vehicular, anti-personnel), demolitions, and direct and indirect fires. The basic advantage of the line formation is its relative ease of control under all conditions of visibility. A disadvantage of the line formation is the possibility that lateral dispersion of the force maybe too great for effective coverage. The line formation is appropriate in close terrain that restricts guerrilla manoeuvre and in open terrain where one flank is restricted by mines, demolitions, or mantraps. Similar obstacles can be placed between the attack element and the kill zone to provide protection from guerrilla counter-ambush measures. When a destruction ambush is deployed in this manner, access lanes are left so that the force in the killing zone can be assaulted. The line formation can be effectively used by a "rise from the ground" ambush in terrain seemingly unsuitable for ambush.

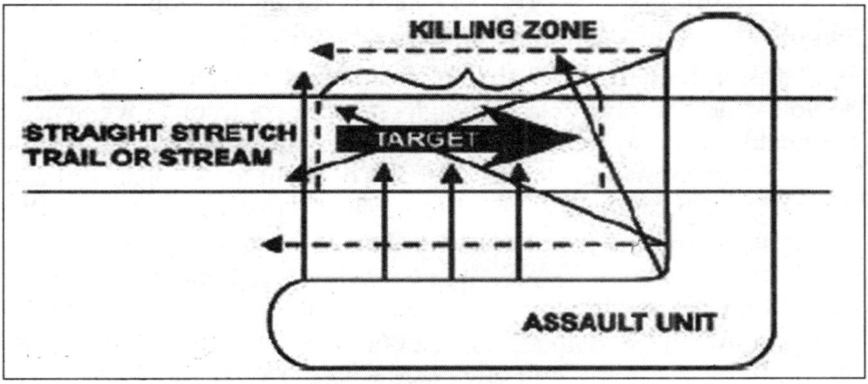

L-formation (destruction) ambush

L-formation: The L-shaped formation is a variation of the line formation. The long side of the attack element is parallel to the kill zone and delivers flanking fire. The short side of the attack element is at the end of, and at right angles to, the kill zone and delivers enfilading fire that interlocks with fire from the other leg. This formation is flexible. It can be established on a straight stretch of a trail or stream or at a sharp bend in a trail or stream. When appropriate, fire from the short leg can be shifted to parallel the long leg if the guerrilla force attempts to assault or escape in the opposite direction. In addition, the short leg prevents escape in that direction or reinforcement from that direction.

Z-formation: The Z-shaped formation is another variation of the L-formation. The attack force is deployed as in the L-formation but

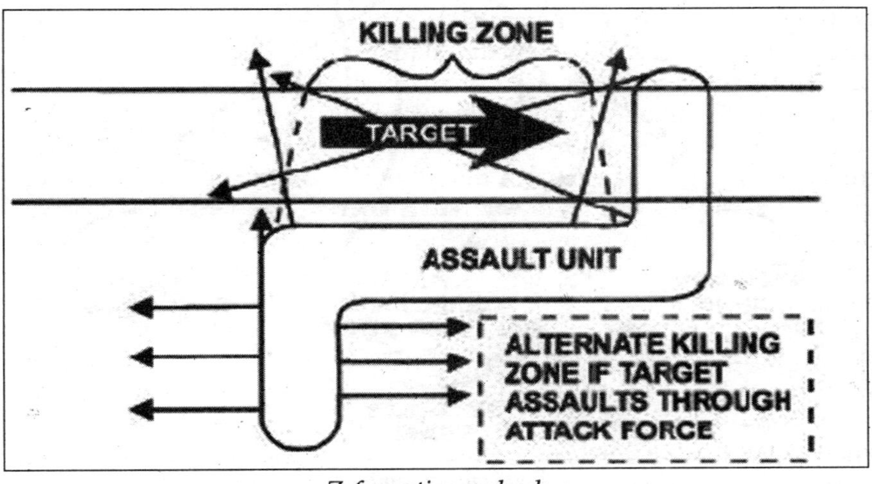

Z-formation ambush

with an additional side so that the formation resembles the letter Z. The additional side may serve to engage a force attempting to relieve or reinforce the guerrillas; restrict a flank; prevent envelopment (of the ambush force); and seal the end of the kill zone.

T-formation: In the T-shaped formation, the attack element is deployed across, and at right angles to, the route of movement of the hostile force so that the attack element and the target form the letter T. This formation can be used day or night to establish a purely harassing ambush, and at night to establish an ambush to interdict movement through open, hard-to-seal areas (such as rice paddies). A small unit can use the T-formation to harass, slow, and disorganise a larger force. When the lead guerrilla elements are engaged, they will normally attempt to manoeuvre right or left to close with the ambush force. Mines, mantraps, and other obstacles placed to the flanks of the

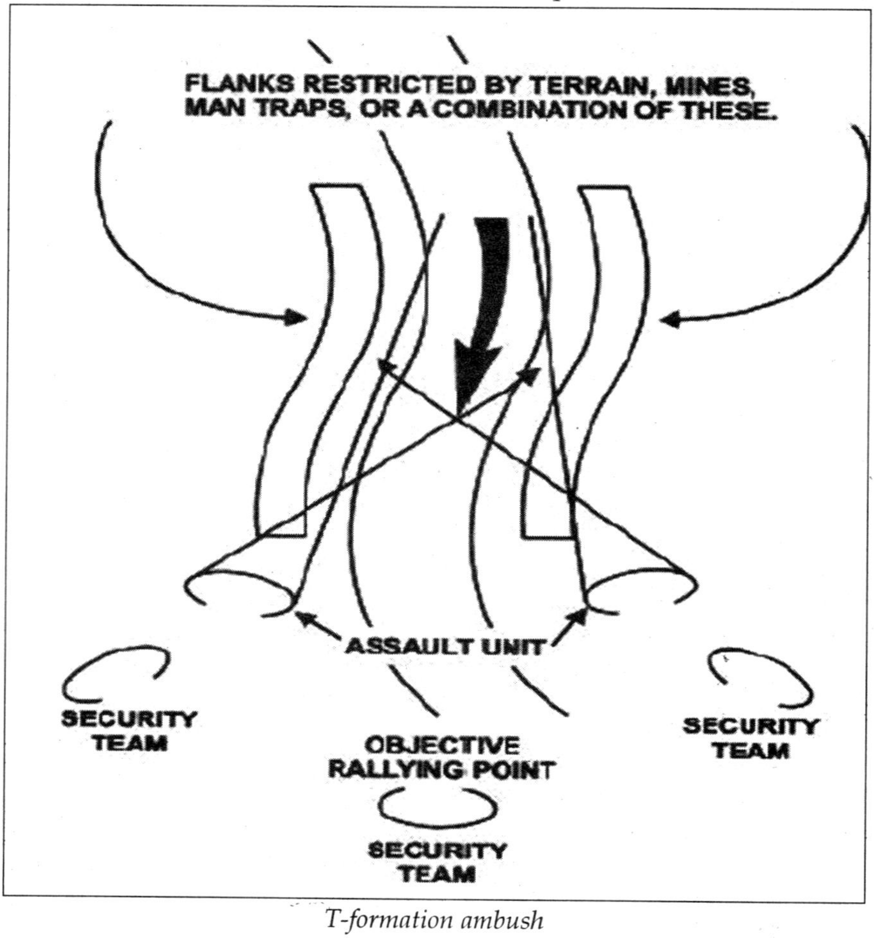

T-formation ambush

kill zone slow the guerrilla's movement and permit the unit to deliver heavy fire and then withdraw without becoming decisively engaged. The T-formation can be used to interdict small groups attempting night movement across open areas. For example, the attack element may be deployed along a rice paddy dike with every second member facing in the opposite direction. The attack of a force approaching from either direction requires only that every second member shift to the opposite side of the dike. Each member fires only to his front and only when the target is at close range. Attack is by fire only, and each member keeps the guerrilla force under fire as long as it remains to his front. If the force attempts to escape in either direction along the dike, each member takes it under fire as it comes into his vicinity. The T-formation is effective at halting infiltration. It has one disadvantage, however. There is a possibility that while it is spread out the ambush could engage a superior force. Use of this formation must, therefore, fit the local enemy situation.

V-formation: The V-shaped attack element is deployed along both sides of the guerrilla route of movement so that it forms a V. Care is

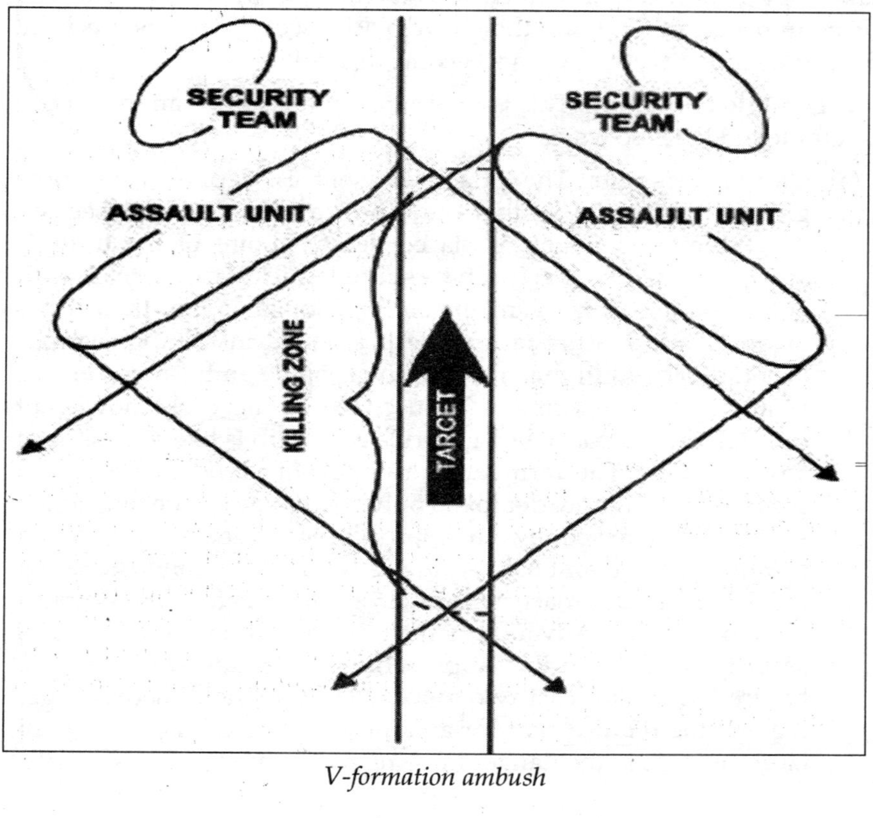

V-formation ambush

taken to ensure that neither group (or leg) fires into the other. This formation subjects the guerrilla to both enfilading and inter-locking fire. The V-formation is suited for fairly open terrain but can also be used in the jungle. When established in the jungle, the legs of the V close in as the lead elements of the guerrilla force approach the apex of the V; elements then open fire from close range. Here, even more than in open terrain, all movement and fire is carefully coordinated and controlled to ensure that the fire of one leg does not endanger the other. Wider separation of the elements makes this formation difficult to control, and there are fewer sites that favour its use. Its main advantage is that it is difficult for the guerrilla to detect the ambush until well into the kill zone. On the other hand, the guerrillas also know that in many places, the troops are obliged to move in an extended file formation. The extended file formation lends itself to be ambushed by the V-formation ambush. Contrary to what natural reactions would dictate, the best course to break out of a V-formation ambush for those who are caught in the kill zone is to charge and rush through the apex of the 'V' using their superior firepower—the enemy cannot possibly take the risk of firing on you close to the apex as then they would be firing into each other. But if they have placed security teams precisely for this eventuality, then things become difficult.

Triangle Formation: This is a variation of the V-formation and can be employed in three ways.

(a) **Closed Triangle:** The attack element is deployed in three groups, positioned so that they form a triangle (or closed V). An automatic weapon is placed at each point of the triangle and positioned so that it can be shifted quickly to interlock with either of the others. Elements are positioned so that their fields of fire overlap. Mortars may be positioned inside the triangle. When deployed in this manner, the triangle ambush becomes a small unit strongpoint which is used to interdict night movement through open areas, when guerrilla approach is likely to be from any direction. The formation provides all-round security, and security elements are deployed only when they can be positioned so that, if detected by an approaching target, they will not compromise the ambush. Attack is by fire only, and the target is allowed to approach within close range before the ambush force opens fire. Advantages include ease of control, all-round security, and guerrillas approaching from any direction can be fired on by at least two automatic weapons. Disadvantages include the requirement for an ambush force of platoon size or larger to reduce the danger of being overrun by a large guerrilla force; one or more legs of the triangle may come under guerrilla enfilade fire; and lack of dispersion, particularly at the points, increases danger from guerrilla mortar fire.

(b) **Open Triangle (Harassing Ambush):** This variation of the triangle ambush is designed to enable a small unit to harass, slow, and inflict heavy casualties upon a larger force without being decisively engaged. The attack group is deployed in three elements, positioned so that each element becomes a corner of a triangle containing the kill zone. When the guerrillas enter the kill zone, the element to the front of the guerrillas opens fire on the lead guerrillas. When the guerrillas counter-attack, the element withdraws and an assault element to the flank opens fire. When this group is attacked, the element to the opposite flank opens fire. This process is repeated until the guerrillas are pulled apart. Each element reoccupies its position, if possible, and continues to inflict maximum damage without becoming decisively engaged.

(c) **Open Triangle (Destruction Ambush):** The attack group is again deployed in three elements, positioned so that each element is a point of the triangle, 200 to 300 meters apart. The kill zone is the area within the triangle. The guerrillas are allowed to enter the killing zone; the nearest element attacks by fire. As the guerrillas attempt to manoeuvre or withdraw, the other elements open fire. One or more assault elements as directed; assault or manoeuvre to envelop or destroy the guerrillas. As a destruction ambush, this formation is suitable for platoon-size or larger units; a unit smaller than a platoon would be in danger of being overrun. Also, control, in assaulting or manoeuvring, is difficult. Close coordination and control are necessary to ensure that assaulting or manoeuvring assault elements are not fired on by another party; and the ambush site must be a fairly level, open area that provides (around its border) concealment for the ambush elements (unless it is a "rise from the ground" ambush).

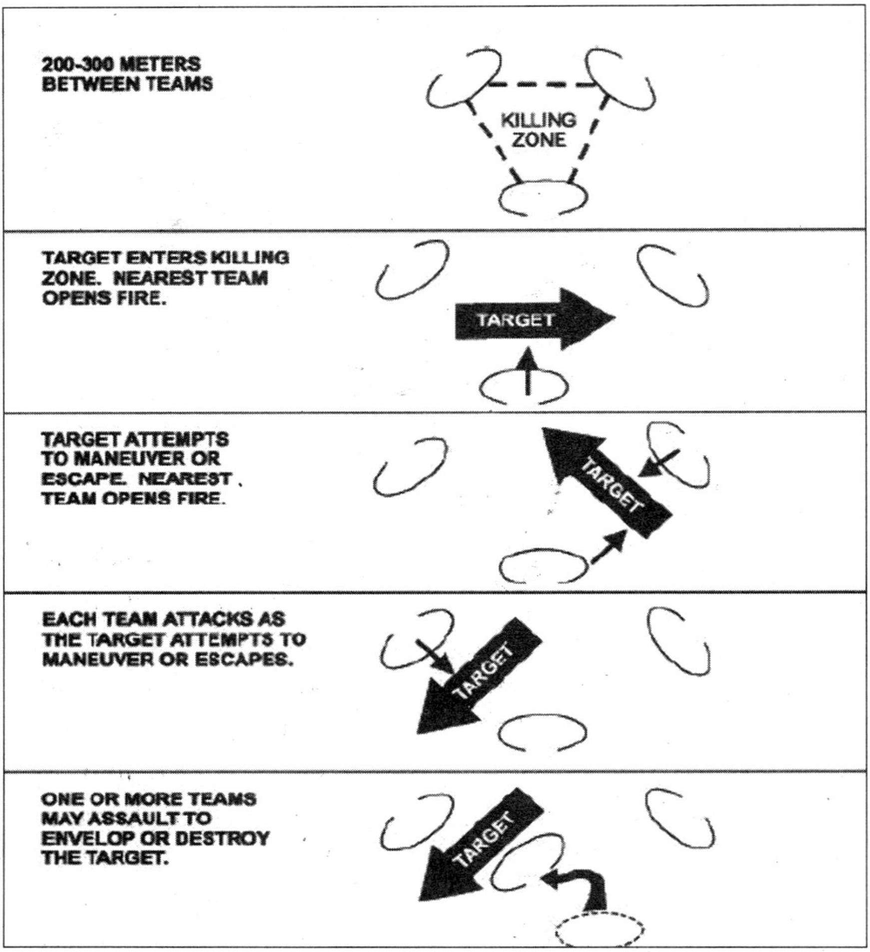

Open triangle formation (destruction) ambush

(d) **Box Formation:** This formation is similar in purpose to the open triangle ambush. The unit is deployed in four elements positioned so that each element becomes a corner of a square or rectangle containing the kill zone. It can be used as a harassing ambush or a destruction ambush in the same manner as the two variations of the open triangle ambush.

(8.8) The Immediate or Hasty Ambush

If your ambush is properly set, the enemy won't walk into it.

There may be occasions when a patrol, without being seen itself, sights an enemy party approaching either on a track, or across a clearing, or in a forest. This is most likely to occur when the patrol has halted and the enemy is on the move. It is obviously better to allow the enemy to approach as close as possible before opening fire on him. If the patrol is on the move there may be time only for a silent signal to be passed through the patrol, to move quietly and quickly into the positions indicated and for the signal to open fire to be given when the enemy reaches the position in which he is most vulnerable. No shot must be fired in the excitement of the moment when the enemy is first sighted; battle discipline is very important. The leading scout must pass a field signal back as he sees the enemy approaching and the patrol commander must give the field signal for the immediate ambush. In some cases (such as when the enemy is very close before the leading scout sees him) there may not be time for this. Patrol commanders must therefore delegate to the leading scout or another member the authority for giving the immediate ambush field signal should circumstances dictate. On seeing the signal, the leading group takes up fire positions that have cover from view and remain still even if they have not assumed a good fire position.

At times, the enemy may be too close for their positions to be adjusted. In that case, other groups further from the enemy must adopt fire positions aimed into the proposed kill zone. The siting of machineguns is critical. The signal to open fire is normally be given by the patrol commander who should be able to see when the machinegun has a good target. Nevertheless everyone must be ready to open fire if the enemy becomes aware of the ambush before the signal is given. Men should remain in position until ordered to move by the patrol commander. Subsequent action by the patrol commander and ambush party is similar to the deliberate ambush, if time and opportunity permits. Other formations and circumstances demand different drills for the immediate ambush. These should be worked out and rehearsed. In open country it may be preferable to carry out a contact drill quietly, if a linear type ambush is not possible and the patrol has been observed by the enemy.

Drill—Immediate Ambush Front: This is employed when leading scouts detect an enemy approaching along the same track who is unaware of their presence, and when there is neither the time nor opportunity to manoeuvre. The actions of individual members of the patrol should be on the following lines:

a. **Action by leading Scout:**

(1) Give silent signal for Immediate Ambush Front, indicating which side to ambush.

(2) Move quickly and silently into cover.

(3) Complete silence and concealment are more important than a good fire position.

b. **Action by Remainder:**

(1) Pass signal back and move diagonally forward into cover on the side indicated and then remain still.

(2) Take up a fire position, at the same time remaining concealed and maintaining silence.

(3) The commander must have a clear view of the killing area.

c. **Springing:**

(1) When the enemy are in the killing area, the commander will shout Fire.

(2) On this signal, everyone will fire, adjusting their positions and standing, if necessary, so as to bring the maximum effective aimed fire to bear on the enemy.

(3) If it is clear that the enemy have seen a member of the ambush before the ambush has been sprung, this man should spring the ambush on his own initiative.

d. **Action if the ambush is not immediately sprung:** If the ambush is not sprung within one minute the enemy may have halted, withdrawn turned off the track or perhaps detected the ambush and be taking counter-measures. In any event, the ambush must not remain in position after one minute has elapsed: at this time, each man must withdraw silently into the jungle for 100 paces at right angles to the track along which the patrol has been moving. When they have all moved 100 paces, which in thick jungle may take some time, the patrol should take up a position of all round defence. The commander should then determine his next course of offensive action.

Drill—Immediate Ambush Rear: This drill is used to meet a threat from the rear. A common tactic, which the enemy may well use, is to follow up or track a patrol to attack it at a convenient moment or when halted: this drill should, therefore, be used at any time when it is known or felt that the enemy is following up and at all halts except for short tactical pauses.

a. **Action by rear man if he detects a following enemy:** Give the Enemy Rear signal discreetly and make sure it is passed forward.

b. **Action by Remainder:** Pass the signal forward quickly and quietly.

c. **Action by Commander:**

(1) When the signal reaches him the commander should proceed as if he was unaware of the enemy until he reaches a suitable ambush position.

(2) He should then give the Immediate Ambush Rear signal which must only be passed forward to the leading scouts.

d. **Action by leading Scout:** On receiving the signal, he will take up an ambush position on the side indicated.

e. **Action by Remainder:** The second man will go about five paces beyond the leading scout and will take up an ambush position on the same side, each following man will then continue five paces beyond the man in front of him and take up a similar position. The rear group, however, will continue along the track for a further 20 paces, before taking up their ambush positions, to lead the enemy into the ambush.

f. **Springing and further action:** As for the immediate ambush front, except that if the ambush is not sprung it will remain in position for 10 minutes before withdrawing silently to the halt or harbour position.

Drill—Immediate ambush flank: This drill is used if the enemy is detected on a flank or the patrol is fired upon.

a. **Action by troops in contact with the enemy:**

(1) Shout Ambush Right or Left according to whether the enemy is on the right or left flank.

(2) Take up a fire position and engage the enemy.

b. **Action by troops out of contact:**

(1) Shout Ambush Right or Left.

(2) Close up in all round defence with the 0 Group in the centre.

c. **Action by commander or senior rank not in contact with the enemy:**

(1) Form up and lead an assault on the flank of the enemy position.

(2) If it is known that only the centre of the column is in contact, the troops to the rear will carry out the flank attack, while the forward troops remain in all round defence and only fire if they positively identify the enemy.

(3) During the attack, a clear signal must be given to the troops in contact to cease fire as the assault goes in.

Drill—Immediate Ambush Contact Front: This drill is used when the enemy is encountered at close range in circumstances where the immediate ambush drill is inappropriate; the enemy may be bivouacked, crossing the front or themselves in an ambush position awaiting the patrol. In any of these or similar situations, the patrol commander must make a plan and the following drill is designed so as to give him the time and opportunity to do this.

a. **Action by leading scout:**

(1) Shout Contact Front (unless the enemy is still unaware of the patrol's presence, in which case pass back silent signal for Enemy).

(2) Take up a fire position, and engage the enemy if surprise has been lost.

b. **Action by Remainder:** Repeat the signal and take up fire positions. Engage the enemy if surprise has been lost.

c. **Action by Commander:** Carry out a quick battle appreciation; if the patrol is part of a larger force he should send back a runner with a description of the enemy position and report on the action he is taking.

d. **Further Action:**

(1) Depending on the strength of the enemy position, either the leading section will deal with it, or the leading platoon or company will attack, possibly using the leading section or platoon as a fire group.

(2) If the enemy position is too strong for the force involved, they should withdraw by fire and manoeuvre, calling for fire support as necessary.

(3) After an attack, the force should reorganise in all-round defence well clear of the enemy position before reporting to their higher formation by radio.

Drill—Immediate Ambush Contact Rear: This action is carried out in exactly the same sequence as above but in the reverse order, the rear man shouting Contact Rear or giving the appropriate signal. Like all the above drills, it is completed as soon as the commander has made an appreciation and given orders.

Drill—Immediate Ambush Contact Flank: Where the attack comes from the flank actions similar to those performed above are done. Despite the difficulty of terrain, where there is an unprotected flank(s) a moving body of troops require flank scouts. Most attacks will come from the flanks or rear.

(8.9) Why some Ambushes Fail, and how to Avoid Failure?

If your positions are firmly set and you are prepared to take the enemy assault on, he will bypass you.

Some of the reasons of failure of ambushes, as gleaned from the experiences of thousands of ambush commanders are:

- Disclosure of the ambush by the noise made by actions like cocking weapons, moving safety catches or changing levers. Check your weapons, make your men practice silent handling and ensure that all weapons are ready to fire.
- A tendency to shoot high at the face of the enemy. This can be corrected by conducting night range practices utilising night vision devices and fixing bayonets when possible.
- Disclosure of the ambush position by footprints made by the ambush party moving into position and by the movement of individuals at the crucial time when the enemy is approaching.
- A lack of fire control, as commanders were unable to stop the firing and start the immediate follow-up.
- Commanders were badly sited with consequent lack of control.
- A lack of all-round observation resulting in enemy arriving in the area of an ambush unannounced.
- Misfires and stoppages through failure to clean, inspect, and test weapons and magazines.
- A lack of a clearly defined drill for opening fire.
- A tendency for all to select and fire at the same targets.
- Fire opened prematurely.
- Ambush training must be aimed at eliminating common faults and improving techniques such as:
- Training of troops to occupy positions without advertising their presence by footprints, movement by individuals when the enemy is approaching, and the noise of weapons being cocked or safety catches and change levers being moved.
- Ensuring the proper positioning of commanders and siting of weapons. A lack of all-round observation can result in the enemy arriving in the area undetected.

- Improvement of fire control and particularly the even distribution of fire.
- Ensuring accurate shooting at moving targets and reduction of the tendency for men to select and fire at the same target; fire high; or fire outside his designated arcs.
- Improving the care of weapons and preventing misfires and stoppages occurring through failure to clean, inspect and test weapons and magazines.
- Developing simple and sound standard operating procedures (SOPs) that all members of the ambush understand.

(8.10) Learning from the enemy: Novel Viet Cong Tactics

If your flank march is going well, the enemy expects you to outflank him.

(8.10.1) Viet Cong Ambushes

The Viet Cong excelled in ambushes. Both offensive and defensive tactics often involved luring ARVN and US troops into a maze of concealed fortifications, or into ambush positions, where they could be bled before the People's Army Forces withdrew. Initial positions were sometimes made to appear deliberately weak, including unmanned bunkers and light sniper-type resistance to bait enemy forces inside the killing zone. In the meantime, more lethal elements manoeuvred and concentrated inside the fortified complex to inflict maximum damage. One important feature of the ambush was that the target units should 'pile up' after being attacked, thus preventing them any easy means of withdrawal from the kill zone and hindering their use of heavy weapons and supporting fires. Terrain was usually selected which would facilitate this and slow down the enemy. The terrain around the ambush site which was not favourable to the ambushing force, or which offered some protection to the target, was heavily mined and booby trapped or pre-registered for mortars.

Ambush units: The NVA/VC ambush formations consisted of lead-blocking element; main-assault element; rear-blocking element; observation posts; and command post. Other elements might also be included if the situation demanded, such as a sniper screen along a nearby avenue of approach to delay enemy reinforcement.

Command posts: When deploying into an ambush site, the NVA first occupied several observation posts, placed to detect the enemy as early as possible and to report on the formation it was using, its strength and firepower, as well as to provide early warning to the unit commander. Usually one main OP and several secondary OPs were established. Runners and occasionally radios were used to communicate between the OPs and the main command post. The OPs were located so that they could observe enemy movement into the ambush and often they would remain in position throughout the ambush in order to report routes of reinforcement and withdrawal by the enemy as well as his manoeuvre options. Frequently the OPs were reinforced to squad size and served as flank security. The command post was situated in a central location, often on terrain which afforded it a vantage point overlooking the ambush site.

Reconnaissance methods: Reconnaissance elements observing a potential ambush target on the move generally stayed 300-500 meters away. Sometimes a "leapfrogging" reconnaissance technique was used. Surveillance units were echeloned one behind the other. As the enemy drew close to the first, it fell back behind the last reconnaissance team, leaving an advance group in its place. This one in turn fell back as the enemy again closed the gap, and the cycle rotated. This method helped keep the enemy under continuous observation from a variety of vantage points, and allowed the reconnaissance groups to cover one another.

(8.10.2) Viet Cong attack doctrine

Viet Cong attacks were invariably characterised by adherence to the principle of 'one slow, four quick'—a doctrine which prevailed in both attack and defence. In offensive operations the 'quick attack' was further broken down to incorporate 'three strongs'—strong fight, strong assault and strong pursuit. Presented in sequence the doctrine can be summarised as follows:

Slow plan: This involved a steady but low-key logistical build-up in forward supply areas, being positioned ahead of the fighting forces to make a solid base for the operation. The degree of planning and preparation necessary to undertake a large operation could take as long as 6 months and often included numerous 'rehearsals'.

Quick advance: This was a rapid movement forward, generally after a circuitous approach march meant to confuse the enemy. Once all the units in the operation were on track, a quick advance was usually made in small and inconspicuous groups to a forward staging area from where the attack would be launched.

Quick attack: Here the attacking forces would be concentrated at the weakest point of the target as identified by prior reconnaissance. The duration of an attack could often be measured in minutes. Surprise was essential and large volumes of fire were poured on the target. Phase 2 of the attack involved the three strongs:

- **Strong fight:** an attempt to achieve and exploit the element of surprise
- **Strong assault:** against a pre-arranged position using concentration of force, effort and mass to overwhelm the defence.
- **Strong pursuit:** the attacking force's reserves would be committed to exploit the breaches in the targets defences so as to deliver a decisive blow.

Quick Clearance: The attacking force would rapidly reorganise and police the battlefield so as to remove weapons and casualties and was pre-planned to prevent confusion on the objective

Quick Withdrawal: Involved a quick egress from the battle area to a pre-arranged rendezvous point where the attackers would again break down into smaller groups to continue their dispersal.

(8.10.3) *Types of ambushes favoured by the Viet Cong*

Mine ambush: This depended on the use of command-detonated mines which were triggered by hidden troops who held a detonating device connected to the demolitions by electrical wire. Mine ambush kill zones might also include punji traps or other homemade traps, landmines and natural obstacles. However, the ambush was always triggered by electrically detonating a mine, when enemy troops moved within the mines killing range.

Bloody nose ambush: This was used by small units against larger enemy forces as a means of harassment, delay and disruption. By positioning the ambush to enfilade an avenue of approach, the NVA/ VC obtained more effective results. Minefields, man-traps, and booby-traps were placed along both sides of the trail and perpendicular to it. As the enemy unit came under fire and attempted to manoeuvre right or left to close with the ambushers, the protective barriers would inflict casualties. As soon as the ambushing element realised that the enemy had advanced into, and taken casualties from, the mine/trap line, the ambushers withdrew to another pre-selected site where they might repeat the manoeuvre.

Flank or linear ambush: This was one of the simplest to set up and operate and was most commonly used by the NVA. It was also easy to get into and away from quickly. The ambush position was laid parallel to the target area. Mines or other obstacles were placed on the other side of the ambush site. Upon command, fire was brought to bear on the kill zone from multiple, overlapping firing positions. The linear ambush pumped bullets into the flank of a surprised enemy column.

The 'L' ambush: L-shaped ambushes included the most effective aspects of both the 'Bloody Nose' and Linear ambush. The short end, or base, of the 'L' was positioned so that at least one machinegun could fire straight down the kill zone, enfilading it. Parallel to the kill zone and tied into the 'L' was a second, flanking ambush. The 'L' shaped ambush could also provide its own flank security. The base of the 'L' might be placed along either flank of the ambush position, not to fire into the kill zone, but to ambush enemy units that were attempting to flank the main ambush position along obvious avenues of approach. In some situations the enemy located a reserve unit in line with the vertical bar of the 'L' forming a 'T' ambush. After the ambush was sprung, the enemy manoeuvred his reserves to block the enemy line of withdrawal. The reserves either close assaulted or set up another ambush along the first linear obstacle to the immediate rear of the kill zone.

The Manoeuvre ambush: This was usually directed against a road bound column of vehicles. The NVA/VC usually sprang it from high ground, near a bend in the road, which allowed cover and longer fields of fire for automatic weapons. Weapons frequently opened fire from positions within forty yards of the road, or less. A road bend was included in the kill zone so that the end of the column was out of sight of the head of the column when the ambush was sprung. Interruption of a column's front-to-rear line of sight increased the likelihood that the head and tail of the column would split and try to fight separately. The ambush was initiated by a small element striking the head of an enemy column and stopping it by fire. Then the main body would attack the column from the rear and/or flank, fragmenting it and rolling it up. The two strikes were timed close enough together so that the target column was engaged from both ends before it could deploy and face toward either danger.

The 'V' ambush: Positioned with its open mouth toward the enemy advance, this was a favourite of the VC. It was used in both fairly open terrain as well as jungle. The ambushers, in good concealment along the legs of the 'V', would wait until the enemy point had passed and then creep close to the trail. The 'V' ambush was virtually undetectable by enemy point or flank security until at least a portion of the enemy force was in the kill zone. Enfilading fire was often directed down the enemy axis of advance, and inter-locking fire from each leg across the 'V'. The 'V' ambush also lent itself to the use of controlled mines and booby-traps.

The 'Z' ambush: Usually laid along a road, the 'Z' ambush was both effective and confusing to the unit being ambushed. This complicated ambush was usually well-planned with low bunkers lining the kill zone, often prepared months prior to the ambush. The ambush position was only occupied after word was received that an enemy battalion or larger unit would be using the road, which passed through the ambush site. The long end of the 'Z' ambush was located on one side of a trail or road enabling the ambushers to employ both enfilading and flanking fire. It was also placed to neutralise attempts to flank the ambush from nearly every direction. Ambushing units deployed along the two short ends of the 'Z' could fire in either direction. The 'Z' ambush was dangerous to ambushers because ambush elements could easily fire into each other.

Jungle terrain offered ideal environments for such methods, but they were also used to cynical effect in civilian areas. Firing a few rounds and withdrawing could not only lure enemy troops into a trap based on civilian structures but could also induce US/ARVN forces to unleash hasty artillery and tactical air strikes after relatively token provocation. This created excessive destruction in the built up areas and radicalized the populace against the attacking troops.

(8.10.4) Clever use of Booby-Traps and Mines

Booby-traps and mines caused immense psychological pressure on US and ARVN troops and also inflicted numerous casualties. By 1970 for example, some 11 per cent of fatalities and 17 per cent of injuries inflicted on US troops were caused by booby-traps and mines. Identified by a variety of markers for friendly forces, these devices slowed operations, diverted resources towards security and clearance activity, damaged equipment, and poisoned relations between soldiers and the surrounding civilian population. Booby-traps ranged from the simple to the complex. Non-explosive traps included the well-known sharpened punji stake coated in excrement for causing infections, and mounted on sapling triggers and placed in shallow, covered pits. Stakes were deployed where infantry would walk or fling themselves to avoid attack such as roadside trenches, or behind logs. One of these devices was to injure a future Chairman of the US Joint Chiefs of Staff, Colin Powell. Another type of trap was a spiked mud ball that swung down on its victim after a trip wire release, impaling him. Other impalement devices included bamboo whips and triggered sapling spikes. Bows with poisoned arrows were also used.

Explosive booby-traps were also employed, some command detonated by hidden observers. They ranged from single bullets, grenades, mud-encased grenades, dud bombs and shells. Anti-vehicle traps ranged from mines to buried artillery rounds. Helicopter traps were often deployed in trees surrounding a potential landing zone, trigged by an observer, or the rotor's wash. Mines caused even more damage than booby-traps. According to one US Army history: "The enemy employed "nuisance mining", that is, scattering mines throughout an area rather than in well-defined minefields, on a scale never before encountered by US forces. Mines and booby-traps were usually installed at night by trained personnel who had detailed knowledge of the terrain. Through ingenious techniques in mine warfare, the Viet Cong successfully substituted mines and booby-traps for artillery. Instead of conventional minefields covered by fire, the enemy hindered or prevented the use of supply roads and inhibited off-the-road operations by planting explosive devices in indiscriminate patterns. While he benefited directly by causing combat casualties, vehicle losses, and delays in tactical operations, equally important was the psychological effect. Just the knowledge that a mine or booby-trap could be placed anywhere slowed combat operations and forced allied troops to clear almost the entire Vietnam road net every day".

(8.11) Using the Claymore mine to great effect in ambushes

There is no such thing as a small firefight.

(8.11.1) Claymore, the Force Multiplier

There is nothing like a Claymore in setting up an ambush. The device is based on the Misznay-Schradin effect—when a thin and broad sheet of explosive detonates, the explosive force is mainly directed perpendicular to the face of the sheet and not in 360 degrees as it happens with any other explosive. Weighing just 3.5 lbs and measuring 8.5"x3.25"x1.375", it spews seven hundred 1/8 inch steel balls in an arc of 60 degrees—this is better than anything your rifles and machineguns can ever muster.

Patrick Camunes reminisces about the Tay Ninh ambush in Vietnam in 1967—a very typical one of the thousands of ambushes they laid in Vietnam:

"As darkness falls, we move to our ambush coordinates in the semi-darkness which is still, except for the buzz of zillions of mosquitoes for which we have no defence. We know that the enemy can pick up the smell of our repellents, as we can pick up the smell of their fermented fish sauce they love so much. So tonight we feed the mosquitoes, and the enemy plans to eat their rice dry... We travel extremely light for

Emplacing the Claymore mine

tonight's deadly mission and have chosen not to use the head-nets for protection against the mosquitoes because they obstruct our vision — a necessity tonight. We carry only the minimum of water and no food, since there will be no time for eating and we cannot afford to compromise the silence.

The ambush has been prepped and is set up in a text book "L" shape fashion. Claymores and trip flares have been set out, checked, and double checked. The "clackers" for the Claymores are within easy reach as are the double stacked clips of M16 rounds taped together. Grenades are also laid out with half of the safety pin straightened out to make it easier to pull, but not so easy to pull accidentally...A silence mode is instilled, and only the occasional low keyed hiss and coded clicks can be barely heard on the radio. There is no need to appoint times for watch; we will all be up tonight.

The one starlight scope our squad is allowed brings a greenish-tint to figures of armed men, barely visible in the darkness, move in front of us! Suddenly my squad is instantly alert and wide awake. We must confirm that there are no friendlies in the area before we blow this ambush..."Confirmation—no friendlies!—blow it! The ambush is set-off by detonating three Claymores wired in series, as instantly 18 more Claymores are blowing and tearing into everything in front of them. The M60 is spreading deadly fire as are M16s on auto and M79s blooping their deadly grenades, and the darkness suddenly becomes alive with our deadly tracer rounds and explosives. 'Cease fire! Cease fire! Cease fire!'...Silence mode is now over, our eardrums are ringing, and our eyes are burning from the smoke as we prepare a hasty exit that we have prepared ahead of time. We have just blown an ambush on a patrol that could be the lead element for a regiment, and no one is in the mood to sit around to confirm it".

The Claymore is so useful that even the naxal insurgents in India try to make local versions of it. The tragedy is that the Indian armed forces do not have it. If the security forces of a nation do not have it, it only speaks volumes about how utterly dumb the nation is—you can see for yourself where your nation stands.

Attempt made by the naxal insurgents in India to make a Claymore mine using a bent steel plate for backing and commercial gelatin sticks for explosive

(8.11.2) *Employing a Claymore mine: Step-by-step Instructions*

The Claymore mine is emplaced in such a manner that:

a. The front of the mine centers on the kill zone.

b. The firing device is at least 16 yards to the rear or side of the emplaced mine and it is fired from a properly covered position or dug up position. Remember, the Misznay-Schardin effect means that the explosive force is 'mainly' directed perpendicular to the sheet—up to 20 per cent of the steel balls would still be ejected backwards towards you!

c. The mine, firing wire, and firing device are camouflaged.

d. The installation is confirmed by conducting a final circuit test.

When the target is in the kill zone, fire the mine by actuating the firing device handle with a firm, quick squeeze.

The firing device is a 'clacker; which produces the required current with a squeeze of the device. During testing and installation, keep the firing device with you to keep anyone else from firing it accidentally. Conduct a circuit test at the firing point. The mine comes with a test set. The flashing light would indicate that the firing device and test set are functioning correctly. Next you test the firing wire and the blasting cap. When doing so, place the blasting cap under a sandbag, behind a tree, or in a hole in the ground to protect the person performing the circuit check should the blasting cap detonate. Now the mine is ready to be installed. Place the firing device on 'safe'; remove the firing device and the test set. Place the shorting plug cover on the firing wire. Tie the shorting plug end of the firing wire to a fixed object such as a stake or tree at the firing position.

Unroll the firing wire to the selected installation position. Lay the firing wire from the firing position to the mine installation site, because the blasting cap end is on the inside of the firing wire spool. Open both pairs of legs to a 45-degree angle with two legs facing to the front and two legs facing to the rear of the mine. Push the legs about one-third of the way into the ground, with the mine facing in the desired direction of fire. In windy areas, or when the legs cannot be pressed into the ground, spread the legs as far as they will go (about 180 degrees) so that the legs are to the front and rear of the mine and the mine will not tip over.

Select an aiming point at ground level about 50 yards (150 feet) in front of the mine. Position one eye about six inches to the rear of the sight. On a slit-type peep sight, align the groove of the sight in line with the aiming point that is about 8 feet off the ground. The aiming point should be in the center of the desired area of coverage, with the bottom edge of the peep sight parallel to the ground that is to be covered with the fragment spray. Secure the firing wire about one yard to the rear of the mine, so the mine will remain aligned even if the firing wire is disturbed. Screw the shipping plug priming adapter, with the blasting cap, into the detonator well. Ensure that the face of the mine marked 'front toward enemy' and the arrows on the mine point in the direction of the enemy. Recheck the aim of the mine. Camouflage the mine. Use the test set again to test the circuit. This is to see if any breaks in the wire have occurred. When retesting the circuit on a claymore mine with the blasting cap inserted in the detonation well, remain behind cover or in a fighting position. Any friendly troops within 250 yards to the front and sides or 100 yards to the rear of the mine must be under cover.

Note: The testing of the circuits can be done with a simple galvanometer also if you do not have the circuit tester. This is best done with one man at each end of the firing wire. To check for a short, separate the two strands (the bare ends) of the firing wire at the firing position. Have the other soldier do the same thing with the other end of the wire at the charge position. At the firing position, touch the bare ends of the two strands to the galvanometer/ circuit tester posts. The needle on the galvanometers should not move, nor should the light on the circuit tester come on. If the needle does not move or if the light does not come on, the wire has a break—replace it. If the wire has no short when tested, test it for a break. Have the soldier at the charge position twist the bare ends of the strands together. Then touch the two strands at the firing position to the galvanometers/ circuit tester posts. That should cause a wide deflection of the galvanometer needle or cause the circuit tester light to come on. If the galvanometers needle does not move or if the light does not come on, the wire has a break—replace it. Similarly, at the firing position, check the blasting cap with a galvanometers or circuit tester to make sure it does not have a short. Remove the short circuit shunt and touch one cap lead wire using the galvanometers, the needle should make a wide deflection. If it does, the cap is good. If the needle fails to move or only makes a slight deflection, replace the cap.

(8.11.3) To emplace a Claymore with a Tripwire

Never interrupt your enemy when he is making a mistake.

Tripwires and booby-traps are things of both beauty and brains. Readers may refer to my treatise *The Ultimate Book of Explosives, Bombs and IEDs* for a detailed exposition of booby-traps of all kinds. In the field one of the most expedient methods of making a tripwire is to use a clothespin. All that you have to do here is to keep the jaws of the clothespin open with an insulator. It should neither offer any great

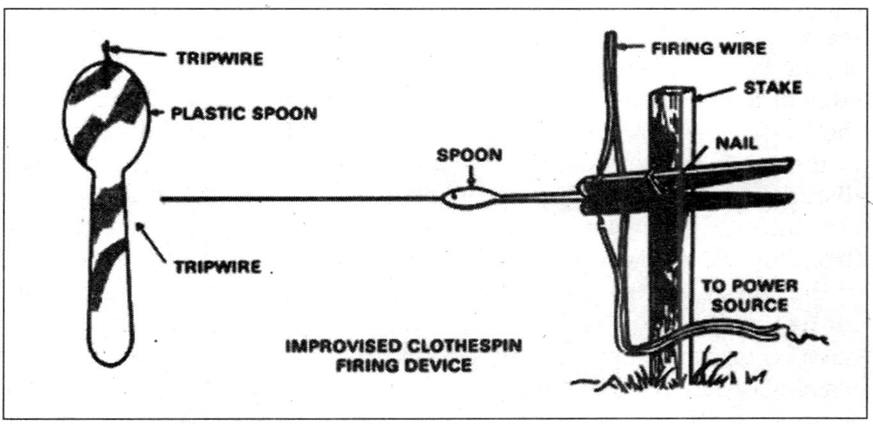

Tripwire connection to plastic spoon and plastic clothespin

resistance to the jaws of the clothespin nor should it be very smooth. The handle of a plastic spoon will do excellently. The clothespin needs to be tied or nailed to a stake. The tripwire will be attached to the spoon. The other end of the tripwire is tied to another stake.

The moment the trip wire is pulled, the spoon will come out and the jaws will close. The closing jaws are used to complete the firing electrical circuit. The tripwire should be about ankle-high and not too tight—too much tension in it will make it unreliable as the tension may pull the spoon out of the jaws of the clothespin before you are ready. Keep in mind that the tripwire is well within the kill zone of the blast of the mine so that one who trips it is caught clearly in the fragments.

Obviously, you would not be using the clacker firing device here. You would require a BA 206 or BA 4386 battery or any other power source that produces at least two volts of electricity.

9

Caught on the Wrong Foot: How to get out alive from Ambushes

Never draw fire; it irritates everyone around you.

(9.1) Death in the La Drang Valley

If you find yourself in a fair fight, you didn't plan your mission properly.

Before I discuss the science of counter-ambushes, you must fully appreciate the extreme gravity of the subject. Ambushes are terrible things; perhaps even butchery is a word too mild for it. Remember, an ambush is the most difficult, most terrible situation which an infantryman can ever face in all forms of combat. The following is a world famous first-hand and most graphic account of an ambush in Vietnam, described by Jack P Smith, one of the few who luckily survived it. The units were the 1st and 2nd battalions, 7th Cavalry Regiment of the US army and the engagement took place in November 1965. Famous as the Battle of La Drang, the battle derives its name from the Drang River which runs through the Valley northwest of Plei Me, in which the engagement took place. The word 'La' means 'river' in the local Montagnard language. Let me also tell you that this was the ambush on which the famous Hollywood movie 'We Were Soldiers' starring Mel Gibson in the lead role is based.

It will make you understand as to what could happen in well-planned ambushes. And do not forget that this could happen to the best-equipped and the best-trained soldiers in the world. Those nincompoops at the helm of affairs in your God forsaken country who start crying themselves hoarse over some incident in which you suffer casualties, I can bet, have not even heard of the La Drang Valley. I had read it as an eight-year-old in 1967, when it was published in the *Saturday Evening Post* and it has been imprinted indelibly on my mind since then. That's the difference between those who know and those who do not know. Next time someone tries to find fault with you for taking casualties in some ambush, make him read this.

"We were being withdrawn to Landing Zone Albany, some six miles away, where we were to be picked up by helicopter. About noon the column stopped and everybody flopped on the ground. It turned out that our reconnaissance platoon had come upon four sleeping PAVN who had claimed they were deserters. They said that there were three or four snipers in the trees up ahead—friends of theirs who did not want to surrender...

I flipped my cigarette butt, lay down and grabbed my M-16. The fire in front was still growing. Then a few shots were fired right behind me. They seemed to come from the trees. There was firing all over the place now, and I was getting scared. A bullet hit the dirt a foot to my side, and some started whistling over my head. This wasn't the three or four snipers we had been warned about. There were over 100 North Vietnamese snipers tied in the trees above us - so we learned later - way above us, in the top branches. The firing kept increasing. Our executive officer (XO) jumped up and said, "Follow me, and let's get the hell out of here". I followed him, along with the rest of the headquarters section and the 1st Platoon. We crouched and ran to the right toward what we thought was the landing zone. But it was only a small clearing—the LZ was to our left. We were running deeper into the bush.

The fire was still increasing. We were all crouched as low as possible, but still keeping up a steady trot, looking from to side. I glanced back at Richards, one of the company's radio operators. Just as I looked back, he moaned softly and fell to the ground. I knelt down and looked at him, and he shuddered and started to gurgle deep in his stomach. His eyes and tongue popped out, and he died. He had a hole straight through his heart...

I had been screaming for a medic. I stopped. I looked up. Everyone had stopped. All of a sudden all the snipers opened up with automatic weapons. There were PAVN with machineguns hidden behind every anthill. The noise was deafening. Then the men started dropping. It was unbelievable. I knelt there staring as at least 20 men dropped within a few seconds. I still had not recovered from the shock of seeing Richards killed, but the jolt of seeing men die so quickly brought me back to life. I hit the dirt fast. The XO was to my left, and Wallace was to my right, with Burroughs to his right. We were touching each other lying there in the tall elephant grass. Men all around me were screaming. The fire was now a continuous roar. We were even being fired at by our own guys. No one knew where the fire was coming from, and so the men were shooting everywhere. Some were in shock and were blazing away at everything they saw or imagined they saw.

The XO let out a low moan, and his head sank. I felt a flash of panic. I had been assuming that he would get us out of this. Enlisted men may scoff at officers back in the billets but when the fighting begins, the men automatically become dependent upon them. Now I felt terribly alone. The XO had been hit in the small of the back. I ripped off his shirt and there it was: a groove to the right of his spine. The bullet was still in there. He was in a great deal of pain, so a rifleman named Wilson and I removed his gear as best we could, and I bandaged his wound. It was not bleeding much on the outside, but he was very close to passing out.

Just then Wallace let out a "Huh!" A bullet had creased his upper arm and entered his side. He was bleeding in spurts. I ripped away his shirt with my knife and did him up. Then the XO screamed: A bullet had gone through his boot, taking all his toes with it. He was in agony and crying. Wallace was swearing and in shock. I was crying and holding on to the XO's hand to keep from going crazy. The grass in front of Wallace's head began to fall as if a lawnmower were passing. It was a machinegun, and I could see the vague outline of the Cong's head behind the foot or so of elephant grass. The noise of firing from all directions was so great that I couldn't even hear a machinegun being fired three feet in front of me and one foot above my head.

As if in a dream I picked up my rifle put it on automatic, pushed the barrel into the Cong's face and pulled the trigger. I saw his face disappear. I guess I blew his head off, but I never saw his body and did not look for it. Wallace screamed. I had fired the burst pretty close to his ear, but I didn't hit him. Bullets by the thousands were coming from the trees, from the LZ, from the very ground, it seemed. There was a huge thump nearby. Burroughs rolled over and started a scream, though it sounded more like a growl. He had been lying on his side when a grenade went off about three or four feet from him. He looked as though someone had poured red paint over him from head to toe.

The amazing thing about all this was that from the time Richards was killed to the time Burroughs was hit, only a minute or two had elapsed. Hundreds of men had been hit all around us, and the sound of men screaming was almost as loud as the firing...The XO was going fast. He told me his wife's name was Carol. He told me that if he didn't make it, I was to write her and tell her that he loved her. Then he somehow managed to crawl away, saying that he was going to organise the troops. It was his positive decision to do something, which reinforced my own will to go on.

A scene of the carnage at the La Drang Valley

Then our artillery and air strikes started to come in. They saved our lives. Just before they started, I could hear North Vietnamese voices on our right. The PAVN battalion was moving in on us, into the woods. The Skyraiders were dropping napalm bombs a hundred feet in front of me on a PAVN machinegun complex. I felt the hot blast and saw the elephant grass curling ahead of me. The victims were screaming—some of them were our own men who were trapped outside the wood line. At an altitude of 200 feet it's difficult to distinguish one soldier from another. It's unfortunate and horrible, but most of the battalion's casualties in the first hour or so were from our own men, firing at everything in sight.

No matter what you did, you got hit. The snipers in the trees just waited for someone to move, and then shot him. I could hear the North Vietnamese entering the woods from our right. They were creeping along, babbling and arguing among themselves, calling to each other when they found a live GI. Then they shot him…This was a massacre, and I was one of a handful not yet wounded. All around me, those who were not already dead were dying or severely wounded, most of them hit several times. I must have been talking a lot, but I have no idea what I was saying. I think it was, "Oh God, Oh God, Oh God", over and over. Then I would cry. To get closer to the ground, I had dumped my gear, including the axe I had been carrying, and I had lost my rifle, but that was no problem. There were weapons of every kind lying everywhere.

All of a sudden a dozen loud "crumph" sounds went off all around me. Assuming that all the GI's in front of them were dead, our mortar platoon had opened up with M-79 grenade launchers. A piece got me in the head. It felt as if a white-hot sledge hammer had hit the right side of my face. Then something hot and stinging hit my left leg. I lost consciousness for a few seconds. I came out of it feeling intense pain in my leg and numbness in my head. I didn't dare feel my face: I thought the whole side of it had gone. Blood was pouring down my forehead and filling the hollow of my eyeglasses. It was also pouring out of my mouth. I slapped a bandage on the side of my face and tied it around my head...I decided it was time to get out. None of my buddies appeared able to move. I crawled over many bodies, all still. The 1st Platoon just didn't exist anymore. One guy had his arm blown off. There was only some shredded skin and a piece of bone sticking out of his sleeve. The sight didn't bother me anymore.

The Cong figured out that the mortar platoon was right by that tree, and three of their machinegun crews crawled up and started to blaze away. It had taken them only a minute or so to find exactly where the platoon was; it took them half a minute to wipe it out. When they opened up, I heard a guy close by scream, then another, and another. Every few seconds someone would scream. Some got hit several times. In 30 seconds the platoon was virtually non-existent.

It also seemed that most of them were hit in the belly. I don't know why, but when a man is hit in the belly, he screams an unearthly scream. Something you cannot imagine; you actually have to hear it. When a man is hit in the chest or the belly, he keeps on screaming, sometimes until he dies. I just lay there, numb, listening to the bullets whining over me and the 15 or 20 men close to me screaming and screaming and screaming. They didn't ever stop for breath. They kept on until they were hoarse, then they would bleed through their mouths and pass out. They would wake up and start screaming again. Then they would die.

I started crying. Sgt. Gale was lying near me. He had been hit badly in the stomach and was in great pain. He would lie very still for a while and then scream. He would scream for a doctor, then he would scream for a medic. He pleaded with anyone he saw to help him, for the love of God, to stop his pain or kill him. He would thrash around and scream some more, and then lie still for a while. He was bleeding a lot. Everyone was. No matter where you put your hand, the ground was sticky. Sgt.

Gale lay there for over six hours before he died. No one had any medical supplies, no one could move, and no one would shoot him.

Several guys shot themselves that day. Schiff, although he was not wounded, completely lost his head and killed himself with his own grenade. Two other men, both wounded, shot themselves with .45s rather than let themselves be captured alive by the gooks. No one will ever know how many chose that way out, since all the dead had been hit over and over again…All afternoon we could hear the PAVN, a whole battalion, running through the grass and trees. Hundreds of GIs were scattered on the ground like salt. Sprinkled among them like pepper were the wounded and dead Cong. The GIs who were wounded badly were screaming for medics. The Cong soon found them and killed them.

All afternoon there was smoke, artillery, screaming, moaning, fear, bullets, blood, and little yellow men running around screeching with glee when they found one of us alive, or screaming and moaning with fear when they ran into a grenade or a bullet. I suppose that all massacres in wars are a bloody mess, but this one seemed bloodier to me because I was caught in it.

About dusk a few helicopters tried landing in the LZ, about 40 yards over to the left, but whenever one came within 100 feet of the ground, so many machineguns would open up on him that it sounded like a training company at a machinegun range.

Bruce P Crandall's UH-1 Huey helicopter bravely does its job even as it comes under intense fire

At dusk the North Vietnamese started to mortar us. Some of the mortars they used were ours that they had captured. Suddenly, the ground behind me lifted up, and there was a tremendous noise. I knew something big had gone off right behind me. At the same time, I felt something white-hot go into my right thigh. I started screaming and screaming. The pain was terrible. Then I said, "My legs. God, my legs", over and over...Still screaming, I ripped the bandage off my face and tied it around my thigh. It didn't fit, so I held it as tight as I could with my fingers. I could feel the blood pouring out of the hole. I cried and moaned. It was hurting unbelievably. The realisation came to me now, for the first time, that I was not going to live.

With hardly any light left, the Cong decided to infiltrate the woods thoroughly. They were running everywhere. There were no groupings of Americans left in the woods, just a GI here and there. The planes had left, but the artillery kept up the barrage...Then the flares started up. As long as there was some light, the Cong wouldn't try an all-out attack. I was lying there in a stupor, thirsty. God, I was thirsty. I had been all afternoon with no water, sweating like hell. By now the small-arms fire had stopped almost entirely. The woods were left to the dead, the wounded, and the artillery barrage.

At nightfall I had crawled across to where Barker, Caine and a few others were lying. I didn't say a word. I just lay there on my back, listening to the swishing of grass, the sporadic fire and the constant artillery, which was coming pretty close. For over six hours now shells had been landing within a hundred yards of me. I didn't move, because I couldn't. Reaching around, I found a canteen of water. The guy who had taken the last drink from it must have been hit in the face, because the water was about one third blood. I didn't mind. I passed it around.

About an hour after dark there was a heavy concentration of small-arms fire all around us. It lasted about five minutes. It was repeated at intervals all night long. Battalion HQ was firing a protective fire, and we were right in the path of the bullets. Some of our men were getting hit by the rounds ricocheting through the woods...About midnight I heard the grass swishing. A few seconds later a patrol of GIs came into view, about 15 guys in line, looking for wounded. They had four stretchers with them, and they took the four worst wounded and all the walking wounded, about 10 or so, from the company. I was desperate, and I told the leader I could walk, but when Peters helped me to my feet, I passed out cold. When I regained consciousness, they had gone. I crawled up to the tree. There were about eight guys there, all badly wounded. Lt Sheldon was there, and he had the only operational radio left in the company. I couldn't hear him, but he was talking to the company commander, who had gotten separated from us. Lt Sheldon had been wounded in the thighbone, the kneecap and the ankle.

Sometime after midnight, in my half-conscious stupor, I heard a lot of rustling on both sides of the tree. The Cong were setting up a machinegun right next to us. I heard the lieutenant on the radio; he was requesting a salvo to bracket us. A few seconds later there was a loud whistling in the air and shells were landing all around us, again and again. I heard the Cong run away. They left some of their wounded a couple of yards from us, moaning and screaming, but they died within a few minutes...Every half hour or so, the artillery would start all over again. It was a long night. Every time, the shells came so close to our position that we could hear the shrapnel striking the tree a foot or so above our heads, and could hear other pieces humming by just inches over us...All night long the Cong had been moving around killing the wounded. Every few minutes I heard some guy start screaming, "No, no, no, please", and then a burst of bullets. When they found a guy who was wounded, they'd make an awful racket. They'd yell for their buddies and babble awhile, then turn the poor devil over and listen to him while they stuck a barrel in his face and squeezed.

About an hour before dawn the artillery stopped, except for an occasional shell. But the small-arms firing started up again, just as heavy as it had been the previous afternoon. The GI's about a mile

A classic picture of grim resolve: a M 60 Machine gunner fires stoically at La Drang – note the improvised firing support made of a fallen tree trunk

away were advancing and clearing the ground and trees of Cong (and a few Americans too). The snipers, all around the trees and in them, started firing back...When the light grew stronger, I could see all around me. The scene might have been the devil's butcher shop.

There were dead men all around the tree. I found that the dead body I had been resting my head on was that of Burgess, one of my buddies. I could hardly recognise him. He was a professional saxophone player with only two weeks left in the Army. Right in front of me was Sgt Delaney with both his legs blown off. I had been staring at him all night without knowing who he was. His eyes were open and covered with dirt. Sgt Gale was dead too. Most of the dead were unrecognisable and were beginning to stink. There was blood and mess all over the place. Half a dozen of the wounded were alive. Lord, who was full of shrapnel; Lt Sheldon, with several bullet wounds; Morris, shot in the legs and arm; Sloan, with his fingers shot off; Olson, with his leg shot up and hands mutilated; and some guy from another company who was holding his guts from falling out.

We were all sprawled out in various stages of unconsciousness. My wounds had started bleeding again, and the heat was getting bad. The ants were getting to my legs...Lt Sheldon passed out, so I took over the radio. That whole morning is rather blurred in my memory. I remember talking for a long time with someone from Battalion HQ. He kept telling me to keep calm, that they would have the medics and helicopters in there in no time. I just couldn't understand at first why the Med Evacs didn't come in and get us. Finally, I heard on the radio that they wouldn't land because no one knew whether or not the area was secure. Then a small Air Force spotter plane was buzzing overhead. It dropped a couple of flares in the LZ nearby, marking the spot for an airstrip. There was silence for awhile, and then they started hitting the LZ with artillery, a lot of it. This lasted for a half hour or so, and then the small arms started again, whistling and buzzing through the woods.

Finally, the firing stopped, and there was a ghastly silence. Then the old man got on the radio again and talked to me. He called in a helicopter and told me to guide it over our area. I talked to the pilot, directing him, until he said he could see me. Some of the wounded saw the chopper and started yelling, 'Medic, Medic'. Others were moaning feebly and struggling to wave at the chopper. Soon after that I heard the guys coming. They were shooting as they walked along. Then I saw them: The 1st sergeant, our captain and the two radio operators. The captain came up to me and asked me how I was. I said to him: "Sorry, Sir, I lost my - axe". He said, "Don't worry, Smitty we'll get you another one".

I was put in a Med Evac chopper and flown to Pleiku, where they changed dressings and stuck all sorts of tubes in my arms. I learned that Stern and Deschamps, close friends, had been found dead together, shot in the backs of their heads, executed by the Cong Gruber had identified their bodies. Everyone was crying. Like most of the men in our battalion, I had lost all my Army friends.

I heard the casualty figures a few days later. The North Vietnamese unit had been wiped out—over 500 dead. Out of some 500 men in our battalion alone, about 150 had been killed, and only 84 returned to base camp a few days later. In my company, which was right in the middle of the ambush, we had 93-per cent casualties - one half dead one half wounded. Almost all the wounded were crippled for life. The company, in fact, was very nearly annihilated.

Our unit was part of the 7th Cavalry, Custer's old unit. That day in the La Drang Valley history repeated itself. (Gen Custer, as you know, was killed with his unit in the Battle of Little Big Horn, a famous battle in the history of the USA).

After a week in and out of field hospitals, I ended up at Camp Zama in Japan. They have operated on me twice. They tell me that I'll walk again, and that my legs are going to be fine. But no one can tell me when I will stop having nightmares".

(9.2) The Scientific Principles of Countering Ambushes

We're moving into the valley of the shadow of death, where you will watch the back of the man next to you, as he will watch yours, and you won't care what colour he is or by what name he calls God. Let us understand the situation. We're going into battle against a tough and determined enemy. I can't promise you that I will bring you all home alive, but this I swear, before you and before almighty God: that when we go into battle, I will be the first to set foot on the field, and I will be the last to step off. And I will leave no one behind. Dead or alive, we will all come home together. So help me God.

(9.2.1) Understanding the Problem

By definition, an ambush contains the element of total surprise; which means the victims of the ambush have no knowledge of how it has been planned, or of what measures may have been employed to prevent escape. Therefore—and this has been proven by the experience of war—the only likely method of survival is withdrawal from the killing zone "the way you came in". All other routes out of the killing zone may be blocked—in a very well-planned and well-executed ambush, even the "back door" would have been closed by the time the ambush is sprung. The established military doctrine in all the forces of the world is "immediate, positive, and offensive action. However, the fact is that this is very likely to have been anticipated by the ones who set the ambush, and often plays into their hands. Remember one thing; the odds are heavily, in fact very heavily, against you if you have got trapped in an ambush. Still, there is something that can be done—people have learnt from innumerous ambushes that there are certain steps that, if taken, will increase the chances of your coming out alive. Respect it; this is a lesson that has been learnt at the cost of nothing but sheer blood.

Everyone must therefore be aware of the threat of ambush and must be proficient in counter-ambush drills. The enemy will be less confident of their ability to execute an ambush if they are unable to achieve worthwhile results from such operations, or if they suffer heavy casualties because of our counter action. The enemy ambush can be beaten or at least reduced in the severity of its consequences by immediate positive offensive measures which are thoroughly understood and practised by all soldiers. Counter-measures against ambushes can be divided into: precautions taken to avoid or detect an ambush; and action on being ambushed.

(9.2.2) Ways to avoid an Ambush

The best way to survive an ambush is not to encounter them. This may be done by denying the enemy knowledge of your movements or by detecting the location of possible enemy ambush sites. For this, patrol movement mustn't be predictable in timing or route, and should avoid the most obvious routes. Rather than moving at a constant speed and direction, the patrol should vary these, with occasional stops to observe both the route ahead, and changes behind. Units should move in such a way that they are close enough together for mutual support, but far enough apart so that one burst of automatic fire wouldn't take out the entire unit. When on foot, if possible, the patrol should move in such a way as to maximise their firepower; for example, with the arrowhead and spearhead formation, they should not allow themselves to be sky-lined. Units on foot should have a point man some way ahead of the main body, and, if possible, a rearguard as well. Those travelling in vehicles follow the same procedures, with lead and trailing vehicles well ahead of, and well behind, the main body of vehicles. To avoid ambush and to reduce critical damage in an ambush:

- Routine movement must be reduced to a minimum. Routes and timings must be varied to avoid establishing a pattern.

- Except in completely secure areas, roads and tracks should never be used if they can be avoided.
- Security of impending operations and movement must be maintained until the last possible moment.
- Plan and use deception whenever possible.
- During movement, full dispersion and movement by bounds must be practised and controlled. All movement must be tactically grouped.
- Thorough reconnaissance to the front and flanks is required. Helicopters are useful for this task and for landing troops to search selected areas if necessary.
- Maps, air photographs, patrol and other reports must be studied to find likely ambush sites. These should be cleared on foot.
- Warning of enemy ambushes may, at times, be obtained from the local population or deduced from some abnormality in their behaviour.
- In order to increase confusion the enemy will aim to destroy commanders and radio operators in the opening volleys of an ambush. Commanders with their radio operators must therefore not be conspicuous and must avoid moving in a set pattern within a column. Badges of rank should not be obvious. Radio operators must be protected and unless the sets are being operated, aerials should be concealed. And remember, not looking conspicuous is not being cowardly. Yes, I am aware of Admiral Nelson insisting upon wearing his ceremonial uniform in the Battle of Trafalgar and the big bright buttons of which drew a sniper's fire that eventually killed him. But leave that to dear Admiral Nelson. I also remember his famous quote "England expects that every man shall do his duty". I too am doing my duty and avoiding getting my ass shot off is also my duty.
- During movement, maximum dispersion commensurate with control must be practised. The aim must be to ensure that the whole of the force is not simultaneously ambushed. Forces that are closed-up make themselves vulnerable to a comparatively small ambush. This is particularly applicable to the rear of a column.
- A pre-planned rendezvous must be known to all ranks and, if possible, should not change en route. This could include, for example, a set distance (500 yards) from the rear of the column and back along the direction of approach. This is probably not

suitable for forces larger than a platoon. Alternatively, it could be the location of the last long halt.

(9.2.3) Recognising Indicators of an Ambush

The Americans paid a heavy price in Vietnam. The observations and experiences of US troops in Vietnam therefore deserve serious thought. They found that there are indeed a number of ambush 'indicators' which, when encountered, gave the commander reason to tighten security and move with caution.

- Tied-down brush which may be a firing lane for an ambush
- Empty villages which may conceal ambushes
- Herds of cattle and well-tended crops in areas which are sparsely populated
- An unusual amount of activity in a specific area
- A steady delivery of small arms fire from one position which, whilst it appeared to be aimed at checking and delaying movement, was actually being used to encourage pursuit
- Sniper fire was used to draw US forces into ambush positions. The snipers would fire harassing rounds and, upon pursuit, fall back and draw the enemy into an ambush.

(9.2.4) Basic Principle of Counter-ambush

In a far ambush, at the initial burst of gunfire from a hostile ambush party, the first impulse would be for each member to seek cover and then retaliate by fire. The security elements would provide the holding fire to allow the assault elements to manoeuvre and establish their positions.

In a near ambush, if all the troops have entered the killing zone of the ambusher, then things become difficult. Quite often the only course of action is to make an immediate frontal attack to wherever you feel the fire is coming from—may be you could ride on your luck and actually see the enemy to shoot at him before you yourself go down. If in case some members escape from the killing zone, the best course is to manoeuvre and counter-attack by outflanking him. But remember that the enemy could have taken the flanking movement into account and the flanking movement itself could run into fire. If it is not so then from vantage points, the assault elements, together with the security force, could attempt to establish fire superiority over the enemy, engage him in this hunting ground, outmanoeuvre him, and neutralise him.

(9.2.5) The importance of immediate offensive action in breaking out

A well-executed ambush is hard to counteract. However, the effectiveness of an ambush can be reduced by the immediate return of fire. Enemy weapons may be silenced, thus creating weak points in the ambush position. Smoke and offensive grenades are effective in executing counter-ambush actions. Smoke will help you create a screen behind which you may locate and take cover. They create confusion, provide a screen for movement, and disrupt the ambush plan. A force laying an ambush has the advantages of selection of site, initiative and surprise. A force moving on foot must always be prepared to counter enemy ambushes. Enemy ambush tactics vary; opportunism and initiative by group commanders and individuals are always required in the counter-ambush battle. Planning should consider the possibility of the enemy using blocking parties to counter our immediate action drill or having mined or booby-trapped the escape routes. The basis of the counter-ambush battle is controlled, immediate offensive action. This involves the immediate return of fire by those caught in the kill zone and a controlled reaction by the rest of the force. It is appreciated that there can be no hard and fast rule for breaking out of an ambush. Try to guess the enemy disposition and strength.

There are, however, two essentials that are common to all counter actions. These are:

- Immediate offensive action must be taken to break out of the kill zone as rapidly as possible.
- Commanders must retain control. Alternative arrangements for command must be made in case the commander is lost in the first contact itself.

(9.3) Breaking out of an Ambush: General Principles

Happiness is a belt-fed weapon.

(9.3.1) When the Entire Force is not caught in the Kill Zone

This drill is particularly suited when only part of the force is caught in the kill zone and the enemy ambush is established in a linear formation. A different drill particularly suited to close country and to restricted enemy fields of fire is an immediate assault in one direction into the ambush. Such a drill must be planned and rehearsed prior to the action. The only orders required, if any, are 'Follow me', 'Charge' or some other simple words to achieve an immediate reaction. We presume a situation where the platoon/squad is moving. The platoon/squad gets into a prepared kill zone. The enemy initiates the ambush with a casualty-producing device, and a high volume of fire.

Near Ambush: Soldiers in the kill zone immediately return fire, take up covered positions, and throw fragmentation grenades or concussion and smoke grenades. If cover is not available, immediately, without order or signal, assume the prone position. Immediately, after the grenades detonate, soldiers in the kill zone assault through the ambush using fire and movement to eliminate the ambush or until contact is broken. Soldiers not in the kill zone locate and place suppressive fire on the enemy, take up covered positions and shift fire as the assault begins.

Far Ambush: In a far ambush, that is, beyond hand-grenade range, soldiers in the kill zone immediately return fire and take up covered positions. The leader identifies the enemy's location and soldiers place accurate suppressive fire on the enemy's position. Soldiers not in the kill zone begin fire and movement to destroy the enemy. The unit moves out of the kill zone, forces the enemy to withdraw, or destroys the ambush. Soldiers in the kill zone continue suppressive fires. Leaders continue to identify the engagement area by using hand-held laser pointers, and ground illumination flares. The team or squad leader in the kill zone identifies the flank elements and leaders of the assaulting force get within the minimum safe distance of the surface danger area. The squad leader orders his squad to shift fires as the assaulting squad fights through the enemy position.

Those who are not pinned by the opening burst of enemy fire must form up to execute an encircling attack. Survivors of the leading group(s) call out "Ambush Left (or Right)" move to fire positions and engage the enemy by a covered and concealed route to a vulnerable flank of the enemy position. The leading group should always be a tactical bound ahead of the patrol commander. This drill can be worked in reverse if the enemy allows the leading elements of a patrol to pass and takes on its rear elements. The time taken to encircle varies according to the nature of the ground and the extent of the enemy position but is rarely less than ten minutes. Commanders select the direction of movement for the assault according to the nature of the ground.

American Counter to Viet Cong 'L'-shaped Ambushes: In the 'L'-shaped ambush, the tactic gets its effects from an intensifying concentration of fire. The NVA/VC normally fought out of natural cover, and the flanking side usually ran parallel to a trail. The twin column company formation was far more properly disposed to cope with the threat than was the wedge or any other eccentric formation, particularly if it was moving with a few flankers out, a practice which should have been adopted whenever conditions permitted. The right-hand column, in the correct position, needed only to face right to engage. The left-hand column moved into line against the enemy force blocking the line of movement. The company CP was located according to the intensity of fire and the availability of cover. So confronted, the enemy lost any initial advantages in fire or manoeuvre, and his problem of collecting forces to alter the terms of the engagement was probably more complex, since he had planned to execute a set piece. NVA/VC reserves were usually placed to support the vertical bar of the 'L', with envelopment of the US force as the ultimate objective, and would be manoeuvred in an attempt to block the US line of withdrawal. Usually this took the form of setting an ambush along the first stream or trail crossing in the immediate rear. Withdrawal over the same route used in advance was therefore to be avoided. The movement away from the 'L' ambush needed to be an oblique from the open flank where the enemy had not engaged.

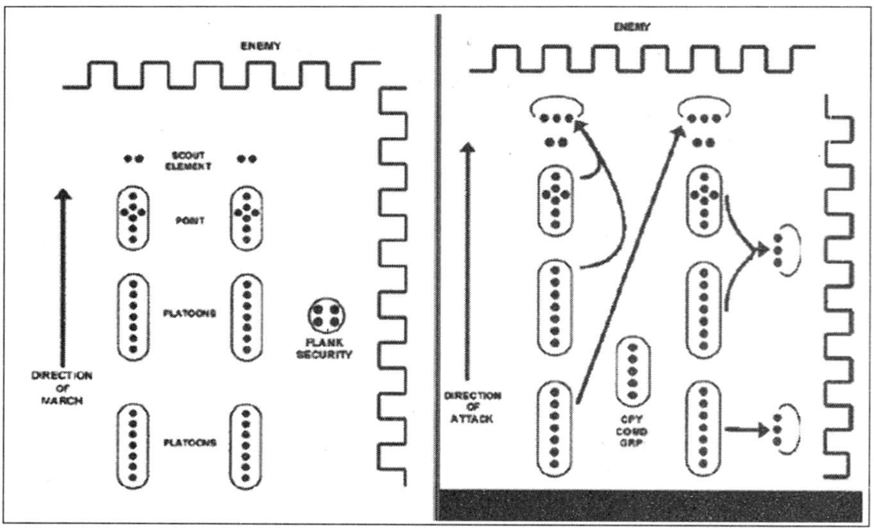

American manoeuvre against Viet Cong L-formation ambush

Whether to accept line-against-line engagement was the prime question for the US force commanders. Initially, he may not have had an option because his position may have been weakened by early losses. At any stage it was preferable to maintain loose contact with the enemy whilst backing away with the main body as promptly as possible. At the same time, the US force commander would call for maximum striking power against the enemy positions. The 'L'-shaped ambush, by reason of its configuration, was an ideal target for artillery and Tac Air operating in combination. The vertical bar was the prime target for the artillery—gun-target line permitting—because it could be worked over with maximum economy and minimum shifting of the guns. The horizontal bar was the proper target mark for Tac Air because the boundaries of the run may be more readily marked manually when a withdrawal was perpendicular to the line of advance than when the strike parallels the line of advance and withdrawal. Other forces that do not have the luxury of artillery support or Tac Air, or are in a situation would obviously find the going tough.

(9.3.2) *Action when the whole of a Force is Ambushed*

Never forget that your weapon and other equipments were purchased from the lowest bidder.

The options become obviously limited in this case. The force must take aggressive action to fight its way out of the immediate kill zone. The following courses are available (or at least, can be tried for want of an alternative—people have tried them and, God willing, they have lived to tell their tales):

- Launch an immediate assault. This is dependent upon the degree of control retained in relation to the enemy's main strength and dispositions.
- Form a hasty defensive perimeter whilst the commander decides whether to attack part of the ambush in order to break out, or whether the force should break down into small groups to filter out. In either case, the force must later reform at a preplanned rendezvous.
- On occasion, during the immediate assault to break out of the kill zone, it may be possible to seize ground on which a reasonable defensive perimeter can be established. The aim would then be to hold this perimeter, to bring in support against the enemy position or to wait the arrival of a mobile relief force. Such action often forces the withdrawal of the enemy ambush and has the advantage that it prevents our own wounded and equipment from falling into enemy hands.

(9.3.3) *Counter-ambush by Night*

As night ambushes are difficult to execute they are likely to be on a small scale only. If a force is ambushed at night, action should be taken as follows:

- They must move out of the kill zone at once. This is especially important if the area has been illuminated.
- They must fight their way from the ambush to a preplanned rendezvous (RV).
- Commanders must retain control. If lost, it must be regained as soon as possible.

(9.4) Immediate Action Drills

When the going gets tough, the tough go on automatic.

(9.4.1) The Why and How of Training in Immediate Action Drills

Why they are called drills? The reason is simple. When you are getting your asses shot off there is little time to think. Hence, knowledgeable people including me have done the job of thinking beforehand. You must practice it till this becomes second nature so that when the bullets start flying, you react without thinking—almost as a motor response. Trust me and all those who have applied mind to it; this will help you when you are in deep shit. Troops moving through close country are likely to encounter the enemy very suddenly at short ranges. To ensure that they react immediately and sensibly to an unexpected contact and to give the commander time to carry out a quick battle appreciation, immediate action drills must be laid down to allow for contact with the enemy from any direction. These drills must be:

a. **Simple:** So that they can be clearly understood by every man and carried out automatically without any further orders.

b. **Immediate:** So that the enemy is caught off balance and the initiative is regained or exploited.

c. **Aggressive:** To inflict the maximum casualties.

If there is one thing that you must remember in all forms of counter-ambush, it is to out-manoeuvre him. Throughout the course of history, this is what the infantries and cavalries have always sought to do—by some manoeuvre, get to the flank of the other guy. Most formations are likely to be strong in a frontal engagement—the flanks are generally not so strong. Hence, they sought to outflank him. You shall also seek to do the same.

Fine. But life is more complex for someone caught in an ambush—the reason is that your enemy is highly devious and he could have positioned himself in many ingenious ways. Hence you shall have to practice and remember many different forms of counters to different situations. Your success will depend on how quickly you figure out the manner in which you are being attacked so that an appropriate response may be mounted. How do you do it? True, the sound of gunfire in a jungle can be quite confusing and with scores of shots being fired, it is difficult to guess from where the shots could be coming. Hence, it is necessary to practice a great deal. You must repeatedly listen to a great many number of shots being fired in the jungle simultaneously from different directions imitating an ambush so that you get better and better at guessing the source of the gunfire. There is no alternative to actually listening to the sound of gunfire in a real jungle. It may be costly but it pays a lot to do a great deal of realistic practice.

One group must act as the attackers and must set up ambush for the other group. The sound must be real and you must use blanks with blank firing adapters so that automatic fire may be simulated—no attacker is going to fire on single shot in an ambush. If your country does not have blank firing adapter, make them get it. Plastic bullets can also be used so that those who commit mistakes on either side, get an attenuated feel of what lies in store when bullets would be real. For God's sake, stop playing with paintballs—you simply do not get enough range with them, and then there is hardly any sound worth its name. Leave that to excitable boys and girls who like to don battle fatigues and play soldiers as long as all they get is some paint blotches. Also please forget about practicing on video simulators—bullshit. Leave that to kids.

The first reaction to any ambush must be to take immediate cover—you can do it by ducking, by hitting the ground and going prone, jumping into some ditch or depression, or going behind some tree or stone. This is necessary to ensure that you do not become a casualty in the first enemy volley itself. That's fine but it would give you only temporary reprieve. You must use this time to think of your response. You are not going to remain behind that cover or on the ground forever. The reason is simple. If the enemy has planned his ambush well, though your hitting the deck or jumping into the nearest ditch may save you from incoming fire for the time being, it will not provide you proper line to return fire effectively. You are not going to remain cooped up there. And if you remain there for long, the enemy may come close and take you out with grenades. In Vietnam, they used to have a lot of gunmen hidden in the trees for precisely this sort of situation who could see soldiers lying prone on the ground or behind cover better from a height.

Training for the Unexpected: Patrol leaders must try to anticipate where contact with the enemy (ambush) is probable. Action to be taken must be planned and rehearsed before the patrol moves out. In a martial arts training environment you can do a simple exercise that will help you learn to "anticipate" contact with the "enemy". This exercise is called Walking the Gauntlet. Read about it in detail in books on Chinese martial arts. It develops alertness, mobility, and attack.

Have several participants line up, spread out evenly, on each side of the room facing inward. Place a student (the trainee) in the middle of the two lines and have him or her walk down the center through the two lines. Prior to conducting the exercise the trainee faces the wall as the instructor selects a couple of attackers on each side of the line. Each trainee that will walk through the Gauntlet will receive a different configuration of attackers. The trainee is then told to turn around and walk through the midst of the participants. The trainee, unaware of who was selected for the attack, cautiously moves through the "crowd" until a noise or aggressive movement from one of the selected attackers catches his or her attention. The trainee quickly defends against the sudden attack. After the appropriate action has been taken against the attacker (be it knife defence training, hand-to-hand, etc), the trainee returns to the place where the attack had just occurred, and picks up where they left off to walk the rest of the Gauntlet.

(9.4.2) The Australian Center-Peel

The basic idea of the Australian Center-Peel is that after the first concerted volley, the entire unit should not be engaging the enemy at the same time. Why should you? Why risk the lives of all the people? The idea is that real contact or fierce engagement should be by turns. By successively peeling out from the killing zone, you increase the chances of your survival. Naturally, you keep coming back because there is no running away from the place in the first place and secondly, because you cannot leave your comrades to face the enemy all the time. The Australian Center-Peel is as brilliant a concept as there could be one—learn it well and make it your second nature.

(9.4.3) Counter to the Classic Linear Ambush

Consider your party in five parts. Call them red, blue, green, brown and black, for example. At contact, all units fire together; after a few rounds, the red unit pulls back through the center of the team and sets up back behind the black unit—far enough away so he can continue to provide sufficient firepower. Those who peel out must try to find some cover if they can. Then the green unit pulls back, and circles around behind the brown unit tapping the blue unit on the way so as to let them know that they are pulling back. Tapping is just a figurative way of describing the phenomenon—they can inform them whichever way they can—over radio, by shouting, whatever. Then the blue unit turns 180 degrees, taps the brown unit on the shoulder, and heads back down the center of the formation. Lastly, the brown unit turns 180 degrees, taps the black unit on the shoulder, and goes down the center of the formation. The entire cycle is then repeated over until contact is broken with the enemy, or at least you find yourself in better situation. Once tapped on the shoulder, usually you fire a complete magazine down range. Call it 'mad minute' or whatever fancy term you may like. But do not waste more than one magazine on full auto or on targets which you cannot see clearly. You have limited ammunition and you must keep the rest for the situation when the bad bandit comes close.

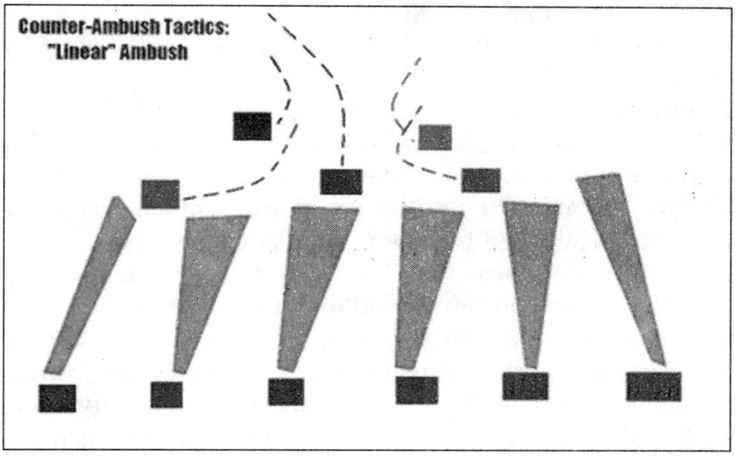

Counter to the "Linear" Ambush

(9.4.4) Counter to the famous L-formation Ambush

This was a favourite of the Viet Cong. Think about it from the enemy's point of view. Basically, he would like to have the long-leg of the "L" along the main location that you will be travelling; the short-leg of the "L" is set up directly in your front—this way, he'll catch you from two separate directions without having to worry about friendly-fire. In the 'L' shaped ambush, the tactic gets its effects from an intensifying concentration of fire. The NVA/VC normally fought out of natural cover, and the flanking side usually ran parallel to a trail.

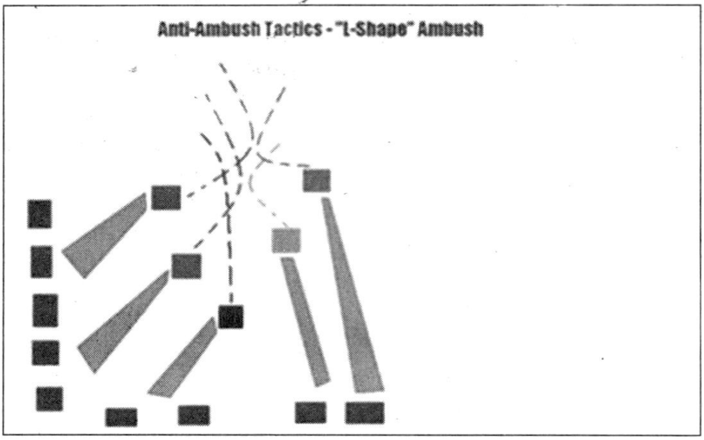

Counter to the L-formation Ambush

The American experience in this regard taught that the two-column company formation was far more properly disposed to cope with the threat than was the wedge or any other eccentric formation, particularly if it was moving with a few flankers out, a practice which should have been adopted whenever conditions permitted. The right-hand column, in the correct position, needed only to face right to engage. The left-hand column moved into line against the enemy force blocking the line of movement. The company CP was located according to the intensity of fire and the availability of cover. So confronted, the enemy could lose any initial advantages in fire or manoeuvre, and his problem of collecting forces to alter the terms of the engagement was probably more complex, since he had planned to execute a set piece.

You can understand this in terms of the Australian Center-Peel also. The basic idea of the counter to the "L" shaped ambush is to fall back. The fall-back route is, however, shifted about 45 degrees to their left; that way, you are falling back from the entire ambush team and not just part of them. The point-man fires a complete magazine once contact is made, falls-back via the center of the formation, taps the red unit, and sets up shop behind the green unit. The red unit finishes what is left of his magazine, falls back via the center, taps the grey unit on the shoulder, and sets up behind the black unit. This cycle is repeated down through the team and over and over again until your team is safe from enemy contact.

(9.4.5) *Counter to the V-formation Ambush*

From the attackers' point of view, this ambush requires a rather precise positioning of attacking fire lest they fire into each other. Falling back in the Australian Center-Peel fashion is a viable option if your line is extended and you are a platoon or more. Those in the rear do stand a very good chance of getting away and also taking cover to return fire effectively. The problem is with those who are well inside the 'V'. Things are difficult for them. They have a simple but effective option that requires some courage. If you are sure that it is a 'V' shaped ambush then you will also be assured that the 'V' shaped ambush has a problem. The apex of the 'V' is its weakest point in terms of the firepower. You must exploit this. If you try to break through the apex or the 'neck' of the 'V', they won't be able to fire there because then they would be obviously firing into each other. You are an army and you have greater firepower. Use it. Focus your firepower on the center of the ambushing force and break through using superior fire power, speed and aggression. In an earlier era, conventional military units were told to take the offence when ambushed—instead of falling back, they were taught to surge ahead. As a rule of thumb it was nonsense but it makes sense in this situation. All your team needs to do is to keep moving and always firing—in a sense, it's like a reversed Australian Center-Peel. If you are a small team, say a section or less, then obviously the chances of mustering an overwhelming firepower to break through are rather bleak. If you survive the first onslaught, then do consider falling back.

(9.4.6) Counter to "Dual-Linear" Ambush

The "Dual-Linear" is a modified broadsides ambushing technique. The enemy squad passes the first ambush team on the right; the second ambush team on the left waits until the enemy enters the team's field of fire and then opens up on them. The ambushed team will usually fall back in some sort of fashion, and that is when the other ambush team on the right comes in. While the enemy is falling back and trying to get fire on the primary ambushing team, the secondary ambush team waits until they arrive in their fire sectors—once the enemy gets in the team's fire-zone, they open up and finish them off. Again, this technique is very simple and easy to set up and is one of the most effective ways to take down a squad. The primary ambushing team—the one that initiated contact first—can also circle around and turn the "Dual-Linear" into an "L-Shape" ambush.

There's really nothing new that I'll discuss that I haven't already done before for other counter-ambushing methods; but one idea that stands out in my mind, and has worked a few times with many forces, is to take the fight to the enemy when ambushed in the "Dual-Linear" type. Unless the ambushing force has a large number of people in it, then, usually, each ambushing unit (primary and secondary) would be half the strength of a normal ambushing force—i.e., split one team into two smaller ones. If that's the case, then your team may have more members then either one of the ambushing teams, and there's a good possibility that your team can take the fight to one of the ambushing units and win; or at least get out of there alive and take out some of the bad guys at the same time. You'll just have to remember that, somewhere, there is a secondary team that can reinitiate the ambush if they get into the right position—keep that in mind.

(9.5) Flanking Movements

If everything is as clear as a bell, and everything is going exactly as planned, you're about to be surprised.

Before you understand the flanking movements, you must understand the terminology associated with various marching formations.

India is the familiar, file or column formation. This formation is used when speed and distance are of essence and immediate contact with the enemy is not expected. The squad leader would set an interval (usually 5 to 7 paces) between each member and designates his position in the squad. This allows each man to fall back into his assigned position after successful contact. **Echo** is the so-called skirmish order. It is used when contact with the enemy is in progress or expected. The squad leader sets the interval for the team and designates each man's position in the formation (P, SL, X, ASL, R). Movement is based on the squad leaders' pace. We have already seen the wedge formation. **Yankee** [Lima (left) or Romeo (right)] is a modified Echo skirmish line that moves at an angle—it is also known as echelon formation. This is often used when a squad is moving along a road, river, or other boundary. The command is "Yankee Lima" or "Yankee Romeo". The foremost man in the squad determines if the formation is a Lima or Romeo (left or right).

Standard drills have been developed for changing formations or marching orders as could be necessary so as to present a less vulnerable target or negotiate difficult or exposed terrain. Thus you have drills for changing from column to skirmish; column to wedge; column to echelon; wedge to column; wedge to skirmish; wedge to echelon; skirmish to column; skirmish to wedge; skirmish to echelon; echelon to column; echelon to wedge; and echelon to skirmish order. Learn them by heart. For illustration, the example of changing wedge to skirmishers (right) is shown in the following diagram.

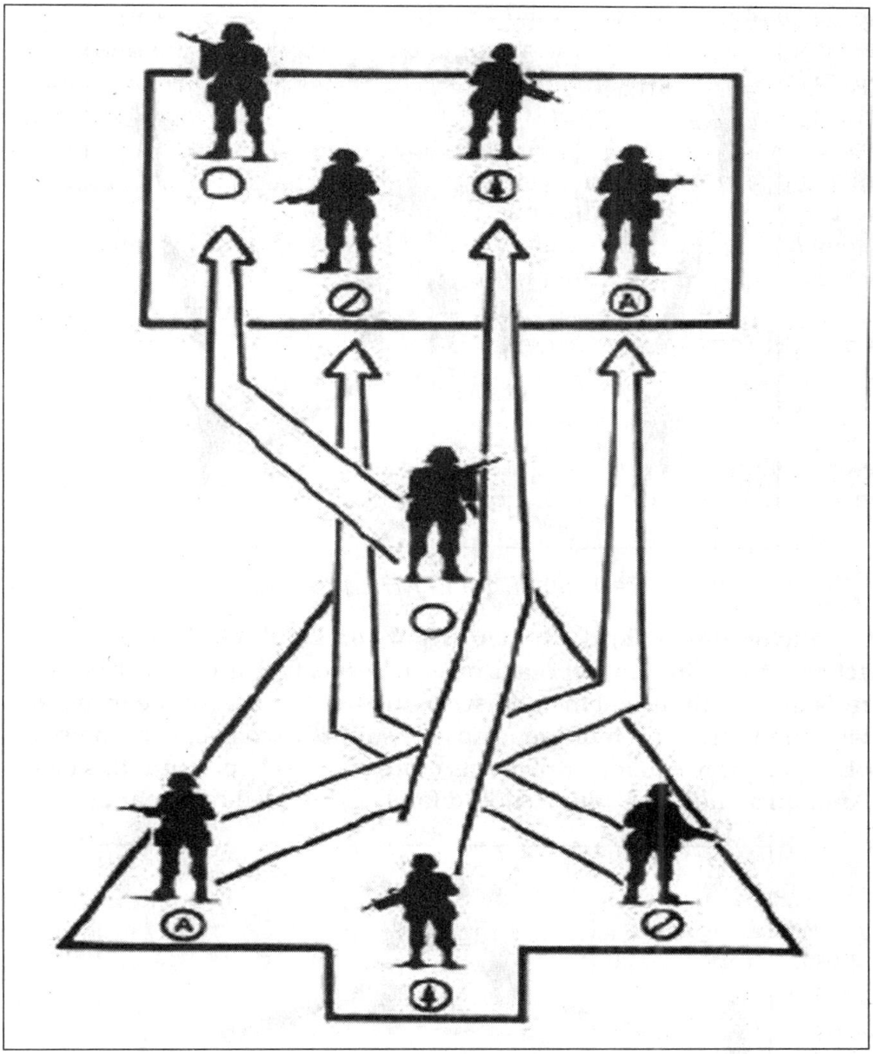

Changing from wedge to skirmishers (Right)

Variations of such basic movements are used for executing various flanking movements.

Bravo [Lima (left), Romeo (right) or Double]: Action Bravo is **a clover leaf assault** where one or more units disengages, leaves the opposition's line of sight, and comes back in on the enemy flank. This can be done on either flank or both. Units that are not in position to execute the movement should provide suppressive fire. It is imperative that the assaulting units completely leave the enemy's line of sight.

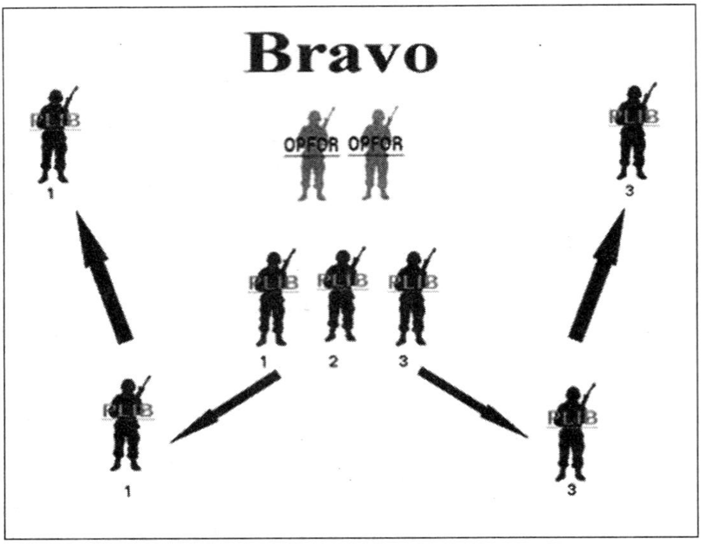

Action Bravo or Clover Leaf Assault

Victor [Lima (left), Romeo (right) or Double]: A Victor is the action of moving an Echo skirmish line meeting a forward point of resistance with the enemy and swinging the "wings" of the formation while the center man or men provide suppressive fire from the point of the V. Large squads or platoons more effectively perform this tactic. After an assault, the squad should fall back into Echo formation.

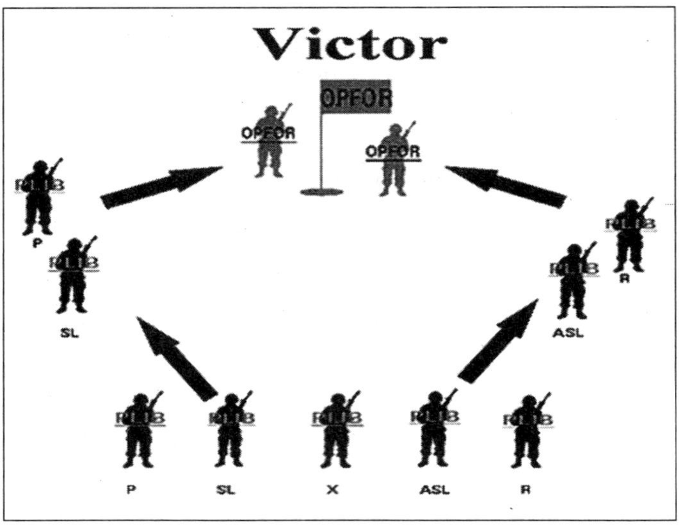

Action Victor

(9.6) Rhodesian Cover or Drake Shooting

When you have a target that has to be suppressed, neutralised or destroyed – do it right now!

(9.6.1) "Kill" the Concealment, Kill the Terrorist

The Drake shooting (also known as the Rhodesian cover shoot) was devised and used by the Selous Scouts to deal with and counter ambushes set by guerrillas in bush country where the enemy had ample concealment and was difficult to locate. In general, Rhodesian cover shooting was the deliberate "killing" of probable cover used by terrorists. No actual visual sighting of terrorists was therefore needed to "take them out", and no time was wasted attempting to identify the exact location of individual terrorists by first searching for muzzle flash or blast, a movement, a shape, and so on. Rather, careful observation of the terrorist`s position was carried out while "killing" their cover. When cover or "drake" shooting, riflemen were to shoot directly into and through the terrorists position, keeping their aim deliberately low, while machine gunners were required to aim at the ground immediately to the front of that cover.

This technique was based on the fact that in a close-quarters firefight, 99 per cent of the combatants seek to hide from incoming fire by hitting the ground and rolling into the nearest cover. Accepting this fact, the Drake/cover shoot concept requires that two rounds be fired into positions of likely cover until all positions are neutralised. Each man of the patrol would concentrate on his assigned arc of responsibility to his immediate front and systematically analyse it. While the Selous Scout analysed his arc he would think "if I was the enemy, which position within my arc would I chosen for cover?" The scout would look at the base of large trees, rocks and thickets, and "double-tap" two controlled shots into each side of the suspected location close to ground level. By placing the shots low into the position, dirt and stones will spray up into the face of anyone hiding there, causing them to take rapid evasive movements and thus exposing them to aimed fire. The trick is to try to place the bullets just above the ground, because a man lying down is no more than 12 inches high. To shoot any higher will result in the bullet winging harmlessly overhead.

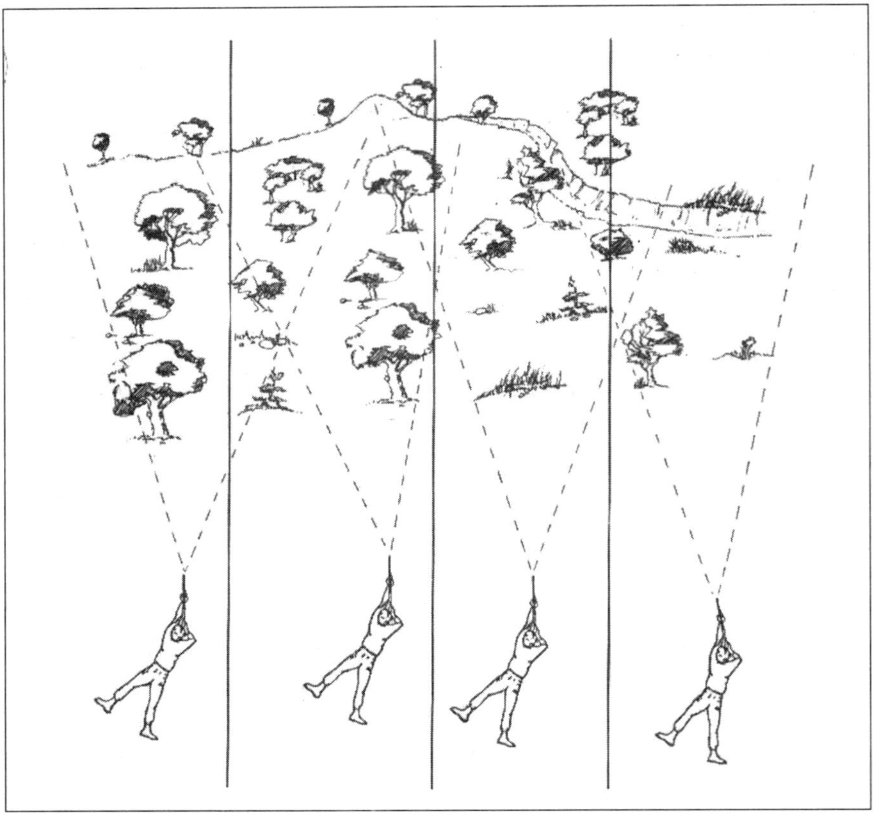

Drake or Rhodesian Cover Shooting

As the scout observed his arc he would start close up, then systematically progress further and further back, widening the arc of fire, until all likely and suspected positions have been engaged. The basic action was to draw the barrel of the rifle or machinegun across the cover area, usually beginning left to right, while squeezing the trigger at appropriate moments so as to "rake" it from one side to the other. Each round or burst was fired in a deliberately aimed fashion.

The method did not replace "fire and movement" procedures, but was rather the primary activity of them. Cover shooting has also been described as a "flushing" action, but this is not strictly accurate. While flushing terrorists from their concealment has obvious advantages, particularly when working with close helicopter support, the first objective of cover shooting was to kill the enemy without the need to see him or locate his exact position first. The method should not be confused with other practices such as walking suppression fire directed "at the jungle". Cover shooting was not a random spraying of bullets, but a deliberate and methodical routine designed to elicit maximum effect.

In its 19 years of existence, most of those fighting at the very forefront of a bush war, the Rhodesian Light Infantry never lost a battle. Well, this sounds impressive but you have also to keep into account the opposition that they had and the sort of terrain in which they operated. Opposition elsewhere may be much stronger both in terms of numerical strength and firepower. The so-called 'Fire Force' of the Rhodesians delivered a party of typically 32 men from the air, organised in 'Sticks' of four each. This maybe too small a number elsewhere in the world. As we have discussed elsewhere in the book, this worked fine because their helicopters went on accurate intelligence, fired from the air to suppress the opposition and then dropped the soldiers to interdict the insurgents running away in a particular direction. This may not be feasible at other places. In places like India, the intelligence is always hopeless and most of the counter-insurgency operations get reduced to jungle bashing. Then some governments may have reservations about firing from the air—it may be bullshit but it is their country and they have to decide. The tree cover or the terrain below may not even permit delivery of effective fire from the air—rockets may be necessary and the governments may not be willing to do that. Finally, the enemy may have solid cover that would not be defeated by rifle fire of even full-length cartridges—it is not uncommon for them to use stone boulders or big solid tree trunks as cover, or even make defensive fighting positions of logs and stones.

(9.6.2) The Mechanics of Rhodesian Cover Shooting

- While the general area of incoming fire would be known, the exact location of individual terrorists may not. It would take too long to locate their exact position.
- Other than employing the normal visual search attributes of, "Shape, Shadow, Shine, Silhouette and Movement", frequently terrorist positions could be detected simply because "something" just did not look right, even though the viewer might be hard pressed to say exactly what he saw.
- This ability is very instinctive, and develops with "bush time". RLI's troops were trained to look through the African bush and to visualise from the shapes and shadows etc as to what might be lying in it, rather than just looking at the bush and so seeing only the obvious.

- When patrolling it was usual to carry out "close to contact" drills when shortening the range to an otherwise oblivious terrorist or group, before making contact, cover shooting, and skirmishing their position. However any targets suddenly sighted within effective range were taken out immediately, usually by snap-shooting from the shoulder with a single round or double tap (usually double). Soldiers would then drop to take cover, roll or "crab" away from the drop position, cover shoot the same terrorist position again, and then cover shoot any other clumps of cover in the near area capable of hiding a terrorist. For those unfamiliar with southern Africa's bush, "other clumps" included the base of trees, rocks, bushes, ant-hills, areas of elephant grass and so on.
- When no clear indication of a terrorist's general position could be ascertained (i.e., a "one burst wonder"), the practice was to "kill" any cover within the active arc to the front of each soldier, beginning with cover nearest to that soldier before moving further out.
- In the case of a sweep line, once a member "walked into" or sighted a terrorist, he immediately shot him, while the other members of the sweep would react to the rifle shot and cover shoot into their own arcs of responsibility directly to their front. In all situations the command "watch my tracer" (or just, "tracer" or "visual"), allowed the rest of the stick to switch their attention to a problem. This did not mean that other areas of possible concealment were then ignored. The affirmative reply to "watch my tracer" was, "seen". Other verbal methods of indicating a target position would be employed if a tracer shot etc would blow the sticks own closing position or ambush.
- It was absolutely essential from the moment of "contact" to react with immediate, accurate, and overwhelming return fire (referred to as "winning the fire fight").
- To "win the fire fight", riflemen would consume the first two magazines as quickly as it remained practical to maintain accuracy, using single rounds or double taps (While trained to use the double tap, the policy was the use of single rounds—aim, squeeze and switch). As with the rifleman's use of magazines, the gunner was free to offload the first one or two belts. Each stick member was responsible for monitoring his own ammunition usage during the fire fight, and running out of ammo was an unforgivable sin!

- Smallish rocks, strange "lumps", or "bundles of rags" were to be killed. In fact anything out of place was to be dealt with—the "rocks" may be heads, hands, or a pattern on a camouflage uniform etc. The soldier then moved his aim to the next area of cover and repeated the process.
- In responding to sudden incoming fire, a sweep or patrol would immediately return fire from either the prone position or from down on one knee, depending on the nature of the surrounding bush. By dropping onto the knee, soldiers often placed themselves below the level of fire from badly trained terrorists, however remaining in position would not be maintained for long.
- The Rhodesians spent quite some time in live-fire training identifying different weapons and their position from the different sounds that they made.
- **Skirmishing:** At some appropriate point after the initial stages of the fire fight, a deliberate attacking movement called a Skirmish was carried out, ending in a run through of the terrorist position. Three basic skirmishing techniques were employed, usually by sweep lines containing a few sticks.
- The first method of skirmishing involved splitting the sweep line into two equal sections, called flanks, with one flank moving forward (say 2-5 yards as an example) while the second flank covered the first. When the first flank went prone and restarted cover shooting, the second flank would then run forward until some yards passed the line of the first, and so on.
- This method is the least likely to result in a "friendly fire" incident, but it is also the easiest to counter. All soldiers running forward did so using open-sighted snap shooting (both eyes open), from the shoulder if a rifleman, or forward of the hip if a machine gunner.
- The second skirmish option had every second member of the sweep line designated as one of the flanks, with each member of that flank passing between and through members of the other, leapfrogging forward so to speak. Obviously, the covering flankers stopped shooting as those moving forward passed them.
- The third option was called a Pepper Pot, and was usually what the second option "degenerated" into as a consequence of the difficult situation. This involved individuals of the sweep line or stick, randomly getting up and moving forward, or going prone and covering, and so on. It is more difficult to implement when in larger numbers, but is also the hardest to counter because prone

troops rise from their positions in a very random and seemingly "uncoordinated" fashion. Sticks of four always used something resembling the Pepper Pot when on the assault, or split pairs if a serious attempt at out-flanking the terrorist position was intended, and so on.

- At no time in the fire fight was any stick member to stop and attend to another wounded member. To do so increased the likelihood of the soldier lending assistance getting hit, and prevented him from continuing with the attack while tending to the wounded man. The exception was a silent machinegun in a 4-man stick, this was to be restarted as soon as possible.
- For the run through, on command the entire skirmish line would rapidly assault the terrorist position by literally running right through it, firing from the shoulder using open sights and with both eyes open. The practice was to aim over and along a line of a "sweeping" barrel and kill anything within the arc of responsibility as the soldier sprinted through the position and out the other side.
- Contrary to American wisdom, the Rhodesians did not use the two-column formation.
- Patrol formations were usually single file, extended line (sweep line), or a "Y" when with a tracker (tracker at the junction of the Y's arms, protection at the forward two arms, and a controller at the back who directed the tracking operation).
- They argued that most people were right handed. They will be "viewed" on the left hand side of trees and other solid objects if they are shooting around them.
- A wounded terrorist in the path of a sweep or patrol would often wait until the "point of inevitability" was reached, before opening fire at very close range. The same could be said for non-wounded terrorists attempting to hide from sweeps, patrols, or helicopters. These were responsible for many of Rhodesia's casualties. In areas of known incursion, helicopters on search missions have fired into very thick cover just to see if anything foolishly fired back.
- Riflemen usually carried 7-8 magazines of the FN-FAL. These would be supplemented with a few extra boxes of 20 rounds each for reloading. The machine gunner generally carried 500-800 rounds in 100 round belts (2 belts x 50 rounds linked together).
- Every third or fourth round of a magazine load was a tracer, and troops generally loaded two consecutive tracers as the final rounds to indicate the end of supply.

- The emphasis was on firepower and not survival in the jungle. Operations were not supposed to be long. The RLI, used chest webbing or "Fire Force jackets" to carry the magazines and one phosphorus grenade, one shrapnel grenade (M962), and one or two smoke grenades of different colours.
- The Phosphorus grenade was also superb for flushing out terrorists from thick or rocky cover, for breaking up enemy skirmish lines, or for taking out a cave or bunker etc.
- Two water bottles (or four depending on the time of year and so availability of water) were carried on the belt, together with essential supplies in two kidney pouches.

(9.7) Halts in Ambush Country

(9.7.1) Different Types of Halts

Because of the cover afforded an approaching enemy, troops are particularly vulnerable when halted. Halts will, however, be necessary for a variety of reasons and can broadly be divided into:

a. Pauses of a few minutes only to reconnoiter, check navigation, listen, or perhaps fill water bottles at a stream. They involve intense vigilance but no deployment.

b. Short halts for up to half an hour for more wide ranging reconnaissance, to make a plan, rest, eat, make radio contact, etc. Providing sentries are posted and everyone remains quiet and alert watching his arc, the immediate ambush drill rear should provide adequate protection for this sort of halt.

c. Long halts when a longer rest, cooking, washing, preparation of a DZ, or ambush can be accomplished.

d. Lying up positions (LUPs) which are used as resting places only. No cooking, washing, establishing of radio contact, or other potentially noisy tasks should be undertaken.

e. Harbour areas which are established to set up a patrol base, assembly area, or for any other longer term function.

Except for a pause, all halts should be preceded by the immediate ambush drill rear to foil any enemy attempt to follow up. For long halts, in lying up positions and harbour areas, it is necessary to take steps to:

a. Reconnoiter a suitable position.

b. Occupy it in all round defense.

c. Ensure that no enemy or local inhabitants are in the immediate area, and

d. Carry out the purpose of the halt.

These steps must be completed quickly and silently with the minimum of orders and all units should evolve a standard drill which should be laid down in SOPs and carried out automatically.

(9.7.2) *Reconnaissance*

After reaching the area in which he intends to halt and completing the immediate ambush drill rear, the commander should carry out a reconnaissance accompanied by his runner and an escort. If a full defensive position, DZ or ambush is to be established, subordinate commanders should form part of this reconnaissance group. When selecting the position account should be taken of those of the following points which are appropriate to the situation:

a. Concealed and easily defended.

b. Easily vacated by day or night.

c. Suitable for radio communications.

d. Covering a suitable killing area (if an ambush is intended).

e. Near water (if cooking, washing, or resupply of water is intended) but note that noisy streams will drown the sound of approaching enemy.

f. Suitable for a DZ or landing point (LP) if required, and

g. Fairly level and dry for a lying up position or harbour.

During the reconnaissance, the unit remains in formation, with each man watching his arc of responsibility. When completed, the runner and half the escort return and bring forward the unit in single file. The commander should remain in the centre of the selected position and visualise the ground as a clock face with the unit entering at 6 o'clock.

(9.7.3) *Clearing Patrols*

Clearing patrols move out to search the immediate area of the position. These consist of the section commander and one man from each group who move out through the left of their rifle group and patrolling clockwise re-enter through their MG position, which must always be manned and warned that patrol is expected. The distances patrols need to clear depend on the maximum range of the noise or smell likely to be created during the work period. If they are likely to be digging a defensive position, cutting LPs or DZ, or any other similar noisy occupation, patrols should move out 300 paces. Where the smell of cooking is the main hazard, this distance can be halved and if no noise or smell is to be made, patrols only move out about 60 paces. Occupation of lying-up position at night does not normally need clearing patrols. As an example of a case when a defensive position is to be dug:

a. Clearing patrols move out on a bearing from the centre of their positions through left hand rifleman for 300 paces.

b. Turn right 2,600 mils.

c. Patrol across 500 paces.

d. Turn right 2,600 mils, and

e. Patrol back 300 paces and enter through gun groups.

This ensures that patrols cover the whole perimeter and do not clash.

(9.7.4) Occupation

A triangular formation is suitable for defence or ambush and ensures that a gun is covering each apex. It can, with minor adoption, be adjusted to suit any size formation and any shape of the ground. The drill for a platoon occupation is as follows:

a. The platoon commander indicates the arc of responsibility and occupation positions. For three sections, the area would be divided, for the first section from 10 to 2 o'clock, the second from 6 to 10 o'clock and the third from 2 to 6 o'clock.

b. In the case of two sections, the first section would occupy from 12 to 6 o'clock and the second from 6 to 12 o'clock.

c. In each section's arc, the scout group occupies the centre with the machinegun (MG) group on its right and rifle group on the left. The scout group and rifle group are about 10 yards and the light machinegun (LMG) group is about 15 yards from the platoon commander.

d. Platoon HQ takes up a position in the centre.

e. Positions, arcs of fire and fixed lines are adjusted, these positions then become the stand-to positions which will be occupied immediately any firing takes place or the silent stand-to signal is given.

10

Convoys and Convoy Security

Even if you can't see the enemy, they still may be able to see you.

(10.1) The Weak Umbilical Cord

(10.1.1) Why Convoys are Attractive Targets?

It is highly likely that an enemy will attempt to ambush vehicle columns. One who doesn't, is certainly dumb. Beat him up before you kill him. Reason is simple. For any government fighting a counter-insurgency war, security forces have to be deployed in large numbers. Modern security forces, by their very nature, are obliged to maintain themselves from the outside. Gone are the days when armies could live off the land by fleecing the local people. This means that the security forces have to get everything ranging from rations, other provisions, ammunition, and medical supplies, to fuel from outside, that is, from zones held by them. Then there is administrative movement of personnel also—people have to come in and go out for myriad reasons. Small units can be maintained through supplies delivered by helicopters, and even personnel can be ferried in them. But large units living in hostile territory for extended periods do need supplies from the land route. All this goes in convoys of vehicles. Why? The security forces think that it is more dangerous to supply piecemeal and in any case, that would not fit into their system of logistics either to which they are used to. They also think that providing security on roads in hostile territory is rather cumbersome. Hence, the fewer times they have to do it, the better.

Convoys are therefore large, very conspicuous objects that move ponderously. A convoy is never safe from a guerrilla ambush. There is no set pattern for a likely area for an ambush. Ravines, defiles, and heavily wooded or jungle-covered areas are most favourable but ambushes are equally likely to be conducted in villages or in flat terrain that offers a minimum of cover and concealment. Shooting at convoys is easy; so is firing RPGs. In insurgencies, it is often extremely easy to mine the roads at will or plant IEDs because the territory is often hostile to the forces and, in a way, the insurgents own the roads. The locals would not dare question them. Above all, the attacker can conceal himself at a safe distance and activate the bombs and fire. Should things go according to plan, he can inflict heavy casualties and cause loss of a great deal of materiel too. If he succeeds in looting arms, ammunition and other valuable things, this damages the credibility of the regime and boosts the control the guerrillas command in the area. Should things not go according to the plan, he can quietly slip away. In fact, in this era of saturation news coverage pining for sensational tidbits, even the mere fact of having fired some rounds on a convoy becomes big news and helps the insurgents in their propaganda war. In short, ambushing vehicle convoys is easy, fun and absolutely risk-free—very tempting indeed! It is therefore essential that the troops in all vehicle columns must be trained in counter-ambush drills.

Before you understand the counter-ambush drills, however, you must first understand the fate that can befall you when your convoy is ambushed. The following story is highly illustrative.

(10.1.2) Ambush on the 8th Transportation Group, US Army

It was late in the day on September 2, 1967, as the 39 vehicles of the 8th Transportation Group departed Pleiku, in Vietnam's Central Highlands, on their return trip to Qui Nhon, on the coast of the South China Sea. At 1855 hours, the convoy was approximately 10 miles east of Mang Yang Pass and six miles west of An Khe. A 5,000-gallon fuel tanker, located near the end of the convoy, was having trouble keeping up and had effectively split the convoy into two parts. There was already a 500-meter gap between the two elements. Suddenly, the enemy sprang an ambush. A 57 mm recoilless-rifle round slammed into the lead M-151 jeep, instantly killing one man and wounding two others. At that moment 29 5-ton trucks were caught in a 700-meter-long ambush. The enemy infantry company hidden in the tree line on the south side of the road, poured rifle and machinegun fire into the trucks. In a matter of minutes, the second, third and fourth vehicles were disabled by recoilless-rifle fire or command-detonated mines. Nor did the enemy neglect the second part of the convoy. The drivers dove for cover alongside the road. They tried to return fire, but they were too disorganised and the enemy was too strong. All the battered Americans could do was call for help. In the gathering darkness A Company, 1st Battalion, 7th Cavalry, located less than a mile east of the ambush site, boarded helicopters and headed out to help their comrades. It took them 15 minutes to get to the ambush. By the time they arrived, it was all over; the enemy had melted back into the jungle. Artillery and gunships hammered the tree line, and an hour later a Douglas AC-47 "Spooky" gunship arrived on the scene to add its miniguns to the defensive effort. The enemy troops were long gone by that time. The Americans lost seven killed and 17 wounded, and 30 vehicles were damaged or destroyed. No enemy casualties were found.

(10.2) Providing External Security to Convoys

(10.2.1) A Critique of the Existing Practices

The primary purpose of all operations orders is to ensure that all blame falls on the line units.

Professionally, it is unrealistic to expect that any force will be able to completely sanitise a stretch of road scores of miles long. We must have the intellectual honesty to admit that, irrespective of whatever we do, determined and skilful terrorists can always mount attacks on the people and the vehicles using the roads. In India the morons have a strange name for this job. It is called 'ROP duty' (road opening party duty). The name is so hopelessly wrong that I consider it a sacrilege to use it myself. Nobody knows what is meant by 'opening a road' and who defined it in the first place? Is the road found closed before they open it? If it is found closed, who had closed it and how? Was the road in the possession of the terrorists? Had they taken complete control of the road before the road opening party moved in? Do the forces drive away the terrorists when they 'open' the road? Do they sanitise the road or secure it so completely that no terrorist can dare to even come near it? It is fondly believed by the Indians that the ROP would prevent any terrorist attack on the vehicles moving on the road; and detect IEDs planted on the road or roadside and remove them or destroy them. Lament their ignorance.

The fact is that they achieve none of these things. What the Indians do is to simply deploy men at regular intervals all along the length of a road without any application of scientific mind, reasoning or knowledge. In essence it is nothing but an extension of the age-old concept of route-lining with which policemen are intimately familiar. The only difference between the traditional route-lining of the police and the so-called ROP is that in the ROP, the men happen to be armed. It is a different thing that their being armed does not make any difference insofar as the purpose sought to be achieved by the ROP is concerned. They are themselves likely to be shot. The following are the intrinsic shortcomings of the existing practice insofar as the IEDs are concerned:

- On an asphalt road or road with a tarred surface, only a dumb terrorist would plant IEDs by tampering with the surface of the road and make it all too obvious. You would be wasting time if you are looking for any recent tampering with the surface of the road.
- On the other hand, there will be a thousand pot holes on the roads in God forsaken countries. If you start checking each one of them, you would not clear even a kilometer in a day!
- If the terrorists have to, they will plant the IEDs in locations like under the culverts or heaps of stones by the side, some rubbish by the side, the untarred footpath, or tunnel under the tarred surface from the sides if the road surface is raised above the sides, and so on. In any case, since they will be inconspicuous, it is difficult to detect them.
- When there would be snow or mud on the sides of the roads in winters or during the rainy season, it would be just not possible or even meaningful to look for concealed IEDs in those places.
- Properly designed IEDs cannot be detected by Deep Search Mine Detectors or explosive detectors.
- Thus to think that the menace of IEDs can be tackled by visual inspection by men, DSMDs or sniffer dogs is sheer ignorance.
- There is no farce bigger than the sniffer dog. The poor dog was never designed by Mother Nature to do things that he is made to do in the ROP. Only the ignorant Indians persist in using dogs for such an arduous task, little realising that the sniffer dog gets tired very quickly and can easily be beaten by a range of substances that decrease his olfactory capacity greatly. Such substances are not esoteric either. In any case, all an intelligent terrorist is required to do to beat a dog is to seal his explosive device hermetically in a PET (polyethylene terephthalate) jar. Unless there is a surface contamination as a result of careless handling, it would beat any explosive detector, not to speak of the poor dog! A sniffer dog could possibly be used for a limited range of tasks like sniffing suspect baggage in an airport on which there could be surface contamination also.

Next we examine the question whether men on the so-called ROP duty can provide any security to the vehicles plying on the road?

- The terrorists could fire at them in a stand-off mode and run away to safety—inflicting casualties in the process.
- There is nothing that can be done about it by the men on the ROP. It is only a fond misconception that if there are armed men available on the roads, they would do something. There is no way these men can make a decent response after such an attack. What would they do, duffers—shoot at what they cannot see?
- Furthermore, a stand-off attack could well be a trap for a well-laid ambush should they desire to pursue deep without adequate strength.
- Suppose there is a road and there are fields on both sides of it. The fields could be in a depth of say, 100-300 yards, after which there could be human habitation, villages, forests, or hills. If a man is standing say, 50 yards deep into the fields and facing away from the road, he could be fired upon by terrorists in a vehicle moving on the road. If he is facing the road, he could be fired at by terrorists sitting in the fields or deeper. Both ways, they stand to get shot and there is nothing they can do about it.
- The man facing the road would not be able to save the man who is facing away from the road—the man who is facing the road can keep a watch on a vehicle that passes him—what he can do about a vehicle that leaves him but fires at the man 50 yards way who is presenting his back to the road. There could be many other vehicles following him and the ROP man cannot open fire at the culprit vehicle even if he has identified the vehicle.
- The men in the ROP cannot do anything for a grenade attack either.
- Therefore the mindless deployment of men in pairs within eye-contact distance of each other is of no deterrence to a terrorist who might fire from a distance or use a rifle grenade or even a small mortar, should it come to that.

(10.2.2) Scientific Way of Providing Security on Roads

There is no utility of a static deployment on the road or outside the road either in pairs or in whichever way. The men should be found only in such strength that if at all they have to mount a response to an attack, they have a respectable level of firepower. They must be kept in a medium vehicle. The vehicle must ideally be a mineproof/bulletproof one or should be improvised so to offer a reasonable degree of protection. This vehicle must randomly (and very deliberately ensuring that it does not follow a set pattern and make itself a predictable target) move up and down its assigned stretch and also halt randomly at places. The idea is that its presence should be seen on the road and secondly that it should be able to respond much faster than men on foot could ever do—it should immediately rush to a place where the attack has been mounted. Suitably protected vehicles moving up and down the road or waiting at some places would have a more visible presence and deterrent value for a potential attacker than isolated men standing on the road or outside the road. Needless to say, various vehicles of a unit must be in constant radio contact with each other and with the base so that information of any incident may be relayed and help sought if necessary.

(10.3) General Principles of Counter-ambush Action for Vehicle Convoys

Have a plan. Have a back-up plan, because the first one probably won't work.

(10.3.1) Briefing on Likely Ambush Sites and Emergency Procedures

The appearance of a unit's road convoys can tell much about its state of operational efficiency. The enemy can read and interpret the signs and tends to look for easier targets than those presented by a well-trained unit. The danger of ambush must not be allowed to become a mental block or "hang up". Troops should be taught that, well-prepared, they are more than a match for the enemy under any circumstances and that the contact afforded by a road ambush gives an opportunity to close with the enemy and destroy them. When troops are efficient, alert and well-disciplined, there is less likelihood of ambush.

Briefing by the convoy commander before the convoy moves off must be detailed and explicit. All drivers and vehicle commanders should be present at the briefing and if possible, the men travelling in the convoy too. The briefing should include: details of timings, routes, speed, density, order of march, maintenance of contact, procedure when contact is lost and action on breakdown; distribution of personnel to vehicles and their conduct in them; duties of vehicle commanders, sentries and details of action on ambush for that particular convoy; and counter-ambush action or action for suspected ambush sites.

As wheeled vehicles have restricted cross-country mobility, their movement is largely on roads and tracks. The enemy is, therefore, likely to take advantage of naturally occurring obstacles such as crossing points, bridges, defiles and wash ways and use these as ambush sites. Roadblocks are normally created to enhance his position and are usually sited on road bends or on tops of crests so that they are not seen until leading vehicles are upon them.

(10.3.2) *Action on Encountering a Likely Ambush Site*

The following actions should be taken if a vehicle convoy encounters an area considered to be a likely ambush site but is not under fire:

- The lead vehicle stops and informs the commander.
- Remaining vehicles maintain convoy spacing and occupants watch their arcs.
- Troops in the lead vehicle dismount and clear the area forward of the road-block on foot. If an armoured vehicle is available it should move forward to give direct fire support.
- The commander orders other troops to clear the road of obstacles. Care must be taken because a roadblock is normally booby-trapped or mined.
- If a column comes under fire when it encounters a road-block, vehicle counter-ambush drill must be carried out.

(10.3.3) *Action on Contact*

No battle plan ever survives initial contact with the enemy.

Every effort must be made to get vehicles clear of the kill zone. When vehicles are fired on, the drivers should not stop, but should try to drive clear of the area. When vehicles are clear of the kill zone, they should stop to allow their occupants to dismount and carry out offensive action. Following vehicles approaching the kill zone should not run through the ambush, but halt clear of the area. Where vehicles have been caught in the kill zone, the troops must debus, get off the road away from the enemy and take cover. Vehicle sentries cover the debussing with fire, including smoke if possible until the troops are in position to return fire. Offensive action is taken after that.

The enemy force may allow the advance guard to pass the site of the main ambush and then block the road and attack the main body and the advance guard separately. At the first indication of an ambush, vehicles attempt to move out of the kill zone. If necessary to halt, vehicles stop in place; they do not drive to the roadsides or shoulders, which may be mined. Specified individuals immediately return fire from inside vehicles to cover dismounting personnel. These individuals dismount last under cover of fire by those who dismounted first. Upon dismounting, personnel caught in the kill zone open fire and immediately assault toward the ambush force and then establish a base of fire. Tanks open fire and manoeuvre toward the ambush force or to the most favourable ground in the immediate vicinity. While the engaged element continues its action to protect the convoy, the commander rapidly surveys the situation and issues orders to the designated attack elements to begin predrilled offensive manoeuvres against the guerrilla force. The fire of the engaged security element is used to fix the ambush force and is coordinated with that of the attacking element.

After the guerrilla force is destroyed or neutralised, security details are posted to cover convoy reorganisation. The convoy commander, using the fastest communication available, briefs his commander on the engagement. Captured guerrilla personnel are interrogated as to where they planned to reassemble, and this information is reported immediately to higher headquarters. After an ambush, patrols may be sent to interrogate and, if necessary, apprehend suspected civilians living near or along the routes of approach to the ambush positions.

(10.3.4) *Action when the Security Element is Weak*

At the first indication of ambush, leading vehicles, if the road appears clear, increase speed to the safe maximum in an effort to smash through the ambush area. Troops from vehicles halted in the ambush area dismount and immediately return fire. Troops from vehicles breaking through the ambush dismount and assault the flanks of the ambush position. Both attacking groups must exercise care that they do not fire on each other. If the enemy force allows the main convoy to pass through and then ambushes the rear guard, troops from the main body return and attack the flanks of the ambush position.

(10.3.5) *The Scientific Method of Debussing*

Debussing must be taught and practised as a drill. To aid debussing, all packs and stores will be stacked in the centre of the vehicle. Troops should hold their weapons at all times and spare machinegun belts should be in pouches, and not in boxes. The following is the procedure when the vehicle is forced to stop:

- The vehicle commander shouts "debus right" or "debus left" to indicate the direction in which the troops will muster.
- Sentries return fire at targets in the direction from which enemy fire is coming.
- Troops debus over both sides of the vehicle and dash in the direction indicated. As few troops as possible should attempt to debus over the tail of the vehicle.

- As soon as the troops are clear of the vehicle, sentries debus and join the remainder.
- The aim must now be to collect the fit men as a formed body for counter-action. Wounded troops must be attended to after counter-action has been taken.

The drill must be practised frequently by vehicle loads. It is desirable that each vehicle load of personnel should consist of a formed body with its normal commander. However, where vehicle loads are made up from a mixed group of soldiers immediately before a journey, two or three practices must be held before the convoy moves off.

(10.3.6) Special Ambush Situation

Attacks against columns protected by armoured vehicles depend on the type and location of armoured vehicles in a column, and the weapons of the ambush force. If possible, armoured vehicles are destroyed or disabled by fire of anti-tank weapons, landmines, and Molotov cocktails, or by throwing hand grenades into open hatches. An effort is made to immobilise armoured vehicles at a point where they are unable to give protection to the rest of the convoy and where they will block the route of other supporting vehicles. If the crew survives an attack but the vehicle is immobilised, the first priority of the others must be to try pushing it to a side so that it does not block the road for others.

(10.4) Scientific Organisation of a Vehicle Convoy so that it may Fight Credibly

Every command which can be misunderstood, will be.

(10.4.1) Various Elements of a Convoy

What we described above, applies to situations where things are not so bad and attacks not so frequent. For really bad situations, the convoy must be able to fight for itself and not depend on others. The security detachment must be organised with adequate combat power to suppress guerrilla ambushes. Its size and composition depend upon the physical characteristics of the area, the capability of the enemy force, and the size and composition of the convoy. In any case, the security detachment should have the following subordinate elements: headquarters element to provide command, control, and communication; medical support element, an armoured element to provide firepower and shock effect; a mechanised or motorised infantry element; and combat engineer element to make minor repairs to bridges and roads and to detect and remove mines and obstacles. For large convoys, the security detachment should include field artillery. Ideally, half of the artillery would be placed well forward in the column and half near the rear of the column. The artillery command and control element would move in the vicinity of the security detachment headquarters. This arrangement allows the most flexibility for providing artillery fire support to elements of the column in the event of ambush. The combined arms security detachment is usually interspersed throughout the convoy so that the various elements can be employed either as a fixing element or attacking element, as required.

The formation of a security detachment and its integration into a convoy varies because the enemy may be expected to observe convoy patterns and prepare their ambushes to cope with expected formations. Tanks lead the convoy to gain maximum advantage from their mobility and firepower. If no tanks are available, a heavy vehicle with sandbags placed to protect personnel from mines should lead the convoy. A strong attack element is placed at the rear of the convoy formation where it has maximum flexibility in moving forward to attack any force attempting to ambush the head or center of the convoy.

If the security detachment accompanying a convoy is too weak for decisive action against a guerrilla attack or ambush, the following principles apply:

- Some of the troops are placed well forward in the convoy, and the remainder are placed a short distance to the rear.
- Radio contact is maintained between the two groups.
- Sharp curves, steep grades, or other areas where slow speeds are necessary are reconnoitered by foot troops before passage.

(10.4.2) *The Convoy Commander, Vehicle Commander and Vehicle Sentries*

The convoy commander should position himself where he considers he can best control the convoy. He must nominate a vehicle commander for each vehicle and brief them thoroughly before moving from the start point. He must always nominate a successor. The task of the vehicle commander is to post sentries, ensure that all personnel are alert, and assist in maintaining convoy formations. He commands the troops in his vehicle should the convoy be ambushed. He must travel in the rear of the vehicle and not in the cabin with the driver. Four sentries should be posted in the back of each troop carrier vehicle (TCV), two at the front, covering 1600 mils each from front to side and two at the rear, covering 1600 mils each from rear to side. These sentries should be armed with automatic weapons. It is their task to take immediate action from those positions should the vehicle be ambushed and to cover the evacuation of the vehicle should it be brought to a halt. Sentries must also assist in control of the convoy by notifying the commander of any disruption in the convoy formation. In addition to the sentries posted in the body of the vehicle, an additional soldier must be detailed to sit in the front seat of the vehicle's cabin beside the driver. The task of this individual, normally called the 'Shotgun', is to assist the driver in controlling or stopping the vehicle in an emergency. If a vehicle is halted by enemy action the 'shotgun' stays with the vehicle to act as close protection for the driver, the vehicle, and any stores it may be carrying. He does not accompany any assault or sweep that may be carried out by the other troops in the convoy.

(10.4.3) Typical Organisation of Occupants in a Vehicle

Encounters with a guerrilla ambush are sudden, short, and unexpected. The opportunity to inflict casualties upon the guerrillas is lost if your troops are not organised and well-drilled to take immediate offensive action. The organisation of a squad as occupants of a 6 by 6 truck is as follows:

1 A vehicle commander is designated for each vehicle. The squad leader is usually the vehicle commander and is positioned in the bed of the vehicle where he can best control the squad and operator of the vehicle.

2 An assistant driver (shotgun rider) capable of operating the vehicle is seated in the cabin with the driver. The shotgun rider is armed with a grenade launcher and an automatic rifle. After debarkation, the shotgun rider remains with the vehicle to act as close protection for the driver and vehicle. He does not accompany manoeuvres executed by the occupant squad.

3 Four comer sentries are positioned in the bed of the vehicle. The two at the front observe an arc of 90 degrees from the front to each side. The two at the back observe an arc of 90 degrees from the back to each side. If the vehicle is ambushed, the sentries fire immediately from their positions within the vehicle. Their fire covers the debarkation of the occupants if the vehicle is halted in the ambush killing area. They also help the vehicle commander by notifying the commander of any convoy formation.

4 If a machinegun team is travelling with the occupant squad, it should be positioned facing out the rear of the vehicle and be prepared to debark expeditiously, bringing fire to bear on the enemy and covering the debarkation of the four corner sentries.

5 The remaining occupants are positioned in the bed of the vehicle, each facing outboard.

6 The maximum number of people in the bed of a hardened 6 by 6 truck should not exceed 13.

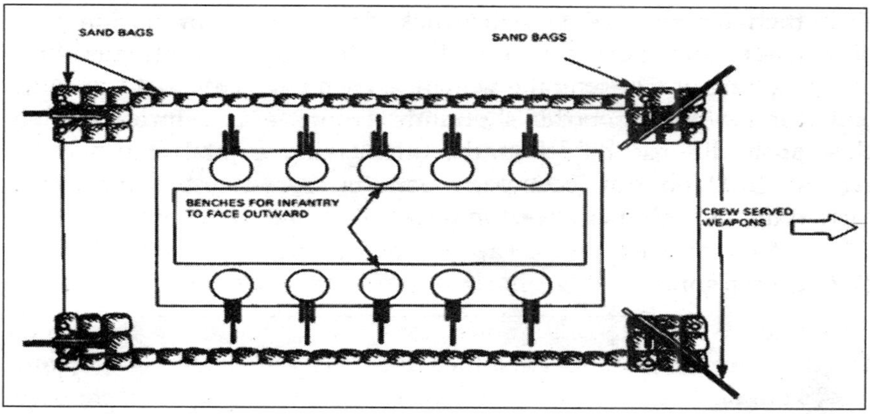

Typical seating pattern of soldiers and positioning of various weapons in a truck

(10.4.4) *Preparation of Vehicles and Improvised Armouring of Vehicles*

Troops travelling in vehicles must have all-round visibility and fields of fire and be able to throw smoke grenades over the vehicle's sides without hindrance. They must be able to exit from the vehicle rapidly with minimum restriction. For these reasons the configuration of vehicles, such as a 6 by 6 cargo truck or a 5-ton vehicle, must be altered suitably. Canvas, bows, windshields, and doors must be removed. The tailgate must be lowered to a horizontal position. Troop movement by troop carrier vehicles (TCV) should be conducted using the center seating method with the troops facing out. A wooden bench or packs rigged down the middle of the bed would provide the troops with seats. A piece of pipe, wood, or metal may be affixed to the vehicle in a vertical position extending above the driver's head. This will prevent decapitation from any wire stretched across the road purposefully to trap standing troops. Machineguns and anti-armour weapons should be distributed throughout the convoy. Where time and the means exist, mounts should be bolted to the truck to provide stable platforms. Ideally automatic weapons should be positioned at each corner. If these weapons are not available, at least two should be carried, with one firmly sandbagged in place on the cab top and one at the rear. As very few forces can afford a large number of armoured troop carriers, the following measures must be taken to "harden" a vehicle and provide its occupants with a degree of protection:

- Sandbags must be placed on the floorboards and bed of the vehicle. For a 6 by 6 truck, a single row of sandbags is placed on the bed of the truck. Then sandbags must be stacked five layers high down each side of the truck. This provides protection from most small arms. A total of 70 to 100 sandbags are required for each truck. The average weight of each bag is about 40 pounds, for a total weight of 2800 pounds. Troops and equipment weigh an additional 2300 pounds, thus giving a total vehicle load of 5100 pounds. This load permits cross-country operations without undue wear on the vehicle. You may, of course, vary the load depending on the capacity of the truck and the local threat perception.

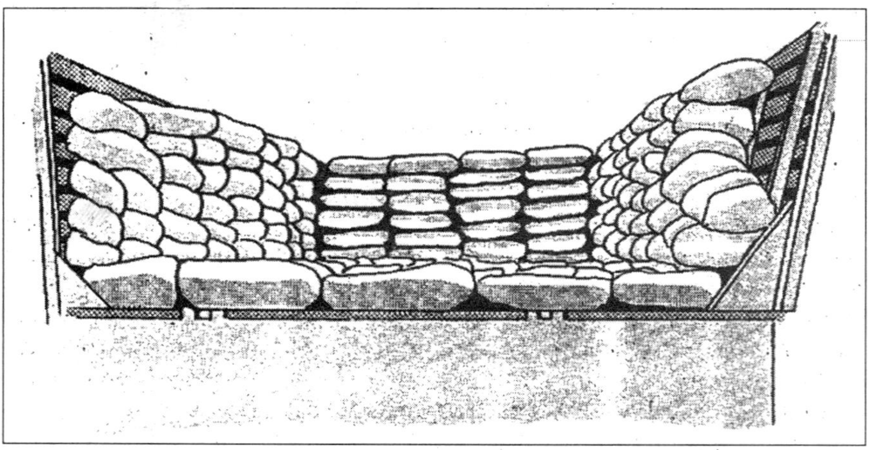

Sandbagging of the body of a truck to protect it from small arms fire and to some extent from IEDs

- To reduce the sandblast effect when a mine is detonated near the vehicle, various materials may be placed on top of the floorboard sandbags (such as rubber mats, light metal plates, plywood, or scraps of runway membrane material). Wetting down the sandbags is also effective but contributes to deterioration of the metal.
- Sections of scrap armour plate, if available, may be used to reinforce sandbags in the bed of the vehicle.
- They can also be used to harden the doors of the driver's compartment because you cannot use sandbags on them.
- Harden the driver's compartment in a similar manner.

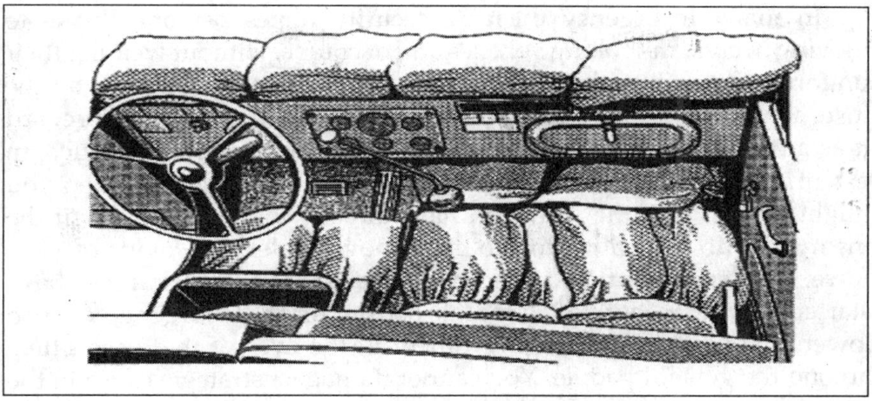

Sandbagging of the driver's compartment

- The windshield glass has a bad habit of shattering and injuring the driver and the occupant of the cabin whenever it faces an explosion.
- The simplest way to deal with this problem is to lower the windshield, place a single layer of sandbags under the windshield, lower the windshield onto the bags, place a second layer of sandbags over the windshield, and then cover both with canvas. This will ensure that the windshield is not damaged by vibrations and also that sand is not blown into the driver's face.

Lowering the windshield and sandbagging it

In many insurgency theatres, security forces personnel take to moving in civilian-looking vehicles and of course, without wearing their uniforms. Arguably, this does reduce the chances of detection by the insurgents and hence reduces the possibility of an attack. But I regard it as an insult. If you have allowed the situation to worsen to such an extent that you are afraid of moving in your own vehicles, then you might as well quit the war. You have already lost half the war if the insurgents do not allow you to even move under the colour of your force. The very news that the security forces are so scared that they have started moving incognito is a morale booster for the insurgents and also lowers the prestige of the government in the eyes of the fence-sitters among the general people. You cannot damage a strategic cause in the name of some tactical expedience. If you have any shame left, you will understand it—otherwise, what can be done for shameless nations?

Moreover, do not think that a civilian-looking vehicle is a guaranteed deception. It is not. There are simple means by which the insurgents may beat it. Civilian-looking vehicles deceive only for a one-way trip. The element of surprise is lost in the return trip as most places may not have an alternative route. You will eventually visit one of your camps only and the camps cannot be concealed. The insurgents may keep innocuous-looking civilian spotters outside your camps, or in the nearby markets etc. To keep a watch on the vehicles going in and out to the camps. Information regarding vehicles of any type would be conveyed to the insurgents through various means. Such cheap stratagems may be tolerated for a few covert operations; if you do it frequently, it will only help the insurgents in their propaganda war that the security forces are shit scared of the guerrillas.

(10.5) Counter-ambush Techniques for Convoys

Incoming fire has the right of way.

(10.5.1) The Basic Techniques

Whatever the precautions and preparations be, the ambush is nearly always an unexpected encounter. Be prepared for the unexpected. Counter-ambush drills are simple courses of action designed to deal with the problem of the unexpected encounter. They call for immediate, positive, and offensive action. The basic action on ambush is to drive through the ambush area or stop before running into it, then to attack the enemy immediately from the flank or the rear. When vehicles are fired upon, the following actions must be taken:

1. Drivers attempt to drive through the killing zone.

2. Personnel return fire immediately.
3. When vehicles are clear of the killing zone, they are halted. Occupants dismount and take immediate offensive action against the enemy positions.
4. Subsequent vehicles approaching the killing zone halt short of the zone. Occupants debark and take immediate offensive action against the enemy positions.
5. Do not enter the killing zone when it can be avoided. Provide flanking support fire into the killing zone.
6. The best way an armoured vehicle can help in counter-ambush action is by moving into the killing zone to engage the enemy at short range. In this way it can give good covering fire to the flanking attack or provide protection for those troops caught in the killing zone.
7. If hardened vehicles are forced to halt in the killing zone, all available weapons are used to return fire immediately. Occupants remain in the vehicle. On the first perceptible slackening of enemy fire, occupants dismount.
8. When riding in a "soft" vehicle and caught in a killing zone, occupants dismount immediately. In both cases, occupants dismount under the covering fires of the four corner sentries, who initially remain aboard. The occupants then deploy to the side directed by the vehicle commander and take the enemy under fire to cover the dismount of the four sentries.
9. After dismounting, if no cover is available, an immediate frontal assault against the enemy is employed.
10. The most logical course of action after dismounting is to take cover, immediately establish a base of fire with a machinegun and/or mortar, and use a manoeuvre element against the enemy ambush positions. Speed of execution is critical.
11. The most effective counter-action to ambushes is a flanking attack by elements not in the killing zone quickly followed by relentless pursuit of the enemy.
12. In actions when no troops have entered the killing zone, the convoy commander launches an immediate flanking attack on the enemy position, using supporting fires from machineguns and mortars.
13. Fire in the killing zone may be from only one side of the road with a small holding force on the opposite side. To contain the

convoy element in the killing zone, the enemy will place mines and booby-traps on the holding force side. Take care when assaulting the main ambush force because mines are commonly used to protect its flanks.

14. In actions where some portions of the vehicles are ahead and out of the killing zone and the remainder are halted short of the zone, the portion that has not yet entered the killing zone initiates the flanking attack. If the convoy commander is not present, the senior vehicle commander takes command and directs the attack.
15. It is possible that the convoy commander may be killed, wounded, caught in the killing zone, or positioned on the wrong side of the zone. It is essential that all vehicle commanders and squad leaders know their responsibilities for organising and directing a counter-ambush action.
16. The techniques outlined above are practiced repeatedly until the reaction procedures become a predrilled response, permitting immediate on ambush and positive action.

(10.5.2) Counter-ambush for an Unblocked Road

Guerrillas are seldom able to contain an entire convoy in a single killing zone. This is because of the extensive road space occupied by even a platoon size convoy, and because security or lack of available forces may limit the size of the ambushing force. More frequently, a part of a convoy, either head, tail, or a section of the main body, is ambushed.

1. That part of a convoy that is in the killing zone and receiving fire must drive out of the ambush if the road to the front is open.
2. Vehicles disabled by enemy fire are left behind or, if blocking the road, are pushed out of the way by following vehicles.
3. Armoured escort vehicles must not block convoy vehicles by halting in the traveled portion of the road to return fire.
4. Vehicles that have not entered the killing zone must not attempt to do so. They should stop and personnel should dismount and take defensive positions.
5. Elements of the convoy should not fire on suspected enemy positions without coordinating with the escort forces.
6. The escort vehicles may have left the road in an attempt to overrun hostile positions.
7. Direct any vehicles mounted with weapons to lay down a heavy volume of fire on the ambush force.

8. Call for support.
9. Direct all non-driving personnel to place a heavy volume of fire on enemy forces as rapidly as possible, as vehicles move out of the killing zone.
10. A motor transport convoy with a limited escort is seldom able to defeat a hostile force and should not attempt to do so. When part of the convoy is isolated in the killing zone, vehicles that have not entered the ambush area should turn around and return to the nearest secured area until supporting forces can clear the ambush.

(10.5.3) Counter-ambush for a Blocked Road

If the enemy has blocked the road, it obviously means that he is well-prepared. Convoy personnel should be aware that a heavy volume of fire is also frequently used by the enemy to slow down a convoy before an ambush. Expect more butchery in this situation. As a rule of thumb, when an element of a convoy is halted in the killing zone and is unable to proceed due to disabled vehicles, a damaged bridge, or other obstacles, personnel must dismount, take cover, and return a maximum volume of fire on enemy positions. That's the best you can do under the circumstances.

1. Security troops from vehicles that have passed through the ambush area dismount and prepare to attack the flanks of the ambush position. Leave a component behind to protect these vehicles.
2. Personnel in vehicles that have not entered the killing zone follow the same procedure.
3. The next step is to outflank the ambush force.
4. Seek support from the base. In such situations, the Americans depend heavily on air or artillery support—it may not be feasible in a counter-insurgency situation.
5. When disabled vehicles cannot be towed, their cargo is distributed among other vehicles if time permits. Try to retrieve critical items like radio. When it is not feasible to evacuate vehicles and/or cargo, they may be destroyed to avoid anything falling into enemy hands.

(10.5.4) Convoy Defence Against Mines and Booby-traps

Mines, IEDs and booby-traps are frequently used by guerrilla forces with great effect. Command-detonated mines are often used to start an ambush. Mines can also be planted along the shoulder of the road.

This is for harassment and interdiction. A booby-trap system may be used against personnel in vehicles. They could consist of hand grenades attached to tree branches over the road where antennas or other projections from vehicles may snag and detonate the grenades. Claymore mines may be suspended from trees and command detonated when a vehicle passes. IEDs are a most formidable enemy. Honestly speaking, there is no dependable solution to the IED menace and a clever enemy can often manage to think ahead of you. Still, for your own satisfaction you must observe the following basic precautions:

1. Prescribe alarm signals.
2. Give instructions for immediate action to take when under attack.
3. Prescribe actions to take in the absence of people on foot. (They will frequently give away the location of any mines or booby-traps).
4. Follow the tracks of the vehicle in front.
5. Avoid driving on the shoulder of the road.
6. Whenever possible, do not run over foreign objects, brush, or grass in the road.
7. Avoid fresh earth in the road.
8. If disabled, steer off the road to allow passage of other vehicles.
9. If disabled and the convoy is moving through the killing zone, mount a passing vehicle.
10. Watch local traffic and the reactions of the local people with the convoy personnel.
11. Make sure that defence procedures are rehearsed before the convoy moves out.

(10.5.5) Convoy Defence for Sniper Fire

If the enemy sniper knows his business, you will be left wondering from where the shot came. The best action to take for protection from snipers is passive, and you should ensure that all personnel wear protective helmets and armoured vests. There is not much to be gained by returning fire as the sniper team would not have more than two guys and concealed as they would be, it is difficult to score a hit. Don't stop at sniper fire even if he hits someone. By stopping you would be giving him more opportunity. Hence, all vehicles should move through the area without stopping. Escort personnel must notify the march element commander by giving a prearranged signal, such as a smoke grenade, thrown in the direction of fire. Any attempt to locate and destroy the sniper must be by long-range fire only.

(10.6) Counter-ambush Action for Watercrafts

Waterways are used as a means to deploy troops into an operational area; or for the logistic support of troops already deployed. Because of their nature, waterways provide ideal ambush locations and accordingly counter-ambush plans need to be made when using them. These plans must take into account the distinctive characteristics of various watercrafts that may be available. Ambushes set on waterways can be avoided or their effects minimised by: protecting critical areas; clearing vegetation from likely ambush sites; using irregular schedules; and patrolling the water-ways and banks, particularly by air. The effects of an ambush can be reduced by: employing tactical spacing and movement; mounting automatic weapons on each boat; and maintaining communications between each boat.

Counter-ambush action is very similar to that with motor vehicles. If ambushed, there should be immediate fire reaction, including smoke and all fire support available; and those boats not ambushed must make for the bank on which the ambush is sited and launch offensive action. During an engagement, boats may be overturned. To reduce its possibility, the centre of gravity must be kept as low as possible and stores should be spread along the length of the floor and not piled. Similarly, troops should sit on the floor or the seats provided and not on top of packs, ration boxes, petrol, etc. Depending on the boat, troops may be seated in linear or double fashion. The boat may still overturn, however. Hence, a life-jacket should be used. However, if it is used it must be appreciated that this may prevent the user from diving and keep the soldier exposed on the surface of the water. All members of the crew and the party should be swimmers or have undergone special waterman-ship training. To get some freedom of movement in water, personnel should remove packs and place them in the boats; webbing equipment should be loosened, and worn over the life-jacket, so that it can be quickly discarded; and the ends of trousers should be pulled out of the boots, and shirts should be buttoned to the neck, and freed of the waistband of the trousers. To ensure that weapons are not lost irretrievably, they should be secured to the boat by quick release ties and in such a way that they can be fired by individuals while sitting in the boat. Since some packs are likely to be lost when a boat overturns, during water moves, at least one spare magazine should be carried in a shirt pocket.

11

Covert and Stealthy Operations

If it's worth fighting for...it's worth fighting dirty for.

(11.1) The Stuff Legends are made of

The only reason that anything ever gets done is because there are pockets of competence in every command. The key is to find them...and then exploit the hell out of 'em.

The Attack on Fort Eben-Emael

In one of the most brilliant commando operations in the history of warfare, an assault force of German Fallschirmjäger (German Air Force Paratroopers) was tasked with assaulting and capturing Fort Eben-Emael, a Belgian fortress whose artillery pieces dominated several important bridges over the Albert Canal which German forces intended to use to advance into Belgium. This was a formidable fortress spread over 75 hectares with 17 interconnected bunkers. The battle (May, 1940) was a decisive victory for the German forces in the Second World War, with the airborne troops landing on top of the fortress through gliders and using explosives and flamethrowers to disable the outer defences of the fortress. The Fallschirmjäger then entered the fortress, killing a number of defenders and containing the rest in the lower sections of the fortress. Simultaneously, the rest of the German assault force had landed near the three bridges over the Canal, destroyed a number of pillboxes and defensive positions and defeated the Belgian forces guarding the bridges, capturing them and bringing them under German control. The airborne troops suffered heavy casualties during the operation, but succeeded in holding the bridges until the arrival of German ground forces, who then aided the airborne troops in assaulting the fortress a second time and forcing the surrender of the remaining members of the garrison. German forces were then able to utilise two bridges over the Canal to bypass a number of Belgian defensive positions and advance into Belgium to aid in the invasion of the country.

The Germans were the first to use gliders in warfare. In this operation, 41 DFS 230 gliders carrying 10 soldiers each were launched behind Junkers Ju 52s, a transport aircraft. This glider was developed in 1933 by the Deutsche Forschungsanstalt für Segelflug (DFS - "German Research Institute for Sailplane Flight") with Hans Jacobs as the head designer. The glider was the German inspiration for the later British Hotspur glider. The glider could carry nine soldiers with equipment or a payload of about 1,200 kg. These engineless aircraft were towed into the air and most of the way to their target by military transport planes or bombers relegated to secondary activities. Once released from the tow craft near the front, given an average speed of 124 km/ph, they were to land on any convenient open terrain close to target hopefully with as little damage to the cargo and crew as possible as most Landing Zones (LZ) were far from ideal. The one-way nature of the missions meant that they were treated as disposable leading to construction from common and inexpensive materials such as wood. Gliders were chosen because landing by parachute caused the troops to be spread over a large drop-zone, whereas gliders could land troops in greater concentrations precisely at the target landing area. Furthermore, the glider, once released at some distance from the actual target, was effectively silent and difficult for the enemy to identify.

For this operation, a detailed study of the Fort, the bridges and the local area was made, and a replica of the area was constructed for the airborne troops to train in. Joint exercises between the parachutists and the glider pilots were carried out in the early spring of 1940, and a number of refinements made to the equipment and tactics to be used. This included arrester parachutes; barbed-wire added to the nose-skids of the gliders to reduce their landing run; and training of the airborne troops with flamethrowers and specialised explosives, the latter of which were so secret that they were only used on fortifications in Germany and not on fortifications in Czechoslovakia similar to Fort Eben Emael.

The German estimated that after sixty minutes, the superior numbers of the Belgian forces defending the Fort and the bridges, as well as any reinforcements sent to the area, would begin to come to bear against the relatively small number of lightly armed airborne troops. The German plan, therefore, was to eliminate within those sixty minutes as many anti-aircraft positions and individual cupolas and casemates as was possible, and at all costs to put out of action the long-range artillery pieces which covered the three bridges. The destruction of these guns was expected to be completed within ten minutes; within this time the airborne troops would have to break out of their gliders, cover the distance to the guns, fix the explosive charges to the barrels of the guns and detonate them, all while under enemy fire.

Hauptmann Koch divided his force into four assault groups—Group Granite (eighty-five men in eleven gliders) to capture Fort Eben Emael; Group Steel (ninety-two men in nine gliders) to capture the Veldwezelt bridge; Group Concrete (ninety-six men in eleven gliders) to capture the Vroenhoven bridge; and Group Iron (ninety men in ten gliders) to capture the Cannes bridge. At 4:30 a.m., forty-two gliders carrying the 493 airborne troops that formed the assault force were lifted off from two airfields in Cologne, the armada of gliders and transport aircraft turning south towards their objectives. There were minor mishaps on the way—both in Group Granite. In one, the tow-ropes on one of the gliders snapped, forcing the glider to land inside Germany. In the other, the pilot of a second glider released his tow-rope prematurely, and was unable to land near its objective.

The remaining gliders were, however, released from their tow-ropes twenty miles away from their objectives at an altitude of 7,000 feet, and they managed to land properly. After the Ju-52's released the gliders and began turning away, Belgian anti-aircraft artillery positions detected them and opened fire. This alerted the defences in the area to the presence of the gliders. Anti-aircraft fire opened up and fierce fighting ensued on the ground. The pillboxes protecting the bridges were attacked with grenades even in the face of small arms fire. Explosive charges were also used on doors to assault them directly. They also disconnected the demolition charges on the bridge so that the Belgian could not destroy them. Group Steel suffered eight killed and 30 injured in casualties. Group Concrete suffered seven dead and 24 injured. The third bridge was destroyed by the Belgians as the German mechanised column moving in to support the Group Iron reached 20 minute early and the Belgians were forewarned. As a result they suffered casualties to the extent of 22 dead and 26 injured.

The fort had formidable firepower—two guns of 120 mm; 16 guns of 75 mm; 12 guns of 60 mm; and 24 machineguns, replete with observation domes and even dummy domes. The Group Granite quickly began attaching explosive charges to those emplacements and turrets on the top of the Fort which housed the artillery pieces that could target the three captured bridges. The attackers carried 28 hollow charges of 50 kg each; 28 hollow charges of 12.5 kg each; 83

charges of 3 kg each; 98 charges of 1 kg each; 2 quick loads of 27 kg each; 8 boxes of 25 kg each; and 33 tubes of 1.5 kg each—total 2401 kg of explosives! The artillery pieces were attacked with exceptional precision. Any exterior entrances and exits located by the airborne troops were destroyed with explosives to seal the garrison inside the Fort, giving the garrison few opportunities to attempt a counter-attack. Having achieved their primary objectives of disabling the artillery pieces possessed by the fort that the fort could have used to bombard the captured bridges, the airborne troops then held it against Belgian counter-attacks from outside, which began almost immediately. These counter-attacks were made by Belgian infantry formations without artillery support and were uncoordinated. This allowed the airborne troops to repel them with machinegun fire. Group Granite suffered six killed and nineteen wounded.

Once the airborne troops had been relieved, an Engineer battalion, in conjunction with an infantry regiment that arrived shortly after the engineers, mounted an attack on the main entrance to the fort. Faced with this attack, the garrison surrendered at 12:30, suffering sixty men killed and forty wounded. The Germans took more than a thousand Belgian soldiers into captivity.

The Gran Sasso Raid to Liberate Mussolini

In September 1943, German paratroopers and Waffen-SS commandos mounted a raid and freed Mussolini from captivity. This was the famous Gran Sasso raid or Operation Eiche (German for 'Oak'). The daring operation was personally ordered by the Fuhrer Adolf Hitler, planned by Major Harald Mors and approved by General Kurt Student, all Fallschirmjäger (German Air Force Paratroopers) officers. Earlier, on 25 July 1943, a few weeks after the allied invasion of Sicily and bombing of Rome, Mussolini was deposed and replaced by Marshal Pietro Badoglio. Mussolini was subsequently arrested. After his arrest, Mussolini was transported around Italy by his captors. Otto Skorzeny, selected personally by Hitler and Ernst Kaltenbrunner to carry out the rescue mission, tracked him.

Intercepting a coded Italian radio message, Skorzeny used his own reconnaissance to determine that Mussolini was being imprisoned at Campo Imperatore Hotel, a ski-resort at Campo Imperatore in Italy's Gran Sasso, high in the Apennine Mountains. On 12 September 1943, Skorzeny joined the team—led by Major Harald Mors—to rescue Mussolini in a high-risk glider mission. The commandos crashed their nine DFS 230 gliders into the nearby mountains, then overwhelmed Mussolini's captors without a single shot being fired. Skorzeny attacked the radio operator and his equipment, and formally greeted Mussolini with "Duce, the Fuhrer has sent me to set you free!" to which Mussolini replied "I knew that my friend would not forsake me!"

The Attacks on the German Battleship Tirpitz

Tirpitz was the second of two Bismarck-class battleships built for the German Kriegsmarine during World War II. In early 1942, the ship sailed to Norway to act as a deterrent against an Allied invasion. While stationed in Norway, Tirpitz was also intended to be used to intercept Allied convoys to the Soviet Union, and two such missions were attempted in 1942. Tirpitz acted as a fleet in being, forcing the Royal Navy to retain significant naval forces in the area to contain the battleship. Operation Source was a series of attacks to neutralise the heavy German warships—Tirpitz, Scharnhorst and Lutzow—based in northern Norway, using X-class midget submarines. The attacks took place in September 1943 and succeeded in keeping the Tirpitz out of action for at least 6 months. The operation was later portrayed in the 1955 war film 'Above Us The Waves', featuring John Mills, which was based on both Operation Source, and the earlier Chariot human torpedo attacks on the Tirpitz.

The vessels were designed to be towed to their intended area of operations by a full-size 'mother' submarine with a 'passage crew' on board, the operational crew being transferred from the towing submarine to the X-craft by dinghy when the operational area was reached, the passage crew returning with the dinghy to the towing submarine. Once the attack was over, the X-Craft would rendezvous with the towing submarine and then be towed home. The craft were about 51 feet long, 5.5 feet in maximum diameter and displaced 27 tons surfaced and 30 tons submerged. Propulsion was by a 4-cylinder Gardner 42 hp diesel engine, converted from a type used in London buses, and a 30 hp electric motor, giving a maximum surface speed of 6.5 knots , and a submerged speed of 5.5 knots. The crew initially numbered three—commander, pilot and ERA (Engine Room Artificer, i.e. mechanic) but soon a specialist diver was added, for which an airlock, known as a wet and dry compartment, was provided. The X class submarines' weapons were two side-cargoes—explosive charges held on opposite sides of the hull with two tons of amatol in each. The intention was to drop these on the sea-bed underneath the target then escape. The charges were detonated by a time fuse.

Six X-craft (X5 to X10) were used—three for Tirpitz; two for Scharnhorst; and one for Lutzow. X9, probably trimmed heavily by the bow in the heavy sea for the tow, was lost with all hands on the passage when her tow parted and she suffered an abrupt plunge due to her bow-down trim. X8 developed serious leaks in her side-mounted demolition charges, which had to be jettisoned; these exploded, leaving her so damaged that she had to be scuttled. X10's attack was abandoned due to mechanical and navigation problems, and the submarine returned to rendezvous with her 'tug' submarine and was taken back to Scotland. Scharnhorst was engaged in exercises at the time, and hence was not at her normal mooring. X6 and X7 managed to drop their charges underneath Tirpitz, but were unable to make good their escape as they were observed and attacked. Both craft were abandoned and six crew members survived to be captured. Although the fate of X5 is unclear, it is believed to have been sunk by a direct hit from one of Tirpitz's four-inch guns before having had a chance to place her charges. Tirpitz was heavily damaged. While not in danger of sinking, she took on over 1,400 tons of water and suffered significant mechanical damage, including shock to the roller bearings in "D" turret aft. Tirpitz could not leave her anchorage until April 1944.

The SAS Attack on Pebble Island

In the Falklands War, three SAS squadrons were deployed each with their own mission. After the British airstrikes on the Argentinean airbase at Port Stanley Argentinean air forces had to disperse to Pebble Island. However, close to Pebble Island lay San Carlos, the intended landing site of the main British ground forces, the planes there included the FMA IA 58 Pucara ground attack aircraft that could devastate the British landings, this threat had to be removed and the job fell to D squadron. However, there was little intelligence on the island. Whatever intelligence was there came from the high speed overflights by British fighters. Hence, a small reconnaissance team was inserted to a land mass opposite Pebble Island by rigid raider. The team then covertly canoed the rest of the way and set up an OP close to the land strip, from there they could see eleven un-camouflaged Pucara and approximately two-hundred men. A subsequent attack by 45 heavily laden SAS men destroyed the aircrafts though there was no opposition from the other side—the air strip had only one sentry!

The SEAL Rescue of Hostages in Somalia

On, January 25, 2012 US Special Operations forces, including members of SEAL Team 6, rescued two hostages who had been kidnapped and held for ransom by Somali kidnappers since October, 2011. The hostages, Poul Thisted, a Dane, and Jessica Buchanan, an American relief worker, were not harmed. Nine kidnappers were killed in the raid and five injured; no American personnel were injured or killed. The kidnappers were not believed to have ties to al-Shabab, the Somali militant group linked to al-Qaeda, or to have been pirates. US officials believe they were interested in receiving ransom for the two Western prisoners.

The pre-dawn raid was carried out by US military helicopters and Navy SEALs operating out of an American base in the tiny East African nation of Djibouti. The operation took place after 2 a.m. local time and lasted about 15 minutes. The SEALs, with other members of the US military, parachuted into Somalia about two miles from where the hostages were being held, walked to the location, and freed the hostages. They were picked up by helicopters, which brought them to the nearby town of Galkayo, where they flew out on a military plane.

(11.2) Insertion

The most dangerous thing in the world is a young officer with a map and a compass.

(11.2.1) *Speed, Intelligence, and Deception*

Insertion is the entrance of a commando force into a hostile area to execute a particular mission. It is the first critical phase of a commando operation. These operations often involve deep penetrations of enemy territory by air, water, or land.

Speed of action is of paramount importance in covert operations. The operation must be conducted swiftly, allowing the commando force to withdraw or get extracted before the enemy can react. One of the major problems facing commando units is the heavy loads carried by soldiers for long operations—after all, since they would not be supplied with anything after insertion, they must have resources to meet any eventuality. But carrying things for all possible eventualities will make the load unbearably heavy. A balance is struck by making three different types of loads: fighting, mission, and existence. The fighting load consists of those items of equipment, weapons, ammunition, food, and water that are common to all soldiers and are necessary for immediate use in combat. These items are normally carried and are retained at all times while in contact with the enemy. The mission load consists of those items of equipment or ammunition that are required by the mission, but are not normally carried by all commandos in a unit. The load may include spare batteries, demolitions, radios, anti-tank weapons, or mines. This load is normally spread out among members of the unit and is rotated often. It may be dropped upon enemy contact, but is normally carried to the objective and either used or emplaced there. The existence load consists of any items designed to provide protection from the elements: sleeping gear, changes of clothes, spare rations, or tentage. This load may or may not be brought into the objective area, depending on the tactical situation. If it is brought, it is normally dropped upon enemy contact or left in an assembly area and retrieved later.

Insertion plans must be based on timely and accurate intelligence. Fail in that and your men will get butchered. The emphasis must be on getting information on the enemy's ability to detect and engage the inserting forces. The type of intelligence needed varies depending on the specific mission, but normally must include the following:

- Current photographs from aerial or overhead reconnaissance.
- Detailed maps.
- Data on the population, terrain, and weather from area studies.
- Current enemy order of battle, enemy troop locations, and enemy capabilities.
- Details on the target area and infiltration routes.

There must always be plans to deny the enemy knowledge of the commando unit's insertion, or to deceive him as to the location or intent of the operation. Feints, false insertions, and other deception operations all add to commando deception plans. Selection of unexpected means, time, place, and routes of insertion, as well as use of speed and mobility, give less reaction time to the enemy. In a military context, planning may include the use of diversionary fires to direct the enemy's attention away from the inserting unit; in a counter-insurgency context, this may take the form of a publicised operation in some other area. In a military context they also use multiple airdrops, water landings, or both; landing a force in an area closer to other potential targets than to the actual targets; diversionary actions such as airstrikes in other than the target areas; and increased reconnaissance flights, either by manned aircraft or remotely piloted vehicles, over false targets. Options in counter-insurgency are rather limited and include leaks of false information and false messages through the media.

(11.2.2) Land Infiltration

Land infiltration to the objective in a military context is normal when the enemy has total air control or effective air defenses in the operational area to be penetrated, or when the objective is close to friendly territory. Commandos can infiltrate over any type of terrain, in any climate. However, thick forests, swamps, and broken or steep terrain offer the best chance for success. In a counter-insurgency context land insertion is possible but be advised that the insurgents may have an elaborate system of civilian spotters sympathetic to them all over the place.

You can try your luck by following the basics, namely, selecting concealed routes for surprise and protection; avoiding obstacles, populated areas, silhouetting (when forced to cross obstacles or ridge lines), enemy positions, main avenues of approach, and movement along often used routes and trails; and selecting the time of infiltration to make use of reduced visibility, such as darkness, rain, snow, and fog, and periods of reduced enemy alertness, such as early morning, holidays, and times following protracted movement or combat. You can further decide whether it will be safer for you to travel together or in small groups along several routes at the same time.

(11.2.3) *Types of Attack*

If you survive the extraordinary things, it will often be the little things that will kill you.

A successful attack depends on concentrating the maximum possible shock and violence against the enemy force. You must combine shock and violence with surprise. The objective is to shatter the enemy's nerve, ruin his synchronisation, unravel his plan, and destroy his unit's cohesion and the willingness of his soldiers to fight. A successful attack combines a scheme of manoeuvre with a coordinated plan of direct and indirect fire support. The focus of an attacking unit's fire and manoeuvre is a weak point, a vulnerable flank, or the rear of an enemy. Once he has identified the point of attack, the leader establishes a base of fire to kill, fix, or suppress the enemy at that point. He then manoeuvres the rest of his force to a position from which it can assault.

- **Hasty attack:** A hasty attack is conducted with the forces immediately available to maintain momentum or to take advantage of the enemy situation. It does not normally allow for extensive preparation.
- **Deliberate attack:** A deliberate attack is carefully planned and coordinated. More time is available to perform thorough reconnaissance, evaluation of all available intelligence and relative combat strength, analysis of various courses of action, and other factors affecting the situation. It is generally conducted

against a well-organised defence when a hasty attack is not possible or has been conducted and failed.

- **Raid:** A raid is an operation involving a swift penetration of hostile territory to secure information, to confuse the enemy, or to destroy his installations. It ends with a planned withdrawal after completion of the assigned mission.
- **Ambush:** An ambush is a surprise attack by fire from concealed positions on a moving or temporarily halted enemy unit. It combines the advantages and characteristics of the offence with those of the defence.

We are more interested in raids. A raid normally involves a swift penetration of hostile territory to confuse the enemy or destroy his installations. Commando units can conduct deep penetration raids when given the appropriate assets for insertion. In a military context it is a strike operation conducted behind enemy lines against strategic objectives, targets of high tactical value, time-sensitive targets, or key personnel and facilities in enemy rear areas. In the context of counter-insurgency operations, however, they must think the destruction of which hurts them bad. For example, the guerrillas could have an arms factory somewhere, or may be some dump of arms and ammunition—destroying them would hurt them. The size of the commando raid force is determined by a detailed analysis of METT-TC (Mission, Enemy, Terrain & Weather, Troops, Time Available and Civil Considerations). The force must be tailored to complete the mission quickly, violently, and with few casualties. Raids are normally conducted in five phases.

Phase 1: The commando force inserts or infiltrates into the objective area.

Phase 2: The objective area is then sealed off from outside support or reinforcement, to include the enemy air threat.

Phase 3: Any enemy force at or near the objective is overcome by surprise and violent attack, using all available firepower for shock effect.

Phase 4: The mission is accomplished quickly before any surviving enemy can recover or be reinforced.

Phase 5: The commando force quickly withdraws from the objective area and is extracted.

(11.2.4) Timing of the Attack

An early morning attack is usually preferable, as it allows more daylight for consolidation and exploitation, although advantage car sometimes be taken of bright moonlight. The best time to attack will depend on the enemy routine, but it is likely to be either:

- Before the enemy 'stand to' at dawn.
- After dawn when they have stood down, and
- Mid-afternoon in the heat of the day when they may be resting.

As night movement is slow, tiring, noisy, and difficult to control, a dawn or night attack will usually entail deployment before last light.

Attacks During Limited Visibility: Attacks during limited visibility achieve surprise, avoid heavy losses, cause panic in a weak and disorganised enemy, exploit success, maintain momentum, and keep pressure on the enemy. Platoons and squads attack whenever possible during limited visibility. Darkness, fog, heavy rain, falling snow, and the smoke and dust of combat create limited visibility conditions that allow infantry platoons and squads to move undetected. When planning attacks under limited visibility conditions, you must consider the increased difficulty with regard to:

- Controlling the movement of individuals and squads.
- Identifying targets and controlling direct and indirect fires.
- Navigating and moving.
- Identifying friendly and enemy soldiers.
- Locating, treating, and evacuating casualties.
- Locating and bypassing or breaching enemy obstacles.

(11.3) Yalghar Ho—The Assault

If you can think clearly, know exactly what's happening, and have total control of a situation in combat, then you're obviously not in combat.

The following elements are required in the assault force:

Assault Groups: These are required to carry out the assault. Enough groups are needed to enable a fresh one to be inserted at each phase of the assault, so that they can pass through each other and hold the ground won until the position has been fought right through and all resistance has been eliminated.

Fire Groups: These are needed to provide close support, usually with machine-guns, light anti-tank weapons and medium anti-tank weapons (LAW/MAW), to each assault phase in turn: there may therefore need to be several fire groups for one attack.

Now pay attention: All your life you must be hearing that the troops must go and 'hit' the enemy. Nobody ever told you how exactly to do it. What is meant by 'hitting'? What do you do when you approach an enemy location? How do you attack him? Do you simply fire on full auto or do something sensible? You have not been told the minor details because they never knew in the first place—the officers have a bad tendency of leaving it to the 'boys' because it is considered infra dig for the officers to even know this, not to speak of doing this—a very clever way of concealing their ignorance. The poor 'boys' have no idea of what to do in any case and they fall back on their commonsense, natural reactions or what they have seen in war movies. That's why casualties occur and everybody tries to cover them up in so many ways. These are the things that you will learn now. *The basic idea is that no one attacks or engages any enemy single-handedly.* Learn to differentiate between bravery and foolhardiness. Fighting battles is teamwork—if you are very keen on individual glory, go into combat sports instead. *One team pins down the enemy with aimed fire or distracts his attention from a position of relative safety at a distance. Under the cover of this distraction, the other team tries to close in and finish the enemy.* How exactly you finish him, depends on what sort of defences he has.

Start lines for fire and assault groups should be as near right angles to each other and as close to the objective as is possible without the attacking troops becoming casualties from supporting fire.

At H-hour, or a clear signal to attack, the fire group should dash forward to their fire positions and engage the enemy with heavy, aimed fire. At the same moment, the first assault group must attack its objective.

Once the main assault has succeeded, fire and breaching groups should assist assault groups to mop up and clear their objectives. Assault groups must hold their objectives until the whole position is cleared to prevent enemy slipping back into cleared areas or escaping by way of tunnels.

Remember, defeating a defensive fighting position that has been built in the manner discussed in this book is a difficult proposition. The earlier method was to lob a grenade or fire a rifle grenade when small arms fire did not work. But grenades lose their effectiveness if there is adequate overhead and rear protection to the position. Then it can be tackled only by a weapon like the M72 LAW. If you have that, do fire it. If you do not have it, you may think of something riskier. One man will engage the sentry by aimed fire so that his attention is occupied by him. While the sentry is thus distracted, another man can try sneaking to his position and planting a charge to reduce the position. The German commandos had done precisely this when they had attacked the Belgian bridges and the fort Eben-Émael.

When an operation is over, the jungle is ideal for breaking contact and carrying our rearguard actions with small bodies of resolute men who can inflict serious delay on a force many times their size. The timing of the withdrawal is, as always, important. Prolonged occupation of a defended area may lead to encirclement and while this may on occasions be acceptable, it will merely present unnecessary difficulties unless it makes a positive contribution to the success of the overall mission.

(11.4) The Myth of the Snipers in Offensive Role

There is nothing more satisfying that having someone take a shot at you, and miss.

I am very well aware of how snipers have been exalted in popular folklore and fiction. Some of it gets percolated in training manuals also. Have an example: "The primary mission of a sniper in combat is to support combat operations by delivering precise long range fire on selected targets. By this, the sniper creates casualties among enemy troops, slow enemy movement, frightens enemy soldiers, lowers morale and adds confusion to their operations...A sniper enhances a unit's firepower and augments the varied means for destruction and harassment of the enemy. His role becomes more significant when the target is entrenched or positioned among civilian or automatic weapons. Such operations can sedulity in the wounding or killing of non-combatants". It's all bullshit. The question is where the hell you get such situations in counter-insurgency? My lord, these are not the plain battlefields of Europe or the rolling hills of Ireland. In a jungle; most of the time the foliage and the terrain would not allow you the luxury of a clear line-of-sight for a distance at which sniper fire could be used profitably. Are you going to use a sniper rifle for taking a shot at 200 yards? In other words, you would have very few opportunities to use the snipers on the insurgent.

Do not be taken in by what you see in Discovery Channel programmes. Snipers do not win wars; they haven't won either. Many of the programmes they show on the Discovery Channel are sponsored by the companies concerned or are made to showcase certain units. Americans love to perpetuate myths of their invincibility. Somebody should ask them the combat record of snipers—what exactly they have accomplished in numerous wars? There are some fundamental issues with respect to utilising snipers in an offensive role in counter-insurgency operations.

- Most of your operations would be night operations whereas snipers work best in daylight only. The US Army FM 23-10 also admits that their AN/PVS-4 sight does not give the width, depth, or clarity of daylight vision; however, a well-trained operator can see enough to analyse the tactical situation, to detect enemy targets, and to place effective fire on them.

- In the sort of operations you would undertake in counter-insurgency, a sniper shot at a distance much before the rest of the team can get into the serious business of shooting, will make the assault party lose the element of surprise much before it makes contact with the enemy.
- Snipers are supposed to shoot high value targets. In a military situation, it is easy to identify a high-ranking officer from his uniform, accoutrements, vehicle or quarters. How the hell do you identify an insurgent leader from a cadre when all of them look equally impoverished?
- A sniper means one man less with an automatic rifle. You cannot afford to lose more firepower with more than one person not having the regular weapon. Hence, if at all you have a sniper team, the spotter will have to carry his regular weapon.

If at all there is a situation where the use of sniper is warranted, the most important equipments I would like them to carry are:

- A 7x50 binocular for first sweeping the area visually. Any higher magnification will defeat the purpose. Once you have a particular area located and identified, it is time to bring in the professional thing.
- An observation telescope (a prismatic optical instrument) of 20-power magnification. Its high magnification makes observation, target detection, and target identification possible where conditions and range would otherwise preclude this ability. Camouflaged targets and those in deep shadows can be more readily distinguished. The team can observe troop movements at greater distances and identify selective targets with ease.
- A sling of the type of US Army's M1907 rifle sling—so that it steadies the aim by wrapping the sling around the non-firing arm in such a way that when the sniper assumes his shooting position, the sling tightens and actually works like a rifle rest to steady the weapon.

Using the US Army's M1907 Rifle Sling to steady the support arm

It is beyond the scope of this book to discuss the training of a sniper and his equipment. Standard texts are available for that. Do not be taken in by fancy items like the Ghillie suit in counter-insurgency operations. It is pure bullshit. Leave it to the stupid Americans. You guys are not going to be static waiting patiently for some high value target to manifest itself after hours—jungle warfare is highly dynamic and mobile—the enemy is not holding a position ready to give battle. He is fleeing half the time and you would be lucky if you get just a glimpse of him. In counter-insurgency, you would not let the sniper team alone. They have to be with the rest of the team and walk with them. A Ghillie suit is inadvisable because it is: unbearably hot; is inconvenient to wear in many weathers, particularly summers; is unwieldy; at many places, not likely to merge with the background, thereby defeating the very purpose of wearing it; the man wearing it can't march with other men; adds bulk to the luggage on back even though it is not heavy; and has a bad tendency of snagging in the bushes and thorns.

Leave the Monstrosity of the Ghillie Suit for exceptional situations demanding its use

(11.4) Counter-Sniper or Sniper Defeat

If you can see the flashes from the enemies' guns in battle, he can see yours too.

(11.4.1) Why Snipers are Valuable to an Insurgent?

On the other hand, do not forget that in counter-insurgency, the enemy can very well use snipers on you because you are big, ponderous, more easily identifiable, and have camps—in other words, you present big, easily identifiable targets. Sniper operations have the same effect in insurgencies as they do in conventional warfare, but the purpose is different. For example, in conventional warfare, a sniper targets leaders in order to cause confusion on the battlefield and disrupt operations. In an insurgency, a sniper will still target leaders, but more for use in propaganda that can be used after a successful attack. Additionally, he can help create and foster a notion that the area of his operations is not secure and the government is powerless to stop him.

The first step in countering snipers is to be aware of the sniper threat. Plans to counter the sniper threat and protect friendly forces from snipers must be integrated into all counterinsurgent operations during the early stages of planning. Enemy snipers in a counter-insurgency environment may vary from well-trained sniper teams to individuals taking shots of opportunity.

There are three types of snipers an insurgent can employ. The lowest is the one who is simply taking shots of opportunity. He may be a good shot but what matters is the opportunity—the damage they might cause is not really significant. Guys of this type have been able to make headlines by taking shots at objects that carry high publicity value—such as helicopters and motorcades of political leaders or senior officers. The second category is a trained marksman. He may have a regular rifle only but he might cause some significant damage. The most dangerous is the specially-trained sniper who is likely to have a proper sniper rifle. He may select his targets with care and could spring some nasty surprises. Identifying the type that is more likely to be found in the field can aid a commander in deciding what countermeasure to use. Since the sniper has the initiative, leaders must enforce strict compliance of the counter-measures. Implementing counter-measures half-heartedly invites casualties from snipers, who can wait hours for the moment when a unit's guard is down.

(11.4.2) Active Counter-measures Against Snipers

Active counter-measures seek to detect and destroy the sniper before he can fire, or engage and neutralise him after he fires.

Observation Posts and Observers: Observation posts should have access to powerful spotting telescopes, medium power binoculars, night observation devices (thermal, if possible), and remote control closed circuit cameras. Additionally, laser countermeasure should be employed, such as laser protective glasses, binoculars with laser filters, and indirect-view optics to protect observers. Additionally, many electronic detection devices are available to aid in the detection of snipers such as acoustic devices. Once detected, snipers can then be neutralised or forced to withdraw. Observers can maintain a constant surveillance over potential sniper positions and detect snipers as they attempt to move into position for a shot. Constantly scanning an area for the minute movements made by a well-trained sniper is exhausting. Therefore, personnel on static OP duty should rotate frequently. Unmanned Aerial Systems (UAS) and rotary wing aircraft should be integrated into an OP plan to give it depth.

Patrols: Constant reconnaissance and security patrols around a unit's position hinder a sniper from getting into a firing position undetected. Small patrols are usually more effective than large ones. A moving sniper who has been discovered by a patrol is at a great disadvantage since he lacks the firepower to fight a long engagement. Small night reconnaissance patrols using night vision devices can be very effective in disrupting and interdicting a sniper. Reconnaissance patrols should move by covered and concealed routes to good observation points; should stop and observe; and then should move to another position. The patrol routes and times must vary, and a reaction force or supporting weapons must be ready if the patrol makes contact. A variation of the ambush patrol is the stay-behind ambush. A small ambush element moves as part of a larger patrol and occupies its position without being observed. It then observes its kill zone, which may be very large if the element has a sniper team with it, and engages enemy snipers as they attempt to move into position.

Your Own Sniper Teams: Your own sniper teams can be a very effective counter to enemy snipers. Not only do they have expert knowledge of sniping and likely enemy hiding places, they can normally engage enemy snipers or marksmen at a greater range than the enemy sniper can engage you. Their precision fires are also much less likely to cause civilian casualties than dozens of rounds from other weapons.

Return Fire and Manoeuvre: If a unit can determine the general location of a sniper, it should return suppressive fire while manoeuvring to engage the sniper from close range. But note that this is not always successful because a well-trained sniper often has a route of withdrawal already chosen. Fire without manoeuvre will not be successful in defeating snipers.

Obscurants: Projected smoke that builds quickly is a good response to protect a unit from further casualties if engaged by an enemy sniper. It greatly limits his ability to acquire targets. The closer the smoke is placed to the sniper's location, the more effective it is. If the location of the sniper is unknown or cannot be reached by projected smoke, a smoke cloud established near the unit can be effective in reducing the sniper's chances of hitting a target and allowing a unit to conduct first aid and Casevac.

(11.4.3) *Passive Counter-measures Against Snipers*

Passive counter-measures prevent the sniper from acquiring a clear target and prevent his fires from causing casualties. Passive counter-sniper measures are rarely successful by themselves. If passive measures are the only measures enacted, they may also create a siege mentality and pass the initiative over to the sniper. They include:

Limiting Sniper Exposure: If soldiers limit their sniper exposure, they can marginalise snipers operations. Some examples include using covered and concealed routes, avoiding lighted areas at night, moving tactically while using travelling or bounding overwatch, and staying away from doors and windows.

Wearing Protective Equipment: Other sniper protective measures include wearing of the Kevlar helmet, protective eyewear, and body armour systems. These should be worn any time soldiers are exposed to potential sniper fire. This decreases the snipers' casualty-producing target area, and which limits his effectiveness.

Using Armoured Vehicles: Whenever possible, move around in the urban area in a protected vehicle with as little exposure as possible. Avoid open-sided cargo vehicles. If it comes to that, one must use improvised vehicular armour against small-arms fire for all unarmoured vehicles.

Erecting Screens and Shields: Simple though it is, its effectiveness can never be underestimated. It is very useful for small camp location where you do not have proper boundary walls. If the enemy can see what you are doing inside barbed-wires and concertina, he can plan his attacks better or may be a sniper can take shots. A screen eliminates that possibility. Similarly, having a simple canvas or plastic screen makes a dangerous alleyway or street crossing safer for foot traffic. In vehicles, adapt screens on windows to allow vision out while hiding personnel inside. At vehicle checkpoints, use moveable concrete barriers to provide protection for personnel at static positions. You can also use common items, such as rubble-filled 55-gallon drums and sandbags, to provide cover.

Denying Enemy Use of Overwatching Terrain: Either occupy overwatching terrain with friendly forces, or modify it to make it less useful to an enemy sniper. Pull down likely hiding places. Clear bushes and rubble. Board or brick up windows. Pile up earth and rubble in front of buildings to block lines of sight for snipers.

(11.4.4) Counter-Sniper Technique

Counter-sniper actions have two parts: find and eliminate the sniper.

Find the Sniper: Once a unit determines it has a sniper or a sniper team in its AOR (area of responsibility), the unit should implement counter-sniper immediate action drills. Allowing the enemy sniper to fight another day is mission failure. First, the unit must find the sniper or the sniper team. Techniques for detecting a sniper consist of identifying likely sniper locations, focusing observation on sniper movement, and seeking audible and visual signs. Backtracking, which involves integrating the following techniques, is used to find the sniper:

Identify Likely Sniper Locations: A sniper is a line-of-sight asset. The larger the sniper kill zone, the closer or the higher he must position himself to cover it. Smaller sniper kill zones create for a narrow, if not linear, line of sight. In such cases, the sniper will always choose a position that offers that offers a line of sight, such as a road or alley, or maybe inside a building, shooting through a window, doorway, or other opening.

Focus Observation on Sniper Movement: Snipers always plan infiltration and exfiltration routes. After identifying possible sniper locations, a unit commander can focus observation on these routes and deny a sniper the ability to reposition. Snipers operate slowly, with calculated movements, to avoid detection. The movement the sniper makes may not be easily detected. Units should look for movement that does not "fit" the environment.

Seek Audible/Visible Signs: Audible/visual indicators help find snipers based on the sniper's firing a shot. Actually, firing a weapon is a sniper's greatest moment of risk; it offers the best opportunity to locate him or his team. The acoustic, light and heat signatures associated with the projection of the bullet from his rifle are his greatest vulnerabilities. The muzzle flash can be detected with infra-red sensors out to a kilometer. Often the muzzle flash and the blast can throw dust into the air. Acoustic sensors can detect a muzzle blast from several hundred meters to more than a kilometer. The bullet's shock wave is a mini-sonic boom. This noise, caused by the bullet travelling faster than the speed of sound, can sometimes be heard more than a kilometer away.

Backtrack Sounds, Sights, and Angles: It is not so difficult in a jungle provided there are not hills around to produce echoes. In an urban area, the backtracking process is complicated by buildings that obstruct the view of the sniper's position. Backtracking is challenging, but it is how you relate shot angles, kill zones, movement, and audible and visible signs to help you find the sniper. Experience and training play a major role in accurate backtracking.

Eliminate Sniper: Once spotted, the enemy sniper must be killed or forced to surrender. To be successful in this goal, the unit must rapidly locate, fix, and finish an active enemy sniper to ultimately kill or capture him.

Avoid the Kill Zone: Figure out his kill zone and stay out of it. A unit may also want to eliminate or at least reduce his targets. If a unit removes its targets, the unit curtails mission success; the sniper will need to move, or at least adjust his position, to remain effective.

Manoeuvre Rapidly: When contact is made, the on-scene commander needs to rapidly calculate the disposition of his forces, the quick reaction force (QRF), and adjacent friendly forces and factor in time/space considerations to determine how to neutralise the threat. Because of the fleeting nature of the sniper, it is often preferable for the on-scene commander to begin to manoeuvre against the hostile sniper with an unengaged portion of his own force rather than wait for a QRF.

Consider Sniper Hunting with Another Sniper: Throughout history, many units engaged in urban combat often employed direct and indirect supporting arms, close air support, or large numbers of ground forces to counter urban snipers. However, the Russian and German forces of World War II found that the best solution to a sniper threat was the employment of their own snipers in a counter-sniper role. Advantages to using a trained sniper to counter enemy snipers include:

- The relative ease of movement over the urban battlefield of a sniper team versus that of a larger ground formation;
- Counter-snipers who "know the habits and modus operandi" of their enemy counterparts; and
- The ability to deliver "precision fire" and the resulting reduction in collateral damage or civilian and friendly casualties.

Confirm that Enemy Sniper is Neutralised: In this context, neutralisation means that the sniper is killed or captured. A dead or captured enemy sniper, besides ending that threat, can be a valuable source of intelligence.

12

Beware of Fancy Stuff

Senior officers think they're businessmen. They think the principles used in business, like "corporate vision" and "TQM (total quality management)" can work in the army. This is because officers spend a lot of time trying to sell things, usually grand ideas and catchy names.

(12.1) The Follies and Foibles of Small Team Operations

The further away you are from your friends, the less likely it is that they can help you when you really need them the most.

(12.1.1) 'American Beauty' Fights for its Life

Small team operations or solo operations like those of Rambo are stuff for Hollywood films. Real life is both different and difficult. In real life, small teams get butchered. When America first landed on the moon in July 1969, the whole world knew about it. But in June in Vietnam, when a US Marine Corps reconnaissance patrol code-named "American Beauty" fought for its life, nobody learnt about it till Jeffrey Grosscup described the horrors of small team operations.

"An order had come down from division headquarters to have reconnaissance teams inserted into the DMZ to confirm enemy presence there. It was already known that there was an NVA battalion there, and the reconnaissance commander, a lieutenant colonel, refused the order, realising that to drop lightly armed teams in the middle of it would be suicidal. That battalion commander was replaced by another who carried out the order...The team went in early on June 6, 1969 with orders to patrol an area four kilometers square. After a 35-minute helicopter flight from Quang Tri in northern I Corps, 'American Beauty' was dropped on the same hilltop they would later fight on with every bit of firepower they had to save themselves. To allow the helicopter landing, American jets had blown away the hilltop foliage, and it was still smoldering when the team went in.

The NVA had to have seen the helicopter insertion...The patrol spent the second night on a mountain precipice to minimise its exposure. "I had my feet wrapped around a tree so I wouldn't roll off when I was sleeping", said a soldier Lake. "We had movement 20 meters from where we were". "Were we watching them or they watching us? I don't know", said Sessums...At about 1630 they stopped to eat, hoping to receive word that they were to be pulled out. They were sitting slightly off a trail with the men back-to-back, observing, listening and ready to eat. "As I looked in the direction we were headed, I saw two jungle hats coming down the trail. They were only 15 meters away. I shot four rounds and the whole team opened up. We killed one and wounded the other".

Having secured the POW, however, they were radioed their orders to get to the landing zone. A Marine observation aircraft was in the area, and the pilot monitored the team's frequency. He radioed, "Be advised you are being attacked from the west". By this time there were fixed-wing aircraft overhead, and the area was raked with bombs. "This hilltop was only 30 yards wide and 20 across. We didn't expect anything could survive the bombing". The team moved out with the hilltop as its objective when the NVA positions exploded with automatic-weapons fire. What followed was little short of butchery.

"As the choppers approached we were ready to make our run", said Lake. "But as they came to hover, the NVA opened up and forced them off". As darkness fell, the team had been able to crawl together behind some fallen trees where they could take cover. "The NVA didn't know where we were", said Lake, "and they didn't come out of their holes to look. Nothing moved". "We carried a strobe light", said See. "I put it in a hat and threw it away from us...the NVA tossed a bunch of chicoms at it. We took a compass reading to the strobe light to mark our position and gave it to the pilot. His machineguns started smoking".

Against orders—First Lt Frank Cuddy came in for the extraction (later awarded the Distinguished Flying Cross). An illumination flare was dropped, and the team was told to be ready. "I was no more than three, four feet off the ground", said Cuddy, "when all of a sudden 15 to 20 NVA were out of their holes firing at us. We were blinded by the muzzle flashes. One came right out of the A-frame and was face to face with me, firing. I stuck my M-16 out the helicopter and emptied a magazine on full automatic". They had to break off the rescue attempt. Eventually Marine units rescued them from the ground. There was no man without an injury".

(12.1.2) *Considerations of METT-TC must decide the Strength of the Group, not Someone's notions of Bravado*

Decisions made by someone over your head will seldom be in your best interest.

The strength of the team for an operation must be decided only on the basis of METT-TC.

(1) **Mission:** The leader considers his mission as given to him by his commander. He analyses it in light of the commander's intent two command levels higher, and derives the essential tasks his unit must perform in order to accomplish the mission.

(2) **Enemy:** The leader considers the type, size, organisation, tactics, and equipment of the enemy he expects to encounter. He identifies their greatest threat to his mission find their greatest vulnerability.

(3) **Terrain:** The leader considers the effect of terrain and weather on enemy and friendly forces using the guidelines below (OCOKA):

(a) **Observation and fields of fire:** The leader considers ground that allows him observation of the enemy throughout his area of operation. He considers fields of fire in terms of the characteristics of the weapons available to him; for example, maximum effective range, the requirement for grazing fire, and the arming range and time of flight for anti-armour weapons.

(b) **Cover and concealment:** The leader looks for terrain that will protect him from direct and indirect fires (cover) and from aerial and ground observation (concealment).

(c) **Obstacles:** In the attack, the leader considers the effect of restrictive terrain on his ability to manoeuvre. In the defence, he considers how he will tie in his obstacles to the terrain to disrupt, turn, fix, or block an enemy force and protect his own forces from enemy assault.

(d) **Key terrain:** Key terrain is any locality or area whose seizure or retention affords a marked advantage to either combatant. The leader considers key terrain in his selection of objectives, support positions, and routes in the offence, and on the positioning of his unit in the defence.

(e) **Avenues of approach:** An avenue of approach is an air or ground route of an attacking force of a given size leading to its objective or key terrain in its path. In the offence, the leader identifies the avenue of approach that affords him the greatest protection and places him at the enemy's most vulnerable spot. In the defence, the leader positions his key weapons along the avenue of approach most likely to be used by the enemy.

(f) **Weather:** In considering the effects of weather, the leader is most interested in visibility and trafficability.

(4) **Troops available:** The leader considers the strength of subordinate units, the characteristics of his weapon systems, and the capabilities of attached elements as he assigns tasks to subordinate units.

(5) **Time available:** The leader refines his allocation of time-based on the tentative plan and any changes to the situation.

(6) **Civil Considerations:** Civil considerations relate to civilian populations, culture, organisations, and political leaders within the area of operation. You must take into account civilian political, economic, and information matters as well as more immediate civilian activities and attitudes in all operations directly or indirectly affecting civilian populations. This is particularly important in counter-insurgency operations because you would be operating amidst civilian populations and there is nothing called war zone. Be extremely wary of civilian collateral damage.

The Indians, in particular, suffer from a great psychological handicap in this regard. Throughout their history and even mythology, they have always idolised warriors who would fight alone. A '*maharathi*' in mythology was a warrior on a chariot who could fight single-handedly with 10000 infantrymen. In the course of history also, they always eulogised warriors and warrior kings who were great swordsmen and perhaps very good in one-on-one duels—the downside was that they neither valued generalship nor learnt to excel as commanders of armies. Precisely for that reason, vast Hindu armies were regularly defeated by all sorts of invaders with relatively smaller armies. For details, readers may refer to '*The Decisive Battles of Indian History*' by Dr Anjali Nirmal.

Due to this sub-conscious hangover, the Indians still dream of great commandos who could be infiltrated into the enemy territory for weeks at a stretch and where they would wreak havoc by their raids. Sheer day-dreaming! Poor buggers never understand that a clever enemy does not have to engage their mythical super-commandos into a frontal battle and discover, to his pain, that man-to-man the commandos are better fighters. Well, they could be but once the enemy finds out that the commandos are in the jungle without any rear support, he has only to engage them in a battle of attrition. All he has to do is to depute four-five guys to engage the commandos by subjecting them to harassing fire form a safe distance from more than one direction. The commandos have no means of finding out the exact strength of the enemy or take the risk of not returning fire adequately—if they do, they face the additional risk of the enemy inching closer. As a result, the commandos will have to use heavy firepower. This will make them expend their precious ammunition. Their perils in the jungle will increase exponentially as they spend their ammunition. Eventually, they will run out of ammunition and will be butchered. A small team would survive only as long as it remained absolutely undetected.

(12.2) An Examination of the Concept of Hunter-killer Teams

Medals are OK, but having your body and all your friends in one piece at the end of the day is infinitely better.

(12.2.1) *The Philosophy of Division of Jobs*

Conceptually, it is a simple division of labour or jobs where a particular task is assigned to one, who is specially suited for the job. Why such an arrangement was needed or evolved? The basic reason is that it minimises the amount of movement carried out by the larger and more conspicuous fire-superiority element. The movement of a larger body could make it vulnerable. The reconnaissance element can better employ stealth and concealment as it searches out targets for the fire superiority element to destroy. The underlying philosophy is that your more valuable asset must not be committed to battle from the very beginning. Generals have always sought to save the valuable for the really critical hour whether to deliver the coup d'grace, the finishing stroke, or to make a last-ditch effort to save the day. Militaries throughout the course of history have followed this concept. The overriding concern was always to save the more valuable asset till it became inevitable to use it. The king saved his favourite son till the very last even if he was a great warrior—if the battle could be managed by lesser warriors, why risk the best warrior in the beginning itself.

Since the Greco-Roman era itself, European armies have had the concept of two types of infantry. Traditionally, light infantry (or skirmishers) were soldiers whose job was to provide a skirmishing screen ahead of the main body of infantry, harassing and delaying the enemy advance. Light infantry was distinct from medium, heavy or line infantry. Heavy infantry were dedicated primarily to fighting in tight formations that were the core of large battles. Heavy infantry originally had heavier arms and more armour than light infantry. Greek light infantry was called *peltast* and the heavy infantry was called *hoplites. Velites* were the Roman light infantry, and the hastati, principes, and *triarii* were their heavy infantry.

The same concept applied to cavalry also and thus you had light cavalry and heavy cavalry. The missions of the light cavalry were primarily reconnaissance, screening, skirmishing, raiding, and most importantly, communications, and were usually armed with spears, swords, bows and later pistols. Light cavalry was popular among the armies and hordes of Central Asia and Southwest Asia. The Arabs, Hungarians, Huns, Mongols, Turks, Parthians, and Persians were all adept light cavalrymen and horse archers. European examples of light cavalry included stradiots, hobelars, hussars, uhlan, chasseurs à cheval, cossacks, chevau-légers and some dragoons. The primary role of the heavy cavalry was to engage in direct combat with enemy forces (that is, as shock troops). They were generally mounted on large powerful horses, and were often equipped with some form of scale, plated, chainmail or lamellar armour as well as either swords, maces, lances, or battle axes. The knights dominated the Middle Ages. Heavy cavalry of the later era included the Gendarme, and the cuirassier. Cuirassiers played a prominent role in the armies of Frederick the Great of Prussia and of Napoleon I of France.

The latter increased the number of French cuirassier regiments to fourteen by the end of his reign, although they gradually declined in importance as the firepower and accuracy of the muskets and rifles of the infantrymen increased. The cavalry still remained battle-deciders though, with Napoleon maintaining several reserve cavalry corps to be employed at the decisive moment in battle to finally break the enemy formations with a devastating charge.

Light infantry sometimes carried lighter muskets than ordinary infantrymen while others carried rifles and wore rifle green uniforms. These became designated as 'rifle regiments' in Britain and Jäger (hunter) regiments in German speaking Europe. In France, during the Napoleonic Wars, light infantry were called voltigeurs. In Portugal, 1797, companies of "Caçadores" (hunters) were created in the Portuguese Army. The Austrian army had Grenzer regiments from the middle of the 18th century, who originally served as irregular militia skirmishers recruited from mountainous frontier areas.

Cynics might argue that it was cruel in the sense that the lesser warriors were thus used as cannon fodder, so to speak—but the counter-argument is that after all, why do you have the lesser warriors in the army, if not for this? Battles were not supposed to be tournaments between the best warriors of the opposing sides. No nation, in the history of the world, sought to settle its disputes by a wrestling, boxing or fencing match between its champion and the champion of the enemy. In a battle you sought to erode the total military potential of the adversary with larger goals in mind. For that, some erosion of the adversary's total fighting ability had to take place. The total fighting ability of a nation was not confined to its best warriors only. You had to kill soldiers, destroy fortifications, burn crops, rage villages and so on.

(12.2.2) *What are Hunter-killer Teams?*

A hunter-killer team is one that separates the tasks of finding targets and attacking them, for handling by separate components of a team or by two different teams. Theoretically, even two individuals can divide the jobs between them. Modern examples of the hunter-killer concept in various spheres of combat include:

- In the context of snipers, two-person sniper teams, one using specialised optical hardware to spot the target as 'hunter' and the other a rifle to actually shoot as the 'killer'.
- In the context of aircrafts, they use pairs of F-4G "Wild Weasels" and F-16Cs aircrafts, where the F-4G "hunters" detect, identify, and locate targets such as radars and then direct the F-16C's weapons to the site.
- In the context of armoured vehicles and tanks in particular, M2/ M3 Bradley Fighting Vehicles work as scouts or 'hunters' and the M1 Abrams main battle tanks act as the 'killers'.
- In the context of helicopters, the OH-6 "Loach" or OH-58 Kiowa act as scouts or 'hunter' and the AH-1 Cobra attack helicopters act as 'killers'.
- In anti-submarine warfare an ASW aircraft may be employed as 'hunter', with surface ships such as destroyers act as 'killers'.

In all these examples, the common thread is that the relatively 'cheaper' 'hunter' element 'locates' a suitable target for the main 'costly' 'killer' element. In other words, the hunter element 'prepares the ground' for the killer element. In general terms, the hunter-killer concept refers to a set of tactics that involve a small reconnaissance element working in concert with a large fire-superiority element. The reconnaissance element searches out targets while the fire-superiority element lies in wait and is called forward for the kill when the reconnaissance element has positively located the target. The idea is that the 'killer' element which is costly and carries more destructive power should not be exposed to battle before the ground is suitably prepared.

The main battle tanks, for example, are very costly pieces of equipment—millions of dollars apiece. And yet a lucky shot from an anti-tank weapon like the RPG costing a few hundred dollars could disable it. An ATGM costing in some thousands could destroy it completely. Obviously, you cannot send the tank the first thing in the battlefield where some infantryman could take a pot shot at it. A main battle tank must fight a worthy opponent—it must destroy other main battle tanks of the enemy. What do you do? You send another vehicle for reconnaissance or spotting the target. That this vehicle must be more agile and smaller, etc. are insignificant things. The significant thing is that it must be 'expendable' if need be. It should not be so costly that you regret its loss. But it should not be too vulnerable either—hence you settle on a Bradley Fighting Vehicle or a Russian BMP which have respectable armour and weapons like the 25 mm cannon, TOW anti-tank missiles and 7.62 mm machineguns.

So is the case with aircrafts. Modern fighter planes are prohibitively costly. You cannot risk them in battle straightaway. They must engage only those targets which are worthy of them. Hence, you send in a relatively cheaper aircraft to do the spotting and reconnaissance. You send in the main fighter only for the kill.

In the context of submarines, you do not want to commit your ballistic missile nuclear submarines for anything other than launching nuclear-tipped missiles and you cannot expect the ponderous machines to waste their energies in protecting themselves either. Hence, the main job of warfare with submarines falls on the so-called hunter-killer submarines. They are designed to pursue and attack enemy submarines and surface ships using torpedoes—this serves the purpose of both offence and defence. They are also able to carry "cruise" missiles for use against shore-based targets. This type of submarine is used to conduct surveillance and for intelligence gathering tasks also.

In the context of anti-submarine warfare in the WWII, it was argued that it was difficult to protect merchant convoys from submarines if the protecting ships were moving along with the convoys. It was found more profitable to make them move ahead and search for the submarines.

Great studies have been conducted regarding the Russian experience in Chechnya in 1994. The Chechen lower-level combat group consisted of 15 to 20 personnel sub-divided into three or four-man fighting cells. These cells consisted of an anti-tank gunner (normally armed with the RPG-7 or RPG-18 shoulder-fired anti-tank rocket launcher), a machine gunner and a sniper. Additional personnel served as ammunition bearers and assistant gunners. Chechen combat groups would deploy these cells as anti-armour hunter-killer teams. The job of the sniper and machine gunner was to pin down the infantry which customarily accompanied the armoured vehicles while the anti-tank gunner would engage the armoured target. Teams deployed at ground level, in second and third stories, and in basements. The reason was that the elevation and depression of the Russian main tank guns were incapable of dealing with hunter-killer teams fighting from basements and second or third-storey positions. Normally, five or six hunter-killer teams simultaneously attack a single armoured vehicle greatly reducing the effectiveness of the tank's machineguns. Kill shots were generally made against the top, rear and sides of vehicles. Chechens also dropped Molotov Cocktails on top of vehicles. The Chechen hunter-killer teams tried to trap vehicle columns in city streets where destruction of the first and last vehicles would trap the column and allow its total destruction.

In response, the Russians attached ZSU 23-4 and 2S6 track-mounted anti-aircraft guns to armoured columns to respond to these difficult-to-engage hunter-killer teams. After considerable losses, the Russians began establishing ambushes on approach routes into a selected area and then running vehicles into the area as bait to destroy Chechen hunter-killer teams.

In popular media, the original concept of hunter-killer teams has been distorted somewhat. You must not get confused by them. For example, the US was reported to be actively considering sending operatives to Yemen to kill al-Qaeda leaders in November 2010 following the failed mail bombing attempt. Gen Charles Krulak had been clamouring for such teams along the Afghan border also—the basic idea was just to be able to bypass the rules of engagement. It was supposed to be simple covert assassination. They were described in the papers as hunter-killers. Strictly speaking, though they would hunt and kill, it was not correct because there was no division of work. The same group was supposed to both locate the enemy as well as kill them.

(12.2.3) Are hunter-killer Operations viable in Counterinsurgencies?

If you survive an ambush, something's wrong.

According to the US army's 1960 Special Forces Manual, "Counter-insurgency Operations" (unnumbered), the basic size prescribed for the hunter-killer teams", was 12—the size of the standard Special Forces "A" Detachment—including local personnel. I do not think that this could be prescribed as a rule of thumb. They are likely to be overpowered and killed. The concept of hunter-killer operations is built around two presumptions. The first is that the preliminary intelligence, on which the hunter teams are sent out, is fairly accurate and that they have only to pin-point the location by actual visuals. This may not be the case everywhere. You know there are countries like your own which have been battling with insurgencies for over 57 years and yet have not been able to eradicate any one of them for good. Obviously, there is something very fundamentally wrong with the intelligence. If they had known something about the sources of strength or weaknesses of the insurgencies, they could have certainly done something in these years. Secondly, the concept presumes that the target would be more or less static and would not be dispersed in a large area. This applies to a target like a small enemy camp in the jungle, a hut, a small clearing, some grove, or something which could be readily surrounded by the assault or killer team.

There would naturally be problems when the enemy has his own system of innocuous-looking civilian spotters to give them advance warning; watchers, watch towers or informers who are spread out under various genuine-looking pretexts. The jungle is not a completely isolated or uninhabited place. Many people could loiter there. The reconnaissance team may make a stealthy entry into the jungle in the night, but there are very good chances that the reconnaissance team would be spotted after the first night in the jungle. As for as you are concerned, any man in the jungle who spots even one of you, could pass on the information to the enemy. As I mentioned above, the small team can survive only as long as it remains absolutely undetected. Once somebody gets a wind of it, the team can be subjected to harassing fire and made to spend its ammunition, after which it can be surrounded and killed.

Then the reconnaissance team will have to contend with many other problems which seem to defy a solution. For example:

- What to do when you have reasons to suspect that a person or persons who are outwardly innocent civilians but for whom you have good reasons to suspect that they have seen you, understood your purpose of being there and are likely to convey the information back to the enemy?
- What to do if you find that some of the approach routes to the proposed observation post or vantage point are mined with IEDs and skirting them is not possible?

- What do you do if you accidentally happen to trigger an IED, even if you do not sustain serious lossess?
- What do you do when you have reasons to suspect that in the vicinity of the enemy position or even en route, there could be such domesticated or semi-domesticated dogs who would take you to be strangers and raise an alarm upon detecting your presence?
- What do you do when you find that there is sporadic or even continuous movement of villagers to the enemy position?
- What do you do when you find that there is sporadic or even continuous movement of combatants to the enemy position and that some of them could venture even in your direction?
- What do you do when the enemy opens, in his opinion, a probing fire towards your location on some suspicion and how to distinguish probing fire from an actual attack?

Supposing the reconnaissance/hunter teams have completed their mission without any mix-up, there could still be surprises in store for the killer teams that follow them:

- There could be hostages, some other non-hostile persons, or some sort of non-combatants inside the target building or area; sometimes there could not be. What sorts of fire would be delivered in each case?
- What do you do if say a few screaming women or children suddenly come out of the hut and start running wildly?
- What do you do if you are surprised by the quality of the retaliatory fire about which you had no inkling? Suppose a few mortar shells are suddenly fired at you and you are not able to make an educated guess about from where they came? How you react to that?
- What do you do when you discover that either human spotters have seen your helicopter used for dropping you and have conveyed the information by some means or the very sound of the helicopter has betrayed its presence directly to the terrorists?

(12.3) The Hoax of UAVs (Unmanned Aerial Vehicles)

(12.3.1) Obvious Limitations of Optical Sensors

Successful counter-insurgency operations require a very comprehensive strategy. Developing a comprehensive strategy and tactics to go with it requires intellectual capacity. And that's missing in India. I don't need to explain that. Anybody who has observed or read about the history of post-independence India knows that Indians simply do not know how to effectively counter terrorism, insurgencies or various sorts of fissiparous tendencies because they are dumb. Their responses are characterised by only one thing: knee-jerk reactions. Who does not know that they have been struggling with terrorism and insurgencies in various parts of the country since 1954 itself and they have not been able to convincingly and emphatically solve anyone of them. Even with regard to the Khalistan movement, the police in India claimed that as late as December 2011, they happened to arrest two terrorists of the Babbar Khalsa International—meaning that some of them are still around! For all other terrorist activities and insurgencies in the country—from the north-eastern states to Kashmir, the Indians have been fumbling everywhere without success. Naxalism (left wing extremism) has flummoxed them since 44 years. In 44 years, they have not been able to take care of a band of rag-tag insurgents whose numbers would, even by the most inflated estimate, not exceed 20,000. When the security forces chase them in the villages, the insurgents flee to the jungles; when they are chased in the jungles, they flee to the villages—and the Indians cannot have enough security forces to remain physically present in every nook and corner of this vast country in spite of having one of the biggest security establishments in the whole world.

India abounds in dumb guys. One of the pieces of wisdom of the dumb guys was to suggest using the UAVs. Desperate to find a technological solution to the problem, they have gone in for all sorts of UAVs—from short-range, short-duration to long-range, long-duration ones. The idea is that the UAV will take images of the jungles from which they will be able to spot the insurgents and then the forces on the ground will go and finish them off! Unfortunately, life is not so simple! The UAV is understandable for high altitude land surveillance and maritime patrol missions. But the jungle is a different story. The optical cameras mounted on the UAV can only see what a human eye can see—and human eyes cannot penetrate the tree canopy. The problem of locating men hidden in a jungle by observing from the air therefore defies a technical solution. There is only one theoretical solution—the FOPEN or the foliage penetrating radar. It is discussed below but more important issues first.

What would you do, if by any chance, you are able to figure out that there are men in the jungle in the open, outside the tree canopy? How can you presume that they are insurgents and they have to be fired upon? You cannot fire missiles on them the way the American drones are doing in Afghanistan or machinegun them—this is your own country. All that you can do is to mount a ground operation. If a big UAV was far, the information won't be actionable as it would take you some time to traverse that distance and, in that time, the guys would run away—by the time you reach the spot, the insurgent would be sipping tea somewhere else. Dropping men by helicopters is not a viable option in the jungle—the helicopter would be heard from miles away and the naxals would run away. If the UAV was small and close, you would be already in hostile environment. The only possible use of small UAVs is to see across difficult obstacles like a hill from its other side without having to climb it.

You hope to fight insurgencies with the help of cameras on UAVs? Use Predator drones to fire missiles if you have to use air power at all

(12.3.2) The FOPEN (Foliage Penetrating Radar)

A foliage penetration radar, such as the one marketed by the SRI International, USA can locate a large class of targets that includes hidden tanks, mobile surface-to-air missiles, rocket artillery systems, supply vehicles and hidden operating bases. That could possibly be of some use in a military context but clearly useless in a counter-insurgency war. What the American agency DARPA (Defense Advanced Research Projects Agency) is trying to develop is Foliage Penetration (FOPEN) Reconnaissance, Surveillance, Tracking and Engagement Radar, or FORESTER that would detect and track moving dismounted soldiers and vehicles at a range of 30 kilometers (20 miles). Its Ground Moving Target Indicator (GMTI) radar also can locate and track people in the open or through light foliage at a range of at least 50 kilometers (30 miles). FORESTER's UHF radar operates in P-band, penetrating foliage very well and is unaffected by obscurants such as snow and particulates. The Americans are interested in it so that they may use it against the drug lords operating their factories in the jungles of various countries of Latin America. Employing the sensor system on the DARPA/US Army A160 Hummingbird UAV helicopter or other suitable platform will provide a robust, wide-area, all-weather, standoff capability. The sensor development is a joint DARPA/Army programme to design and integrate a long, lightweight, electronically scanned and mechanically positioned, multi-channel radar. Syracuse Research Corporation (SRC) is the prime contractor. Cost is one of the major factors in the programme. The sensor system is being designed for a manufacturing cost not to exceed $2.5 million per unit, with a goal of $1 million per unit in quantities of 50 or more". In any case, the device is yet to become commercial. The technological challenges were brought to fore in September 2010 by the crash in the jungles of Belize of a radical, new-technology robot helicopter equipped with a radar intended to penetrate jungle canopies from above. The tests were terminated for the time being after the crash of the trials aircraft. Subsequent developments are not known.

(12.4) Fancy but Unsuitable Weapon Systems

Night vision devices will only fail at night. They will function perfectly once the sun rises.

(12.4.1) The CGRL

The 84 mm CGRL (Carl Gustav Recoilless Rifle—mistakenly called a rocket launcher by the ignoramuses—there is actually no rocket in it) tops the list of the monumental blunders committed by the Indians in CI operations. It is the most-fitting example of the intellectual bankruptcy that has engulfed and consumed Indian forces since long. The Carl Gustav is an old (1948) Swedish-designed anti-tank weapon which, in its era, was more powerful than its contemporaries like the American Bazooka and the German Panzerschreck. With muzzle velocity in the range 255-290 m/s, it was capable of engaging stationary targets at 700 meters. The basic problem of the weapon is its weight. A loaded weapon weighs 10.4 to 14.2 kg for various models. Precisely for this reason, it cannot be expected that troops operating in jungles would be able to carry it on their backs and that too for several days. The warhead alone weighs about 3.2 kg. After all, you would not be carrying just one warhead! As such, it is absurd to even think of using it in anti-personnel role in the jungle. You are not going to get a clear line-of-flight in the jungle for even 100 meters.

It makes some sense in anti-armour role, particularly against lightly armoured fighting vehicles of today or tanks of an older generation. The Germans use it for battlefield illumination. In that role, the FFV545 an illuminating starshell, can be fired up to 2,300 m maximum range, but with an effective envelope of 300 to 2,100 m. Suspended by parachute, the starshell burns for 30 seconds while producing 650,000 candela, providing a 400 to 500 m diameter area of illumination. For full effectiveness, illumination rounds have to be fired at a very high angle, creating a danger for the gunner as the back blast from firing can burn him. FFV502 is an HEDP round with the ability to be set to detonate either on impact or one-tenth of a second afterwards. However, for the safety of the firer, the arming distance for the fuze of the warhead is up to 40 meters. That becomes a problem in the jungle, even if you have taken one inside. You may not get enough clear line-of-flight to reliably arm the warhead. As such, the FFV502 warhead can be used in bunker-busting role, but by the regular infantry only which has its load-carrying resources nearby. Commandos operating in jungle on their own do not have the luxury of carrying this heavy a weapon on their backs. Moreover, in counter-insurgency situations, you may come across a number of enemy bunkers. People have found over 100 of them in one location! You cannot carry a 100 of the CGRL warheads!

US Special Forces fire the CGRL in a training exercise in Basrah, Iraq: it can be used profitably only in such terrains against armour and not in a jungle

Remember that the warhead of a CGRL cannot distinguish between a brick wall encountered in rural areas, a layer of sandbags, and a concrete wall. The result is that you may not get detonation of the warhead where you need it. It simply goes through such weak structures like a hot knife blade through butter. Reliable detonation can be had only at sufficient range and proper resistance offered by the structure. Other nations of the world have applied their mind to it and have developed specific weapons for dealing with such situations. In other words, they have understood that an anti-tank or anti-armour warhead cannot be properly used in anti-bunker role, so to say. In fact, they call such munitions, BDM or Bunker Defeat Munitions as against anti-tank munitions.

The M141 BDM (Bunker Defeat Munition), for example, addresses the specific need to destroy structures such as bunkers and other fixed enemy positions, and incapacitate the enemy personnel located within these targets by shrapnel. The dual-mode fuze is the key to beauty of the M141 BDM. The warhead function, in quick or delay mode, is automatically determined by the fuze when the rocket impacts a target. The M141 BDM is fired at hard or soft targets without any selection steps required by the gunner. Warhead detonation is instantaneous when impacting a hard target, such as a brick or concrete wall, or an armoured vehicle. Impact with a softer target, such as a sandbagged bunker, results in a fuze time delay that permits the rocket to penetrate into the target before warhead detonation into splinters. This too is, however, 7.1 kg in weight and, as such, not suitable for jungle commandos. Moreover, it is a disposable weapon, meaning one tube and one warhead is an integrated package. You cannot expect the commandos to be carrying several of these. Once again, the device is useful for regular infantry only.

(12.4.2) Bullpup Rifles

Don't center on your pants. Keep your concentration here and now, where it belongs.

Why people are fascinated by the bullpup rifles like the Israeli X95 or the Austrian Steyr AUG? They look futuristic or cool, and this is the real reason so many people are enamoured of them. Ignoramuses in the media keep on lamenting how impoverished the Indian forces are. It is generally believed that the Indians are failing in their counter-terrorist mission because they do not have the latest weapons and gadgetry. Probably under this pressure, the Indian morons have purchased a large number of these rifles for CI ops. I leave the other reasons for the journalists to speculate. Other than the fact that science fiction films and television shows have a penchant for featuring bullpups, there is no reason why bullpups should be called the future of assault rifles. Quite like adolescents, the media is fascinated by gadgets—unfortunately, many people in the forces also get fascinated. When they watch foreign TV channels or surf the Internet, they get to see a lot of gadgets being used by foreign forces. Naturally, they latch on to the catchiest objects in the business of counter-terrorism—weapons and gadgets fit the bill perfectly. The general refrain becomes: if we had such-and-such thing, we would have wiped off the terrorists a long time back. Little do they realise that fancy weapons are either simply fancy weapons or an adolescent's fancy—having a fancy weapon does not mean that you will win in all combats; not having a fancy weapon does not mean that you will lose all combats.

How The Higher Rate of Automatic Fire Amongst Rifles Does Not Offer Any Significant Advantage?: One of the USPs of the X95 is the higher rate of fire at 750 to 900 rounds per minute. This is inconsequential. Most people do not know that a little difference in the rate of automatic firing does not make any difference to the human target in front of the bullets. The point to be understood is that when one is spraying bullets on full auto in a room or in the open, he is not firing all the 750 bullets. All he can fire is one magazine of 30 rounds. It does not really make any difference whether he is pouring out 30 rounds in 3 seconds (at the rate of 600 rounds per minute) or 2.4 seconds (at the rate of 750 rounds per minute)—the human targets in front of him will not be able to tell the 'perceived' difference of 0.6 seconds—one cannot say that the target can take evasive action, if the rate of fire is 600 rounds per minute and cannot take such evasive

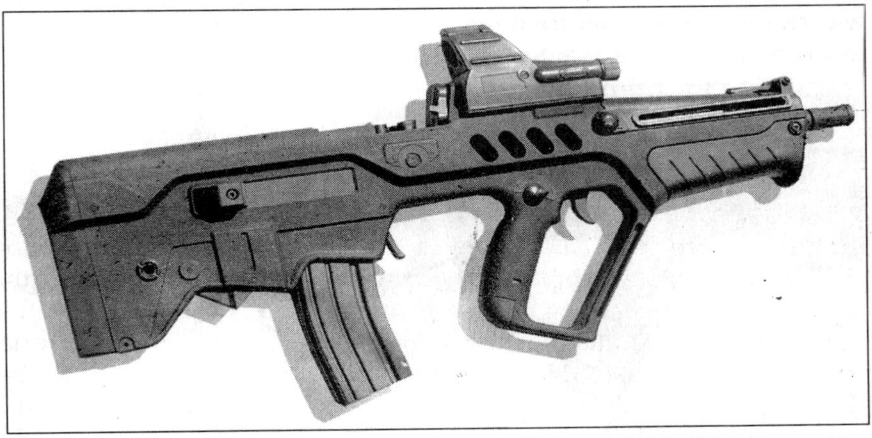

If looks could kill, the X95 sure would do; unfortunately, you need more than just futuristic looks in the jungle

action, if the rate of fire is higher—human reflexes are, in any case, far slower. Further, when we take into account, the fact that anyone of the bullets could be fatal; the difference becomes even more insignificant. It must also be kept in mind that on a mission when one is carrying only 150 rounds or so, he cannot really afford to waste ammunition in some frenzied automatic fire except in a desperate situation. As shown above, even in that situation, the little difference in rate of fire does not make any difference. And when one is firing single-shot, the question of rate of fire does not even arise.

The Experience of other Bullpup Designs in the World: The very short service of the Tavor with the Israelis is not sufficient to prove that it is a great weapon or greater than 'the legend called the AK rifle' which has seen service with over 100 million users! The fact is that in spite of all the hype surrounding bullpups, many armies that have fielded bullpups have found them wanting. The British L85 (SA 80) has gone through a 20 years saga just to get it to function reliably! The new Chinese fashionably flaunted QBZ-95 made by ChiCom is being "supplemented" by the conventional layout QBZ-03. The French are thinking about replacing the FAMAS. The only bullpup that doesn't seem to garner severe criticism is the Steyr AUG. But the fact about the AUG is that the rifle has not seen the kind of widespread combat

It would be instructive to analyse the Chinese experience with bullpups. In the late 1980's Chinese designers developed a 5.8 x 42 mm cartridge, designated DBP87, which was claimed to be superior to both the 5.56 mm NATO and the 5.45 mm Soviet cartridges. This cartridge develops a muzzle velocity of 930 meters per second from a standard barrel, with a bullet weighing 4.26 grams. As soon as the ammunition was ready, the PLA began to develop an entirely new and supposedly much more modern family of small arms for it. This family, known

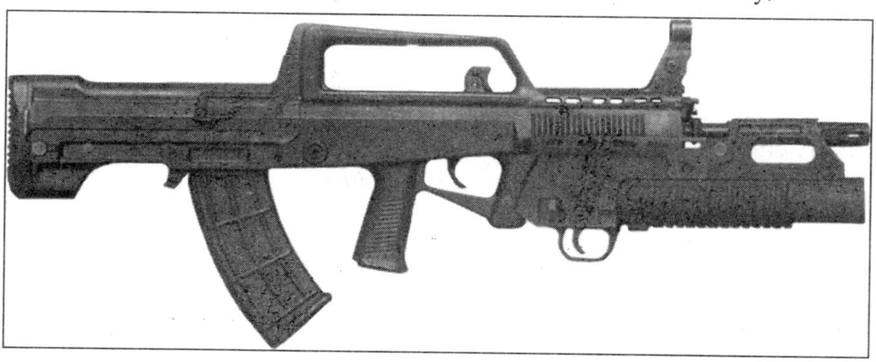

The Chinese QBZ-95 Bullpup Rifle: A design that was eventually found to be unsatisfactory

as QBZ-95 ('Qing Buqiang Zu' = Light Rifles family-1995), was first displayed outside the PLA in 1997. When China took over Hong Kong; it was observed that the Chinese guards were armed with a bullpup rifle.

For various reasons the bullpup Type 95/QBZ-95 assault rifle was eventually found unsatisfactory in PLA service. Though they flaunted it as late as during the 60th anniversary parade; in the field formations it was, however, already on the way out. It was decided to develop a new 5.8 mm assault rifle of conventional layout instead of playing further with the QBZ-95 or trying to modify it. The new weapon is known as QBZ-03 (Type 03/2003) and it is replacing the QBZ-95 issued earlier.

Problems with the Bullpups in General: Bullpups are unbalanced. In simple words, they do not have a good heft. A conventional rifle is balanced in between the dominant and support hands; and there are good reasons for that. A human being naturally handles things better that balance in the palm, or in front of it. Because the weight of the receiver, trigger group, and ammunition in a bullpup configuration is all concentrated in the stock, the center of gravity of a bullpup gun is quite a bit further toward the rear than conventional designs and this has a bearing on the heft of the rifle for most shooters. I must say that heft is an important factor—if the great Winchester rifle would be remembered for one thing besides the repeater action, it is its excellent heft which enabled strong men to fire it with one hand from horseback! If there is one department in which the M16 scores over the AK, it is its heft.

An unbalanced rifle means that it does not lend itself to carry with a single bare hand. On long marches, it is not always possible to carry the rifle in high port carry position. If there is no imminent danger, most men prefer to carry them in one hand. Since with a loaded magazine, most of the weight is to rear, the rifle tends to swivel back in the grip, straining the wrist. It is not possible to carry it with one hand comfortably for long. Then magazine changes are much slower because they require more repositioning, and are difficult to see (if necessary) without fully dismounting the rifle from the aimed position. Charging the rifle and manipulating the operating handle is rather awkward, and sometimes can't be done without dismounting the rifle, or reaching over with one's support hand. Agreed that a lot of this can be worked around with training, but the simple unassailable fact is that bullpups are ergonomically incorrect for human beings. The rule of thumb in designing a great weapon is that you don't train someone to do something ergonomically incorrect; you must redesign the weapon to fit human ergonomics.

My considered opinion is that bullpups are likely to remain nothing more than a niche weapon, to be preferred where OAL (overall length) is the most critical factor, but a SMG or collapsible or folding stock are inappropriate choices for whatever reason. Precisely for this reason, they are more suitable to urban combat.

13

Guerrilla Innovations that may Confound you

Sometimes it is like being pretty much the ham in a bad ham sandwich.

(13.1) The Misery Called IED

(13.1.1) 'Bobcats' Narrate their Experience of Vietnam

From an operational point of view, the IEDs have two ways to torment you. They can damage a vehicle and that could be all. They could also be used to set up more deadly ambushes against the survivors or those in the rear in other vehicles. Or they could be used as antipersonnel landmines against foot soldiers.

"The soldiers of the 1st battalion, 5th Infantry, 25th Infantry Division, were learning more and more about the booby-traps used by the VC. There were hand grenades with trip wire; the unexploded cluster bomb units rigged with tip wire; the Chicom Claymore designed to explode in a 360 degree circle, the artillery and bomb duds, rigged to be tripped or command detonated. They were in the ground, on the ground, hung in trees or bamboo clusters, ankle high, knee high, waist high, head high or higher. You would find them on trails or footpaths. They could be encountered in tunnels or attached to spider hole covers. One was even found attached to a pineapple growing in a garden. And there were the sharpened bamboo sticks, referred to as punji stakes. Some of the men started referring to the area as the "Christmas Tree" because it was 'decorated' with so many booby-traps and mines".

(13.1.2) How Insurgents defeat Conventional anti-mine Systems and Measures?

The insurgents have become cleverer than what they used to be some decades ago. Earlier, it was hoped that one could detect the metal used in the IED through various means. But, to your dismay, they are not obliged to use metal. It is not at all necessary for them to use a metal container in the IED (presumably to yield shrapnel) that could possibly be detected by a DSMD (Deep Search Mine Detector). Why should they? They only need blast overpressure. It is a fine point and I will explain it at some length.

It is not really necessary for the IEDs to have explosives in metal containers that the security forces so eagerly hope to get detected by the DSMDs (Deep Search Mine Detectors). It is one of the secrets of the science of explosives. Many of the dumb terrorists and most of the dumb officers of the security forces do not know that their intended damage is caused by that part of the explosive force that is directed upwards and not what is directed to the sides. The blast overpressure releases itself primarily through the path of least resistance. Supposing they had a metal container, the tensile strength of the sides of the container is not a critical issue as the force of explosion encounters solid ground after that. If the ground is not very solid in the sense that they had dug a larger pit first and then filled it up with loose soil after planting the container, and that's usually the case in which the benefit of reflection of shock waves is denied to them, it will at best waste itself in creating a crater—this is what we find after an IED attack—a crater. The crater is a waste of explosive energy in so far as the lethality of the attack on a vehicle passing overhead is concerned—what matters is what goes up. Vertically, the explosive force will encounter a much weaker resistance for most containers will have a lid and which will not be a welded one. Hence, in practice, it does not make much difference whether there is a metal container for the explosive or not. Eventually, it is simply the blast overpressure of the explosion released through the top which does the damage. And for that a plastic container is as good or bad as a metal container. Once they understand it, they would not use metal containers. And all that they have to do is to lay the plastic jerrycan sideways.

An IED consisting of explosive in a plastic container and no shrapnel (one does not need shrapnel if the target is a vehicle) will have only a detonator as the metallic part. If the detonator is triggered by detonating cord, even electrical wire would not be there.

The problems with regard to IEDs buried on dirt or muddy tracks are well-known and need not be narrated at length. The process of digging the earth to bury the IED does not become apparent because the ground is broken anyway or is covered with mud or water in potholes. Hence, you never know when you could be driving over an IED or take some evasive action. The additional problem is that the road or track could be so narrow that there is no way you can avoid obvious potholes without landing off-road in some ditch or very rough ground.

The most challenging problem is posed by IEDs planted beneath asphalt or concrete surfaces. The real menace of this device comes not as much from the explosive as from the extremely clever manner of planting it. The IED is planted under the concrete surface of the road by making a hole from the side of the road without disturbing the top surface in any way. Since there is often a pronounced slope on one side of the road, if not on both sides, digging from the side is not a problem. In several instances, there are reasons to believe that even if the IED has not been inserted from the side, it is planted in such a manner that the tarred surface of the road is still not disturbed. How? There are only two ways. The first is that the device is planted even before the surface was tarred. This calls for a foresight in the terrorist which is rather difficult to come by. The second is that the device could be inserted when the tarred surface undergoes some repair work like patchwork and when digging would obviously not arouse any suspicion. All that they have to do is to get hold of the contractor who has undertaken that work and either frighten the shit out of him or simply subvert him. The involvement of the contractor is actually very likely because even if they dig a particular place where no repair works are going on, the restoration of the surface would call for molten coal tar etc. And this can be had through some contractor only. There are reasons to believe that some problems of reliability owing to long-term burial underground notwithstanding, many insurgents prefer to leave IEDs planted under road surfaces. In fact, many of them are learnt to leave a proper male-female type connector out by the side of the road. They do so because leaving an IED planted in some place makes planning an attack on short notice infinitely easier. An attack can be planned on minutes' notice—all that they have to do is to plug in the socket and unspool a wire to a battery pack some distance away.

Some roads are concrete topped. The concrete top is essentially in the nature of a plate overlay only on the soil underneath. This improvised technique of road construction is adopted in many places because it is a much faster method of construction in comparison to macadam asphalt tarmac. The concrete top does not pose any problem to one who digs from the side to plant his IED. Further, the plate does not provide much strength or resistance to explosion from under it. The resistance that it can offer depends on its coupling with the soil underneath. Once that coupling is weakened by digging from the side, the plate is only as strong as the thickness of 6-12 inches of non-reinforced structure would permit.

Concrete-topped road attacked by IED

I may further mention that radio waves are not the only means of activating a device by wireless remote control. And hence jammers cannot help for long. If it comes to that, activation can be made by even an ultrasonic whistle (used for calling dogs, and available commercially for a rather low cost). The man can stand in full view and trigger the device in an innocuous manner. Even if he has used wires, it is generally not practical to locate the wire by raking the sides of the road. Those desirous of learning in detail about the whole business of explosives and IEDs must refer to my treatise *The Ultimate Book of Explosives, Bombs and IEDs.*

Some duffers have toyed with the idea of using a tractor/JCB for snagging and pulling out IED wires. Contrary to popular notion the tractor is of practically no use for this particular purpose. The tractor plough is not able to dig deep enough on hitherto unploughed surfaces to be useful in snagging IED wires. When the mine is buried on the road (usually tarred), you expect the wires to be taken out from somewhere outside the tarred surface and then to wherever the terrorist operator is. In some places you may have sufficient road surface outside the tarred surface (we may call it unpaved pavement) on which the entire tractor can run; in some places, the unpaved pavement may be narrow and the wheels of only one side may be accommodated. In some places, the unpaved pavement may have a pronounced slope and even one set of wheels cannot operate on that; in other places it could be very uneven or full of stones. All these factors severely restrict the driving of tractors thereon. In any case, even in the ideal condition of there being such a large unpaved pavement that the entire tractor may run on it, the tractor plough can barely scratch the ground with hardly two inches of penetration. Even in those places where the ground is a little softer the penetration is not more than three inches. The plough works best only on ground which has already been ploughed once. A terrorist, who has experimented even once with the tractor, would learn to bury his wire deeper than the depth to which the ploughshare digs. The tractor/JCB loses any practical relevance as an IED wire-weeding device because the penetration is inadequate; the unpaved pavements are so irregular; and you cannot have the time to run it over the same surface more than once. In any case, who in the world has got so much time that he would move in an operational area with the speed of a tractor plowing a field?

(13.1.3) How IEDs Attack Mine-Protected Vehicles (MPVs)?

The only medal you really want to be awarded is the Longevity Medal.

Dumb Indians place great faith in the vehicle called MPV and the companies are laughing all the way to the bank capitalising on the stupidity of the security establishment. Now that the insurgents have started attacking them successfully, the naxals have scored a great psychological victory with such strikes. The general feeling is that the forces' ultimate weapon has been beaten. It's like your champion boxer getting bashed up in the ring.

What is a MPV and How it Works?: The vehicle is in the 12.5 ton class—both imported and indigenous. They are all equally good or bad because the basic design concept is the same. The passenger compartment of the MPV is a steel box raised much higher above the ground than that of other vehicles. The explosive force of a landmine or the IED dissipates itself in a solid sphere by an inverse cube law, because the volume of a sphere is proportional to the cube of the radius. This means that if you double the distance, the force is reduced eight times. Then the bottom of the steel box is shaped like a 'V'. This helps deflect the explosive force to the sides and thereby reduces the force that would otherwise act against a flat hull and tend to break it. The downside is that it raises the center of gravity of the vehicle and increases the chances of rolling over.

How it is Attacked?: A clever insurgent need not bother with procuring factory-made anti-tank mines or even military high explosives like RDX to attack both unarmoured and armoured vehicles like the MPVs. He does not need to blast the vehicle to pieces. In other words, he is not interested in what is known as C-Kill (Catastrophic Kill). His purpose is eminently served if the vehicle is even toppled to a side, preferably down a slope. If the MPV topples on a road which has got slope on one or both sides, the MPV rolls down. Rolling down is enough to injure the occupants seriously. Even otherwise, toppling would result in serious injuries as they bang against the body of the vehicle. Further, toppling often results in the rear door and top hatches opening under the impact. The insurgents are known to come close and shoot the occupants—those who survive the blast, fall to the bullets.

Low detonation velocity explosives like gelatins, emulsions and slurries are particularly useful in this role as they have a heaving effect instead of a shattering effect. Used in quantities as low as 10 kg, they are enough to topple the MPV. Then there are other uses also. Even for a MPV, it is only the hull that is protected against blasts. The wheels, the differential, the axle, and the transmission shaft etc are all unprotected. They can be damaged by a blast that would not be able to damage the armoured V-shaped hull. That renders the vehicle immobilised and then the insurgents can attack it by other weapons. This is called a M-Kill (Mobility-Kill).

A MPV attacked by an IED

Even the half-educated savages called naxals know this. Don't believe this? You could read the January-June 2005 issue of their magazine called *Awam-e-Jung*. It describes in great detail how to attack MPVs and laughs at the stupidity of the Indian security establishment. It is only the Indian security establishment and the companies who do not know this. Why? The reason is simple. The security establishment is intellectually bankrupt anyway and the Indian companies are nothing but peddlers of goods produced abroad. The western companies make their MPVs to withstand factory-made mines and high detonation velocity military explosives (like RDX) of the type they encounter in Iraq and Afghanistan. Insurgents in India are not so well-equipped. Mostly they would use low detonation velocity gelatins, emulsions and slurries because in this nation they produce about 1.89 million tons of them and it is very easy to obtain them. In India you are likely to encounter mostly propulsive (heaving) explosives. And they do not have a solution for this. Precisely for this reason, blast trials of MPVs conducted with high detonation velocity explosives like RDX give results that are misleading for other contexts. The hull remains intact but is bodily pushed away.

Heaving effect: Note the size of the crater produced by the IED

Too much has been made of troops not using seatbelts inside the MPVs. This is neither fair nor scientifically supported. A balance has to be struck between turning the vehicle into a sealed steel coffin, and injuries sustained due to not wearing the seatbelts—troops trapped inside a disabled vehicle the doors of which may get jammed also can still be killed by noxious fumes that can be created on the spot by setting fire to plastics and rags.

Where and how the Indian Manufacturers Fail?: The American response to the IEDs they encounter has been changing according to the situations they face. They have the Bradley Fighting Vehicle, the Stryker and now the MRAP (Mine Resistant Ambush Protected) vehicle. The Bradley weighed a massive 27.6 tons. It was found to be ponderous and was successfully attacked several times. Then they tried the Stryker which weighed 18 tons and was faster. That enabled it to run away and it fared better. The MRAP is 14 tons plus and is only better than the old Humvees in terms of protection. But its much higher speed is a plus point. The point to be noted is that the Americans have never applied mind to the problem of 'heaving' explosives. And since they did not apply mind, the dumb Indians, who only buy seond-hand technology, also did not apply any mind. They will have to ditch the habit of riding piggy back on someone else's research. Foreigners would not understand your problems and solve them for you. You have to work for yourself. Get out of the mind-set that if you have the money, someone else can do the research and then you can buy it.

(13.2) An Improvised big Blunderbuss

Move away from your attacker. Distance (lateral and diagonal preferred) is your friend.

It is an improvised firearm resembling the Blunderbuss of yore. It can be thought of as a crude but huge shotgun. The naxals call it Big Gun or Challenger; their stupidity is pardonable—the sheer ignorance of the Indian officers is unpardonable, however, when they call it by various (and wrong) names such as Claymore mine, directional mine, etc across the country. It is not a mine by any imagination nor is any high explosive used in it. Though crude, it is an extremely clever device and extremely effective for its cost and ease of operation. Anybody can fashion a crude firearm. The ingenuity of this device is seen in its triggering mechanism. Normally, one would expect a firearm to be operated directly by the user as he holds it. This device, however, lends itself to be operated by remote control through wires. That makes it ideally suited for a guerrilla. He can plant the device and then take position at a safe and vantage point. From there he can watch his quarry approaching and can trigger the device at the exact moment he wants without any risk to himself. Not only that, he can easily run away after that to safety. Since the device is made so cheap, it can be easily abandoned or may be even retrieved later if the soldiers fail to retrieve it first. This is the first insurgent weapon that uses electrical ignition of the propellant and that too by an extremely cheap method—using the most abundantly available electrical detonator so that they are saved the trouble of fabricating anything at all.

The device is a nearly 2.5 feet long GI pipe of 3-inch diameter—commonly used in bore wells. It is fairly thick, about 4 mm, and weighs 5.6 kg but is still quite portable. One end of the device is hammered and flattened to close it. Then a touch hole is drilled into it. An electrical detonator is inserted into it and the wires are taken out to the battery pack and switch. Ignition is by an electrical detonator which sets off the propellant. Theoretically even the filament of a flashlight bulb could be used but why bother with it when you get factory-made detonators in such large quantities. The propellant is simple black powder - about half a kg. Crude shrapnel consisting of numerous metallic things, nails, scrap iron or whatever available are used. The shrapnel is packed in the tube (barrel) with tight wads of paper which also serves as an improvised gas seal. The device is concealed in the bushes and supported by some stones. It can be mounted on trees also. Upon ignition, the shrapnel are projected in an arc. The device is concealed in the bushes and supported by some stones; it can also be planted on a tree. The shrapnel are projected in an arc of about 20 yards to a range of about 50 yards where they can easily injure half a dozen of men very badly.

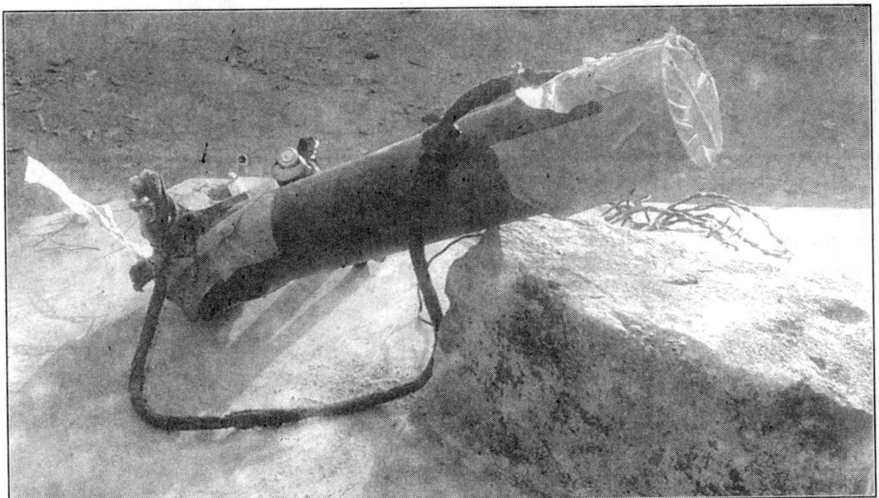

The big Blunderbuss like device invented by the naxal insurgents: note its portability and remote controlled electrical ignition

The electrical ignition enables him to activate the device from even 200 yards or more. If he does not have a clear line-of-sight himself, he can act on the signal of a spotter. Therein lies its tactical advantage. A man hiding 200 yards away can easily inflict casualties of 6-10 by the device and then run away to safety. Not only that, the device can be used to set up a deadlier ambush.

(13.3) Improvised Mortars

These pants may not look like much, kid, but they've got it where it counts.

Mortar fire is for the intelligent terrorist. In its impact, mortar fire is better than the RPG because it is a NLOS (non-line of sight) weapon. It is therefore extremely difficult to ascertain the firer's position and mount a pursuit and search operation. The mortar bomb can hit you through the roof.

Terrorists across the world have made improvised mortars successfully. The Irish Republican Army did it very systematically. In the latest phase of the Al-Aqsa Intifada the Gaza Strip has witnessed a significant development with the use of improvised mortar systems against Israeli Defense Force (IDF) bases and Jewish settlements in the Gaza Strip. The latter are well protected with secure perimeters but cannot defend themselves against indirect fire from nearby Palestinian areas. Attacks are now taking place from the Gaza Strip into Israel itself. Mortar rounds are fired from improvised tubes and with improvised propellant charges.

Barrack buster is the colloquial name given to several improvised mortars, developed in the 1990s by the engineering group of the Provisional Irish Republican Army (IRA). The Irish Republican Army improvised the so-called Mark 15 with one meter long metal propane cylinder with a diameter of 36 cm that contained around 70 kg of home-made explosives and with a range up to 300 yards. The cylinder is an adaptation of a commercial 'Kosangas' gas cylinder for heating and cooking gas used in rural areas in Ireland. The barrack buster belongs to a series of home-made mortars developed since the 1970s. The first such mortar—Mark 1—was used in an attack in May 1972 and it was soon followed by the first of a series of improved or differentiated versions stretching into the 1990s:

- **Mark 1 (1972):** Consisted of a 50 mm copper pipe filled with 10 ounces of plastic explosives. Propelled and detonated by two commercial low-caliber cartridges.

- **Mark 2 (1972–73):** An 8 inch length 57 mm steel pipe filled with two pounds of explosive and detonated by a 12 gauge shotgun cartridge.
- **Mark 3 (1973–74):** A 60 mm mortar barrel with a static firing pin on the plate and a range of 260 yards. Propelled by a dried mixture of rags and sodium chlorate and detonated by a charge of ammonium nitrate.
- **Mark 4 (1974):** Basically an Mk 3 with a larger charge of propellant which extended its range to 400 yards. The bomb was filled with 1 pound of ammonium nitrate and aluminium powder.
- **Mark 5 (1974):** Never used in any known attack, the security forces learned of it after the discovery of an IRA workshop at Cushendall, Antrim, in 1974.
- **Mark 6 (1974–94):** A 60 mm conventional mortar with a bipod and base plate and a range of 1,200 yards. The shell was propelled by a charge of homemade gun powder, ignited by a .22 cartridge. The warhead, made of 3 pounds of Semtex, was detonated by another .22 cartridge on impact. The bomb armed itself "by means of a wind-driven propeller, which is an integral part of the striker".
- **Mark 7 (1976):** Longer version of Mark 6.
- **Mark 8 (1976):** Longer version of Mark 6.
- **Mark 9 (1976–?)**
- **Mark 10 (1979–94):** A large caliber mortar containing 44–220 pounds explosives. It was used in several attacks using configurations with multiple launching tubes, "often launched from the back of transit type vans". Three such mortars using a mixture of ammonium nitrate and nitrobenzene—known as "Annie"—as warhead were used on 7 February, 1991 in an IRA attack on 10 Downing Street in London against British Prime Minister John Major and his War Cabinet during the first Gulf War.
- **Mark 11 (1982–?):** The mortar had a range of 550 yards.
- **Mark 12 (1985–?):** Fired horizontally against armoured vehicles as well as RUC/Army bases. Also referred to as Improvised Projected Grenade. Had a warhead made of 40 ounces of Semtex and TNT.
- **Mark 13 (1990–?):** A spigot mortar, usually lobbed to the intended target from the back of a heavy vehicle.

- **Mark 14 (1992–?)**
- **Mark 15 (1992–):** First mortar known as "barrack buster". It came to be the "standard IRA large caliber mortar system" and described as having "the effect of a 'flying car bomb". It has a caliber of 320 mm and loads with 196–220 pounds explosives and a maximum range of 275 yards. It has also been used in configurations with multiple launch tubes with an attack using 12 tubes. Two British helicopters, one Lynx from the Army and an RAF Puma, were brought down by this type of mortar between March and July 1994.
- **Mark 16 (1991–?):** A shoulder fired weapon for use against armoured vehicles. Used successfully in late 1993 and early 1994. Also described as Projected Recoilless Improvised Grenade. The projectile consisted of a shaped charge with armour piercing capabilities, made of a tin can of 1 pound filled with 600 g of Semtex.

The Mark 15 'Barrack Buster' improvised mortar of the IRA

(13.4) Improvised Rockets and RPGs

(13.4.1) 107 mm Factory-made Rocket or Improvised Rockets

The 107 mm rocket of the Type 63 MBRL (Multi-Barrel Rocket Launcher) of China was a great favourite of the Mujahideen during the war in Afghanistan against the Soviets and then in their internecine warfare and it was used literally by the thousands. In India, it has not yet been found outside Kashmir. The rocket itself is small and can be cradled in one's arms, making it eminently portable. The rocket is a smooth cylinder with a tapering head without the tell-tale fins of a rocket but with Vernier exhausts. Do not commit the folly of confusing it with an artillery shell as many people do. The rocket can be and has been fired from improvised launching pads of iron, wooden planks or the like also, though then the flight becomes inaccurate. Still, with some luck it can land somewhere inside a large or somewhere close enough to cause panic.

The Qassam Rocket of the Palestinians and their Improvised Launching Pads

Those who cannot get this, have taken to making their own rockets. Believe me, it is easy and you can get ranges of several kilometers! The Palestinians now excel in it with their series of Qassam rockets. The point being emphasised here is that making such rockets is not beyond the capability of Indian terrorists including the naxals. The naxals had, in fact, made a very serious attempt at making one.

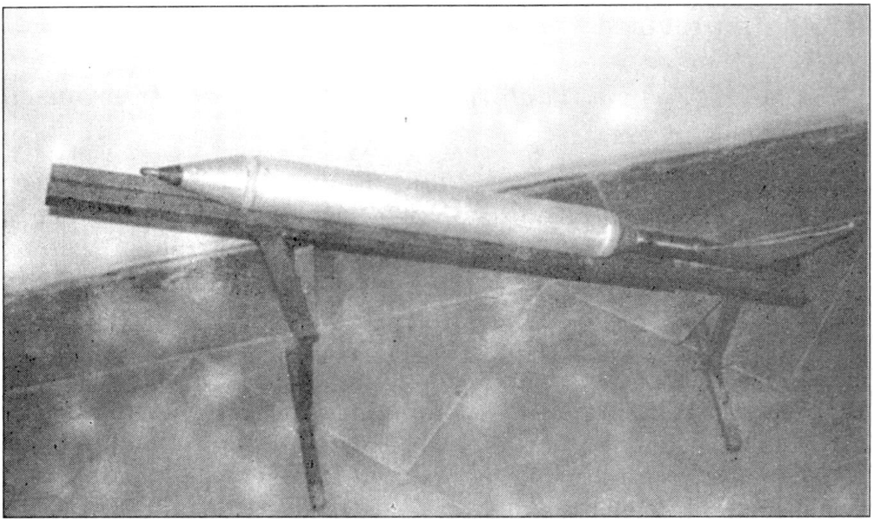

The Indian naxals' attempt at making a rocket

(13.4.2) The RPG and its Improvised Versions

The factory-made RPG is a great weapon—the signature weapon of the rebels all over the world. Next to the AK, it is the most beloved weapon of the guerrilla—as I have discussed earlier, it has been used to attack everything ranging from a room in a house, to trucks, armoured vehicles, and even helicopters. Do not be under the impression that the RPG is found only in Afghanistan, Iraq and at worst in Kashmir. For

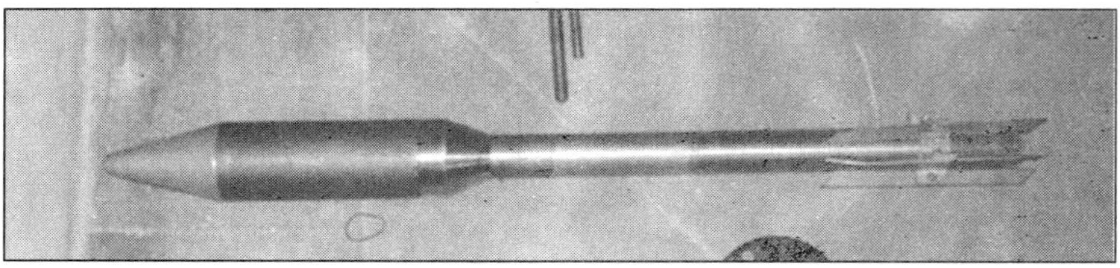

The naxal attempt at making the rocket and warhead of the RPG-7

your information, the naxals have made a serious attempt to fabricate a device similar to the RPG. In September 2006, the Andhra Pradesh police had recovered 900 improvised rockets and 27 launchers in two separate raids in Mehboobnagar and Prakasam districts. It is a different thing that due to certain technical mistakes the devices would not have functioned quite as intended; the point to be understood is that they did make a serious attempt. Nothing prevents them from trying again or correcting those mistakes in future. Hence, you must be prepared

The launching tube of the improvised RPG-7

for them. It would require a separate dissertation to explain what mistakes they had committed. But you must understand that they were not insurmountable problems.

14

Desirable Weapons and Equipments

The cavalry doesn't always come to the rescue. When you are in deep shit, you will have to fend for yourself.

(14.1) Commando Mortars

The object of using a mortar in a jungle is to deliver shrapnel on ill-defined or unseen (as against sharply defined or easily and clearly identified) targets where bullets cannot find their targets—particularly when the line of sight is not clear. The 51 mm Indian mortar, though a hopelessly inaccurate weapon, is still used because of the bang it makes, both on firing and on impact—not because you can really hit anything it with it. Firing a mortar instills some confidence in the troops and frightens the enemy. Mortar fire can be used to drive enemies from cover to create targeting opportunities for rifles or machineguns. The mortar also gives the team an organic capability for large scale illumination or smoke screening—using para-illuminating bombs and smoke screens must be made into an integral part of training.

The Indian 51 mm mortar is a hopelessly inaccurate weapon and is essentially a copy of the British 2" mortar of the Second World War that leaves much to be desired. If you could hit something with it, the mortar bomb can, of course, do damage which the .50 heavy machineguns or the 40 mm automatic grenade launcher cannot. The mortar is also a good reply to the RPG-7. Therefore, what you need for jungle operations is the so-called commando mortar. Commando mortar refers to a class of infantry light mortars designed for maximum portability and rapid deployment with a reasonable degree of accuracy. They are handheld and feature an integrated base plate. Commando mortars often feature design simplifications such as straps instead of bipods, carrying handles, and limited aiming equipment.

Famous models include the M4 60 mm Arsenal Commando Mortar M6C-210 (South Africa); the L9A1 51 mm mortar (UK); the M70 60 mm Yugoslavian mortar; the Antos 60 mm Czech Ultra-Light Commando mortar; and the Hirtenberger 60 mm Austrian mortar etc. Commando mortar straps are marked with measurements, with the intent that the mortar man simply steps on a marked point of the sling and pulls the sling taut, at which point the mortar will automatically be angled so as to fire to the range marked at that point of the sling. This is such a simple and yet so greatly useful feature that its significance cannot be overemphasised.

The Arsenal Commando Mortar M6C-210: note the range marking points on the strap

The South African M4 commando mortar has a carrying handle at its centre of gravity that mounts the trigger and a bubble sight. More importantly it can be carried ready loaded. In the event of an ambush the mortar-man simply drops the base plate to the ground, aims and fires. Unless the mortar-man is one of the first casualties the unit can respond with mortar fire within seconds of being fired upon.

The Yugoslavian M70 is also a trigger or trip-fired mortar and not drop-fired. The base plate is very small and rectangular in shape with a welded on socket. The mortar has a canvas hand-grip around the barrel to compensate for the heat of firing. The sight is a simple vile level and rifle like "iron sight". The mortar-man can also use a cord tied to the sight mount marked with knots to represent the tube elevation for various ranges. This cord, hanging down from the sight-mount indicates the correct elevation when the knot corresponding to that elevation is on the ground.

The Czech 60 mm Ultra-light Commando Mortar ANTOS is an extremely light weapon in which most parts are made of aluminium alloys and plastic materials. The firing mechanism is trigger type with fixed striker. The handgrip with trigger allows easy carrying and firing in oval and flat trajectories. It has got a very interesting liquid sight. The liquid level against the scale shows directly the range of fire for primary and full charge of the 60 mm mortar bombs delivered with the ANTOS mortar. The sight scale is divided; half of the scale for each charge with marked ranges of fire for the applied charge without need to use standard range tables.

The Czech 60 mm Ultra-light Commando Mortar ANTOS

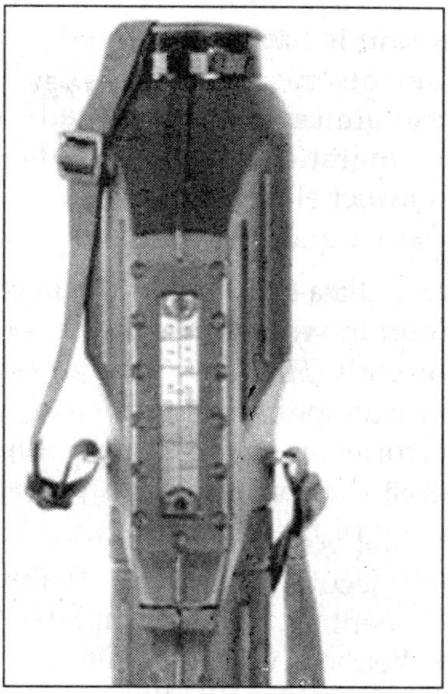

The Unique Liquid Sight of the ANTOS Mortar

Other nations also felt the necessity of laying down mortar fire at ranges well below 500 yards. The British army, when they modified their old 2-inch mortar to make their L9A1 51 mm mortar, they did invent something called SRI (Short Range Insert—which increases chamber volume, thereby reducing the chamber pressure) which could bring down its minimum range from 150 yards to 50 yards or so.

(14.2) The XM - 25 Individual Semi-automatic Airburst System (ISAAS)

The XM – 25 Individual Semi-Automatic Airburst System (ISAAS), also known as the Counter Defilade Target Engagement (CDTE) System, and previously referred to as the Air-Burst Assault Weapon or Air-Burst Weapons System, is semi-automatic firing 25 mm ammunition, including a high-explosive air-bursting (HEAB) round. The weapon weighs 12 to 12.5 pounds, is 29.5 inches long, and has a magazine capacity of 6 rounds. The XM – 25 is a gas operated, rotating bolt, semiautomatic weapon. It is designed using bull-pup layout, with the magazine and bolt located in the butt-stock. It uses detachable, single stack magazines, which hold 6 rounds. The accuracy of the weapon comes from a clever idea. There is a range-finding day/night sight, combined with ballistic computer, which will automatically pre-set the aiming reticle in the sight for measured range and programme the 25 mm grenades to explode in air exactly over or next to the target.

The XM-104 sighting unit is battery-operated, but, shall it fail due to battery run-out or damage, the XM-25 could still be used as a direct-fire weapon with the grenades automatically set to point-impact detonation mode. The point-detonating capability will be useful in anti-vehicle operations also.

The 25 mm HEAB (High Explosive Air Burst) programmable ammunition will have at least three times longer effective range against point target, when compared with current 40 mm systems such as M-203 single-shot or Milkhor Mk.1 multi-shot grenade launchers. The XM-25's HEAB 25 mm round would be capable of defeating an enemy behind a wall, inside a building or in a foxhole giving soldiers a 300-500 per cent increase in hit probability, according to weapon specifications.

The XM-25 Air Burst Assault Weapon was developed from the air-burst portion of Objective Individual Combat Weapon (OICW), termed OICW Increment 2. The complete system, the XM-29 Integrated Air Burst Weapon, was to be OICW Increment 3. The XM-29 OICW programme, if you can recall it, was suspended in 2004 due to impossibility of reaching weight goals, and subsequently split up into two OICW Block 1 systems – the XM8 5.56 mm modular carbine, and the XM-25, 25 mm semi-automatic grenade launcher, along with XM-104 target acquisition / fire control system (FA/FCS, also known as 'computerised sight'). It is possible that in the future the XM-8, XM-25 and XM-104 will be again combined into single modular system. However, current plans are to produce and test XM-25/XM-104 system as a stand-alone weapon.

By the time of writing this book, several pre-production XM-25 weapons were being tested in the field by US Armed Forces operating in Afghanistan.

(14.3) The M-72 LAW

By them we live; for them we would die; whatever
the mission; we'll give it a try.

Remember the famous scene in First Blood Part II where Rambo pretends to be dead and lures the Soviet Mi-24 Hind gunship to land. Suddenly, Rambo comes to life and destroys the Soviet helicopter with a shoulder-fired rocket. That was the legendary M-72 LAW (Light Anti-tank Weapon). There is no weapon as useful as the M-72 LAW for dealing with improvised or properly-made fortifications—its use by as many as 23 countries itself attests to its greatness. The improved M-72 consists of a 60 mm unguided rocket prepackaged at the factory in a telescoping, throwaway launcher. Quite often people think that the UBGL would work where rifle bullets would not work. However, in the absence of specific air-burst capability (such as in the XM-25 HEAB grenade) the regular UBGL 40 mm grenade would be squarely defeated by even a simple barricade of stone boulders and it is extremely difficult to ensure that a UBGL lands only a couple of yards behind such a barricade. The M-72 is the answer to all these problems. It is just 2.5 kg in weight and therefore scores heavily over all other anti–armour weapons. Carrying it in jungle over long distances is therefore not a problem. It is very accurate over the ranges you are likely to encounter in jungle operations—about 220 yards. It is also a throwaway weapon—that is, you do not have to haul the tube back. The M-141 Bunker Defeat Munition and the SMAW (Shoulder-Launched Multi-purpose Assault Weapon) may be technologically more advanced but they are heavier—the M-72 LAW is the weapon for the jungle warrior. Although generally thought of as a Vietnam War era weapon. Its low cost and low weight prompted the US Marine Corps Systems Command in 2011 to place a 15.5 million dollar contract order with Talley Defense for 7,750 M-72 A-7s. What more needs to be said in its praise.

If the insurgents have made this sort of improvised fortifications, there is no way you can ever reduce them with rifle, machinegun or UBGL fire – you have no option but to use the M-72 LAW.

The great M-72 LAW: note the exceptionally small size and light weight making it eminently useful in the jungle

(14.4) Hand Grenades like P2A1 or Norinco Type 86

If you are in the enemy's range, so is he in your range.

The HE-36 grenade used by the Indians is a pitiable anachronism. Essentially, a copy of the First World War Mills Bomb of the British, the grenade has several drawbacks. In the first place, the splinters fly off to such ranges that it necessarily demands throwing from a cover—a situation which could be realised in the trenches of WWI, not in jungles of today. Secondly, the splinters are so few in number (just about 49) that the probability of scoring a hit is very low. There have been instances when as many as 17 grenades were required to take out a man hiding in a cornfield of the size of a badminton court. Thirdly, the fuze is neither very accurate nor very reliable. If it functions properly in the 7-second mode then there have been instances when people have actually thrown it back! There is a recent but equally pathetic invention by the DRDO, India. The Multimode Grenade developed by the DRDO either throws big splinters in one mode (quite like the old HE-36) or no splinters at all in the other mode. The other mode involves the explosion of only the explosive and it depends only on the blast overpressure, hoping to stun some dumb guy.

In counter-insurgency operations you require a grenade, which produces a large number of very small fragments. This has got two advantages. The first is that, a greater number of fragments has a greater probability of hitting greater number of human targets. Secondly, the smaller fragments, having poorer aerodynamic characteristics don't go far and, in any case, much less than the distance to which the grenade can be thrown. Hence, it would not be necessary for the soldier to take cover after throwing the grenade. This is a very useful feature in actual combat because quite often, if one has to throw the grenade to a reasonable distance, it may not always be possible for him to find a suitable cover before throwing. Even the Pakistanis have made an excellent grenade of this type—the P2A1—the Indians have not even been ashamed of it. The weight is 480 g. Its body is of plastic with steel balls. The number of steel balls is 5000 (approximate diameter 2-2.3 mm). The weight of the explosive is 95 g of plasticised PETN.

The Pakistani P2A1 grenade fashioned after the Austrian Arges 84 grenade

The Chinese Norinco Type 86 is also an excellent grenade. This weighs just 260 grams and has 1600 steel balls (approximate diameter 2.5-3 mm). Its small size is a great advantage.

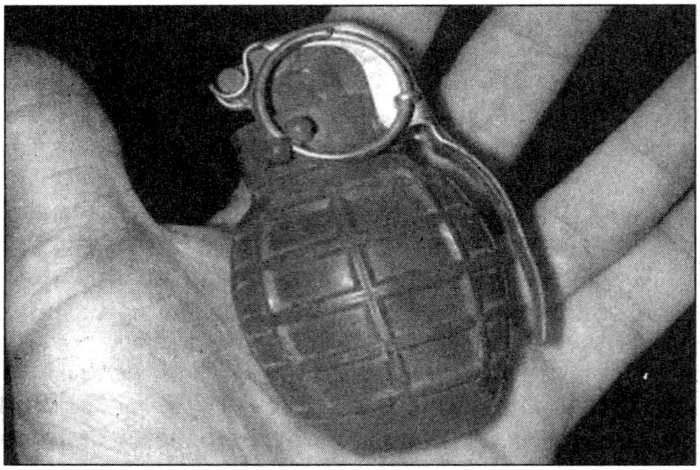

The Chinese Norinco Type 86 Grenade: Note the small size

(14.5) Sawn-off 12 Gauge Shotgun

Do not be fooled by what you see in Hollywood movies. This is not a gangsters' weapon. It is very useful in jungle warfare. You may have a suspicion that the insurgents could be hiding in some bushes. What do you do? Well, one response could be to shoot in the bushes. But you cannot afford to waste your precious rifle ammunition shooting in them. Then what do you do? You could lob in some grenades. Well, grenades would work provided they are of the Arges 84 type, with a large number of fragments. But you would have rather few grenades only—say, two per man. You cannot waste them on mere suspicion. You would need them when things go bad, such as during an ambush.

From a purely tactical perspective, this is the problem of what the forces elsewhere in the world call 'brush clearing'. In such situations, we should adopt the time-honoured and battle-proven practice of the US Marines in this regard. The Marines use a Remington 870, Mossberg 590 or Benelli M1014 pump action shotgun and use the SSG load (15 pellets of .269 inches diameter each to the ounce) to clear brush. The SSG load is critical—anything less would be useless. I have reservations about a pump action gun because it becomes a dedicated weapon and deprives the man of his rifle. You must use a regular break-hinge double-barrel shotgun in a sawn-off configuration which may be carried slung on the hip as an additional weapon. The most suitable shotgun for the CI ops is therefore a sawn off double barrel (internal hammer) shotgun with pistol grip (and not a full stock).

The great advantage of the break-hinge design is the speed of reloading and its ability to be carried as an additional weapon on the hip.

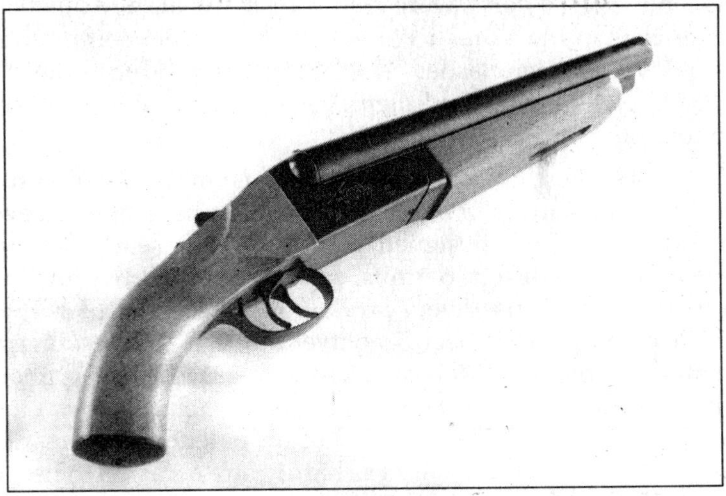

The 12 gauge sawn-off double barrel shotgun with pistol grip for brush clearing in the jungle

(14.6) The AGL (Only if it is used in its Proper Role)

You yell; we shell.

The AGL (Automatic Grenade Launcher) is not for the foot soldier. It is useful to him only if it is mounted on a vehicle or on a helicopter. Reason? It is only in these two situations that you can have sufficient ammunition with it. You cannot carry that much on your already strained backs and there is little point in carrying an automatic grenade launcher with only a handful of grenades to go with it. Get it? Unless mounted on a vehicle and with sufficient ammunition to boot, the AGL is a useless weapon—another example of the monumental follies which the Indians have been committing. If you got to use the weapon, use it properly; otherwise forget about it.

The AGL was developed independently both by the USA and the USSR. The AGL was developed by the USA because they were flummoxed by the 'human wave' tactics of the Chinese they encountered in the Korean War and then again in Vietnam where frenzied attacks by massed bands perplexed them. This weapon was supposed to provide the infantry with close to medium range fire support against enemy personnel in large groups and unarmoured targets like trucks and other such equipment against which the firepower of the machinegun was not so effective. The idea was to let the splinters do what the bullets could not do. By an extension of the argument it was also mounted on riverine crafts and helicopter gunships also. The Soviets, on the other hand, were disturbed by what they saw befalling the Americans in the Korean War—their fears were compounded by the Sino-Soviet border clashes. The Americans produced their Mk 19 in 1968. The Soviets designed their AGS-17 in 1967 but could try it in combat only in Afghanistan.

The AGL's best use on the ground is made by mounting it prominently on sturdy vehicles (the Americans mount it even on Humvees) on specially designed platforms with nearly 360 degrees traverse and, if the design permits, some armour plate protection for the firer. This may be used very profitably in situations like ambushes on vehicle convoys. The sheer firepower of the AGL does have a very demonstrative role. A MMG can also be mounted on the same truck, quite like the Soviets did it. The very sight of a vehicle having an AGL and a MMG has a very salutary effect on potential adversaries and their desire to attack you. There was hardly any occasion to use it from the ground by the foot soldiers on the move—it is way too heavy for them unless they happened to be defending a static position. Further, there was a simple problem. If the weapon was really to be fired in automatic mode, one could not expect the infantry to carry all the ammunition unless they were firing from a static well-stocked, well-defended position.

Automatic grenade launcher mounted on a vehicle

There are basically two design approaches to the problem of mounting the AGL on a helicopter. The first is a turret mounted in the nose of the helicopter. The Americans did so with the UH-1 Huey. The second is to use a gun pod. This is what the Soviets did with the Mi-24 Hind gunship. A gun pod is a detachable pod or pack that contains the weapon(s). A gun pod can have more than one weapon or one type of weapon. It is mounted externally and can be removed. The Mi-24 Hind used the gun pod called GUV-8700 (9A669). In Afghanistan, the AGL on the Mi-24 Hind gunship helicopters was used to spray shrapnel in villages from a flying platform. The Soviets also mounted it very profitably on several vehicle mounts and turrets along with machineguns, guided rocket launchers and sighting equipment—the wise idea being to use it as a direct fire support weapon.

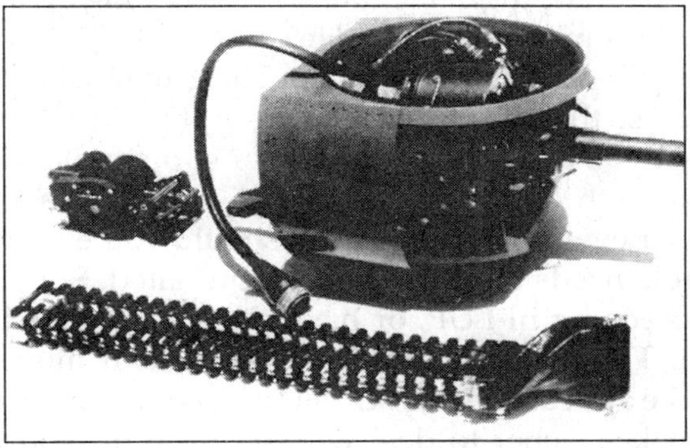

The M-75 grenade launcher in the M-5 Turret system

The M-5 Turret mounted in the nose of the UH-1 Huey Helicopter

(14.7) Other useful Equipment

(14.7.1) The Machete

I am very much aware of the aura which has been built around the commando knife in films—starting from the US Marines' iconic Ka-Bar to the Jimmy Lile and Gil Hibben knives used by Rambo—but the reality is different. The short reach of the knife limits its use greatly. I do not envisage a situation where you would have to use the commando knife for slitting the throat of a sentry from the rear! Commando knives are glamorous but real jungle warriors use machete instead because it is a workhorse.

Machetes come in a great variety. The so-called bush style machete is the best. For soldiers, the blade cannot be very long because carrying it on the waist becomes a problem. He cannot carry it in his hands all the time as campers and survivalists do. The grip must have a knuckle bow or D-guard so that the machete does not slip out of the hand when wielded violently and perhaps with wet or slippery hands. The spine must have saw teeth. The machete can easily double as a thrusting or slashing knife or even as a short sword should you ever need to fight with it. This role needs to be properly appreciated. Suppose the men are sitting or sleeping in LUP, or have simply concealed themselves in some bush. They cannot afford to make much movement there. Suppose a snake appears nearby. Obviously, commandos cannot have a stick or a snake-catcher to deal with it. What do you do with the snake? You cannot allow the snake to slither all over you and have faith in the myth that if you lie still, it will go away. The damn thing may misinterpret any innocuous or inadvertent movement of the sleeping or unaware man and may bite. With the machete lying naked by your side you can simply hack the snake from a safe distance—that's where a 12 inch blade with a 5-inch grip comes handy. The double-edge is a very important feature—you can hack the snake by wielding it in either direction. And remember, forget about the snake catcher. By God, man you are in the jungle to fight—not to protect animal species. You have no qualms about killing other humans and are you supposed to bother about snakes! Well, ethical issues apart, how the hell are you going to carry a 5-foot snake catcher on you? End of the matter.

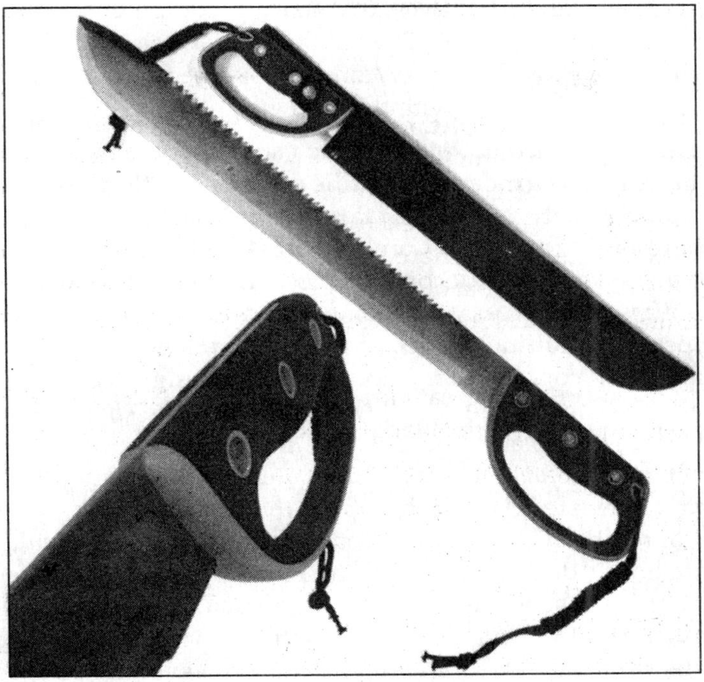

A typical bush style machete with 12-inch blade and secure grip

There are many uses of the machete. In much of the world, machetes are a part of daily life. Just a few of the scores of uses of the machete include: cutting and maintaining trails in the jungle; brush clearing; firewood and tinder gathering; clearing a new campsite; cutting undergrowth at the place where you may have to sleep; snedding, or removing side branches from a main trunk for making posts and poles; pruning and trimming bushes and trees; killing snakes etc quietly and in one swift motion which might slither by when you are waiting in the LUP and cannot afford to move or wield a stick; cutting trees to make sticks for fording or for climbing hills; slaughtering caught or trapped wild game, poultry and other livestock; nut/fruit-splitting: the survival fruit coconut being a classic example, and which would not lend itself to smaller knives; butchering and meat processing: quickly break deer or large livestock carcasses into manageable pieces; shelter construction; cutting poles and roofing materials; and creating the lattice in wattle and daub housing and cutting straw in straw bale construction.

In the show *Dual Survival* on the Discovery Channel, survival experts Cody Lundin and Dave Canterbury take on some of the planet's most unforgiving terrain to demonstrate, in their own way, how the right skills and some creative thinking can keep you alive—and they carry only a machete each, not even fire starting equipment. Commandos need a machete that has a 0.125 inch thick blade made of 1095 Carbon steel with black powder epoxy/zinc phosphate finish or black oxide coated 440C stainless steel with the total weight about 450 g.

Regarding the iconic *khukhri* which some people happen to like, I must state that it is a most unscientific design—a reflection on the poor intellectual capacity of the Nepalese who designed it in the ancient era—there is no reason that anyone must endure it now. It is good to look at, to keep as a decorative piece, and as a memorabilia—the British officers unnecessarily romanticised it. Shorn of that it is just a chopper—the cutting power of the *khukhri* comes from its weight and top heavy construction—not from any design feature. You use any blade that heavy and it will work as good. The *khukhri* is actually hybrid of an axe blade and a knife. Being unbalanced and highly asymmetric, the *khukhri* has a definite tendency of turning in the wrist if the strike deviates even slightly from the perpendicular—a situation which cannot be always guaranteed. The *khukhri* is a particularly bad and unscientific design. A *khukhri* has a heavy top which is tilted away from the spine. As long as the blade strikes an object at ninety degrees, the *khukhri* tries to turn on an axis which runs transverse to the wrist. No problem so far—that's with all blades. However, when the *khukhri* happens to strike an object at some angle, the moment of inertia of the tilted heavy top makes it rotate on an axis that runs through the spine of the blade. This makes the entire weapon rotate in the grip and has the highly deleterious effect of loosening the grip. Precisely for this reason, an axe which has got a long blade becomes difficult to control and can profitably be used only for simple tasks like splitting logs kept vertically and stable on a surface. If used for swinging against a standing tree trunk or any other live branch which could be situated oddly, it tends to turn. For that, one needs a blade that is broad and shorter.

(14.7.2) Marine Binocular

In jungle warfare the basic purpose is to scan an area. This requires that the field of view should not be small in the angle sub-tended. Higher magnification results in a smaller field of view. If the field of view is small, scanning becomes difficult as even identifying a spot amongst similar features becomes difficult. Further, the slightest shake of the hand results in the place getting lost. (Field of view is measured in width at factor 1000—that is, X-number of feet or meter at 1000 yards or meter). Hence, binoculars with lower magnification are more useful for such applications. The bigger field of view makes scanning easier and allows one to fix a spot therein. Further, shaking of hand does not make much difference. It has been calculated that the maximum magnification that you need is seven. A larger field of view contributes significantly to a more natural viewing experience. In jungle operations you need a marine binocular. Do not be confused by the name. You need a marine binocular because in the jungle you and your equipment may be exposed to rain or you may have to trudge through water. If you have ever used a binocular in rain, you would know that it leads to fogging inside a regular binocular. Nitrogen-filled marine binoculars prevent this. Further, the objective lens must be larger for use in low-light conditions – something that we encounter frequently. For general low-light conditions use, a 50 mm objective gives maximum brightness. Binoculars concentrate the light gathered by the objective into a beam, the exit pupil whose diameter is the objective diameter divided by the magnifying power. For maximum effective light-gathering and brightest image, the exit pupil should equal the diameter of the fully dilated human eye—minimum 7 mm. Then it should have a long eye relief. Eye relief is the distance from the rear eyepiece lens to where the image is formed. It determines the distance the observer must position his or her eye behind the eyepiece in order to see an unvignetted image. The longer the focal length of the eyepiece, the greater the eye relief. Eye relief is particularly important for eyeglass wearers. The eye of an eyeglass wearer is typically further from the eye piece which necessitates a longer eye relief in order to still see the entire field of view. Binoculars with short eye relief can also be hard to use in instances where it is difficult to hold them steady. The double-Porro-prism design gives a Z-shaped optical path to shorten the optical path and erect the image. This feature results in binoculars that are wide, with objective lenses that are well-separated but offset from the eyepieces. Image stabilisers make things unnecessarily complicated and hence you don't need them.

(14.7.3) Hydration Packs

The Camelbak Company wisely writes on its products: 'hydrate or die'. Nothing could be far from truth. The basic idea of hydration pack is that you must be able to sip water on the move without taking off the backpack—long flexible drinking tube allows the wearer to drink hands-free.

(14.7.4) Protecting your Rifle Barrel from Mud

There is a serious problem experienced during night operations whenever it has been raining and the jungle floor is both muddy and slippery. Though the problem has been experienced since long, nobody applied an innovative mind to it. In pitch dark conditions, it is just not possible to get a feel of the ground in front of you. Slipping, tripping and falling are unavoidable and people do fall often. When people fall, they try their best to keep the barrel clear off the ground. However, this cannot be guaranteed all the time. At times the barrel may touch the ground and the mud may get in. Stopping and cleaning the barrel while on march is ruled out. Hence, whether the mud has actually got in the barrel or not is a moot question; the mere suspicion of the barrel having touched the ground is enough for the man to quietly refrain from using the weapon thereafter and you are less by a rifle.

I have made a simple but very clever innovation to solve this problem. The innovation is to fix a balloon on the muzzle to make a 'Mud-Protective Balloon Cover'. The balloon keeps the mud out and in case of a doubt; one can always feel the surface of the balloon on the muzzle opening with fingers in the dark to check whether there is something sticking or whether the membrane has been ruptured. If some mud is found sticking to the membrane, it can be cleaned with

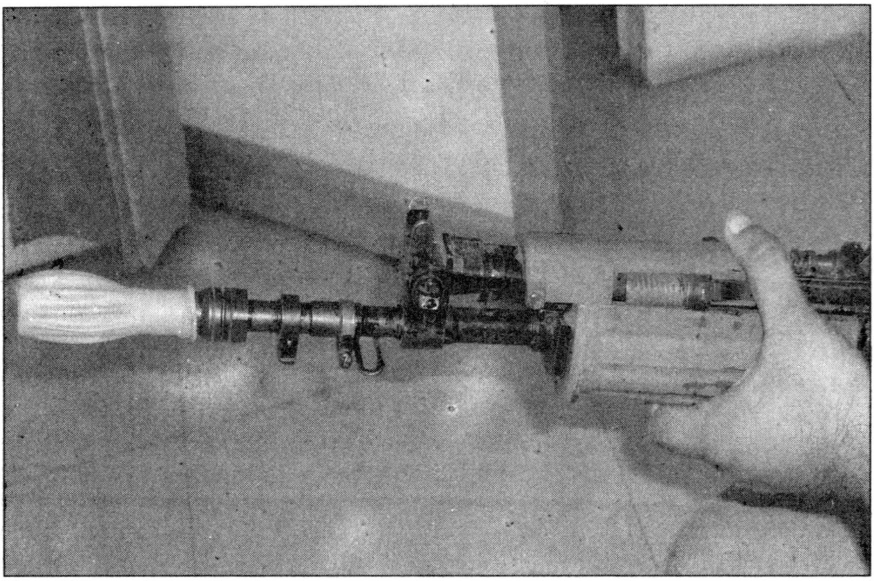

The Balloon over muzzle system to keep mud out

fingers even in pitch dark. If the membrane is ruptured, however, one would refrain from using the weapon till it is cleaned. The great advantage of a balloon is that it is eminently cheap and one can fire safely through them without any danger of the bullet encountering any resistance.

(14.8) The Ideal Load Bearing System

No matter how much you do, you'll never do enough.

Anyone who has hiked with a heavy load on his back; has suffered pain in the back, shoulders and waist from packs that hung too low; has got burns in his underarms from shoulder straps that cut into the body; and who has felt suffocated from chest straps that were too tight, would know how acutely he would have felt the need of a backpack that was scientifically designed. If you are soldier, you would know how difficult it is to get critical items out of a backpack if it is not properly designed—may be you would be obliged to fumble for long or stop and unload the whole thing! Most people won't ever think about it, but US military backpacks represent years and years of development, testing and heavy use in the field right from the First World War—and above all, responding to the needs of the soldiers. The following would also show you that if you care for your soldiers, you have no option but to apply that much research effort on something which is apparently so simple and trivial.

The M-1956 Load-Carrying Equipment (LCE) was the first major redesign of load-carrying equipment for soldiers of the US Armed Forces. The LCE was made of cotton canvas webbing like earlier equipment, yet introduced sliding clip fasteners that replaced the wire hooks dating back to the earlier M-1910 design. The LCE consisted of equipment belt, suspenders for carrying load, field pack, entrenching tool carrier, ammunition cases, canteen cover, pouch containing first aid, and sleeping bag carrier. In field use; however, soldiers found the field pack insufficient for more than a day's needs and often augmented their kit with a second or larger pack. This led to the development of a slightly larger pack with a rounded shape, the M-1961 Rucksack. Between the LCE and the Army's next major revision in 1967, a series of interim experiments were conducted using lighter materials. In 1962, tests on a nylon-constructed set of LCE revealed a substantial reduction in weight—nearly two pounds.

The Lightweight Individual Clothing & Equipment (LINCLOE) programme of 1965 applied a 'systems analysis' approach to redesigning load-carrying gear. During the early part of the Vietnam War, environmental conditions in Southeast Asia exposed the shortcomings in the webbing, cotton duck and canvas of the LCE. Cotton absorbed water thereby increasing weight; in addition, cotton duck, canvas and webbing were adversely affected by mildew and dry rot. LINCLOE developed the M-1967 Modernised Load-Carrying Equipment (MLCE) that was made with different materials that were more appropriate for use in tropical environments. It replaced cotton with nylon, and steel and brass with aluminium and plastic. Velcro fasteners, also called "hook and pile" fasteners, replaced the LTD fasteners and zippers of the LCE.

In 1974, they developed the All-Purpose Lightweight Individual Carrying Equipment (ALICE). One of the primary design goals of the ALICE was to reduce weight on the individual soldier. The fighting load, such as weapons and ammunition, is distributed on the belt and suspenders while the existence load, such as food supplies, is intended to be carried in the field pack. In 1988, they developed the Individual Integrated Fighting System (IIFS). In the IIFS, the fighting loads are carried on the vest and in the Combat Patrol Pack; existence loads are carried in the Combat Field Pack M-1990 (CFP-90). The CFP-90 is a top-loading pack constructed of water-repellent back-coated nylon fabric and an internal frame of two removable aluminium staves. The pack has two compartments: a main compartment with a false bottom and an internal compartment for communications equipment or a hydration unit. The smaller Combat Patrol Pack carries part of the fighting load and is attached to the top of the larger CFP-90 field pack.

Introduced in 1997, the Modular Lightweight Load-Carrying Equipment (MOLLE), is the current standard-issue military backpack for the US Army. The MOLLE uses a modular attachment system called the Pouch Attachment Ladder System (PALS), a series of evenly spaced horizontal rows made of heavy-duty nylon webbing sewn onto the load-bearing equipment. Smaller attachments, such as knife sheaths, holsters or other containers equipped with PALS webbing can easily be attached to the MOLLE. This allows soldiers to customise their field pack to a considerable extent to meet a variety of mission-specific needs. There are three components to the MOLLE system: The Fighting Load Carrier (FLC), also called the Load-Bearing Vest (LBV); the Modular Pouches, and the Hydration Bladder. The Fighting Load Carrier, also called the Load-Bearing Vest (LBV), is able to accommodate more ammunition than the load-bearing equipment and suspenders of the ALICE system. The FLC uses no metal clips and utilises an H-harness on the back for better ventilation. Fatigue is mitigated by a connecting device between the load-bearing vest and the main rucksack that transfers the carrying load on the shoulders to the hips. Stored underneath the rucksack is the Army's new modular sleeping bag. Detachable pouches on either side of the main pack hold a Meal, Ready-to-Eat (MRE) and a tube from the hydration unit delivers water. However, there were complaints with the MOLLE, mainly that the external plastic frame of the main pack was prone to breakdown under field conditions and a number of lower back injuries

The MOLLE (Modular Lightweight Load-Carrying Equipment): The US Army's current Standard-Issue Military bacpack

were attributed to the ball-and-socket mechanism between the frame and waist-belt. In addition, the straps were too short to accommodate body armour.

Though the Marines had initially taken the MOLLE, the Marine Corps initiated their own development programme that produced the Improved Load Bearing Equipment (ILBE) system. The Marine Corps specifically requested a backpack with reduced volume, greater load-carrying capability, less complexity than the MOLLE, and the ability to carry 60 mm and 81 mm mortar rounds on the outside of the pack. The ILBE was approved by the US Marine Corps in 2004, and is the current standard-issue backpack for Marines. It is somewhat narrower but longer than the MOLLE. Designed by a company called Arc'teryx, the ILBE contains three components: the ILBE Main Pack, the ILBE Assault Pack, and the ILBE Hydration System. The ILBE was designed for three specific load configurations to respond to the contingencies faced by Marines in the field: the Existence Load, the Approach March Load and the Assault Configuration. The Main Pack carries the main load of the ILBE three-part system. Made of Cordura 725, the pack is also fitted with PALS grids for MOLLE-type pocket attachments, allowing soldiers to customise their pack. Unique to the ILBE packs is the ability to carry 60 mm and 81 mm mortar rounds on the outside of the pack. The Assault Pack carries the main fighting load of ammunition for the ILBE. Equipped with PALS webbing, it is designed to carry up to 40 pounds and consists of two storage compartments in addition to an inner-pocket to hold the hydration unit. The ILBE Hydration System is a bladder-type hydration unit that holds 100 ounces of water.

In the Existence Load configuration, all three components are utilised. This is the heaviest configuration as the soldier carries necessities for extended missions in which quick resupply is not possible. A fully loaded ILBE can weigh as much as 120 pounds. The Approach March Load uses only the ILBE Main Pack and hydration unit and is intended for extended missions away from supply lines. The Assault Configuration is the lightest of the three configurations and utilises only the ILBE Assault Pack and hydration unit. This configuration allows for maximum combat effectiveness and mobility.

In late 2009, the Marine Corps, however, announced that they were looking into a replacement for the ILBE. A 2009 survey of Marines had revealed, among other shortcomings, that the ILBE does not integrate well with the Modular Tactical Vest (MTV) body armour that was developed to protect against roadside bombs. But a replacement has yet to come. This also shows that however well-researched a product be, it is only after extensive field use that its specially good points or shortcomings emerge. Forces like the Indians which lay down specifications for generations, are simply dumb.

15

Scientific Principles and Practices of Camp Defence

When you have sufficient supplies and ammo, the enemy would take two weeks to attack. When you are low on supplies and ammo the enemy decides to attack that night.

(15.1) The Great Significance of Proper Camp Defence

If you fortify only your front; you'll get your rear shot up.

(15.1.1) The Attack on Nui Ba Den

Guerrillas like to attack on the camps of security forces because it brings them disproportionately high publicity. If by any chance the attack is successful, they can inflict heavy losses and it also demoralizes the force greatly. Then the insurgents are able to claim it to the fence-sitters amongst the target population that they are so powerful that they could attack the forces right in their homes and a regime that could not protect its forces could have no pretensions about its authority to rule in that area. In other words, a successful attack on the camps of the security forces puts a question mark before the regime's very claim to offer security to others against the depredations of the insurgents. It is therefore necessary that the business of camp defense be undertaken in a scientific manner; one who does not, pays a heavy price as Ed Tatarnic describes in his account of the attack on Nui Ba Den.

"The United States Army had a two-acre camp built among the rocks and boulders on the summit of Nui Ba Den, rising 3000 feet above the paddy fields . It was first captured by Special Forces in a helicopter assault in May 1964. Nui Ba Den was a highly sensitive, complex and covert military communications station used as a listening post to capture enemy signals. At the time of the attack, there were 140 soldiers there. The NVA attacked the camp on May 13, 1968. During the attack 24 Americans were killed and 2 were taken prisoner.

Although the summit was controlled by the US Army, all the rest of the mountain and surrounding area was Viet Cong controlled. The post was therefore maintained by helicopter. Special Forces personnel had concerns regarding the defence of Nui Ba Den and made these known to the CO months before the May 1968 attack. These concerns included the concertina wire was only one strand and it was 50 meters down the mountain.

One suggestion was to build concrete bunkers into the military crest of the camp, but this was not done. Instead small houses were built near the perimeter and these had poor lines of fire. By not having concrete bunkers, the wood would rot due to the monsoon rains and they could not be reinforced with sand bags. Regardless, the CO said the sand bags were on order but they never arrived. An American General inspecting the mountain camp questioned the construction of the bunkers but was told the bunkers were for the CIDG (Civilian Irregular Defense Group) and not Americans. The General asked what difference that would make but the comment was shrugged off. The bunkers were not manned at all times, only every 3rd or 4th bunker during the day and only every second bunker during the night. Further recommendations included installing trip flares and cementing claymores into the bed rock and reinstating listening posts but none of these were done.

At 2145 hours the camp on Nui Ba Den came under attack from combined 82 mm mortar and rocket propelled grenades. It was at this time that the communications antenna was blown out by rocket propelled grenades or satchel charges and the radio went silent. The enemy moved uphill eastward toward the pagoda at the top of the mountain blowing up the generator on the way. RPG fire set many bunkers on fire. They also used tear gas to flush out the American soldiers from the bunkers. Generally, US soldiers were split into small pockets of resistance and stayed this way throughout the night.

At approximately 2330 hours a Light Fire Team and mini-gunship arrived and were directed by a lone radio operator working under the Red Horse re-transmission. The supporting forces providing fire and illumination during the attack were B Troop, 3rd Squadron, 17th Air Calvary (UHIC) gunships; 5th Air Command Squadron (C-47 Flare and gunships); Tay Ninh Artillery B Battery 2/23 Artillery. The LFT drew heavy anti-aircraft fire from the base of the mountain. The LFT saturated an area about 75 meters outside the perimeter to prevent any further infiltration.

It was determined that the size of the attacking VC force was between a reinforced platoon and a company size. The VC advantage was their ability to closely approach and break into the perimeter undetected and their thorough knowledge of the locations of key installations such as VHF antenna towers and the generators".

(15.1.2) *Why you must have a SOP for Camp Defence?*

An analysis of the incidents of attack on the camps of security forces in India shows that in each one of them, the response of the security forces was characterised by only three words: chaotic, panic-stricken and haphazard. Moreover, they had never understood the special concepts of preparing camp defenses especially for such situations. The common thread that has emerged in all the instances is that in the absence of a scientifically prepared SOP for dealing with such situations, nobody knew what to do and responses were characterised by natural instincts or were simply knee-jerk reactions. In the first place, utter confusion was found to prevail. Fear gripped people and men were found to have fired more to relieve themselves of the anxiety induced by fear than to actually hit the terrorists. In other words, in the initial moments people fired randomly just for the sake of firing. There has been a serious lack of fire discipline and command-controlled fire. Camp defence is something which the stupid Indians take in a most routine manner without any application of scientific mind. Whatever they have by way of standing instructions pertaining to camp security has in fact never envisaged the sort of situations that the forces have had to encounter. Had they been useful, the terrorists would not have been able to inflict so many casualties in attacks on Indian camps.

(15.2) Possible Modes of Attack

Firing from a stand-off position or firing on the run: This is the simplest way of attacking though, in terms of real damage, the least effective. There is little which can be done to prevent the physical action of firing from a distance. Little damage can be inflicted on the enemy by returning the fire randomly or in the general direction; however, it serves a limited purpose. It tells the enemy that you are alert and that you have sufficient firepower and thereby deters him from any further adventure. Do not waste too much ammunition in the process and do not take such firings as challenges or affronts and jump out of the camp in hot pursuit. The fire could easily be a bait to bring you out into a trap. Do not respond to a challenge in a knee-jerk fashion. The correct procedure is to mount a pursuit and search operation in the suspect location with sufficient preparedness.

Hand grenades or rifle grenades: In those areas where camps happen to be situated amidst populated areas, lobbing of grenades is quite a popular method for the ease of its execution and also because the damage potential is not dependent on its accuracy. Innocuous looking persons lob the grenades underhand from close to the location and become a normal man the next moment. Western forces operating in foreign lands can afford to keep the local population strictly away from their camps so as to maintain a stand-off distance—it is not so easy for forces that are combating insurgencies in their own country. Firing of a rifle grenade from UBGL is equally easy and has the additional advantage of longer range and accuracy. There is little that you can do about this.

Mortar and Rocket Fire: Excellent methods of non-line-of-sight attack and that too from a very safe distance. There is little that can be done if your camp is struck by mortar fire except taking the best cover that you can. So is the case with improvised rockets or 107 mm rockets. Since RPG-7 has a shorter range and a flatter trajectory, it is not such a wise idea to attack a camp with a RPG.

Suicidal (Mistakenly Called Fidayeen) attacks: The so-called Fidayeen attacks have acquired an aura of their own. The very mention of the word Fidayeen is enough to send shivers down the spines of most personnel. The basic difference is that the attacker does not seek to run away. Since he is prepared to die, he is capable of inflicting more casualties than one who is intent upon running away. A suicidal attack, in order to be successful, must first breach the perimeter security. Once he has breached your perimeter security, he can use firearms, grenades and IEDs etc upon you.

(15.3) Various Methods of Breaching Perimeter Security

The enemy invariably attacks on two occasions:
a. When they're ready.
b. When you're not.

Making a Frontal Suicidal Assault: Making a frontal suicidal assault does not mean that they will use only the front gate. It means that the attacker is not taking any protective cover and is facing you frontally. He can try to breach perimeter anywhere. The purpose is to overwhelm the defences by the sheer volume of fire delivered through firearms or grenades. While one or more of them could be killed in the process, the remaining could force their way through. Success depends on the degree of surprise. From the point of view of the forces, their only option is to deliver heavy and accurate fire on the intruders. Needless to say, success depends on the alertness of the person who has detected the terrorist first. That's why it is necessary that in such situations, all personnel must carry their weapons at all times.

Entering Surreptitiously: In contrast to the above, this method involves deceit. The guerrilla would try to enter the premises by scaling walls, cutting wires or slipping underneath under the wires under the cover of darkness. Defeating this requires adequate perimeter security both in terms of the physical barriers and also perimeter lighting. While generators and flood lights/security lights are all in order and useful and must be available, there is no substitute of a hand-held lights as all other systems can fail under an attack. An explosion can cause a short circuit somewhere and render all electrical systems useless.

Effecting Entry under the Cover of Diversionary Fire or some other Activity: This is a more intelligent method. The idea is to create a diversion by fire, grenade explosion, IED or car bomb at some point or more than one point along the perimeter and while the attention of the personnel is engaged in the above, enable some others to enter through some other point by overcoming the physical barriers or overwhelming the sentries there. All personnel need to be briefed regarding this possibility. The natural reaction of most troops is to physically rush to or focus their attention on where the first shots have landed. It needs to be drilled in their minds that the persons charged with perimeter security on other points shall continue to man their locations and be alert there irrespective of what is happening elsewhere in the camp.

Car Bombs or, more generally, VBIEDs (Vehicle Borne IEDs): There is nothing better than a car bomb or VBIED for confounding the sentry or crashing through physical barriers. There is no limit to the ingenuity in which IEDs may be carried on vehicles. The only way of reducing the effectivity of the VBIED is to have sufficient stand-off distance—the explosive power falls off with the cube of the distance and doubling the distance from the bomb means that you reduce the power of the explosion by eight times. You must accomplish this either by suitable barricading near your location. Be very alive to this threat if you have your post in a populated area. There are several simple ways of creating barriers. Take four-five feet long pieces of angle iron. Drive them half way into the ground. Space them four-five feet away. This stops four-wheelers. Create a hedge hog and it will defeat a two-wheeler also.

(15.4) Response to Breach of Perimeter Security

The enemy never watches until you make a mistake.

Caltrops and other Obstacles: Supposing that the terrorists somehow succeed in breaching the perimeter, what needs to be done after that? Your first task must be to make his progress difficult. A terrorist has to cover some ground before he enters a room or building. Some ingenuity must be exercised to make it difficult for the terrorists to make a dash for a vulnerable place. From the gate or perimeter breaching point to the building they have to traverse some space. It is this space that must be made difficult. A caltrop is a four-pronged object. Whichever way you throw it, one prong always points up. In Vietnam it was made of pieces of barbed wire also. You could also consider simply strewing the land with a large number of pieces of barbed wire or concertina. By strewing the ground with such obstacles, you reduce the terrorist's speed and render him vulnerable to fire while he is in the open.

Covering Dead Ground: Wherever a sentry has to protect a dead ground or an open space in which your own men are not to be found, they must do it with grenades. A suicide attacker could indeed survive the fire of the sentries, if they are firing from semi-automatic weapons because he has the advantage of the darkness and also the fact that he could be running in an erratic manner. To prevent this, you must saturate the dead ground with shrapnel of grenades or automatic fire. It is a good idea to supplement his rifle with a sub-machinegun. A sub-machinegun firing on full auto is very useful in saturating a dead ground not longer than 50 yards with bullets and in an emergency the sentry can fire it with one hand also.

Why Immediate Response is Vital?: The success in repelling or neutralising an attack depends on how quickly the fire is returned. Camp defence does not mean only perimeter security. We must also provide for fighting if an attack takes place. Don't leave the job to the sentries alone. The sentries could have been injured in the first attack itself. When an attack takes place, every second counts in the first few minutes. The battle is effectively won or lost in the first few minutes. The terrorists require some time to rush through the land between the entry point and their target (such as the barracks). They are exposed in that duration. Even after they enter a building they require some time to occupy a vantage position. It is those moments that they are most vulnerable and may be attacked. Remember that once they have taken up defensive positions, it becomes a battle of attrition. Then you have to proceed like a regular house intervention. A situation where you find people scurrying for their weapons kept in their rooms or under their beds after they hear the shots is a sure recipe for disaster. Life and death depend on how quickly fire is returned.

Raising a Distinctive Alarm: There ought to be a special alarm to tell people that the perimeter security has been breached and the camp is under a attack. The special alarm will be used only for this purpose and nothing else so that it is never misunderstood. A special alarm is necessary because the usual whistle has become too common by overuse. I have used the FOX40 Pealess Sonik Blast whistle which, with over 120 decibels output, can be heard over a mile away amidst ambient noise.

Immediate Reaction of those who have not spotted the Intruders: All those who are inside somewhere at the time of the attack must refrain from rushing out lest they become inadvertent casualties. Those who are caught in the open must rush to the nearest cover and assess the situation from there for further action. To save sleeping men from getting slaughtered, in any barrack where men are sleeping, irrespective of the number of men sleeping, at least one man must remain awake by rotation. The idea is that not all men must be found sleeping together to be killed together when someone enters the room.

Impeding their Progress: You shall not allow an attacker to simply barge into a building and kill your men at will. For this you must impede his progress at every stage—at every turn or landing, for example. You must therefore have a defensive fighting position made at all such places and drill must be devised that they come to be manned the moment the alarm is raised. But you have to explain it to your men that it is their responsibility that all such defensive fighting positions must be immediately manned the moment they understand that there is a problem. It should be an automatic reaction. Pay special attention to the armoury and the approach to it. You don't want the attacker to take control of the armoury and kill you after commandeering your own weapons, and decamp with looted weapons. Soldiers must roll grenades down the stairs if they feel that a suicide attacker is charging upstairs. If he is running upstairs, he has obviously killed the men downstairs and they need not worry about injuring their own men.

Firing, Engaging and Neutralising the Terrorists after their Position is Ascertained: You must presume that the attacker has already done a reconnaissance of your location and knows where he has to go. Once it is ascertained that the intruders are in a certain location, they will be engaged by the standard methods of fighting in built-up areas. The first step is to isolate the building. After the building is isolated, the second step is to cover all its entry/exit points including windows with fire. For this purpose, it may be necessary to build temporary DFPs (defensive fighting positions) at vantage points.

(15.5) Scientific Design of 'Defensive Fighting Positions' and the Method of Firing from them

Never share a fox-hole with anyone braver than yourself.

Most people in the armed forces do not have any idea of how to construct proper 'defensive fighting positions' that are especially suited for anti-terrorist operations. All of them are found to be in a time warp in this regard. Most armies still suffer from the hangover of the bunkers and pillboxes that were designed and constructed in the two World Wars for infantries to defend a place far away from the bunker/pillbox. They are singularly useless in an anti-terrorist or counter-insurgency situation. Why? The bunkers and pillboxes were constructed with two purposes in mind. The first was to protect the soldiers from artillery or small arms fire. Much emphasis was therefore laid on overhead protection because soldiers in open trenches used to be exposed to them earlier. In an anti-terrorist or counter-insurgency situation, you should normally not expect shrapnel coming from overhead. Hence, you can save yourself the trouble of providing protection against bullets and shrapnel from the top. The second objective of the bunkers and pillboxes was to strafe the enemy as he came from a certain direction. Thus they had prescribed fields of fire for each weapon in the bunker or pillbox. Machineguns were mounted elaborately and supports were provided even for rifles so that men could fire conveniently for long.

All these bunkers and pillboxes are useless in an anti-terrorist or counter-insurgency situation. The simple reason is that they cater only to a situation where the enemy would come only from a certain direction and only in a certain fashion. Thus, you could have bunker to cover a bridge or a mountain pass because the enemy could come only through that. Weapons were therefore so sighted that they could fire right at the expected zone. Generally, this distance used to be of the order of hundreds of yards if not thousands. You could afford to have a small loophole or firing port and poke the barrel of the gun out of it. Even if you could not see very well through that loophole, you could rest assured that the bullets would be hitting the right place.

The position in an anti-terrorist or counter-insurgency situation is materially different, however. The terrorist or guerrilla is not going to behave like regular enemy infantry troops. He is not fool enough to come rumbling through that mountain pass, lane or bridge that you so assiduously seek to cover with your fire. His purpose is to attack your camp or location with small arms and grenades. And remember that you are not living in a fort. He would therefore take the advantage of the cover of darkness or bad weather and sneak in close to your camp before he opens fire. How in the world you retaliate with weapons that are sighted to fire at say, 300 yards?

There is no way you can shoot at him effectively if you are hiding behind a wall of sandbags or concrete and have left only a small loophole. The loophole or the firing port is so small that if you poke the barrel of your gun out of it, you cannot see a thing outside; if you try to peep outside, you cannot fire through it. You are thus severely handicapped. Hiding in that bunker will save your life but will do nothing towards protecting your camp. If the guerrilla manages to somehow bypass your bunker, he is free to wreak havoc elsewhere even as you would remain safe. You must therefore leave the firing port to the tanks. You are a soldier defending a camp and you need different devices.

A classic infantry pillbox/bunker with a small firing port designed to cover a fixed spot/zone with the fire of a mounted weapon – unfortunately; this won't do in guerrilla warfare

For an anti-terrorist or counter-insurgency situation, you require defensive fighting positions from which you have an all-round view and above all, the flexibility to manoeuvre your weapon and be able to fire close. The requirements are met by two basic design considerations. If you have to fire from a rifle at distances of say 100 yards or less, you must be raised above the ground. The height to which you need to be raised depends on the ground you have to protect. You must either build the entire defensive fighting position above the ground or provide platform inside the position so that you are raised above the ground. In order to be able to fire at close distances, remember that you shall fire from a standing position.

Forget all that they taught you about the battle-crouch position with the barrel of the rifle placed on the wall in front of you. You are not going to kneel either. Remember that the terrorist is highly mobile. He could actually be running and jumping like a rat, scurrying from one position to another. Moreover, there could be several of them. Hence, what you need most is flexibility of movement and also flexibility in pointing the barrel of your rifle. This means that the only position from which you can and you must fire is the standing position and you should be able to move freely inside your defensive fighting position. From this will be dictated how you must make the loophole and how big it should be. You will find that the very concept of a loophole becomes dubious for such a situation. If you make a loophole, you are doomed. In an anti-terrorist or counter-insurgency situation the more you can see outside the better. Then the question arises as to how you will get some cover. Obviously, if you are exposed, you cannot fight. This means that we have two conflicting requirements. The secret of making a proper defensive fighting position lies in reconciling these two conflicting requirements.

From my research I have determined that this would require openings (now that we are no longer calling them loopholes or firing ports) that are not only substantially bigger but have a vertical orientation so that you may point the barrel down and fire close to you. Visualise the opening like a wide vertical slit. Okay, that solves the problem of firing close to you. Now how do you fire from it? Obviously, if you stand right in front of it, you will be shot. What is the solution, then? Once again, I have determined form my research that you can still have cover and fire near you. The secret is that you must stand sideways (so as to present a smaller target) to a side of the opening and then fire instead of firing from a frontal position. You should have such openings on all the sides that you intend to cover from that position. A sentry post should therefore have vertical pillar like structures for firing sideways in different directions without facing the opening directly.

You require firing ports like this which give you more flexibility: you shall fire from it standing sideways to the port sans a mounted weapon – note the widening in the center to allow more traverse

Henceforth, you shall not commit the mistake of mounting a LMG in the bunker. The primary weapon of a bunker in counter-insurgency situations should be the rifle only for the flexibility it offers. The LMG will only be a support weapon in case the barrel of the rifle overheats. You do not require a mount or support for it.

(15.6) Proper use of the AGL and the MMG in Camp Defence

When you have secured the area, make sure the enemy knows it too.

The AGL has some role in camp defence, provided the gunner is able to:

- Open fire at the instant desired;
- Adjust fire on the target;
- Regulate the rate of fire; and
- Shift fire from one target to another.

Engage fleeing targets as soon as possible and with all available fire. Observation and adjustment of fire is the most important element of fire control. It is continuous throughout the action. The gunner must be trained to observe and adjust fire without command and to check the lay of the gun frequently. Adjustments may be made before or after firing.

The MMG is useful in camp defence for reasons similar to that for the AGL. A long automatic burst going very far has a salutary effect on the adversary. The size and nature of the target determine how the gunner applies his fire. He must manipulate the machinegun to move the beaten zone throughout the target area. The rate of fire must be controlled to adequately cover the target but not waste ammunition or destroy the barrel.

- Distributed fire is delivered in width and depth such as at an enemy formation.
- Concentrated fire is delivered at a point target such as an automatic weapon or an enemy fighting position.
- The rates of fire that can be used with the machinegun are sustained, rapid, and cyclic. These rates enable leaders to control and sustain fire and prevent the destruction of barrels. More than anything else, the size of the target and ammunition supply dictate the selection of the rate of fire.

When engaging an area target, the gunner must fires in the center of mass, then traverse and search to either flank. Upon reaching the flank, he must reverse direction and traverse and search in the opposite direction in the manner illustrated below. The leader may indicate the width and depth of the target.

(15.7) Physical Security of Camps

Physical security is defined as a part of security that is concerned with physical measures designed to safeguard personnel; to prevent unauthorised access to equipment, installations, material, and documents; and to safeguard against espionage, sabotage, damage, and theft. The objectives of a terrorist with respect to static locations could include: inflicting injury or death on people; destroying or damaging camps, property, equipment, or resources; stealing equipment, materiel, or information; and creating adverse publicity. The terrorist or the aggressor has a wide field of choice to achieve these objectives and the security systems must be designed to protect against each one of them.

Protective Barriers: Common barriers such as barbed wire or concertina protect against human intrusion. A great advantage with concertina is the ability to deploy quickly. When used as the perimeter barrier for a restricted area, the ideal way to lay concertina is between poles with one roll on top of another or in a pyramidal arrangement (with a minimum of three rolls).

Observation Towers: All observation towers should be located to provide maximum observation and should be constructed for protection from small-arms fire. However, during inclement weather and during a blackout, towers lose the advantage of a greater range of observation and must be supplemented by on-ground observation. They must have appropriate Surveillance, Target-acquisition, and Night-observation (STANO) equipment. All camps using towers must have a support force available for emergencies. You must ensure that towers have overlapping, mutually supporting fields of observation and fire and that they are provided with a backup fortified defensive fighting position, as appropriate.

Perimeter Barrier: When the perimeter barrier encloses a large area, an interior all-weather perimeter road should be provided for security-patrol vehicles. Clear zones should be maintained on both sides of the perimeter barrier to provide an unobstructed view of the barrier and the ground adjacent to it. If it is not possible due to whatever reason, compensate for it by increasing the height of the perimeter barrier, increasing security-patrol coverage, adding more security lighting, or installing an intrusion-detection device along that portion of the perimeter.

Security Lighting: Optimum security lighting is achieved by adequate, even light on bordering areas; glaring lights in the eyes of an intruder; and little light on security-patrol routes. In addition to seeing long distances, security forces must be able to see low contrasts (such as indistinct outlines of silhouettes) and must be able to detect an intruder who may be exposed to view for only a few seconds. Higher levels of illumination improve these abilities. High brightness contrast between an intruder and the background should be the first consideration when planning for security lighting. With predominantly dark, dirty surfaces or camouflage-type painted surfaces, more light is needed to produce the same brightness around installations and buildings than when clean concrete, light brick, and grass predominate. When the same amount of light falls on an object and its background, the observer must depend on contrasts in the amount of light reflected. His ability to distinguish poor contrasts is significantly improved by increasing the illumination level. The observer primarily sees an outline or a silhouette when the intruder is darker than his background. Using light finishes on the lower parts of buildings and structures may expose an intruder, who depends on dark clothing and darkened face and hands. Stripes on walls have also been used effectively, as they provide recognisable breaks in outlines or silhouettes. Providing broad-lighted areas around and within the installation against which intruders can be seen can also create good observation conditions. An open yard adjacent to a perimeter (between guards and fences) must be illuminated according to the perimeter's illumination requirements. Where lighting is necessary in other open yards, illumination should not be less than 0.2 foot-candle at any point. A secure auxiliary power source and power-distribution system for the facility should be installed to provide redundancy to critical security lighting and other security equipment. Auxiliary power sources must be available for critical electrical loads and must be secured against direct and indirect fires as well as sabotage.

16

Field Management of Gunshot Wounds and other Penetrating Injuries

Never stand when you can sit, never sit when you can lie down, never stay awake when you can sleep.

(16.1) What is Field Management of Wounds and how does it differ from First Aid?

Anything you do can get you killed, including nothing.

The battlefield is a place that has many crisis situations at the same time—bullets flying all over the place, landmines exploding, people getting shot up, limbs getting shattered, the wounded screaming, and the survivors finding themselves unable to help under fire. Then depending on the inefficiency of the country you unfortunately happen to be fighting for, medical evacuation of casualties could take a long time—in God forsaken countries like India where helicopter pilots are notorious for inventing a million excuses for why they cannot fly and land at some place at some given time, the evacuation could be even 24 hours away. Americans are known to evacuate their wounded soldiers by helicopter within an hour; even if that meant more than one helicopter getting shot in the process—the Indians take their own sweet time—*sab chalta hai*! Life is cheap in India anyway. So what are you going to do? Wait till the stupid pilot arrives and bleed to death in the meantime—certainly not if you love your life. It is therefore necessary that you must learn procedures that will help save your and your comrades' lives. The Americans value the life of every single soldier. That's why they have taken great pains and devoted enormous resources to carry out research in this field even when they are confident that they would evacuate their wounded quickly. The United States Army Institute of Surgical Research, for example, has a full-fledged Combat Casualty Care Research Programme, precisely to develop methods and techniques by which soldiers may help themselves in the battlefield. They have done so because they do not want to take any risk with any life. The soldier must get the best field management of his wounds as soon as he is wounded so that his chances of surviving without any disability are increased greatly.

This is real and practical field medicine as the soldiers would apply it to themselves in the field. This is not what hospitals understand by emergency medicine. This is not about first aid either—first aid is for school kids; this is about serious injuries sustained in the battlefield. Most general medical practitioners are not familiar with the knowledge which is presented here for the simple reason that they do not get to study such things in India. I am very much aware of the best practices of what is described as emergency medicine in the world. Nothing of that sort, however, can be applied in the field by soldiers upon themselves. The methods of hospitals have any relevance only when the casualty reaches the hospital. The methods presented here are designed to keep him alive till he reaches the hospital. These methods have been developed by outstanding scientists who also understood the peculiarities and intricacies of the battlefield. They are all based on solid science and have found application in numerous wars of the US army since Vietnam where they have proved eminently successful.

When most people start talking about help in the battlefield they tend to drift towards too much of everything, too much expertise and too much gear to carry. On the contrary, these procedures are based on what the soldiers, as against paramedics or trained combat medics, can be taught to do to themselves with the minimum stuff to carry, or things which may be improvised right there. The emphasis is on effective procedures. They teach one to handle trauma when a hospital's institutional facilities are not available. Elsewhere in the world, the Army Medical Corps actually runs courses on such procedures. In India I am doing it for the first time. This is extremely valuable knowledge; cherish it—you will not find it anywhere else. This goes much beyond what you are normally taught in managing casualties—that is, the A, B, C, D, E's; Airway, Breathing, Circulation, Disability, Exposure—leave that for the magazines. The philosophy must be very clear—I am not going to let my man die simply waiting for him to receive proper medical care in the trauma center; we shall do everything in the meantime to save him. We shall not be afraid of any possible complication for no complication could be worse than imminent death. In any case, all of the possible consequences can be managed in a hospital.

(16.2) Do not be unduly afraid of Battlefield Wounds, they can be managed

The only thing more accurate than enemy fire is friendly fire.

(16.2.1) *What Battlefield Data Say?*

Lay people have an unfounded fear of gunshot wounds. This notion is fostered further by the wrong depictions in TV and films. The reality is different. The US army has analysed data collected over decades. The figures speak for themselves:

- Deaths from isolated wounds to the head = 62 per cent
- Deaths from isolated wound to the chest = 28 per cent
- Deaths from isolated wounds to the abdomen = 9 per cent
- Deaths from isolated wound to the extremities = <1 per cent

It means that while one can die from a gunshot wound but the odds are against it most of the time provided blood loss is controlled. The men need to understand that getting shot does not necessarily mean sure death. This chapter is about allaying that fear and doing something effective about it.

External bleeding is generally described in terms of the origin of the blood flow by vessel type. Soldiers must know this so that they may themselves assess the severity of the wound to some extent. Knowledge would help allay unfounded fears. The basic categories of external bleeding are:

Arterial bleeding: As the name suggests, blood flow originating in an artery. With this type of bleeding, the blood is typically bright red in colour, due to the high degree of oxygenation. Blood typically exits the wound in spurts, rather than in a steady flow. The amount of blood loss can be copious, and can occur very rapidly.

Venous bleeding: This blood is flowing from a damaged vein. As a result, it will be a darker red to burgundy in colour (due to the lack of oxygen being transported) and will flow in a steady manner. Caution is still indicated; while the blood loss may not be arterial, it can still be quite substantial, and can occur with surprising speed without intervention.

Capillary bleeding: Capillary bleeding usually occurs in superficial wounds, such as abrasions. The colour of the blood may vary somewhat (distal portion of circulation with oxygenated and unoxygenated blood mixing), and will generally ooze in small amounts, as opposed to flowing or spurting.

Internal Bleeding: Signs of internal bleeding include firmness in the abdomen after injury, vomiting blood, blood in urine or feces, large bruises over the flank or abdomen, pale skin, cool and clammy skin, rapid heart rate, weakness, thirst, dizziness, shortness of breath. There is little you can do about them.

(16.2.2) The Great Significance of Stopping Blood Loss

Blood loss is the most important reason why people die of gunshot wounds and other battlefield injuries. The medical fact is that unless one gets hit in the heart or aorta (major blood vessel from the heart) he shouldn't bleed out so fast that having a decent chance of survival would be ruled out. Severe bleeding means the loss of more than 1000 ml (1 liter) of blood. How do you judge it? This flow of blood can soak a paper or cloth handkerchief in a few seconds. In such a situation, the bleeding will cause the death of the casualty in seconds to minutes. The average adult male has about 5 liters of blood in the body. Typically blood pressure begins to drop (hypotension) when 20-30 per cent is lost. Death can occur when 40 per cent of blood loss occurs and the volume is not replaced. Soldiers in battle are to be found in a situation where replacing blood loss in the field by them would not be practical. In fact, any IV infusion of plasma expanders or whatever would not be possible. We have therefore to look for means of stopping blood loss before it becomes critical. The main principle of field trauma care for the "lay" person is to stop ongoing blood loss.

There are five areas from where people can bleed large amounts causing shock. They are the chest, abdomen, pelvis/retroperitoneum, long bones (e.g. femur) and at the scene (bleeding from an open wound onto the ground). There is not much which the men in the battlefield can do about head wounds. They are best avoided by proper helmets. Next to them are chest wounds, abdominal wounds and wounds in large limbs—the classic soldier's wounds in field. We must focus on them.

(16.3) How to Control Bleeding in the Field?

Pressure, pressure, pressure! It cannot be overstated that simply putting direct pressure on a bleeding wound will stop or control most bleeding. This is particularly true for wounds on all places except chest, abdomen (where you cannot apply pressure) or when a limb is shattered by massive trauma or when a major blood vessel is torn along its length. One should press with whatever amount of force it takes for the bleeding to slow down and finally stop. Placing pressure on the wound will constrict the blood vessels manually, helping to stem any blood flow. When applying pressure, the type and direction of the wound may have an effect, for instance, a cut lengthways on the hand would be opened up by closing the hand in to a fist, whilst a cut across the hand would be sealed by making a fist. A victim can apply pressure directly to his own wound, if his consciousness level allows. Direct pressure can be used with some foreign objects protruding from a wound also, and to achieve this, padding is applied from either side of the object to push in and seal the wound—objects must not be removed in the field.

1. Remove clothing cover from the wound so you can examine the source of blood—i.e. exit and entry wounds. Clothing must be cut using scissors and not by knives as that could result in undesirable force getting applied to the body of the injured person. Soldiers must carry small scissors for this purpose.
2. Apply pressure directly to the wound with the heel of your hand using the cleanest available bandage, sterile gauze pad, or cloth compress.
3. **Field Improvisations for applying Direct Pressure:** Ideally a barrier, such as sterile, low-adherent gauze should be used between the pressure supplier and the wound, to help reduce chances of infection and help the wound to seal. Other soldiers assisting a patient are always advised to use protective latex or nitrile medical gloves to reduce risk of infection or contamination passing either way. These are not costly items and can be carried by the soldiers. An excellent field improvisation, however, is sanitary napkins for holding pressure on bleeding wounds. Sanitary napkins can be used as improvised bandages that would soak up a lot of blood and help in stopping bleeding. The packet comes sealed and is therefore more contamination-free (though not sterile) than ordinary cotton or bandages that we, in any case, use so liberally. Use of cotton bundle must be avoided because it leaves fibers in the wound. Gauze is better. But carrying gauze enough for large wounds could be a problem. The usual amount which they carry in their first-aid kits is hopelessly insufficient. There have been occasions when four-five people got injured simultaneously and the soldiers fell short of dressing.
4. Remember that direct pressure works most of the time for external bleeding. It can stop even carotid and femoral bleeding. Even just a firmly applied thumb may work with big bleeders in small wound tracts. One soldier in the US army has used a thumb successfully in two casualties. One had carotid bleeding – the other had femoral bleeding.

5. Bleeding control requires very firm pressure. You are doing it for stopping bleeding. The blood vessels are deep inside the limbs. The pressure must reach them. Do not be afraid of hurting the victim. He may even scream. Stuff a rolled up handkerchief in his mouth to muffle the scream if the battlefield situation demands so. Do not bother about the pain to him. He is not going to be hurt more by the pressure than by the bullet or splinter that has hurt him in the first place.
6. Maintain pressure for a minimum of 10 minutes to allow several blood vessels to close by vascular spasm and allow early blood clot formation. Do not peek at the wound during this period as this will prolong bleeding.
7. If direct pressure fails to stop bleeding, check to see that you are applying pressure at the correct location. You should be pressing directly on the bleeding point. Try repositioning your pressure and hold again for another 10 minutes.
8. Once bleeding has subsided, apply a pressure dressing. Cover the wound with the cleanest available bandage, sterile gauze pad, or cloth compress and wrap firmly with rolled gauze or elastic bandage. Do not apply dressing so tightly as to compromise circulation where the victim loses feeling in fingertips or toes.
9. When applying bandages to stop bleeding, add new bandages over the old; do not remove bandages when they become soaked.
10. **Do not bother about the Pressure Points taught in books on First Aid:** In a civilian scenario, laymen are taught to stop bleeding by applying pressure to the pressure points. The idea is to compress the nearest leading (proximal) side of the artery feeding that area. The idea is fine. However, there are limitations of this when it has to be used by soldiers in the battlefield. Finding the pressure points on a patient who is lying naked on a table is one thing—finding them correctly in the heat of the battle when the solider could be encumbered with his uniform, flak jacket, magazines, rucksack, etc is quite another. Above all, the soldiers would have to know the correct pressure points. This requires substantial training. Then he has to make a correct assessment as to which artery could be feeding a given area. He may commit mistakes on both scores.

(16.4) How Tourniquets, if used properly, are a most Valuable Aid?

(16.4.1) *Do not be Fooled by the Notions of the Ignorant*

The use of tourniquets is in fact widespread in military applications, and has the potential to save lives during major limb trauma. Those scientists in the US army, who have conducted extensive research into it, strongly contest the reluctance that is often associated with the use of tourniquets in civilian practice. Tourniquets stop blood flow to any part beyond the point of application. This means that the tissues there are getting deprived of oxygen carried by the blood. If the tourniquet is left in place for a long time—remember, a long time—it will lead to necrosis of the tissue and may result in amputation of the limb. But there are many myths associated with amputation and the actual necessity of it. Much of the amputation that is carried out by dumb doctors is often a result of a medieval hangover. In the medieval ages, the only treatment of battlefield injuries was amputation because no other treatment was available. This memory lives in the collective subconscious of many medical practitioners and particularly amongst army surgeons, who have little experience of anything else. Peer-reviewed published studies have shown that in cases of major limb trauma, there is no apparent link between tourniquet application and morbidity of the limb. Precisely for this reason, many armies insist that the soldiers carry a tourniquet as part of their personal first aid kit. The US army does it and I am going by their opinion. Should anyone have objection, he must disprove their studies first by publishing peer-reviewed papers with sufficient case-studies to support it. I am not going to accord any credence to the notions of medical practitioners over the research findings of those who conduct path-breaking research themselves. In any case, the issue before field medicine is: what do you choose—life or limb? My contention is that we must choose life over limb. My man could bleed to death right before the eyes of his comrades if his bleeding is not stopped. Am I going to not allow a tourniquet on the argument that it might result in his losing a leg? Certainly not! A tourniquet is the last resort method of bleeding control. In combat settings, they are the biggest lifesaver on the battlefield! Use them without fear at all. They are not a problem if not left in place for too long. Damage to the limb is rare if the tourniquet is left on for less than two hours.

(16.4.2) *The Mechanical Advantage Tourniquet* (MAT)

This is one of the great inventions. Why it was needed in the first place? Because improperly devised tourniquets fails to achieve the required pressure to compress the arteries and may even increase bleeding by impairing the venous blood flow instead. The MAT (Mechanical Advantage Tourniquet) is well-designed and can be rapidly applied to any extremity with even one hand—you can imagine how convenient it is to an injured soldier. With its easy, fast and secure one-handed operation, blood flow can be stopped in less than 10 seconds. Here is how the tourniquet is applied.

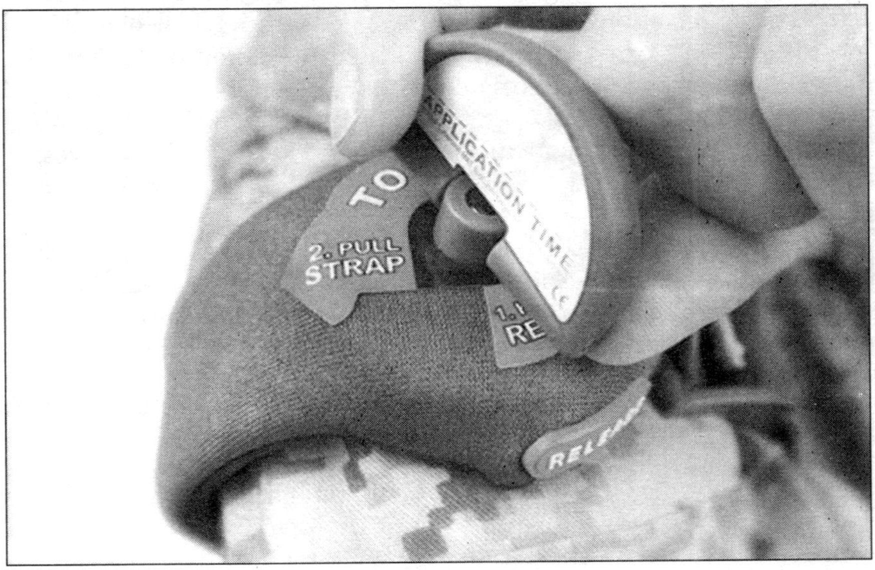

The Mechanical Advantage Tourniquet

Proper Application of Tourniquets: A tourniquet should be applied to the limb between the bleeding site and the heart, as close to the injury as possible (not more than 2-3 inches away) and tightened just to the point where the bleeding can be controlled. It should not be placed over a joint space (as the artery dives deep there and can't be compressed by the bone). Further, a tourniquet should not be applied over exposed muscle without skin (to avoid slipping). Tourniquets can be very painful. Do not bother about it. This is a critical moment. You are saving a life. It should be evaluated and removed as soon as possible and converted to a pressure bandage if possible. Pressure bandages are sometimes confused with tourniquets in non-trained civilian use. A pressure bandage is applied either directly to the wound or just above the arterial path to slow blood flow and reduce blood loss, without occluding blood flow to the injury. If a tourniquet is loosened after some time, don't take the tourniquet off and discard it. You may need it back on if the bleeding starts up again.

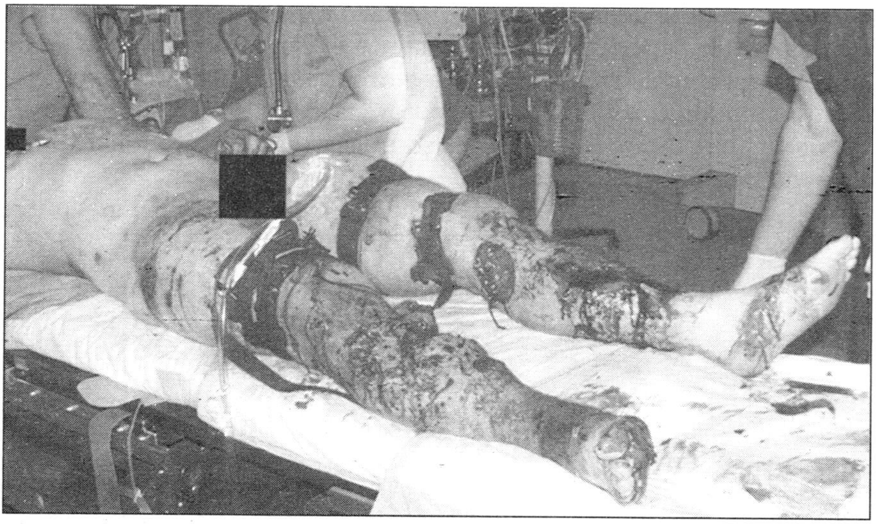

Illustrating how lives have been saved with mechanical advantage tourniquets even when there were such horrible injuries

Constructing an Effective Field-improvised Tourniquet if you have to: Use a 2- to 4-inch wide bandage or strip of strong cloth that will not cut the skin. Wrap the bandage around the limb several times then tie a knot, leaving loose ends long enough to tie another knot. Put a sturdy stick or rod over the knot then tie it in place with a knot formed with the loose ends. Twist the stick until the bandage is tight enough to stop the bleeding and then secure it so that it does not untighten itself. Every 10-15 minutes briefly release the tourniquet to see if it is still needed to control the loss of blood. As soon as bleeding stops, remove the tourniquet.

(16.5) Why you should not bother about Suturing a Wound?

This is a myth propagated by innumerous films where a gutsy hero like Sylvester Stallone is seen suturing his own bullet wound. Leave that to the films. In films even rifle bullets merely get stuck in his biceps which he plucks out with a hot knife. In real life, they can go right across the torsos of not one but two men! Nothing could be more unscientific than suturing up a bullet wound. A bullet or splinter contaminated by powder residue and gases, passing through used cloth and dirty skin creates a contaminated wound. Closing the skin over trapped-blood, dead tissue, and foreign material creates a buffet table for bacteria. Don't even think of suturing it.

The science of surgery divides wounds into four categories: Clean, clean-contaminated, contaminated, and dirty/infected. The differences between each class are determined by the amount of bacterial contamination expected in the wound. The first two categories are for patients in a hospital. A clean wound occurs when prepared (cleansed) skin is opened in a controlled fashion and no internal organs are entered. Hernia repair is a good example. Clean-contaminated wounds also happen in operating rooms, as when an internal organ is operated upon under controlled circumstances, often with antibiotic coverage. A good example is an appendectomy. Contaminated wounds include open fresh traumatic injuries or surgery with bacterial contamination from an internal organ. Slashing your hand with the same knife you have been using to clean fish or game would be a good example of the former. Dirty and infected wounds contain dead tissue, pus, foreign material (e.g. wood, grass, etc), gross contamination (e.g. dirt, manure) or are contaminated wounds that have received no treatment in the first hours after injury.

Infection rates by classification are: Clean: 1.5-3.9 per cent; clean-contaminated: 3.0-4.0 per cent; contaminated: 8.5 per cent; and dirty wounds: 28-40 per cent. Obviously, the dirtier the wound is the greater likelihood of a subsequent infection. This is especially true if you suture up the wound and trap the contamination inside. Bacteria in a warm, closed space feed on bloody injured tissue and are able to multiply rapidly. Using chemical-bulldozers they are able to spread into the surrounding healthy tissues causing an infected wound that is red and drains pus. If drainage doesn't occur they can spread through tissue planes causing fasciitis, the so-called flesh eating disease, or spread throughout your entire body causing fatal infection. Even surgeons in a hospital will usually leave a dirty wound open initially. This allows the fluid and bacteria to drain from the wound and antibiotics to kill the invading bacteria. After the wound has been repeatedly cleansed and treated with antibiotics, closure can be accomplished with little chance of infection.

(16.6) What to do after the bleeding has been stopped?

Debridement and irrigation of the wound: Once the bleeding has been stopped, gently clean out any gross debris, such as wood particles and dirt or grit, but don't do it so vigorously that it restarts the bleeding. Foreign materials such as mud, clothing, and unattached bone fragments must be removed. Mud/dirt in an explosive wound must be excised. As the US army surgeons say, "The solution to pollution is dilution!" The single-most effective method of reducing bacterial counts on wound surfaces is irrigation that is, washing the wound. The best way of washing a wound is by a 35 ml syringe with 19-gauge cath because it generates 7-8 psi pressure and is found vastly superior to the bulb syringe. If you don't have that, just pour water. The irrigation stream should not be directed into puncture/narrow-based deep wounds—if these wounds are to be irrigated they should be opened. In the battlefield, potable, non-sterile, well-chlorinated water will suffice and the US army has not found it associated with increased infection rates. All that you have to see is that it shouldn't be grossly dirty or contaminated. Again, do not clean so vigorously that you restart any bleeding.

In fact, it has been found that the use of even famous antiseptics like Betadine offers no additional advantage. The downside is that it is cytotoxic! Irrigation with potable water is most certainly better than no irrigation! The use of antiseptics in care of open wounds has little to no demonstrated benefits in preventing infection or enhancing healing of open wounds. They are toxic to neutrophils; retard wound contraction and epithelialisation; and lead to increased inflammation, tissue necrosis and endothelial cell damage.

Bandaging: Place sterile gauze or even clean cloth into the wound as deep as you can without causing undue pain. Cover the site with more gauze pads, and wrap the site with gauze or an elastic bandage. If it is near a joint, try to immobilise the joint to prevent further bleeding and pain. The wound may seep a lot of fluid and the dressing may need to be changed frequently in the first 48 hours. Make an effort to cleanse the site with water and then replace the gauze pack. Removing the pack will help to remove a lot of the debris that you couldn't easily get out initially.

Further Wound Management: If victim has bones or internal organs protruding do not attempt to push these back inside the body. Cover the exposed tissue with moist sterile cloth or bandages or whatever is the cleanest that you can manage in the field.

(16.7) The correct use of Antibiotics in the Field

Infection is a late cause of morbidity (sickness) and mortality (death) in battlefield wounds. The CoTCCC [Committee on Tactical Combat Casualty Care (US Special Operations Command)] has shown that antibiotics must be given within 30-60 minutes of wounding to be effective for prophylaxis and must have good tissue penetration ability. Antibiotics are clearly not effective to prevent infection if given more than 4-6 hours after wounding. The CoTCCC has recommended that casualties must receive antibiotic treatment as soon as possible. The CoTCCC has identified the antibiotics that provided the most "bang for the buck". The following medications have been chosen for their, broad coverage, minimal side effects, resistance to heat or cold, simple dosage requirements, and minimal storage requirements.

Moxifloxacin is the oral antibiotic of choice chosen after a very careful review of a long range of antibiotics. The dosage is one 400 mg tablet by mouth, once a day. This should be administered to all casualties who can tolerate oral medications as soon after injury as possible. It is a broad spectrum antibiotic with few side effects. Its great value has been confirmed by multiple subsequent reviews of this topic, the most notable of them being by O'Connor [Military Medicine 2003]. The next choice of oral antibiotic is Levofloxacin.

Cefotetan is the parenteral (injectable) antibiotic drug of choice. If it is presumed that soldiers would find it difficult to give IV injection over 3-5 minutes in the field, the IM dosage is 2 grams. This should be given to casualties who cannot take oral medications. This includes casualties who are unconscious or those who have significant facial wounds. Ertapenem is the recommended alternative to cefotetan in the event it is not available. The dosage is 1 gram administered IV or IM. This should be given to casualties who cannot take oral medications. For IM use, reconstitute the contents of a 1 gram vial of ertepenam with 3.2 ml of one per cent lidocaine injection (without epinephrine). Shake well to dissolve and administer into a deep muscle mass (gluteal, lateral thigh). The reconstituted solution should be used within 1 hour after preparation. Almost everybody can be taught to give IM injection in deep muscle. The next choice is Ceftriaxone. It is good and may be used but its limitation is that it does not cover anaerobic bacteria. It is recommended for abdominal injuries. For injuries to the extremities, cefazolin is the next choice.

(16.8) Management of Acute Pain in the Field

The CoTCCC has applied a great deal of mind to it. Tremendous research has been done into it. The US army has devised a system of a Combat Pill Pack where all these medicines are kept in the rucksack. These are carried by everyone in the field and self-administered as soon as possible after sustaining a wound. Their well-considered findings are that if the solider is able to fight, he should be given Meloxicam 15 mg once a day, and Paracetamol 650 mg two bi-layer caplets 8 hourly.

The 8-hour Bi-layer Caplet is a clever invention. The outer layer of the caplet is designed to dissolve quickly to provide quick relief whereas the second layer gives relief for 8 hours. The CoTCCC recommends this medication because it acts quickly and helps to bridge the gap until the Meloxicam takes effect. Medications like aspirin, Motrin (Ibuprofen), and Toradol (Ketorlac) have been found to interfere with blood clotting and should not be used by combat troops in theater.

If the soldier is unable to fight, he should be given Oral Transmucosal Fentanyl Citrate (OTFC), 800 μg transbuccally. It is an opiod that provides a means of delivering effective, rapid onset pain relief without starting an IV. This medication is produced in a lozenge form. it should be given only to patients who can no longer participate in combat operations. It should be administered by taping the "lozenge-on-a-stick" to the patient's finger and placing the lozenge in the patient's mouth. If the casualty becomes drowsy the arm will fall, pulling the OTFC out of the casualty's mouth, preventing overmedication. This medication has been used extensively in Special Operations forces in the GWOT and has worked very well. Multiple studies have demonstrated its safety when used at the recommended dosing levels, but note that you must not use two when one will do! It is recommended to reassess the situation in 15 minutes. Add second lozenge, in other cheek, as necessary to control severe pain. Respiratory depression is very unlikely especially if only 1 lozenge is used. It saves the time of starting an IV and works as well as IV morphine. It is a great invention and must be procured at all costs.

(16.9) Management of Chest Wounds in the Field

(16.9.1) *What is Tension Pneumothorax and why it is an Extreme Emergency?*

Direct pressure does not work for chest wounds because it is often hard to compress chest bleeding as the structures that are bleeding are protected by the bony rib cage. Chest wounds tend to become serious for the following reason. The pleura is a thin layer of tissue that line the inner side of the thoracic cavity as well as the lung itself. In the undamaged chest/lung, there is no space between the pleural layers because they ride close to one another. In the damaged chest/lung, air may flow between the two pleural layers, creating an unnatural space. As this space grows, it leads to a condition known as a pneumothorax. If bleeding is present, you get hemothroax. When both air and blood are present, you get hemopneumothorax.

Tension pneumothorax is the accumulation of air under pressure in the pleural space. This condition develops when injured tissue happens to form a one-way valve, allowing air to enter the pleural space but preventing the air from escaping naturally. Every breath adds more air into the air space outside the lung. The air can't be exhaled because it's outside the lung; no way to escape and pressure builds up. This results in what we call collapse of the lungs. One collapsed lung should not kill a man, but the elevated air pressure outside the collapsed lung in a tension pneumothorax can impair the function of the good lung and the heart by preventing them from expanding normally. This can kill a man. It is therefore an extreme emergency and must be treated right there in the battlefield itself. The classic signs of a tension pneumothorax are deviation of the trachea away from the side with the tension, a hyper-expanded chest, an increased percussion note and a hyper-expanded chest that moves little with respiration. However, these classic signs are usually absent and more commonly the patient is tachycardic and tachypnoeic, and may be hypoxic—exhibited by respiratory distress, cyanosis, and loss of consciousness. Look for respiratory distress as the first sign.

Sucking Chest Wound (Open Pneumothorax): It takes a hole in the chest about 2 cm in size or bigger for this to occur. In a sucking chest wound, air enters the pleural space through a wound in the chest wall. The elastic lung deflates and pulls away from the chest wall. On inspiration, the air now enters the chest through the hole instead of into the lungs. The affected lung cannot be fully re-inflated by inhalation. This is treated by applying an occlusive dressing completely over the wound during expiration. The reason is that at this point in the breathing cycle, there is relatively less air in the pleural space. Once the wound has been occluded with a dressing, air can no longer enter or exit the pleural space. The injured lung will remain partially collapsed, but the mechanics of respiration will be better. Negative pressure during inhalation retracts the dressing over the wound. The lung now has a better chance of re-inflating. Monitor for possible development of subsequent tension pneumothorax because air can still leak into the pleural space from the injured lung. Allow the casualty to be in the sitting position if breathing is more comfortable. If signs of a tension pneumothorax develop, remove the occlusive dressing for a few seconds and allow the tension pneumothorax to decompress!

Occlusive Dressing: This is required for needle chest decompression also to function properly. The purpose is to prevent entry of air into the wound. If conscious, victim should be placed in sitting position leaning towards injury. If unconscious, he should be lying on injured side. Some very clever inventions exist to do this.

Asherman Chest Seal: The ACS™ (Asherman Chest Seal) is a sterile occlusive dressing for treating open pneumothorax and preventing tension pneumothorax in chest injuries from gunshots, stab wounds, or other penetrating chest trauma. The unique one-way valve is designed to let air and blood escape while preventing re-entry of either. Proven to be more effective treatment than standard petroleum gauze, the ACS is standard issue for the US Army, the British Army and the US Navy. The ACS is 5.5″ in diameter, includes a gauze pad (4″ x 4″) to clean and dry the wound, and is translucent so the wound can be observed.

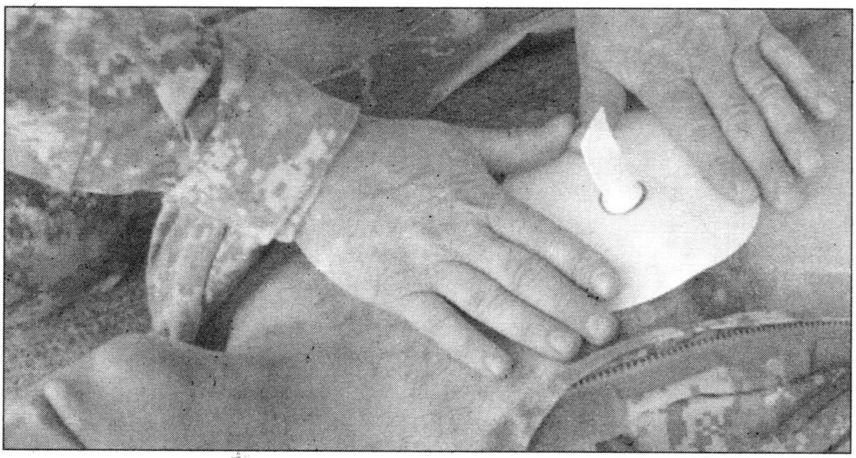

Applying the chest seal

Bolin Chest Seal: It is claimed that this performs better than Asherman chest seal when blood is present. Sucking chest wounds caused by gunshots, stabbing or fragmentation during military operations, require an emergency first aid solution that is fast, direct, and effective: the Bolin Chest Seal (BCS) is specifically engineered to meet these critical needs. The patented failure-proof triple-valve design of the BCS allows air and blood to escape while preventing the re-entry of either, thereby eliminating any unwanted gas or liquid exchange at the trauma site. The large (6″ diameter), rugged polyurethane disc structure of the BCS can cover practically any size chest trauma site. The thickness of the disc prevents any disc wrinkling from occurring during application. In addition, the wound side of the disc is covered with a thick layer of jell-based adhesive, strong enough to not only seal over hair and blood but also flexible enough to be removed and reapplied to the trauma site if required. These critical characteristics of the BCS ensure that treatment of pneumothorax and prevention tension pneumothorax can be accomplished quickly, directly, and effectively.

Field Improvised Chest Seals/Occlusive Dressing: The improvised occlusive dressing can consist of any material that will ensure an airtight seal over the wound (e.g. plastic wrap, MRE wrapper, Vaseline gauze, aluminium foil—any plastic-like material can work well for this purpose, including Ziplock bags, cellophane wrappers, and latex gloves). The correct technique is to tape all four sides of the dressing. The last edge is taped after the patient exhales forcefully. The dressing should be large enough to cover at least 2 inches past the wound on all four sides. If tape won't stick to a wet or bloody chest, large trauma dressings can be held down with cravats that surround the chest. If an exit wound is present, it too must be covered. Soldiers have used even duct tape very successfully. In fact, it is strongly recommended that soldiers must not bother with zinc tape and the trouble of cutting it. Plastic tape must be used.

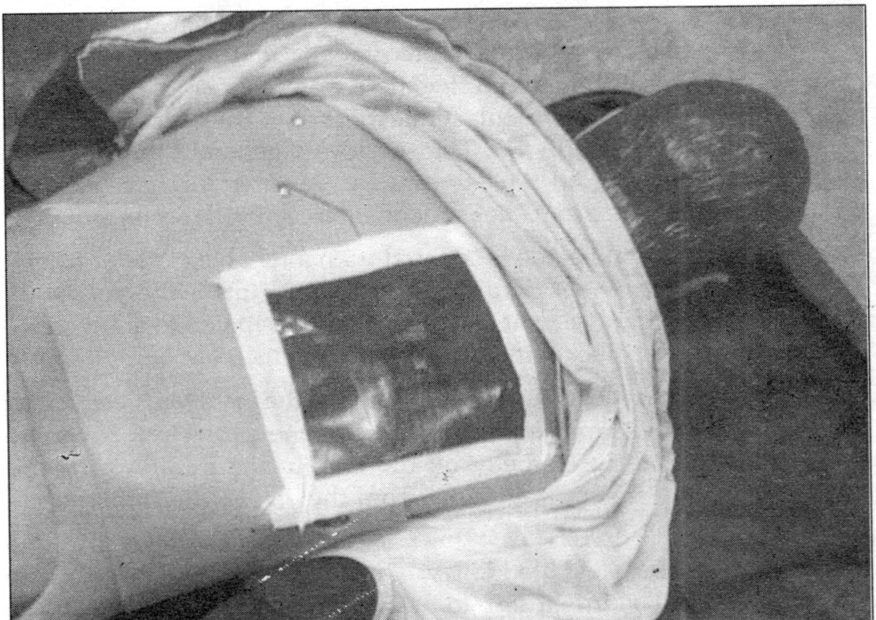

Field improvised chest seal/Occlusive dressing

It is often recommended that one should not close the bandage on the fourth side. This is supposed to allow the chest to achieve its usual negative pressure state. The CoTCCC has, however, found that there is no evidence to show that a three-sided dressing is more effective than a simple occlusive dressing. It further argues that four-sided simple occlusive dressings are easier to apply than constructing 3-sided dressings and wasting precious time in that.

(16.9.2) *Needle Chest Decompression*

An excellent technique to relieve tension pneumothorax is needle chest decompression on the side of the injury. Here is how to do it in the field.

1. A 14 - gauge angiocath-type (catheter over needle) needle is required.
2. The needle is a 14 - gauge needle that is 3.25 inch in length. A study by Dr Harcke in 2008, published in Military Medicine has shown that several casualties died from needles being too short to get through the chest wall. Old 2-inch needles were too short. 3.25 inch needles will get through the chest wall in 99 per cent of individuals. Multidetector computed tomography scans from 100 virtual autopsy cases were used to determine chest wall thickness in deployed male military personnel. Measurement was made in the second right intercostal space at the midclavicular line. The mean horizontal thickness was 5.36 cm (SD = 1.19 cm) with angled (perpendicular) thickness slightly less with a mean of 4.86 cm (SD 1.10 cm). Thickness was generally greater than previously reported. An 8-cm angiocatheter would have reached the pleural space in 99 per cent of subjects in this series.
3. The rigid metal needle is covered with a flexible catheter (tube). The needle provides rigidity needed in puncturing the chest wall. When it is removed, the flexible catheter remains to allow air to escape the air pocket that is causing the tension pneumothorax.
4. **Prepare Catheter/Needle Unit:** Remove the catheter/needle unit from its packaging and then remove the protective covering. Insert the needle/catheter all the way to the hub. Ensure you remove the small plastic plug from the end of the catheter hub prior to insertion.
5. **Location for Needle Entry:** 2nd intercostal space in the midclavicular line. It is 2 to 3 finger widths below the middle of the collar bone. The insertion site is located in the second intercostal space (the area between the second and third ribs, counting from the top) at the mid-clavicular line (an imaginary line perpendicular to the ribs approximately in line with the casualty's nipple) on the same side of the chest as the penetrating wound. The 1st rib cannot normally be felt. The 2nd rib can be felt just below the collar bone. The 2nd intercostal space is the area between the 2nd and 3rd rib.

6. **Precautions:** The needle goes on the same side of the chest as the injury. Ensure that the needle entry into the chest is not medial to the nipple line and is not directed towards the heart. Enter over the top of the third rib. This avoids the artery and vein on the bottom of the second rib. Care must be taken to enter on 90 degree angle to chest wall. Going over the top of the rib avoids the neurovascular bundle (nerve, artery and vein) that runs along the bottom of the ribs.
7. Clean area with Betadine or other antiseptic.
8. Re-identify 2nd intercostal space in the midclavicular line.
9. Firmly insert the 14 gauge needle/catheter over the top of the third rib into the pleural space at a 90 degree angle to the chest wall. You will feel a "pop" as the needle enters the chest cavity. Listen for a decompression air rush (hissing sound) from the needle. This indicates that you have entered the chest cavity.
10. Aspirate as much air as necessary to relieve the patient's acute symptoms.
11. Remove the needle from the catheter. Withdraw the needle from inside the catheter while holding the catheter hub to keep the catheter in place. The catheter will remain as a means for air trapped in the chest to escape to the atmosphere.
12. **Secure the Catheter:** Use the strip of tape to secure the catheter hub to the chest wall. If possible, allow the patient to sit up.
13. **Monitor Casualty:** By allowing trapped air to escape from the plural area, the casualty's respirations should quickly improve. Applying airtight material over the wound and having a catheter release trapped air permits the affected lung to re-inflate only "somewhat" but not completely. If possible, monitor the casualty until medical care arrives or until the casualty is evacuated to the nearest medical facility. Be prepared to take measures to treat for shock. Observe the patient for recurrence of progressive respiratory distress symptoms and prepare for a chest-tube insertion if necessary.
14. If the catheter becomes clogged with blood or tissue it can cause the respiratory distress to reoccur. If this happens you can attempt to flush the catheter with a small amount of sterile fluid (one cc) or place an additional needle catheter next to the first. If this is successful remove the first catheter you placed.

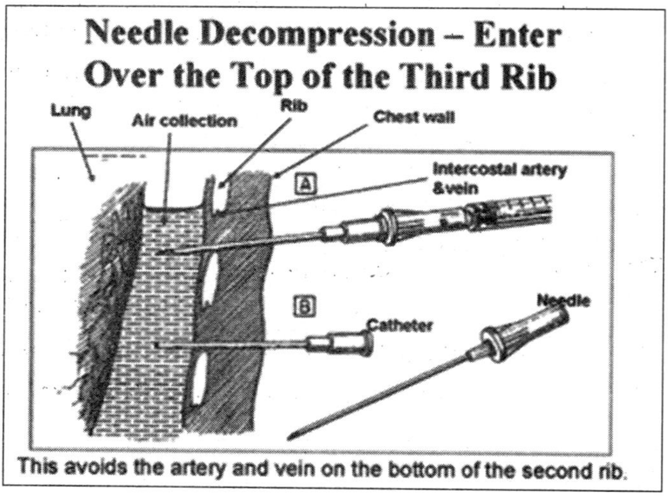

Needle Chest Decompression

Allaying the Fears related to NCD: A frequent question that occurs is: what will happen if the casualty does not have a tension pneumothorax and you perform a needle chest decompression? Will it cause more harm? The answer is NO; it will not cause any additional harm. Let's look at why. If the casualty already has a hole in his chest, he already has a pneumothorax and actually probably has a combination hemo-pneumothorax. If he has penetrating trauma to that side of the chest, there is already a collapsed lung and blood in the chest cavity. The needle won't make it worse if there is no tension pneumothorax. If he does have a tension pneumothorax, you will save his life.

(16.10) Gunshot Wounds to the Head, Face, Neck, and Abdomen

Gunshot wounds to the head are typically fatal if the bullet crosses both of the brain hemispheres or hit the brain stem which is responsible for control of basic vital functions. There is no real treatment in the field to help this. Head elevation or seated positioning is all that you can do till he is sent for medical care. There is some chance in all other cases. Scalp wounds bleed profusely and may require prolonged pressure. Position the casualty with head and shoulders slightly raised.

Gunshot wounds to the face and neck are often troublesome. Since the face and neck have excellent circulation, bleeding is often heavy. In addition, the airway can become obstructed by blood, teeth, and swelling. Manual pressure should be applied to a bleeding wound and leave the victim in the upright position. Direct pressure should be strong enough to stop the bleeding. Avoid pressing over a large area as you can compromise blood flow to the brain or shift the trachea causing an airway obstruction.

The civilian practice is to often place a cervical collar and back-board to immobilise a gunshot victim. However, the US army has found that the incidence of spinal cord injury caused by movement is exceedingly rare and therefore time should not be wasted with immobilization of the victim. Paralysis following gunshot wounds happens instantaneously when the bullet rips through the spinal cord. It generally does not occur with moving fractures or other means. Don't worry about it.

Gunshot wounds to the abdomen can cause bowel damage as well as significant bleeding. Manual pressure with a dry dressing is indicated for an actively bleeding wound but oftentimes it is difficult to compress the internal bleeding source. The position for the victim must be lying on his back with knees raised.

(16.11) Penetrating Eye Injuries

Penetrating Eye Trauma: Penetrating injuries can result in eye infections that can cause permanent blindness. If a penetrating eye injury is noted or suspected, cover the eye with a rigid eye shield (and not a pressure patch). Ensure that the 400 mg Moxifloxacin tablet is taken right away. A rigid shield will protect the eye from any pressure. Pressure patch or bandage could force the interior contents of the eye to come out – this is a bad thing! Rigid shield should be in first aid kits and medical sets. Tactical eyeware can be used to protect the eye if no eye shield is available.

(16.12) Hemostatic Dressings

Combat Gauze: The Combat Gauze is a new hemostatic dressing. It is impregnated with kaolin, a material that causes the blood to clot. Combat Gauze has been shown in lab studies to be more effective than the previous hemostatic agents like HemCon and QuikClot powder granules. Two research studies by both the Army (USAISR) and Navy (NMRC) have confirmed this. The Committee on Tactical Combat Casualty Care recommends Combat Gauze™ as the first-line hemostatic agent. It is packaged in 3 in x 4 yd lengths and the weight is just 0.8 oz. It can be fitted to any size or shape wound, is non-allergenic, and is easily removed once clotting occurs. It provides the ultimate in stopping power for traumatic wounds. It is an advanced hemostatic agent combined with the simplicity of gauze. It is easy to use, easy to remove, generates no heat and greatly improves hemorrhage control in the most demanding tactical conditions. Gauze-type agents are easier to use on the battlefield than powder-type agents. It is especially true for wounds with big bleeder at the bottom of a narrow wound tract.

The concept that blood and plasma develop clotting properties when exposed to glass or related materials has been known for about 50-60 years. This process can take place even when calcium and platelets are absent. In 1958 Dr Margolis from Oxford, England published a paper titled "The Kaolin Clotting Time". In this study he developed a system to diagnose plasma clotting defects by using recalcified plasma where the contact surface and the number of platelets were kept constant. In his study, Dr Margolis quickly recognised that instead of relying on the walls of glass tubes as the activating surface, he could get the same activation effect by adding kaolin to the process. Further studies discovered that exposure of human plasma to kaolin (or glass-like substances) initiates a group of reactions known as contact activation phase which include the activation of the intrinsic blood coagulation sequence, the kinin-forming pathway, the plasma fibrinolytic system and the generation of permeability factors.

Directions for Use:

1. Open clothing around the wound.
2. If possible, remove excess pooled blood from the wound while preserving any clots already formed in the wound.
3. Locate source of most active bleeding.
4. Pack Combat Gauze™ tightly into wound and directly onto bleeding source. More than one gauze may be required to stem blood flow.
5. Combat Gauze™ may be re-packed or adjusted in the wound to ensure proper placement.
6. Quickly apply pressure until bleeding stops. Hold continuous pressure for 3 minutes.
7. Reassess to ensure bleeding is controlled.
8. Combat Gauze may be repacked or a second gauze used if initial application fails to provide hemostasis.
9. Apply Bandage over Combat Gauze. Leave Combat Gauze™ in place.

   Wrap to effectively secure the dressing in the wound. The wound may be secured with any compression bandage, Ace™ wrap, roller gauze, or cravat.

10. Ensure bleeding has stopped and apply a pressure bandage over the wound. Watch for rebleeding.

Other Hemostatic Products:

The HemCon Bandage is composed of Chitosan, which is a biodegradable, nontoxic, complex carbohydrate of chitin, found in the exoskeletons of shellfish. The RDH or Rapid Deployment Hemostat Bandage is derived from single-cell algae and the mechanism of the material is to act as a catalytic surface that accelerates the normal clotting process. TraumaDEX is a wound-dressing agent material naturally synthesised from potato starch. The particles accelerate natural blood clotting by concentrating blood solids such as platelets and red blood cells.

(16.13) How to handle Snake Bite in the Jungle

A jungle warrior is always at the risk of getting bitten by a snake in the jungle. What is he supposed to do? Terrible myths exist regarding snake bites and their filed treatment. Scientific research has proved that they are perfectly useless. Snake bite kits are found in many survival kits, but most are worse than useless. It is best to abide by the classical physician's dictum, "primum non nocere", Latin for "first do no harm". The old fashioned snake bite kits often included can cause additional damage, potentially more dangerous than the snake bite itself, and don't work worth a damn anyway.

Don't make a cut: One of the famous old wives' tales is to make deep cuts at the bite mark—the belief was that the resulting blood flow would carry away the venom. The traditional "Cutter" kit and its clones, with a razor blade to cut an "X" across the fang punctures are now universally derided by knowledgeable experts. If you own one, throw it away! Really! Leave these dramatic measures to the movies where it is make believe and no one is really hurt. Unfortunately, it does not work. The venom travels rather fast.

Don't suck: You cannot suck or drain an appreciable amount of venom from the bite using oral means. And remember that any open lesion in your mouth (such as mouth ulcers) or esophageal tract would result in you getting poisoned too.

Don't use tourniquets: The use of tight tourniquets made of rope, belt, string or cloth have been traditionally used to stop venom flow into the body following snakebite. Do not waste time with tourniquets. They have the following drawbacks and problems:

- Risk of ischemia and loss of the limb.

- Increased risk of necrosis with 4/5 of the medically significant snakes of India.
- Increased risk of massive neurotoxic blockade when tourniquet is released.
- Risk of embolism if used in viper bites. Pro-coagulant enzymes will cause clotting in distal blood. In addition, the effect of the venom in causing vasodilation presents the danger of massive hypotension when the tourniquet is released.
- They do not work! Venom was not slowed by the tourniquet in several experimental studies, as well as in field conditions. Often this is because they are tied on the lower limb or are incorrectly tied.
- They give patients a false sense of security, which encourages them to delay their journey to hospital.

Don't wash the wound: Victims and bystanders often want to wash the wound to remove any venom on the surface. This should not be done as the action of washing increases the flow of venom into the system by stimulating the lymphatic system.

Use extractor, but quickly: The only kit worth carrying is the Sawyer "Extractor". This has proved very effective with insect bites, if used promptly. It will also improve your chances somewhat after a snake bite, reportedly removing about 35 per cent of the venom, if treatment is started within three minutes, without causing further injury or trauma. The Extractor uses a venom pump suction device, akin to a syringe but it creates suction when the plunger is depressed, with various form fitting adapters to create a very strong vacuum, sucking the venom out through the original punctures. It has been identified that suction more than 270 mm Hg can initiate the flow from the puncture marks. The device needs to remain on the site for 30 minutes.

Doubtful Utility of Pressure Immobilisation Method (PIM): Pressure Immobilisation has gained some supporters on television and in the herpetology literature. PIM was developed in Australia in 1974 by Sutherland. His research involved tying monkeys to wooden frames and injecting venom, then seeing if a pressure bandage would slow the absorption. He achieved some good results but there were mixed findings. He only used 13 monkeys which is not an adequate sample. He argued that a crepe bandage and an integral splint be applied over the wound to a pressure of 55 mm Hg. Further work done by Howarth in the 90s showed that full immobilisation was crucial. If the victim walked for 10 minutes after application the PIM would be ineffective. Most importantly, he found that pressures above the ranges specified would actually increase the flow of venom. Gray found that pressures under the recommended range may also increase venom flow. Work carried out by Norris in 2005 showed that only 5 per cent of lay people and 13 per cent of doctors were able to correctly apply the technique! That alone rules it out for soldiers in the field.

Correct Protocol for Treatment of Snake Bite: The only effective method of treatment is the anti-snake venom. Snakebite can often cause severe pain at the bite site. This can be treated with painkillers such as paracetamol. Adult dose of 500-1000 mg 4-6 hourly. That's all you can do in the field. Try to get him evacuated as quickly as Anti Snake Venom (ASV) in India is polyvalent, i.e., it is effective against the four common species; Russells viper (Daboia russelii), Common Cobra (Naja naja), Common Krait (Bungarus caeruleus) and Saw Scaled viper (Echis carinatus). There are no currently available monovalent ASVs primarily because there are no objective means of identifying the snake species in the absence of the dead snake. Remember that it may lead to anaphylactic shock also in case of a mismatch and hence doctors must use it judiciously only when there is definite evidence of systemic envenoming manifest by coagulopathy (tested by 20WBCT—20 minute Whole Blood Clotting Test); neurotoxicity (manifest by ptosis, external ophthalmoplegia, and muscle paralysis etc). In the Indian context and in the vast majority of cases, one of the following two categories will be the sole determinant of whether ASV is administered to a casualty: cardiovascular abnormalities: hypotension, shock, cardiac arrhythmia and abnormal ECG; and persistent and severe vomiting or abdominal pain.

Research is currently going on to develop Enzyme Linked Immuno Sorbent Assay testing for snake species and the level of envenomation. It may be years away, however. There are known species such as the Hump-nosed pitviper (Hypnale hypnale) where polyvalent ASV is known to be ineffective. In addition, there are regionally specific species such as Sochurek's saw scaled viper (Echis Carinatus Sochureki) in Rajasthan where the effectiveness of polyvalent ASV may be questionable. Dr Narayan Chandra Ghosh has described several homeopathic medicines for treatment of snake bite in his classic work "Comparative Materia Medica". But I do not think that anybody conducted scientific trials to validate the claim. This is one field where research could be undertaken.

17

Combat Fitness, Food and Innovative Training for Jungle Warfare

Pull up! All pants pull up!

(17.1) Combat Fitness distinguished from Sports Fitness

When Daniel Craig stepped out of the surf on a Bahamas beach, he melted women around the world and spiked browser searches from guys looking for that incredible James Bond physique. Fitness marketers capitalised on the moment by offering the usual bodybuilding-style workouts and labelling them Bond. But anyone who knows anything about tactical operations wasn't fooled. A guy like Bond needs more than show muscle to save the world—he needs serious go muscle— because it isn't enough to look pretty when Blofeld comes calling. Crisis response demands a physical training programme tailored to the specific needs of the warrior: tireless stamina, extreme range reactive strength, ballistic speed, the agility and coordination of a Free Runner, and active recovery.

The exercise regimens used by many forces are not fundamentally different from the training regimens used by athletes—if it is so, it is a classic example of their intellectual bankruptcy. Conventional exercises used by sportspersons develop what is known as 'sports fitness'. Commandos who have to fight in jungles must seek 'combat fitness' against 'sports fitness'. Jungle warriors in particular have to do hard work—they are not going to compete in a sports stadium. The closest approximation of the objective of making them 'tough' and capable of hard work like loaders is found in the labourers working in wholesale grain or vegetable markets and farm labourers. It is easy to make rippling muscles by working out on low weight-high repetitions in a gym. That would not help you one bit in becoming a hard-working jungle warrior. Six-packs are good for impressing girls—they would not help you haul 55 lbs of backpack for miles in a jungle and yet be alert enough to shoot back when you are ambushed. Some elite forces have understood it, but the Indians are intellectually incapable of understanding it. I will therefore explain the concept.

After Afghanistan 2002, the US Army's Official After-Action Review for Recent Operation Anaconda Combat concluded: "While we work daily to max the Army Physical Fitness Test (APFT), our runs, push-ups and sit-ups betray us when we put our LBE, rucksack, helmet and weapon on. We all know of the "jack rabbits" who can run two miles under 12 minutes, but who turn into "slugs" when you put a heavy load with useful equipment on them. The reality is that the Army Physical Fitness Test (APFT) is a sports-oriented test, and not a combat-oriented test of physical fitness. This is a violation of the most basic fitness principles which is to train for the specific tasks to be done. Compounding this, the sit-up exercise is universally recognised by health/sports experts as being harmful to the lower back...The terrain and altitude make combat in mountains extremely physically demanding. Units need to get away from the normal PT routines before deploying to the mountains. Push-ups, sit-ups and 5-mile runs will not prepare soldiers. They need to have the ability to spend time in the mountains to physically adapt to the terrain and altitude. Soldiers were not used to steeper slopes and wasted time and energy. Hence, emphasise ruck marches (6-8 mile) with heavy loads... And note that any reasonable timing would do. What is important is that the solider must not collapse under the weight. A minute here or there does not make any great difference in combat. The enemy is not running away. Any war, regular or counter-insurgency, is a complete activity—it is not dependent on the speed of marching. Leave that to showcase bullshit".

After the Falklands War, the British had also realised that the intent of physical training was not to develop professional athletes or weightlifters. The purpose of physical conditioning was to develop combat stamina—that is, the ability to march long distances with heavy loads.

(17.2) The Concept of Toughening

When the going gets tough; just whip the lad out!

Toughening is a concept that is not generally known to those who focus only on sports fitness. It is described as the capacity to do gruelling physical work without getting exhausted or developing musculo-skeletal problems like sprains, slipped discs, joint pain, etc. It is different from anaerobic, glucose-lactic acid or cardio-respiratory capacity that we talk of in the context of sports because it entails things more than them.

There are many real life examples of toughened people both in India and abroad. In the Indian context we have the labourers (beldaar/palledar) who work in wholesale grain and vegetable markets. They load/unload gunny bags usually weighing 100 kg on to and from trucks using ramps. An average beldaar/palledar of about 60-70 kg body weight is able to load gunny bags weighing up to 100 kg about 50 times non-stop, and bags weighing 50 kg or more up to 100 times. They are able to carry bags of 130 kg also. Farm labourers, particularly those who dig up fields with *fawdas* (for want of a suitable English word, we may call it a shovel, though in a *fawda* the blade is almost perpendicular to the handle whereas in the regular shovel the blade is in line with the handle) have this capacity. The Indian wrestlers of yesteryears also used to have enormous capacities of doing literally back-breaking work. Most of them were able to do thousands of push-ups and squats—a typical figure used to be 2000 Indian style push-ups and 4000 Indian style squats. Earlier in the western world also, miners (when they used pick and shovel in the mines), farmhands and lumberjacks (when they used heavy axes) used to have this sort of physical capacity. The concept of a 'toughened up' man was so well-understood in the western world earlier that there was a saying that this was what distinguished boys from men. Men could do gruelling, punishing work; boys, even if large muscled, could not.

In the Western armies, till the First World War, soldiers were purposefully made to develop the capacity to do gruelling physical work. It was required in preparing defensive earthworks for infantry; redoubts for cannon; mines for demolition through explosives; living and fighting trenches; and communication trenches—all these activities demanded a great deal of digging and shovelling. They had to push and pull heavy cannons across the battlefield on rough or broken ground—the lightest and the most abundantly used 12-pounder gun of the 19th century weighed up to 1200 kg with its carriage and it was generally not horse-drawn in the battlefield. Its wheels did not even have ball-bearings. Then there was pitching of tents and long forced marches with full loads when the infantry was not mechanised. Soldiers used to be toughened people.

(17.3) Field Expedient Toughening Exercises

(17.3.1) The Basic Principle

The basic principle of these toughening exercises is simple—they try to emulate load-bearing movements that take place in daily life as closely as possible—and they also call for high repetitions. In essence it requires that as many muscle groups be involved in the movements as possible. Gym exercises with weights (and particularly those on machines) isolate specific muscle groups. As such they have value in creating muscle definition and strength in a limited range of movement of the joints. However, they do not prepare a man for hard work in real life where the range of motion is larger and where muscles usually do not get isolated. There is one more important difference between barbells and real life weights. Barbells/dumbbells and weights on machines afford an excellent grip. Real life weights do not have such grips and thus handling them becomes more difficult. Secondly, the toughening exercises focus on the center, the fulcrum of the human body, that is, the pelvic joint and musculature associated with it, that is, the lower back region in everyday language. In fact, one of the well-known ways of describing strong men in the past in the western world was to say that he had 'strength in his loins'.

When we handle weights in real life, muscles do not get isolated. A whole group of muscles is obliged to act in a synergetic fashion. This synergetic action is not to be found when muscles get isolated on a machine. Weights which have a large volume and are irregular or awkwardly-shaped, exert many torques on the body which need to be countered by many muscle groups. When 'concentrated' weights are handled, they exert only one torque and thus fewer muscles are required to counter them.

This can be felt at any time in real life. Lifting a 30 kg dumbbell in the hand and walking with it is materially different from lifting a 30 kg large suitcase and walking with it. The dumbbell is a concentrated weight and has good grip. The grip of the suitcase is not so good. Then the very fact that the suitcase is large and thus does not allow the same freedom of movement to the lower body (it keeps on bumping on to the legs) makes carrying it difficult. Carrying a 32 kg LPG cylinder perched on the shoulder is different from carrying the same thing on the chest. Carrying a 60 kg barbell across the shoulders and walking with it is easier—carrying a 60 kg man slung across the shoulders is difficult. Lifting a 50 kg barbell in a 'snatch' movement overhead is easy—lifting a 50 kg stone, bag, or box is not. Precisely for this reason, one of the mandatory items in 'strongmen' contests is carrying of a round stone across the chest. Carrying a bag up a ramp on your back is not the same as carrying the same weight hung from the arms, or carried across the chest. Suppose one has to swing a bar-like object of 10 kg. This could be designed in many ways. One could have a uniform cylindrical iron piece in which the weight is uniformly distributed over the length. One could also devise a hammer-like device with a wooden pole of say 2 kg, and an 8 kg block of iron at one end. While the total weights of both the devices are same, swinging the hammer-like device is more difficult because the weight at the end has two effects. Firstly, it increases the torque (F x r) which it exerts on the hand. Secondly, it has a greater moment of inertia (∑mr2) which resists change in angular momentum.

Incidentally, it was precisely for this reason that wielding a battle-axe was difficult and only strong men wielded it in battle. Further, this had a pronounced bearing on sword designs. Those who understood the concept well-designed their swords in such a manner that the moment of inertia was as low as possible. The samurai sword *katana* for example, is a double-handed sword in which the grip is long (nearly one-third of the total length) thereby reducing the 'r' in the torque. On the other hand, in the single-hand-grip European broadsword, most of the weight of the blade is away from the grip, thereby increasing both 'm' and 'r' for the moment of inertia. The result was that the *katana* could be wielded with great dexterity whereas the broadsword could not be wielded so.

The physics and kinesiology of handling awkwardly-shaped weights needs to be understood carefully. Those with only an elementary knowledge of physics could argue that the 'work' done in physics depends only on the weight and the height to which it is displaced; and hence the work done (W = F x d) would be the same whether you lift a 50 kg barbell or a 50 kg bag. A finer analysis, coupled with some knowledge of kinesiology proves it to be a rather simplistic notion. While the total work done by the human body in terms of the energy spent remains the same in the two situations, the 'perceived work load' differs. The perceived work load depends on what muscles are involved. If those muscle groups are made to work which are not used to load, the man tires faster. This can be understood with a simple example. Consider the squat movement with a barbell. One can handle higher weights when the barbell is placed on the back of the shoulder—the so-called 'back squat'. The reason is this that in this position, a large number of muscles of the lower back help in rising from the squat and the load on the quadriceps is proportionately reduced. On the other hand, when the barbell is held in front of the shoulders—the so-called 'front squat'—the quadriceps are obliged to bear a greater load without the same help from the lower back muscles, and performing the squat appears to require greater effort. For this reason only, one can lift even greater weights in the so-called 'hack lift' or 'behind the back dead lift' because you get greater support from the back. Conversely, suppose that the same weight is lifted in 'hack lift', 'back squat', and 'front squat'—the degree of tiredness one would perceive would be the least in hack lift, more in back squat and the most in front squat.

(17.3.2) Description of the Exercises

Carrying Weight up a Ramp on your back: For this exercise you first wear a specially made harness. The weight has to be in a gunny bag because they are large. Two grips may be improvised at one end of the bags to facilitate holding the bags. Load the bag on to your back. You need not do it yourself. In fact, if you are assisted in the process, the assistant gets exercise in hoisting the bag. The point to be noted is that one must bend suitably at the waist. One who stands upright is likely to topple over. Take care not to strain the back. Take careful steps and climb the ramp on to the truck. Wear jungle boots for a better grip. Drop the weight in the truck and then carry another. Those who finally unload the bags from the truck, will get additional exercise.

Digging a Wrestling Pit with a huge Shovel (*Fawda*): If I have to select just one exercise for best all-round effect, it would be this. This was a favourite of great Indian wrestlers like Gama. The general practice was to dig the *akhaara* (wrestling pit) thrice with it. You need not do it thrice. Even once is enough. One great advantage of the exercise is that there is very little risk of injury. The sheer size of the blade of the shovel (*fawda*) makes it very special. The blade is 16 inches long, 14 inches wide at the base of the handle and 11 inches wide at the cutting edge. The handle is 3 feet long with a circumference of 5.5 inches. The shovel must be 9 kg in weight—neither more nor less.

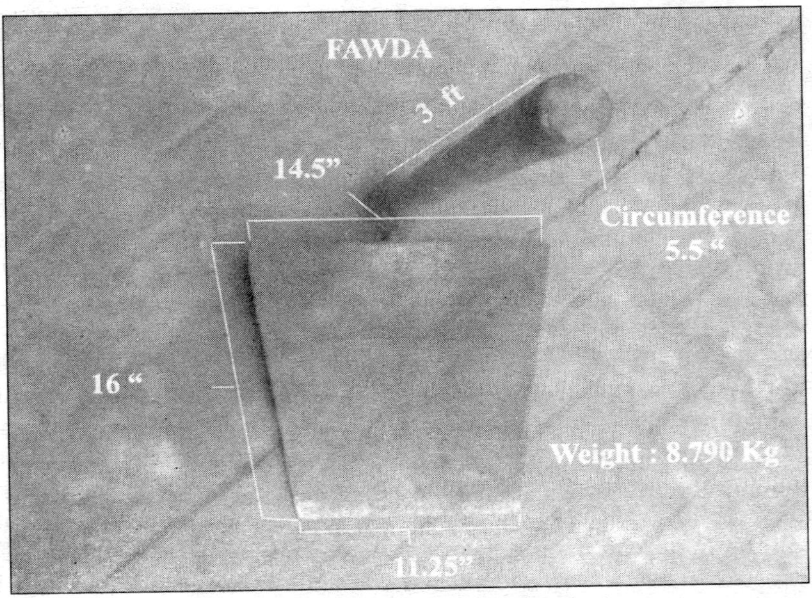

The 9 kg heavy shovel (Fawda) for digging

Levelling a Dug Up Pit with a Concrete Slab (Sledge Dragging): This is a sequel to the above. In this exercise, you drag a heavy concrete slab (22.5 inches x 20.5 inches) across a dug up pit in a fashion very much similar to an ox pulling a plough. Resistance to the movement is offered by the weight of the slab and the dug up ground. The weight and size of the slab are critical at 46 kg. Make the slab heavier and it would tend to sink in the ground thereby it making pulling very difficult. Make it lighter and you would not get enough resistance. This is also a great exercise and makes one tough like an ox. You can also use barbell discs or a tractor tire on plain ground. You can also pull backwards.

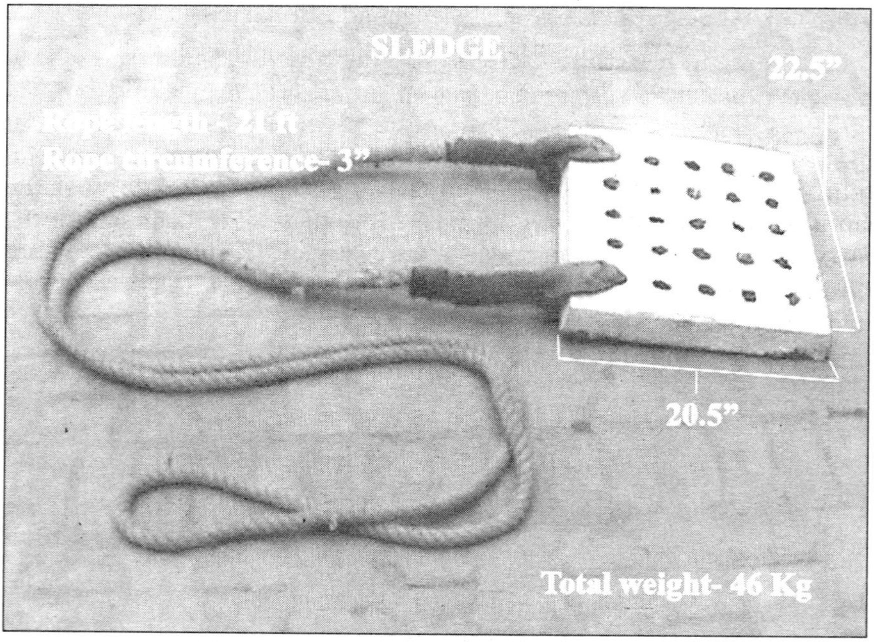

The 46 kg concrete Slab Fro-Dragging on a dug up pit

Carrying Irregular Weight across the Chest and Walking: In this exercise you carry an irregular large-size weight held across the chest and walk. Once again it involves many muscles. Strong men carry huge stone boulders. To lift stones you need to clamp your arms around the centre and squeeze using the biceps and chest muscles, then row the stone up to your knees. From here you need to drive with the legs and hips to roll the stone up your torso and if powerful enough, to your shoulder. You can exercise your imagination and use anything. The stones may be carried and placed on a platform of some height for added workout.

Carrying a stone across the chest

Carrying Weights in both Arms and Walking (Farmer's Carry): In this exercise you carry two irregular weights slung down from the hands and then walk. In the western world, they call it 'The Farmer's Carry' and is a standard exercise for strongmen. This would also give soldiers good practice for carrying stretchers.

100 The Farmer's Carry

Flipping a Heavy Weight (Tyre/Log Flipping): This exercise is a classic demonstration of load-bearing movements in which a very large numbers of muscles come into play. A big tyre like a tractor's is a large unwieldy object. You do not get a good grip. You squat, meaning that the muscles of the leg will be exercised. You straighten your back—this means that the back muscles are exercised. You use your arms in a bent fashion—this means that the arm muscles are also exercised. One of the famous exercises used by strongmen, in the western world, they use heavy tyres of earthmoving machinery weighing from 250 to 700 kg. You can use any heavy weight available for flipping. For example, you can use even huge logs or concrete sleepers and flip them from end-to-end.

Tyre flipping

Swinging a Weight Overhead (Wine Keg/Heavy Bag Toss): This exercise is actually an improvement over the 'snatch' which is the best all-round exercise using barbells. One of the famous exercises used by strongmen, in the western world, they use wine barrels, heavy bags or similar objects for swinging it overhead and back. Once again, note how several muscles are called into play.

Keg toss

Hitting a Tyre with a Sledge-hammer: This exercise involves swinging a heavy jackhammer down onto an inflated tyre and then controlling the rebound. You exert both in swinging it and in controlling the rebound. Swinging a heavy axe onto a tree is also very good but where would you get so many trees to chop—the jackhammer is a non-destructive option.

US Marines' Exercises: The US Marine Corps has devised its own set of exercises for toughening that includes asymmetric push-ups with one arm on a raised platform, the mountain climber, and exercises with medicine ball, etc for the beginners. Trained commandos typically perform:

Cable commando pull-ups 5, 5, 5 with incline push-ups 25, 25, 25

Cable crawl 50ft x 2 with a set of regular crunches on each end 50, 50

Dummy drag 40 yards x 2 with regular push-ups 25, 25

Log squats 6, 6, with elevated crunches 50, 50

Ammo can lift. They pull a 50 lb ammo can up about 20 ft with a rope and let it down twice without stopping for one set; 2 sets with wide push-ups 25, 25.

12 ft log flip 40 yards x 2 with Hello dollies 50, 50,

Barrel lift and carry. They carry a 55 gallon drum (with about 50 lbs of water in it) 25 ft and put it on a 4 ft wall. Then they take it down and carry it 25 ft and put it on a 3 ft wall for 1 set.

2 sets with narrow pushups 25, 25,

Wheel-barrow push.

(17.4) Combat Load

In the 19th and earlier centuries, the haversack (containing food, clothes, blankets, etc) of the soldiers usually did not exceed 30-40 lbs (that is, 13.6 to 18.2 kg). It got reduced substantially during the two World Wars, only to pick up again. The general standard for the US Marines is that the average commando carries not more than 30 per cent of his body weight on his back for long marches. The average 'assault load' is also not more than 30 per cent of the body weight. The strong men among them are able to carry up to 40-45 per cent of their body weight in 'approach marches' for up to 8 hours. In the US Army the fighting load is actually just 48 lbs (that is, 21.8 kg, according to the FM 21-18) and the marching load is 72 lbs (that is, 32.7 kg, FM 7-10 refers). This 48 lbs includes only one MRE weighing 1.3 lbs (that is, just 0.6 kg) and 3 liters of water in a hydration pack weighing a total of 6.906 lbs (3.14 kg). This means that they do not intend to march for more than a day with this. The 'existence load' in the US Marines' ILBE can be up to 120 lbs. The maximum weight of the existence load is such that the average infantry marine will be able to conduct limited movement within the confines of Naval shipping, embark and debark aircraft or amphibious craft, and limited marching from the landing zone into a secured area. The SAS, of course, claim that they marched with this for long.

(17.5) Food for Combat

Hot garrison chow is better than hot C-rations, which, in turn is better than cold C-rations, which is better than no food at all. What is often more important than why.

(17.5.1) Food and Water for How Long?

There is considerable debate in the world about the capacity of the Special Forces to remain unsupported in the jungles. Special Forces elsewhere in the world generally do not undertake long operations. Usually, it is one day and often not more than three days in any case—most of the military rucksacks are designed for three days only (such as the MOLLE 3-day assault pack). I am aware of the stories that are told about the SAS that a party stayed in the Malaysian jungle for as many as 89 days. These are all fake legends carefully woven to bolster their image. The average man tends to believe in whatever he gets to read because his critical faculties are not developed. No one has ever asked probing and critical questions: what did they eat for 89 days; did they carry all the stuff on their backs; if yes, how; what was the stuff and what was its weight; if not, how did they get the food; if they went to some village, the secrecy of the operation must have been blown; did they hunt game; if so, how could they do it noiselessly; if not, was the risk worth taking; how did they solve their water problem; was there enough natural water in the jungle; what could they have done had there not been enough water; what did they do all these days; did they march in the jungle; if yes, how many km on an average per day; how did they meet their caloric requirements; what was their condition after the mission; and finally my lord, what did they achieve by this feat? Ask such questions and the legend is busted. The length of an operation depends on the circumstances. It must depend on the mission and the factors that limit the duration of the mission. There are other limiting factors also besides food and water. If you are engaging the enemy sporadically, you will soon run out of ammunition and you cannot last long. One hypothetical situation in which you may have to remain in the jungle for long is a mission in which you have accurate intelligence about some deep enemy location that is not (it is to be hoped that) protected by spotters on the way. You have only to reach there stealthily and destroy that facility. May be traversing that distance would take several days but once you reach there, the results of the attack would be very rewarding. Well, for such an unlikely mission, the troops must be trained to march in the jungle for several days and be equipped to be self-sufficient in respect of food and water for this duration. Living in the jungle indefinitely is not a problem; living unsupported and unobserved is. You may live permanently in the jungle but you will have to be supplied with food from outside by helicopter and that is the end of any pretensions to stealth.

(17.5.2) Desirable Characteristics of Food for Combat

Besides their arms and ammunition, the most important items soldiers have to carry are food and water. Now there are some special requirements of the food that the Special Forces have to carry. Considering that they have to carry all the stuff on their backs, the food must be as low in weight as possible—one food packet made by the DFRL (Defence Food Research Laboratory), India weighs 1.714 kg

It should also have a high density so that it occupies as small a volume in the backpack as possible. Special Forces can neither waste their time nor afford the luxury of reconstituting food.

Common Requirements

- Because the soldiers have to march with all their weapons and provisions on their backs and since there cannot be any supply line, the weight (including that of packing and accessories) must be as low as possible. The food packet made by the DFRL (Defence Food Research Laboratory, India weighs 1.714 kg. Compare this with the MRE (Meals Ready to Eat) which typically weighs 600 g (510-740 g, depending on the menu) only!
- There should be no necessity of reconstituting it because potable water is scarce and the soldiers do not find it convenient to add water, heat and so on.
- Soldiers would prefer food which may be eaten straight out of hands without using any utensils at all; not even a plastic plate. Just to illustrate the point, imagine the convenience of eating a 'parantha roll' straight from the hand as against eating vegetable pulao or chapaties and vegetable curry from a dish.
- The packing should be such that it should open easily and the contents must come out of it easily; the soldiers must not need a scissors to cut it open and scrape the food with a spoon.
- For a given weight, the density must be as high as possible so as to reduce volume in storage.
- The food must appeal to the palate of the soldiers who have to use it, though need not be restricted to the regular items of food that are eaten across the country.
- The bottom-line is that it should not merely be 'preserved food'—it should cater to those aspects which are specific to jungle operations.

Food for Long Operations

- Must be balanced in all the major nutrient groups.
- The fiber content of the food must be normal so that it does not lead to constipation.

Food for Marches/Operations up to 48 Hours

- As against the food for long operations, it must be purposefully low in fiber content so that it does not compel the man to evacuate his bowels frequently.

- Precisely for this reason, traditional Indian food items like pulao, daal, chapaties, potato-peas curry, biriyani, or sooji halwa are unsuitable for this purpose, having normal/high fiber content.
- It need not necessarily be a complete food in the sense that it need not have the prescribed ratio of proteins, carbohydrates and fats in it. It can focus on complex carbohydrates to keep a man going—the body would not suffer irreparably in two days, and he can replenish after he comes back to base.
- It should also have high glycemic index items—that is, simple sugars for instant bursts of energy, if required.

(17.5.3) Combat Food in the US Army over the years

Learning this would show you how much mind other nations have applied to the matter. The information furnished would also make you take a hard look at your own R&D because others had done much more nearly a century ago!

Iron Ration (1907-1922): Three-ounce cakes (made from a concoction of beef boullion powder and parched and cooked wheat); three one-ounce bars of sweetened chocolate; and packets of salt and pepper.

Reserve Ration (1917-1937): 12 ounces of bacon or one pound of meat (usually canned corned beef), two 8-ounce cans of hard bread or hardtack biscuits, a packet of 1.16 ounces of pre-ground coffee, a packet of 2.4 ounces of granulated sugar, and a packet of 0.16 ounces of salt.

C-Ration (1938-1945): Each daily ration (i.e. enough food for one soldier for one day) consisted of six 12 oz. cans (three M-units and three B-units),

M (meat) unit: Meat and beans, meat and potato hash, or meat and vegetable stew. "Meat & Spaghetti in Tomato Sauce" was added in 1943. In mid-1944 Chopped Ham, Egg, and Potato; Meat and Noodles; Pork and Rice; Frankfurters and Beans; Pork and Beans; Ham and Lima Beans; and Chicken and Vegetables were introduced in an attempt to increase the C rations' period of continuous use.

B (bread) unit: 5 hardtack crackers, 3 sugar tablets, 3 Dextrose energy tablets or loose candy, and a packet of beverage mix (instant coffee, powdered lemon drink, or boullion soup powder). Later revisions added orange drink powder (1944), sweetened cocoa powder (1944), and grape drink powder (1945) to the list of beverages.

Another B-unit: Consisting of pre-mixed oatmeal cereal, was introduced in 1944 as a breakfast ration that was usually paired with the "Ham, Egg, and Potato" Meal.

D-Ration (WWII): High energy emergency ration. Four oz bar of chocolate, sugar, oat flour, cacao fat, skim milk powder, and artificial flavouring.

K-Ration (WWII): Short duration complete food for airborne troops, tank crew, and other more mobile forces.

- **Breakfast Unit:** Canned entree (chopped ham and eggs, veal loaf), biscuits, a dried fruit bar or cereal bar, Halazone water purification tablets, a 4-pack of cigarettes, chewing gum, instant coffee, and sugar (granulated, cubed, or compressed).
- **Dinner Unit:** Canned entree (processed cheese, ham, or ham and cheese), biscuits, 15 malted milk tablets (early) or 5 caramels (late), sugar (granulated, cubed, or compressed), salt packet, a 4-pack of cigarettes and a box of matches, chewing gum, and a powdered beverage packet (lemon (c. 1940), orange (c. 1943), or grape (c. 1945) flavour).
- **Supper Unit:** Canned meat, consisting of either chicken paté, pork luncheon meat with carrot and apple (1st issue), beef and pork loaf (2nd issue), or sausages; biscuits; a 2-ounce D ration emergency chocolate bar, Tropical bar, or (in temperate climates) commercial sweet chocolate bar; a packet of toilet paper tissues; a 4-pack of cigarettes; chewing gum, and a bouillon soup cube or powder packet.

C-Ration (Type E, 1946-48): Essentially a mixture of C-ration and K-ration

Type C-2 to C-4 Rations (1948-1958):

- 2 Cheese bars (1.5 net ounces)
- 2 "Cereal Class 5" bars (1.5 net ounces)
- 3 Type XII Style 1 Enriched chocolate bars (1 ounce)
- 1 "Jelly Bar" (2 ounces)
- 2 "Fruit Cake Bars" (2 ounces)
- 3 sticks topps peppermint chewing gum
- 3 Domino sugar packets
- 2 Nestea "soluble tea product" packets
- 1 packet of pure soluble sugar

- 1 packet of "Soluble cream product"
- 1 bottle Water Purification Tablets, Individual, Iodine

MCI (Meal, Combat, Individual) Ration (1958-1980): The MCI consisted of a rectangular cardboard carton containing 1 small flat can, 1 large can, and two small cans. It consisted of an "M"-unit can (meat-based entree item), a "B"-unit (bread item) composed of the Crackers & Candy Can and the flat Spread Can, and a "D"-unit can (dessert item). The "M" unit came in 12 basic varieties grouped in 3 menus of 4 different entrees (later supplemented by "Alternate" variant entrees):

- M-1: Beefsteak, Chicken or Turkey Loaf, Chopped Ham & Eggs, or Ham Slices (Cooked in Juices or Fried).
- M-1A: Tuna Fish.
- M-2: Meat Chunks w/. Beans in Tomato Sauce, Ham & Lima Beans, Beef Slices w/. Potatoes in Gravy, or Beans w/. Frankfurter Chunks in Tomato Sauce.
- M-2A: Spaghetti w/. Meatballs in Tomato Sauce.
- M-3: Beef in Spiced Sauce, Boned Chicken or Turkey, Chicken w/. Noodles in Broth, or Pork Steak Cooked in Juices.
- M-3A: Meat Loaf.

The "B" unit came in three different varieties:

- B-1: 7 Crackers and 2 Chocolate Discs (Types: Solid Chocolate, Chocolate Creme, or Chocolate Coconut) and Peanut Butter Spread.
- B-2: 4 Hardtack Biscuits (often referred to by troops as "John Wayne cookies") and a cookie sandwich or fudge disc. Plus Cheese Spread (Types: Processed Cheese w/. Pimentos, or Processed Cheese w/. Caraway Seeds). Spread Alternate: Plain Cheddar Cheese.
- B-3: 4 Cookies and a packet of Cocoa powder. Plus Jam Spread (Types: Apple, Mixed Berry, Seedless Blackberry, Mixed Fruit, Grape, or Strawberry).

The "D" unit came in three different types:

- D-1 (Fruit): Halved Apricots, Sliced Peaches, Quartered Pears, Fruit Cocktail. D-1A (Fruit): Applesauce.
- D-2 (Cake): Pound Cake, Fruitcake, Cinnamon Nut Roll. D-2A (Cake): Date Pudding and Orange Nut Roll.
- D-3 (Bread): White Bread. (There were no alternates).

LRP Ration (Vietnam War Era): For use by Special Forces when the regular MCI would be considered too heavy. It was freeze-dried ration that needed 700 ml water to cook it. It was its main drawback. From where were the soldiers expected to get 700 ml oz drinking water? Menus consisted of a main entree and a dessert item. Entrees included:

Menu #1: Beef Hash,

Menu #2: Chili con Carne,

Menu #3: Spaghetti with Meat Sauce,

Menu #4: Beef with Rice,

Menu #5: Chicken Stew,

Menu #6: Pork with Scalloped Potatoes,

Menu #7: Beef Stew, and

Menu #8: Chicken with Rice.

The dessert unit included one of the following: A Cereal Bar, a Fruitcake Bar, chocolate discs (2), a packet of individually-wrapped pieces of candy (Brachs caramels or Charms hard candies), or even freeze-dried fruit (pears, peaches, or apricots)

MRE (Meals, Ready to Eat) [1981 Till Date]: General contents include:

- Main course (entree)
- Side dish
- Dessert or snack (often commercial candy, fortified pastry, or HOOAH! Bar)
- Crackers or bread
- Spread of cheese, peanut butter, or jelly
- Powdered beverage mix: fruit flavoured drink, cocoa, instant coffee or tea, sport drink, or dairy shake.
- Utensils (usually just a plastic spoon)
- Flameless ration heater (FRH)
- Beverage mixing bag
- Accessory pack:
- Xylitol chewing gum
- Water-resistant matchbook
- Napkin / toilet paper

- Moist towelette
- Seasonings, including salt, pepper, sugar, creamer, and/or Tabasco sauce

The choices for the main course include chicken fajita; chili w/ beans; beef ravioli; maple sausage; Mediterranean chicken; beef patty; beef brisket; meatballs w/marinara sauce; beef stew; chili and macaroni; vegetable lasagna; spicy penne pasta; cheese tortellini; ratatouille; southwest beef & black beans; pork rib; pork sausage w/ gravy; chicken w/ noodles; beef roast w/ vegetables; spaghetti w/ meat sauce; lemon pepper tuna; sloppy joe; chicken pesto pasta; and buffalo chicken.

FSR (First Strike Ration): Compact, eat-on-the move ration concept from the United States Army, designed to be consumed during the first 72 hours of conflict. Eat-out-of-hand foods that require little or no preparation by the Warfighter. Innovative packaging technologies enable the beverages to be reconstituted and consumed directly from the drink pouch. When compared to three meals, ready-to-eat, the FSR reduces the weight and volume of one day's subsistence by approximately 50 per cent.

Menu 1: Filled French toast pocket, Bacon cheddar pocket sandwich, Pepperoni pocket sandwich, Jalapeño cheese spread, Wheat snack bread, Energy beverage (2), Mini First Strike™ Bar (mocha), Mini First Strike™ Bar (chocolate), Peanut butter dessert bar, Beef snack (BBQ), Beef snack (teriyaki), Zapplesauce®, Trail mix, Caffeinated gum.

Menu 2: Brown sugar cinnamon toaster pastry, Italian pocket sandwich, Chunk chicken, Tortillas, Peanut butter, Cracker, Energy beverage (2), Mini First Strike™ Bar (apple cinnamon), Mini First Strike™ Bar (cran-raspberry), Mocha dessert bar, Beef snack (BBQ), Beef snack (teriyaki), Zapplesauce®, Trail mix, Caffeinated gum, Fat free mayo, Hot sauce.

Menu 3: Lemon poppyseed pound cake, Honey BBQ beef pocket sandwich, Albacore tuna, Tortillas, Cheese spread, Cracker, Energy beverage (2), Mini First Strike™ Bar (mocha), Mini First Strike™ Bar (cran-raspberry), Chocolate banana nut dessert bar, Beef snack (BBQ), Beef snack (teriyaki), Zapplesauce®, Trail mix, Caffeinated gum, Fat free mayo, Hot sauce.

Accessory Packet A: Apple cider, Salt, Matches, Tissue, Zip-lock pouch, Towelette (2), Spoon.

Accessory Packet B: Lemon tea, Salt, Matches, Tissue, Zip-lock pouch, Towelette (2), Spoon.

Accessory Packet C: Coffee, cream substitute, sugar, salt, matches, Tissue, Zip-lock pouch, Towelette (2), Spoon.

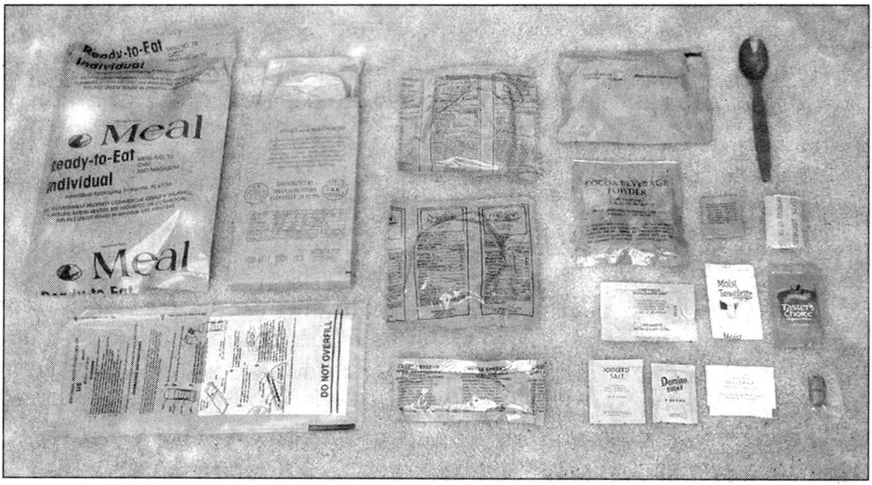

Contents of the US Army's MRE (Meals Ready to Eat) Packet

(17.5.4) The Indian Scene

Compare this with the pathetic research of the Indians. The MRE developed by the Defence Food Research Laboratory consists of four Chapaties (preserved), Sooji halwa (300 g), Vegetable pulav (300 g), Potato Peas Curry (300 g), Chocolate bar and Tea (3 servings). Items like spoon, tissue paper, matchbox, specially designed foldable stove and fuel tablets for warming the food are also included. The products like sooji halwa, vegetable pulav and potato peas curry are processed in a specially designed bulk sterilizer. Since one packet weighs 1.714 kg, troops are forced to depend on their own improvisations that includes eating Sattu (flour of roasted chickpeas, barley etc) with water/salt/lemon/raw onions/pickles etc; and chiwra (beaten rice) with jiggery/water/milk powder/sugar etc. The basic problem with such food is that they do not satisfy the desire of a man to have at least one hot meal a day. Having at least one hot meal also helps in proper bowel movement. Sattu is said to be useful in summers but it has a problem—it increases thirst and thus increases water consumption. It also has a tendency to cause constipation if only this is taken continuously for 2-3 days. Eventually, the troops have to fall back on noodles to satisfy their desire of a hot food.

(17.5.5) *Beware of Indians' Quackery*

Never underestimate the ability of the top brass to foul things up.

At least in India, the whole nation is consumed by an overwhelming desire to find miraculous solutions to complex problems. And they don't have to go far to find such miracles. For every problem that defies solution, they have their ayurveda and the yogis.

In May 2010, a claim was made over TV channels in India that an 83-year-old man called Prahlad Jani in Ahmedabad has a yogic '*siddhi*' (miraculous power) that has enabled him to survive for 70 long years without a grain of food or even a drop of water! Even a layman would understand that it is pure bullshit. No mortal man (or for that matter the lowliest life form) can survive without food and water. But the Indian establishment was taken in by this fraud. What is most frustrating in India is that even the DRDO (Defence Research and Development Organisation) was also taken in by this. They wanted to learn from him so that the soldiers could learn to survive without food—how stupid! They believed that Mr Jani could hold the key to understanding how humans could be taught to survive for long periods without sustenance. "It is possible that it will be able to help save human lives during natural disasters, high altitude, astronauts, sea journeys and other natural and human extremities, and soldiers, who often have to survive without food or water for long spells", said a spokesman for the team. "We can educate people about the survival techniques in adverse conditions with little food and water, or nothing at all". He added: "If his claims are verified, it will be a breakthrough in medical science".

Gentlemen, the fact is that there is no scientific temperament in this country. Indian scientists, like Indian doctors, are merely practitioners of science as the doctors are practitioners of medicine—they are not scientists by attitude. They are as irrational as the common people. Dr G Ilavazahagan, director, DIPAS (Defence Institute of Physiology and Allied Sciences) had said, "The exercise of taking this yogi under a medical scanner is to understand which energy supports his existence, if not food or water. And if at the end of three months by which we plan to come out with observations based on this 15-day check up, we are able to reach to an explanation of this hypothesis, it would tremendously benefit mankind". Well, it is nearly two years now and the DRDO has not been able to find anything of consequence. Even interim results have not been shared for peer-review as they had promised. There has been no publication in any research journal of repute. Fact is, they would never be able to find anything because there is nothing to be found at all.

In February 2012, the newspapers reported: "Soon, herbal energy bars to help jawans keep off hunger, sleep". It was claimed that traditional herbs that helped sages to go without food for months may come in handy for soldiers of paramilitary forces to beat hunger and sleep as they lie in wait during operations in conflict zones. The Mysore-based Defence Food Research Laboratory (DFRL) is planning to develop an anti-sleep and anti-hunger energy bar for jungle operations. Dr K T Jayakrishnan, an ayurveda practitioner, said: "There are herbs to increase alertness and help a person to stay awake for a longer period without damaging the nervous system. *Aswagandha* and *sankupushpam* are some of the herbs that can be used. Similarly, there are herbs that can increase and decrease hunger". Sages used these herbs to help them go without solid food for up to six months. Well, they want to make sages out of you—you won't be a soldier anymore. The simple fact is that no such claim has ever stood the test of scientific scrutiny. We have heard tales of yogis going without food or water for 60,000 years (Muni Parashar, the father of Ved Vyasa, is said to have done that) in the age of the *Mahabharata*. In living memory, there is no verifiable record of any such feat. For details on busting such myths, readers are referred to my work *Yoga and Other Quackery Exposed*. These guys are wasting their time and making a fool of the nation in the process.

(17.6) Getting Potable Water in the Jungle

(17.6.1) Avoid Dehydration at all Costs

In hot conditions with no water, dehydration can set in within an hour. Since you're in the hot and humid jungle you also need to worry about heat stroke. Drinking water will cool you down and lower your core temperature. Knowing the signs and symptoms of dehydration can help you prevent a more serious condition. The stages are:

Mild dehydration: Lack of saliva; decreased frequency of urine; decreased output of urine; and deep colour and strong odor in urine.

Moderate dehydration: Even less urine; dry mouth; dry and sunken eyes; and rapid heartbeat.

Severe dehydration: No urine; lethargy and irritability; and vomiting and diarrhoea. At this point, your body will go into shock. Your skin will turn a blue-grey colour and be cold to the touch because of a drop in blood pressure. Shock is followed by coma and organ failure, and you know what that means—certain death, the opposite of survival.

In the jungle, the hot and humid conditions can cause you to lose about 25 per cent of your body water per day. The water leaves your body as sweat, urine and even in the air you breathe. If you're busy hunting, fishing, gathering wood and building a shelter, you can lose even more fluids than that. All soldierly activity, such as arching long distances, carrying heavy loads on your back, bounding, running, taking cover, and fighting, would require even more water. This means you need to drink at least two gallons of water per day to function at your physical peak. Forget about the 3-liter hydration pack. That's for far more congenial climates and activities.

And you are not likely to get that quantity of water from vegetation like some vines and roots as some self-styled experts of jungle survival would tell you. Vines with rough bark and also shoots about five centimeters thick may have some water. But you have to learn by knowledge which can be the water-bearing vines, since not every vine have got drinkable water. Once again the quantity would not be enough. It may quench your thirst and may save some stupid camper from immediate death but this is not the stuff for soldiers. The buri, coconut, as well as nipa palms all have a sweet liquid that's potable. To get the fluid, you have to flex any blooming stalk associated with one of these brilliant palms downwards, and cut off the tip. In the event you cut a thin piece from the stalk every twelve hours, the flow can replenish, to be able to gather as much as a liter daily. Nipa palm shoots grow from the bottom, to enable you to just work at ground level. On developed trees and shrubs associated with some other varieties, you will have to climb them to attain a blooming stalk. Now not all of you can climb a palm tree! Further, though the milk coming from coconuts has considerable water content, it might have a powerful laxative within ripe nuts. Consuming an excessive amount of the milk may lead you to shed more pounds liquid than you consume. Soldiers are strongly advised to desist from doing such things.

(17.6.2) *Chemical Sterilization of Water in the Jungle*

Water is the number one thing you need to survive any environment on earth—you simply can't live without it. For this reason, the number one tool you can have to survive in the jungle is means of purifying the water you drink. I am a strong votary of chemical sterilisation of water.

Iodine used for water purification is commonly added to water as a solution, in crystallised form, or in tablets containing tetraglycine hydroperiodide that release 8 mg of iodine per tablet adaptation to chronic tetraglycine hydroperiodide. The iodine kills many — but not all – of the most common pathogens present in natural fresh water sources. Carrying iodine for water purification is an imperfect but lightweight solution for those in need of field purification of drinking water. Kits are available in camping stores that include an iodine pill and a second pill (vitamin C or ascorbic acid) that will remove the iodine taste from the water after it has been disinfected, such as those marketed under the Potable Aqua Plus name. The addition of vitamin C, in the form of a pill or in flavoured drink powders, precipitates much of the iodine out of solution, so it should not be added until the iodine has had sufficient time to work. This time is 30 minutes in relatively clear, warm water, but is considerably longer if the water is turbid or cold.

A potentially lower cost alternative to using iodine based water purification tablets is the use of iodine crystals, commonly sold under the Polar Pure name. A small amount of water is poured into a small glass bottle containing 0.25 ounces of iodine crystals, shakes and waits 60 minutes, and then pours off only the amount of liquid solution needed into a larger source of untreated water such as a canteen. After waiting 20 minutes, lengthened if treating cold water instead of warm water, potable water is then available from the treated water. An advantage of using iodine crystals is that only a small amount of iodine is dissolved from the iodine crystals at each use, giving this method of treating water a capability for treating very large amounts of water, around 2,000 liters (500 gallons), with but a small bottle of crystals. Ingestion of the actual iodine crystals must be avoided when using this method. Unlike tetraglycine hydroperiodide tablets, iodine crystals have essentially an unlimited shelf life as long as they are not exposed to air for long periods of time and are kept under water.

Chlorine bleach tablets give a more stable platform for disinfecting the water than liquid bleach (sodium hypochlorite) as the liquid version tends to degrade with age and give unregulated results unless assays are carried out - not practical on the spot. Still, despite chlorine-based portable water purification falling from favour in tablet form such as in halazone tablets, chlorine-based bleach may nonetheless safely be used for short term emergency water disinfection. Two drops of unscented 5 per cent bleach can be added per liter or quart of clear water, then allowed to stand covered for 30 to 60 minutes. After this treatment, the water may be left open to reduce the chlorine smell and taste. Guidelines are available online for effective emergency use of bleach to render unsafe water potable. The Centers for Disease Control & Prevention (CDC) and Population Services International (PSI) promote a similar product (a 0.5 per cent - 1.5 per cent sodium hypochlorite solution) as part of their Safe Water System (SWS) strategy. The product is sold in developing countries under local brand names specifically for the purpose of disinfecting drinking water.

Chlorine-based halazone tablets [Dichlorosulfonamidobenzoic acid] were formerly popularly used for portable water purification. Chlorine in water is more than three times more effective as a disinfectant against Escherichia coli than an equivalent concentration of iodine. Halazone tablets were thus commonly used during World War II by US soldiers for portable water purification, even being included in accessory packs for C-rations until 1945. The primary limitation of halazone tablets was the very short usable life of opened bottles of halazone tablets, typically 3 days or less, unlike iodine-based tablets which have a usable open bottle life of 3 months. Neither chlorine (e.g., bleach) nor iodine alone is considered completely effective against Cryptosporidium, although they are partially effective against Giardia. Iodine should be allowed at least 30 minutes to kill Giardia. Chlorine is considered slightly better than iodine against Giardia.

Sodium dichloroisocyanurate has largely displaced halazone tablets for the few remaining chlorine-based water purification tablets available today. Sodium dichloroisocyanurate is often abbreviated to NaDCC and is compressed with effervescent salts, usually adipic acid and sodium bicarbonate to form a rapidly dissolving tablets. Diluted to 10 parts per million available chlorine (ppm av.cl) when drinking water is mildly contaminated and 20 ppm when visibly contaminated.

For campers, whose water requirements may be little, they prefer water filters. Some of them like the LifeStraw enable you to suck directly from a water source. I do not recommend them. You have to bend down like an animal to suck water—that's unnatural. Secondly, you can use it to drink only—soldiers typically store 3-5 liters in their backpack so that they may take a glug anytime. They need water for cooking also. The sucking device would not let you do any of that. Some manufacturers realised that problem and made things like Combat Water Filter also. All you do is drop the suction tube into the water and pump the lever to draw the water into a bottle. Most models use a ceramic filter to get rid of particles as small as 0.2 microns. A micron is tiny—just 0.000039 inches, to be exact. So 0.2 microns means your pump will supposedly rid the water of bacteria and harmful parasites. But for soldiers it is found to be a very slow method even when the ceramic is clean—it becomes progressively slower as dirt accumulates on the other side. Pumping even one liter out takes considerable time and it is tiring too. Soldiers may not get that much time in one place. Why take unnecessary risk or complicate life. And you cannot expect them to be cleaning the ceramic regularly either. Then ceramics are fragile. The filter element tends to break in the rough and tumble of jungle. Once it develops even a crack, it becomes completely useless as the pathogens will pass through. They need a device which filters the turbidity, without bothering to remove pathogens from it and then kill the pathogens chemically. Simple and quick—you can continue with your activity while the chemical works. Take any stagnant water also, filter it and treat it chemically and drink it.

(17.7) And Thou shalt do something Innovative in Training

(17.7.1) Realistic Jungle Firing Training

Jungle firing practice must simulate real life situations as closely as possible. The standard business of firing on a range has little to do with real life. Only fools do it. Nowhere in real life are you going to get targets that would stand still waiting patiently for you to lie in a prone position, take your sweet time in aiming and then shooting at them. Snap shooting also does not bring you closer to real life. In real life you have to shoot at men who are clever bastards; who could be hiding or changing their positions continuously. But armed forces of this country are notorious for their intellectual bankruptcy. Many fools think that the conventional firing practice on the range could be brought closer to real life if the men are made tired. In reality, after various types of runs, exercises and negotiating obstacles only all you really get is a tired, panting man shooting at clear targets. That's the Achilles' heel. In real combat, you may be tired after a long march but that is not critical. What is critical is that targets in the jungle shall necessarily be concealed amidst vegetation and the response has to be quick. The bad guy has you already in his sights. You do not have much time to respond. React quickly or you will be dead before you can say 'Oh Shit!' Hence your practice targets also need to be partially concealed amidst bushes in the first place. You will have to modify the targets accordingly—beat up anybody who suggests using targets replete with bulls' eye etc. You could, at best see the bad guy's cap, some clothing or something of that sort.

When you hear the enemy shot, you are likely to be standing or moving. *From that position, you must learn to immediately take the nearest available cover and retaliate credibly.* There are two things in it. The first thing is what I called the 'nearest available cover'. Your first priority is to reduce the chances of getting hit in the first burst or first few shots itself. OK, that done, what you ought to do next. The second thing is what I called 'retaliating credibly'. That's no less important. You are not going to simply hide in a hole forever—after all, you are there to fight and shoot at the bad bandit. How do you do that? Here comes the important concept that I have developed. The secret is that there shall always be a dynamic trade-off between the best cover and the best firing position for a given situation and that there cannot be a fixed rule for all situations.

A common thing that they teach you in conventional training is to adopt a prone position. Yes, I do know that the moment you adopt a prone position, you reduce your area by about 85 per cent and hence your chances of getting hit are proportionately reduced. That's fine, but once you are down, you may not always get proper aim at the possible targets because your field of view is restricted accordingly. The enemy himself could be in a prone position and you may have to try to see through undergrowth on the jungle floor which may make it very difficult to see beyond a few meters. What do you do then? In such a situation, if you have to return fire reasonably, you will have to raise your head and body. Get the picture? This means that, in every situation, you will have to decide how you would return the fire credibly without getting shot cheaply. Sometimes you may have to adopt a kneeling position by the side of some waist high bush; sometimes you may have to stand by the side of some tree. Do not think that prone position is the rule. The hostile fire could well be coming from a height such as from a hill or the insurgent could be on a tree from where he could be seeing the ground in front of him clearly. From his perspective, a prone body could be offering a target of greater area than one who is crouching behind some bush or standing sideways behind a tree trunk.

Hence, in training the soldiers must learn to take whatever improvised cover they can take on signal (a shot itself) and return the fire from all three positions: standing, kneeling and lying down, as the case could be. They must also practice to change positions after firing a couple of shots from one location and then change location to fire again—practice this by crab rolling, duck walking, crouch sprint, kitten crawl; and so on. The effect of fire should be evaluated in all modes of firing—single shot, short bursts of full automatic, full automatic one magazine, and three-round bursts separately. This will give the trainees a first-hand idea of the effectiveness of various types of fire in various situations involving multiple targets.

Then there is the factor of poor visibility. Most encounters in the jungles in counter-insurgency operations take place in low or very low-light conditions of night. Hence, the targets may not be visible at all and if there are hills around then reflection of sound may further confuse regarding the direction of the source. Hence, a direct clue to their locations could perhaps be obtained only from the muzzle flash of the enemy's weapons. In realistic training you must try to simulate this to the extent possible. To simulate this condition, practice must be done in real-life darkness of varying degrees. The targets should once again be partially concealed in bushes as in good light conditions. Muzzle flash may be simulated by momentary lighting of bulbs placed in front of the targets. They must learn to assess the location of the enemy by the flash and then deliver fire on the target. Batteries may be kept on the firing side and wires can be run up to the targets. The bulbs will light up only for a moment. They must be small, directional and under no circumstances should light up the target completely. I do not expect a man-sized target to be hit often under such conditions. The essential idea of firing in such conditions is that even if our shots land somewhere close to the target, it would be sufficiently unnerving for the bad bandit. Hence, we will be using larger targets for this.

Firing in low-light conditions is a challenging task any day and demands some out-of-the-box thinking. The binocular NVD is way too heavy (2.34 kg) to be of any use in the field by troops on the move. A monocular NVD is good for observation during movement or from temporary halts/LUP when one is not expecting to shoot; but a definite encumbrance when one is shooting or is required to shoot on short notice—one cannot observe through it with one hand and one eye thus occupied, and shoot at the same time. Monocular night vision sights mounted on rifles are useful only if we have them on every rifle; otherwise those without it would remain severely handicapped.

For firing in instantaneous response, as would be necessary in ambushes etc. during low-light conditions, illuminated 3-dot iron sights are extremely useful. This allows one to align the sights quickly without any encumbrance or weight added to the rifle and have a rough idea of where the shots are going—obviating the main problem of the shots going wildly astray in the dark as the foresight gets lost in the background. Tritium sights seem to serve the purpose well.

(17.7.2) Endurance Marches

Boxers are produced by practicing real boxing, not in the gyms. You can bench-press as much as you like and curl 300 pounds; nothing will prepare you for taking that left hook on your chin. You can shadow box the whole evening and still would not know how much a punch hurts. For that you must practice real boxing in which punches connect. That's why the PKA (Professional Karate Association) scorns at the karate schools where people get black belts without having ever received a punch. Such black belts have been beaten black and blue in real street fights because they never knew how it feels to take a punch and how they must tolerate pain. In other words, training must correspond as closely to the real life activity as possible. Merely strengthening the body by exercises in the gym would not prepare a man for combat.

In jungle warfare, a primary activity is marching long distances over rough, broken and undulating ground amidst rain, cold and mud with heavy loads. This must be practiced as such in endurance marches. Running 10000 meters on an excellent track does not prepare you for this. General Augusto Bayo, who had trained the Cuban guerrillas, had set a standard in this regard. That was an endurance march of 15 hours with full combat load covering 30-50 km depending on the terrain. It is still an excellent standard and all jungle warriors must practice it. About 45 km must be covered in this period in a terrain which is not hilly. Incidentally, the US army (according to the FM 21-18) does a forced march of 52 km in 21.84 hours which comes to 45 km in 18.9 hours with a similar combat load.

In such marches, particularly in hot weather, one must be extremely careful about the danger of dehydration. Pay special attention to water and electrolytes. As thirst is not a reliable indicator of dehydration, one must constantly monitor his urine output and its colour. It is better to have specially formulated good quality 'hypertonic sports drinks' made elsewhere in the world, the sugars (dextrose/sucrose/fructose etc). and salts (sodium/potassium/calcium) of which may form an "active pump" that transports fluid to cells more quickly than water alone. Some of them, such as Isostar are available in tablet form also.

The second major problem is that of blisters in the feet. Elsewhere in the world where long hikes have become a way of life, an entire industry is supported by this need and the subject itself has been raised to the level of a science with experts like John Vonhof writing whole books like 'Fixing Your Feet: Prevention and Treatments for Athletes'—the products devised by this industry include specifically designed shoes with cushioned inner soles; double-layered socks of moisture-wicking material (such as polypropylene or CoolMax); moleskin for padding or various types of 'sports tape' for taping 'hot spots'; Dr Scholl's blister treatment; and blister-preventing lubricants like BodyGlide etc.

The third problem is that of carrying the weapon. The three-point sling poses a problem in a long march. On long marches like this it is difficult to carry the weapon all the time in a modified port carry as it becomes tiring. The benefit of the three-point sling in allowing more control of the weapon in tactical situations is fine. However, when hauling the weapon over long distances, I find that the three-point sling is not the right equipment and the right equipment would be something similar to the proprietary 'CrossFire Two Shoulder Carry Sling'.

The CrossFire Two Shoulder Carry Sling

This sling permits the rifle to be carried slung to the back of an arm in the old-fashioned GI 'sling-arms' carry position (stock hanging down and barrel pointing up) but has an extra loop which goes across and over the head, thus distributing the weight to two shoulders, thereby reducing fatigue—it also frees one from the necessity of tugging forward on the sling in the old fashioned way.

Appendix A

Search of Individuals

Techniques of Searching Individuals

It is not as simple a task as it is commonly believed to be. The Western forces have made a complete science of it. Even for something like frisk search the searcher stands behind the suspect and his assistant takes a position from which he can cover the suspect with his weapon.

Frisk Search

The frisk is a quick search of an individual for weapons, evidence, or contraband. It should be conducted in the presence of an assistant and a witness. In conducting the frisk, the searcher stands behind the terrorist. The searcher's assistant takes a position from which he can cover the terrorist with his weapon. The terrorist is required to raise his arms. The searcher then slides his hands over the individual's entire body, crushing the clothing to locate concealed objects.

Wall Search

The wall search is based on the principle of rendering the suspect harmless by placing him in a strained, awkward position and affords the searcher a degree of safety. It is particularly useful when two searchers must search several suspects. The searcher approaches the suspect from the right side. The searcher's weapon must not be in such a position that the suspect can grab it. When searching from the right side, the searcher places his right foot in front of the suspect's right foot and makes and maintains ankle-to-ankle contact. From this position, if the suspect offers resistance, the suspect's right foot can be pushed back from under him. When searching from the left side of the suspect the searcher places his left foot in front of the suspect's left foot and again maintains ankle-to-ankle contact. The searcher must crush the suspect's clothing between his fingers; he should not merely pat it—that is the difference between a professional's work and a cursory search. When two or more suspects are to be searched, they must assume a position against the same wall or object but far enough apart so that they cannot reach one another. On completing the search of one suspect, he is moved to the left of the line and resumes the position against the wall. Thus, in approaching and searching the next suspect, the searcher is not between his assistant and a suspect. Any upright surface can be used such as a wall, vehicle, or tree.

(1) **Position of Terrorist:** The terrorist must face the wall (or other object) and lean against it, supporting himself with his upraised hands placed far apart and fingers spread. His feet are placed well apart, turned out, parallel to the wall, and as far from the wall as possible. His head is kept down.

(2) **Position of Searcher's Assistant:** The searcher's assistant stands on the opposite of the terrorist (from the searcher) and to the rear. He covers the terrorist with his weapon. When the searcher moves from his original position to the opposite side of the terrorist, the assistant also changes position. The searcher walks around his assistant during this change to avoid coming between his assistant and the terrorist.

(3) **Position of Searcher:** The searcher approaches the terrorist from the right side. The searcher's weapon must not be in such a position that the terrorist can grab it. When searching from the right side, the searcher places his right foot in front of the terrorist's right foot and makes and maintains ankle-to-ankle contact. From this position, if the terrorist offers resistance, the terrorist's right foot can be pushed back from under him. When searching from the left side of the terrorist, the searcher places his left foot in front of the terrorist's left foot and again maintains ankle-to-ankle contact.

(4) **Initial Position:** In taking his initial position, the searcher should be alert to prevent the terrorist from suddenly trying to disarm or injure him. The searcher first searches the terrorist's headgear. The searcher then checks the terrorist's hands, arms, right side of the body, and right leg, in sequence. The searcher repeats the procedure in searching the terrorist's left side. He crushes the terrorist's clothing between his fingers--he does not merely pat it. He pays close attention to armpits, back, waist, legs, and tops of boots or shoes. Any item found that is not considered a weapon or evidence is replaced in the terrorist's pocket. If the

terrorist resists or attempts escape and must be thrown down before completing the search, the search is restarted from the beginning.

(5) **Switch of Multiple Terrorists:** When two or more terrorists are to be searched, they must assume a position against the same wall or object but far enough apart so that they cannot reach each other. The searcher's assistant takes his position a few paces to the rear of the line with his weapon ready. The search is started with the terrorist on the right of the line. On completing the search of one terrorist, the searcher moves the terrorist to the left of the line to resume his position against the wall. Thus, in approaching and searching the next terrorist, the searcher is not between his assistant and a terrorist.

Strip Search

Strip search is usually necessary when the individual is suspected of being a guerrilla leader or important messenger. You must search not only his person but his mouth, nose, ears, hair, armpits, crotch, and other areas of possible concealment also. The following are the basic methods of searching of individuals. The search should be conducted in an enclosed space such as a room or tent. The searching technique can be varied. One method is to use two unarmed searchers while an assistant, who is armed, stands guard. The terrorist's clothing and shoes are removed and searched carefully. A search is then made of his person to include his mouth, nose, ears, hair, armpits, crotch, and other areas of possible concealment.

Search of Females

The terrorists make full use of females for all types of tasks where search may be a threat. COIN forces must fully employ female searchers. If female searchers cannot be provided, a doctor should be used for searching female terrorists. The search of females is an extremely sensitive matter. When male soldiers must search females, every possible measure must be taken to prevent the slightest inference of sexual molestation or assault.

Search of Built-Up Areas: Cordon and Search Operations

Techniques

Search techniques in built-up areas are practised by police and military forces operating in populated areas. These techniques are required for searching either a few isolated huts or buildings, or for searching well-developed urban sections. Search operations in built-up areas require thorough preparation and rehearsal. In larger towns or cities, the local administration may have detailed maps showing relative size and location of buildings. Remember that a search operation can turn into a full-fledged encounter with the terrorists anytime. Terrorists who are hiding inside may decide to slug it out instead of escaping or surrendering. Hence, you must always go into a cordon and search operation with the full preparation of an encounter. Special emphasis should be given to the following:

(1) Divide the area to be searched into zones, and assign a search party to each. A search party consists of a search element (to conduct the search), a security element (to encircle the area and prevent entrance and exit, and to secure open areas), and a reserve element (to assist, as required).

(a) The search element conducts the mission assigned for the operation. Normally, it is organised into special teams.

(b) The security element surrounds the area while the search element moves in. Members of the security element orient primarily upon evaders from the populated area; however, they can cut off any terrorists trying to reinforce. Checkpoints and road blocks are established. Subsurface routes of escape, such as subways and sewers, must be considered when operating in cities.

(c) The reserve element is a mobile force within a nearby area. Its specific mission is to assist the other two elements should they meet resistance they cannot handle. In addition, it is capable of replacing or reinforcing either of the other two elements should the need arise.

(2) Consider any enemy material found, including propaganda signs and leaflets, to be booby-trapped until inspection proves it is safe.

(3) Thoroughly search underground and underwater areas. Any freshly excavated ground can be a hiding place. Use mine detectors to locate metal objects underground and underwater.

(4) Deploy rapidly, especially when a guerrilla force is still in the area to be searched. The entire area to be searched is surrounded simultaneously. If this is not possible, observed fire must cover that portion not covered by soldiers.

Approach

On some operations, the situation may allow mounted movement directly into the area to be searched. On others, the situation may dictate dismounted movement into the area. Emphasis is placed on rapid and coordinated entrance into the area.

Surrounding the Area

During darkness, troops approach silently by as many different routes as possible. At first daylight, the area can be occupied by a chain of observation posts with gaps covered by patrols. Normally, a large area cannot be completely surrounded for any length of time because of the number of troops required. If necessary, troops dig in, take advantage of natural cover, and use barbed wire to help maintain their line.

Reserves

If there is a chance that hostile elements from outside the area could interfere, measures are taken to prevent them from joining the inhabitants of the area under search. Air observers can assist by detecting and giving early warning of any large-scale movement toward the occupied area.

Search Parties

(a) The officer in command of the operation informs the inhabitants that the area is to be searched, that a house curfew is in force, and that all inhabitants must remain indoors. This method prohibits movement of civilians, allows them to stay in their dwellings, and discourages looting. The disadvantages are that it makes control and interrogation difficult and gives inhabitants time to conceal evidence in their homes. Alternatively, he may require the inhabitants to gather at a central point and then have the search party move in and begin the search. Search parties are usually composed of search teams.

(b) When a decision is made to gather inhabitants at a central point, the head of the house should accompany the search party when his house is searched. If this is not done, he can deny knowledge of anything incriminating that is found, or he can accuse the troops of theft and looting. In order to avoid accusations of theft or planting of incriminating evidence, witnesses should be present during the search. This method provides maximum control, facilitates a thorough search, denies terrorists an opportunity to conceal evidence, and allows for detailed interrogation. It has the disadvantage of taking the inhabitants away from their dwellings, thus encouraging looting which, in turn, engenders ill-feelings.

(c) In the third method, the head of each household is told to remain in front of his house while all others are brought to a central location. During the search, the head of each household accompanies the search team through his house. Looting is minimised, and the head of the household can see that the search team did not steal property. This is the best method for controlling the population.

(d) Buildings are searched from top to bottom, if possible. Mine detectors are used to search for arms and ammunition. Every effort is made to avoid unnecessary damage. Each house or building searched is marked with a coded designation. This same designation can be used to list occupants who must be accounted for in subsequent searches, and the designation helps ensure that no building is overlooked in the search.

House Search

Each search party assigned to search an occupied building should consist of at least one local policeman, a protective escort, and a female searcher, if appropriate. The search party must first assemble everyone. The civil police may give the necessary orders and do the actual searching. The object of this search is to screen for suspected persons. Apprehended persons are evacuated as soon as possible. Troops may perform this task. Escort parties and transportation must be planned in advance.

Village Search

Prior to conducting search operations in a village, a reconnaissance patrol is sent out to gain information about the village and its inhabitants. The patrol avoids detection. A portion of the patrol maintains surveillance over the village while the remainder of the patrol returns with information. This is done to detect any changes which may take place prior to the security element going into position. Information of value to a commander includes: size and exact location of the village; fortifications (mantraps, spike traps); warning systems. tunnel systems; where does the terrorist live; does he live in the forest at night and inhabit the village during the day, or does he stay in the village night and day; does he inhabit one or more huts; and how many people are there in the village?

Places Requiring Special Attention

Cattle pens, wells, haystacks, gardens, fence lines, and cemeteries should be investigated. Regardless of the terrain, the search unit checks possible locations for caches of materiel or terrorists in hiding. In areas where tunnels have been reported, it is imperative that the search unit have a tunnel reconnaissance team attached. This team should be composed of volunteers trained for this type of operation. They should have special equipment such as flashlights or miner helmets, protective masks, communication with the surface, and silencer-equipped pistols. They should know how to sketch a tunnel system, and they should recover all items of intelligence interest.

Appendix B

Combat Tracking

In all operations, you must be alert for signs of enemy activity. Such signs can often alert you to an enemy's presence and give your unit time to prepare for contact. The ability to track an enemy after he has broken contact also helps you regain contact with him. Tracking is a precise art. You need a lot of practice to achieve and keep a high level of tracking skill. You should be familiar with the general techniques of tracking to enable you to detect the presence of a hidden enemy and to follow him, to find and avoid mines or booby- traps, and to give early warning of ambush.

Tracker Qualities

Visual tracking is following the path of men or animals by the signs they leave, primarily on the ground or vegetation. Scent tracking is following men or animals by their smell. With common sense and a degree of experience, you can track another person. However, you must develop the following traits and qualities:

- Be patient.
- Be able to move slowly and quietly, yet steadily, while detecting and interpreting signs.
- Avoid fast movement that may cause you to overlook signs, lose the trail, or blunder into an enemy unit.
- Be persistent and have the skill and desire to continue the mission even though signs are scarce or weather or terrain is unfavourable.
- Be determined and persistent when trying to find a trail that you have lost.
- Be observant and try to see things that are not obvious at first glance.

- Use your senses of smell and hearing to supplement your sight.
- Develop a feel for things that do not look right. It may help you regain a lost trail or discover additional signs.
- Know the enemy, his habits, equipment, and capability.

Fundamentals of Tracking

When tracking an enemy, you should build a picture of him in your mind. Ask yourself such questions as: How many persons am I following? How well are they trained? How are they equipped? Are they healthy? How is their morale? Do they know they are being followed? To find the answer to such questions, use all available signs. A sign can be anything that shows you that a certain act took place at a particular place and time. For instance, a footprint tells a tracker that at a certain time a person walked on that spot.

The six fundamentals of tracking are:

- Displacement.
- Staining.
- Weathering.
- Littering.
- Camouflaging.
- Interpretation and/or immediate use intelligence.

Any sign that you find can be identified as one or more of the first five fundamentals. In the sixth fundamental, you combine the first five and use all of them to form a picture of the enemy.

Displacement

Displacement takes place when something is moved from its original position. An example is a footprint in soft, moist ground. The foot of the person that left the print displaced the soil, leaving an indentation in the ground. By studying the print, you can determine many facts. For example, a print that was left by a barefoot person or a person with worn or frayed footgear indicates that he may have poor equipment.

How to Analyse Footprints?

- Footprints show the following:
- The direction and rate of movement of a party.
- The number of persons in a party.

- Whether or not heavy loads are carried.
- The sex of the members of a party.
- Whether the members of a party know they are being followed.

If the footprints are deep and the pace is long, the party is moving rapidly. Very long strides and deep prints, with toe prints deeper than heel prints, indicate that the party is running. If the prints are deep, short, and widely spaced, with signs of scuffing or shuffling, a heavy load is probably being carried by the person who left the prints.

You can also determine a person's sex by studying the size and position of the footprints. Women generally tend to be pigeon-toed, while men usually walk with their feet pointed straight ahead or slightly to the outside. Women's prints are usually smaller than men's, and their strides are usually shorter.

If a party knows that it is being followed, it may attempt to hide its tracks. Persons walking backward have a short, irregular stride. The prints have an unusually deep toe. The soil will be kicked in the direction of movement.

The last person walking in a group usually leaves the clearest footprints. Therefore, use his prints as the key set. Cut a stick the length of each key print and notch the stick to show the print width at the widest part of the sole. Study the angle of the key prints to determine the direction of march. Look for an identifying mark or feature on the prints, such as a worn or frayed part of the footwear. If the trail becomes vague or obliterated, or if the trail being followed merges with another, use the stick to help identify the key prints. That will help you stay on the trail of the group being followed. Use the box method to count the number of persons in the group. There are two ways to use the box method—the stride as a unit of measure method and the 36-inch box method.

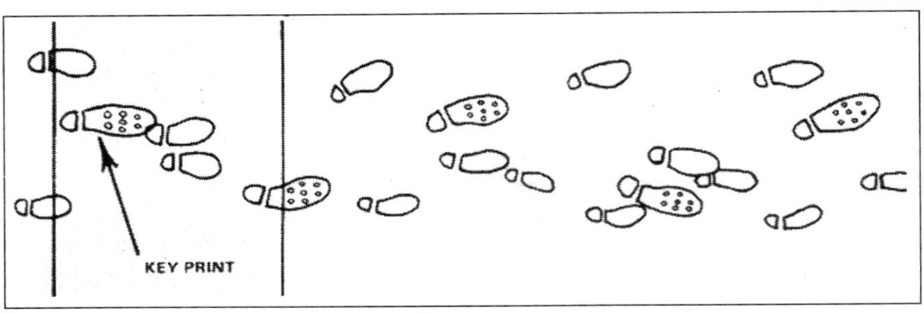

The stride as a unit of measure

The stride as a unit of measure method is the most accurate of the two. Up to 18 persons can be counted using this method. Use it when the key prints can be determined. To use this method, identify a key print on a trail and draw a line from its heel across the trail. Then move forward to the key print of the opposite foot and draw a line through its instep. This should form a box with the edges of the trail forming two sides, and the drawn lines forming the other two sides. Next, count every print or partial print inside the box to determine the number of persons. Any person walking normally would have stepped in the box at least one time. Count the key prints as one.

To use the 36-inch box method, mark off a 30- to 36-inch cross section of a trail, count the prints in the box, then divide by two to determine the number of persons that used the trail.

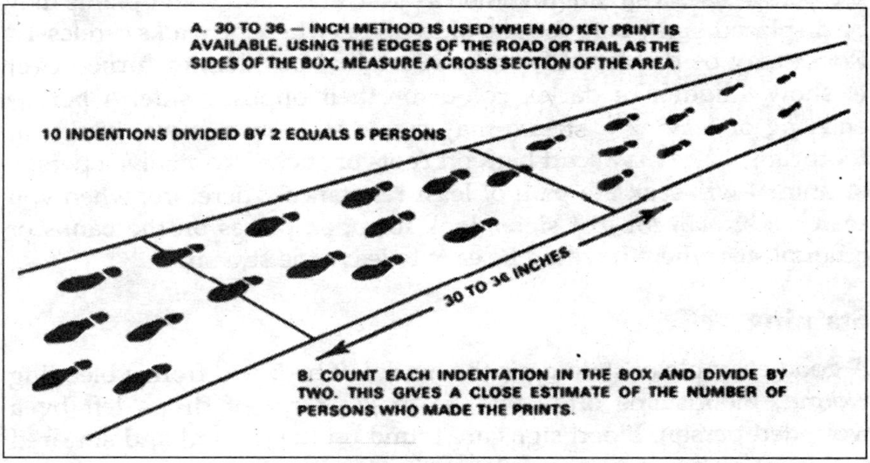

The 36-inch box method

Other Signs of Displacement

Footprints are only one example of displacement. Displacement occurs when anything is moved from its original position. Other examples are such things as foliage, moss, vines, sticks, or rocks that are moved from their original places; dew droplets brushed from leaves; stones and sticks that are turned over and show a different colour underneath; and grass or other vegetation that is bent or broken in the direction of movement.

Bits of cloth may be torn from a uniform and left on thorns, snags, or the ground, and dirt from boots may make marks on the ground. Another example of displacement is the movement of wild animals and birds that are flushed from their natural habitats. You may hear the cries of birds that are excited by strange movements. The movement of tall grass or brush on a windless day indicates that something is moving the vegetation from its original position.

When you clear a trail by either breaking or cutting your way through heavy vegetation, you displace the vegetation. Displacement signs can be made while you stop to rest with heavy loads. The prints made by the equipment you carry can help to identify its type. When loads are set down at a rest halt or campsite, grass and twigs may be crushed. A sleeping man may also flatten the vegetation. In most areas, there will be insects. Any changes in the normal life of these insects may be a sign that someone has recently passed through the area. Bees that are stirred up, and holes that are covered by someone moving over them, or spider webs that are torn down are good clues. If a person uses a stream to cover his trail, algae and water plants may be displaced in slippery footing or in places where he walks carelessly. Rocks may be displaced from their original position, or turned over to show a lighter or darker colour on their opposite side. A person entering or leaving a stream may create slide marks, wet banks, or footprints, or he may scuff bark off roots or sticks. Normally, a person or animal will seek the path of least resistance. Therefore, when you search a stream for exit signs, look for open places on the banks or other places where it would be easy to leave the stream.

Staining

A good example of staining is the mark left by blood from a bleeding wound. Bloodstains often will be in the form of drops left by a wounded person. Blood signs are found on the ground and smeared on leaves or twigs. You can determine the location of a wound on a man being followed by studying the bloodstains. If the blood seems to be dripping steadily, it probably came from a wound on his trunk. A wound in the lungs will deposit bloodstains that are pink, bubbly, frothy. A bloodstain deposited from a head wound will appear heavy, wet, and slimy, like gelatin. Abdominal wounds often mix blood with digestive juices so that the deposit will have an odor. The stains will be light in colour.

Staining can also occur when a person walks over grass, stones, and shrubs with muddy boots. Thus, staining and displacement together may give evidence of movement and indicate the direction taken. Crushed leaves may stain rocky ground that is too hard for footprints. Roots, stones, and vines may be stained by crushed leaves or berries when walked on. Yellow stains in snow may be urine marks left by personnel in the area.

In some cases, it may be hard to determine the difference between staining and displacement. Both terms can be applied to some signs. For example, water that has been muddied may indicate recent movement. The mud has been displaced and it is staining the water. Stones in streams may be stained by mud from boots. Algae can be displaced from stones in streams and can stain other stones or bark. Water in footprints in swampy ground may be muddy if the tracks are recent. In time, however, the mud will settle and the water will clear. The clarity of the water can be used to estimate the age of the prints. Normally, the mud will clear in one hour. That will vary with terrain.

Weathering

Weather may either aid or hinder tracking. It affects signs in ways that help determine how old they are, but wind, snow, rain, and sunlight can also obliterate signs completely. By studying the effects of weather on signs, you can determine the age of the sign. For example, when bloodstains are fresh, they may be bright red. Air and sunlight will change the appearance of blood first to a deep ruby-red colour, and then to a dark brown crust when the moisture evaporates. Scuff marks on trees or bushes darken with time. Sap oozes from fresh cuts on trees but it hardens when exposed to the air.

Footprints

Footprints are greatly affected by weather. When a foot displaces soft, moist soil to form a print, the moisture holds the edges of the print intact and sharp. As sunlight and air dry the edges of the print, small particles that were held in place by the moisture fall into the print, making the edges appear rounded. Study this process carefully to estimate the age of a print. If particles are just beginning to fall into a print, it is probably fresh. If the edges of the print are dried and crusty, the prints are probably at least an hour old. The effects of weather will vary with the terrain, so this information is furnished as a guide only.

A light rain may round out the edges of a print. Try to remember when the last rain occurred in order to put prints into a proper time frame. A heavy rain may erase all signs. Wind also affects prints. Besides drying out a print, the wind may blow litter, sticks, or leaves into it. Try to remember the wind activity in order to help determine the age of a print. For example, you may think, "It is calm now, but the wind blew hard an hour ago. These prints have litter blown into them, so they must be over an hour old". You must be sure, however, that the litter was blown into the prints, and was not crushed into them when the prints were made.

Trails leaving streams may appear to be weathered by rain because of water running into the footprints from wet clothing or equipment. This is particularly true if a party leaves a stream in a file. From this formation, each person drips water into the prints. A wet trail slowly fading into a dry trail indicates that the trail is fresh.

Wind, Sounds, and Odors

Wind affects sounds and odors. If the wind is blowing from the direction of a trail you are following, sounds and odors are carried to you. If the wind is blowing in the same direction as the trail you are following, you must be cautious as the wind will carry your sounds toward the enemy. To find the wind direction, drop a handful of dry dirt or grass from shoulder height. To help you decide where a sound is coming from, cup your hands behind your ears and slowly turn. When the sound is loudest, you are probably facing the origin of sound. When moving, try to keep the wind in your face.

Sun

You must also consider the effects of the sun. It is hard to look or aim directly into the sun. If possible, keep the sun at your back.

Littering

Poorly trained units may leave trails of litter as they move. Gum or candy wrappers, ration cans, cigarette butts, remains of fires, or human feces are unmistakable signs of recent movement. Weather affects litter. Rain may flatten or wash litter away, or turn paper into pulp. Winds may blow litter away from its original location. Ration cans exposed to weather will rust. They first rust at the exposed edge where they were opened. Rust then moves in toward the center. Use your memory to determine the age of litter. The last rain or strong wind can be the basis of a time frame.

Camouflage

If a party knows that you are tracking it, it will probably use camouflage to conceal its movement and to slow and confuse you. Doing so, however, will slow it down. Walking backward, brushing out trails, and moving over rocky ground or through streams are examples of camouflage that can be used to confuse you. The party may move on hard surfaced, frequently traveled roads or try to merge with travelling civilians. Examine such routes with extreme care, because a well-defined approach that leads to the enemy will probably be mined, ambushed, or covered by snipers. The party may try to avoid leaving a trail. Its members may wrap rags around their boots, or wear soft-soled shoes to make the edges of their footprints rounder and less distinct. The party may exit a stream in column or line to reduce the chance of leaving a well-defined exit.

If the party walks backward to leave a confusing trail, the footprints will be deepened at the toe, and the soil will be scuffed or dragged in the direction of movement. If a trail leads across rocky or hard ground, try to work around that ground to pick up the exit trail. This process works in streams as well. On rocky ground, moss or lichens growing on the stones could be displaced by even the most careful evader. If you lose the trail, return to the last visible sign. From there, head in the direction of the party's movement. Move in ever-widening circles until you find some signs to follow.

Interpretation/Immediate use of Intelligence

When reporting, do not report your interpretations as facts. Report that you have seen signs of certain things, not that those things actually exist. Report all information quickly. The term "immediate use intelligence" includes information of the enemy that can be put to use at once to gain surprise, to keep the enemy off balance, or to keep him from escaping an area. A commander has many sources of intelligence. He puts the information from those sources together to help determine where an enemy is, what he may be planning, and where he may be going. Information you report gives your leader definite information on which he can act at once. For example, you may report that your leader is 30 minutes behind an enemy unit, that the enemy is moving north, and that he is now at a certain place. That gives your leader information on which he can act at once. He could then have you keep on tracking and move another unit to attack the enemy. If a trail is found that has signs of recent enemy activity, your leader can set up an ambush on it.

Tracking Teams

Your unit may form tracking teams. The lead team of a moving unit can be a tracking team, or a separate unit may be a tracking team. There are many ways to organise such teams, and they can be any size. There should, however, be a leader, one or more trackers, and security for the trackers. A typical organisation has three trackers, three security men, and a team leader with a radio-telephone operator (RO). When a team is moving, the best tracker should be in the lead, followed by his security. The two other trackers should be on the flanks, each one followed and overmatched by his security. The leader should be where he can best control the team. The RO should be with the leader.

Tracker Dogs

Tracker dogs may be used to help track an enemy. Tracker dogs are trained and used by their handlers. A dog tracks human scent and the scent of disturbed vegetation caused by man's passing. Tracker dogs should be used with tracker teams. The team can track visually, and the dog and handler can follow. If the team loses the signs, then the dog can take over. A dog can track faster than a man tracks, and a dog can track at night. A tracker dog is trained not to bark and give away the team. It is also trained to avoid baits, cover odors, and deodorants used to throw it off the track.

Counter-tracking

In addition to knowing how to track, you must know how to counter an enemy tracker's efforts to track you. Some counter-tracking techniques are discussed below:

While moving from close terrain to open terrain, walk past a big tree (12-inch in diameter or larger) toward the open area for three to five paces. Then walk backward to the forward side of the tree and make a 90-degree change of direction, passing the tree on its forward side. Step carefully and leave as little sign as possible. If this is not the direction that you want to go, change direction again about 50 meters away using the same technique. The purpose of this is to draw the enemy tracker into the open area where it is harder for him to track. That also exposes him and causes him to search the wrong area.

When approaching a trail (about 100 meters from it), change your direction of movement and approach it at a 45-degree angle. When arriving at the trail, move along it for about 20 to 30 meters. Leave several signs of your presence. Then walk backward along the trail to the point where you joined it. At that point, cross the trail and leave no sign of your leaving it. Then move about 100 meters at an angle of 45 degrees, but this time on the other side of the trail and in the reverse of your approach. When changing direction back to your original line of march, the big tree technique can be used. The purpose of this technique is to draw the enemy tracker along the easier trail. You have, by changing direction before reaching the trail, indicated that the trail is your new line of march.

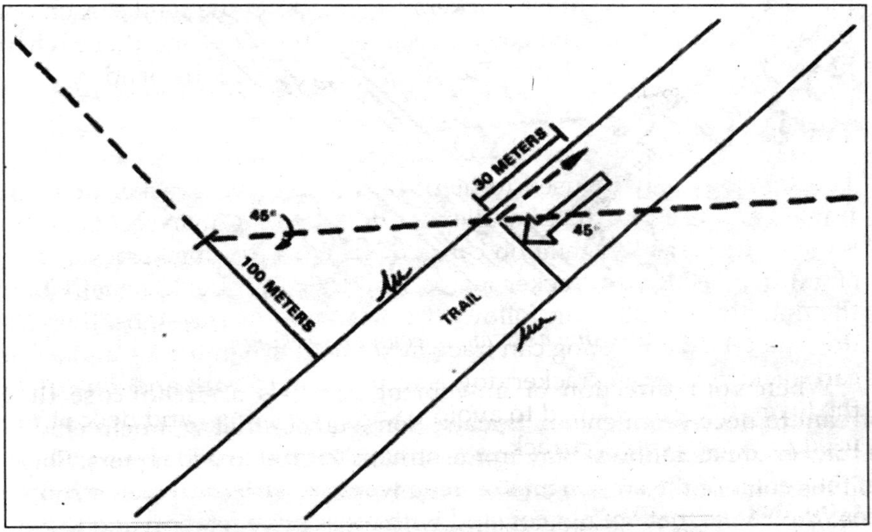

Approaching trail in counter-tracking

To leave a false trail and to get an enemy tracker to look in the wrong when leaving a stream: To further direction, walk backward over soft ground. Continue this deception for about 20 to 30 meters or until you are on hard ground. Use this technique when leaving a stream. To further confuse the enemy tracker, use this technique several times before actually leaving the stream.

Leaving false trail when leaving a stream

When moving toward a stream, change direction about 100 meters before reaching the stream and approach it at a 45-degree angle. Enter the stream and proceed down it for at least 20 to 30 meters. Then move back upstream and leave the stream in your initial direction. Changing direction before entering the stream may confuse the enemy tracker. When he enters the stream, he should follow the false trail until the trail is lost. That will put him well away from you.

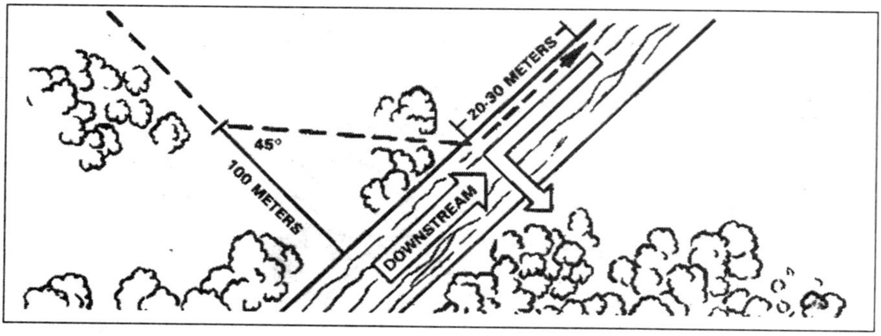

Crossing a stream in counter-tracking

When your direction of movement parallels a stream, use the stream to deceive an enemy tracker. Some tactics that will help elude a tracker are as follows: Stay in the stream for 100 to 200 meters. Stay in the center of the stream and in deep water. Watch for rocks or roots near the banks that are not covered with moss or vegetation and leave the stream at that point. Walk out backward on soft ground.

Walk up a small, vegetation-covered tributary and exit from it.

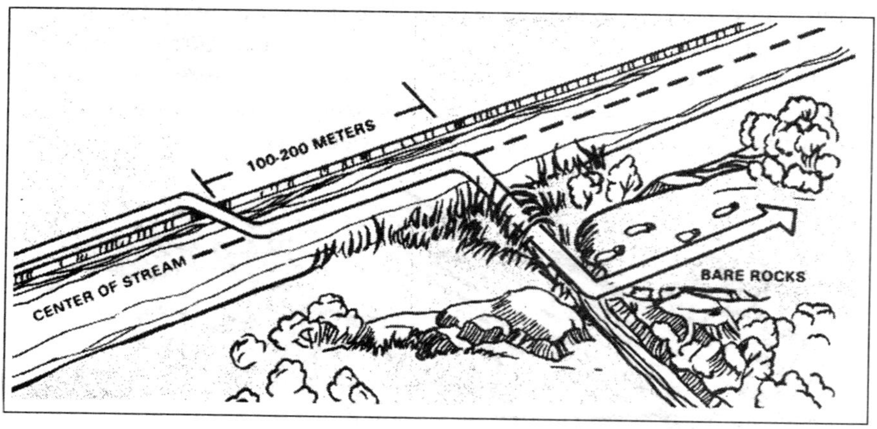

Parallel trail in counter-tracking

When being tracked by an enemy tracker, the best bet is to either try to outdistance him or to double back and ambush him.

Appendix C

Vessels for Operations in Water

Over the years, increasingly sophisticated methods of inserting specially trained soldiers from the sea using traditional and new vessels or vehicles have been developed as seaborne, riverine and maritime operations are carried out in many conflicts. Insertion via the enemy's coastline or movement along it by "island hopping" are favoured Special Forces tactics as units operating at night in small craft are invariably difficult to spot. Canoe or kayaks have been used in Operation Rimau, a commando reconnaissance mission mounted against the Japanese fleet based in the strategic port of Singapore during World War II. Even in recent conflicts, the two-man Klepper canoe, made of wood and treated cotton, enabled British SAS units to silently infiltrate the enemy's coast and inland waterways. Light assault boats have been employed by British and Malayan forces in Borneo and the Malay peninsula during the insurgency years of the 1960s right through the 1980s. Riverine patrol/assault vessels were utilised extensively by the US Special Forces, especially the US Navy SEAL teams in Vietnam conflict of the 1970s.

For Special Forces or commando units operating in the riverine and coastal areas, anything from local canoes to landing craft, have been employed. The ability to deploy Special Forces teams in the face of adverse sea conditions is of great advantage, not least in the area of surprise. The need for fast clandestine insertion of commandos has led many militaries to procure fast assault boats, either rigid raider craft or rigid inflatable boats. They are increasingly popular, being flexible and quite inexpensive. Such fast small craft are intended to insert reconnaissance units during the earliest stages of an amphibious operation or straight into battle in actual counter-insurgency or anti-terrorist operations.

Inflatables and Rigid Raiders

Initially, inflatable boats were developed for use in the navy for transporting torpedoes and other cargo as well as other applications. Today, Special Forces organisation around the world use inflatable boats, particularly RIBs, for many applications inshore and offshore. During the Falklands conflict, British patrols were then inserted by the boat close to the shore to begin their reconnaissance of the Argentinean positions prior to the main amphibious landings on West Falkland. SAS patrols landing by sea along a hostile shoreline are usually inserted by Rigid Raider boats. The boats are five-meter long, have fiber-glass hulls and are fitted with 140 hp Johnson outboard engines, or similar, and can reach speeds of up to 35 knots. Their low silhouette, coupled with modified, near-silent engines, make vessels such as these practical and effective craft for the clandestine infiltration and extraction of SF patrols along enemy-held coastlines. US Navy SEALs also use these agile rigid inflatable boats or RIBs which has hard fiberglass hulls with inflatable sides. They also developed the STAB or SEAL team assault boat, a lightweight outboard engine-powered vessel based on a commercial trimaran design.

Another example of such a fast amphibious, albeit bigger, assault boat is the Swedish CB90H. The CB90H has a welded aluminium construction with a reinforced bottom to withstand rough landings on all types of shoreline through its forward blow ramp. Standard displacement is 16 tons, fully manned and tanked. The boats have a loading capacity of 21-armed soldiers or up to 4.5 tons of cargo. Two tailor-made water jet propulsion units, each turned by a 460 kW diesel engine, provide unusual manoeuvrability and continuous speeds exceeding 40 knots. Machineguns can be mounted in a fixed installation, or stabilised and remotely controlled from a monitor in the wheel-house. Other available weapon systems include mines or guided-missiles, which can be carried on board. A newly developed, gyro-stabilised twin-barrel 120 mm mortar makes the CB90H even more flexible for naval applications worldwide.

The Zodiac Company has been continually developing its standard inflatables and now offers five distinct ranges, each designed specifically for a family of uses. In the 50 years that Zodiac has been developing these standard inflatables, they have acquired an unmistakable Zodiac "look" that many forces have purposefully continued to use. Well-known throughout the world as the definitive Special Forces boat, the FC range is used by more elite soldiers and sailors than any other craft worldwide. It is the only craft of its type that has actually been used in combat in different theatres and comes through with flying colours.

This is a result of its unique patented hull shape and various floor systems that allows it to carry combatants in a variety of missions. The hull shape is especially important as it can get a large load on the plane as well as give the driver unsurpassed manoeuvrability in different and often dangerous conditions. Continually being updated for its ever-changing roles, the FC range is Zodiac's most recognisable military boat.

Zodiac has recently unveiled Armorflate (patent pending), the world's first inflatable bullet resistant system for Combat Rubber Raiding Craft (CRRC). The inflatable Armorflate system made its debut on the legendary Zodiac F-470 CRRC, which has been used for decades by military and Special Forces operations worldwide. The Armorflate system is available with soft armour made from a ballistic material provided by Simula, Inc. The soft armour package folds and stores on the inflatable tubes in minimal space and when needed can be inflated rapidly (about 40 seconds) to provide armour protection for CRRC occupants, the boat and the engine. Hard armour panels can be inserted in pockets on the inflated soft armour panels to provide upgraded protection. The armour is combined with Zodiac's high-pressure fabric panels.

Another maker of specialised inflatable rubber boats is Sillinger. The company's UM range of inflatable boats in the UM range have proved their efficiency and reliability over a long period of time. They have become indispensable to military and professional users. In order to satisfy as many requirements as possible, Sillinger has designed the boats in the UM range in two distinct versions—folding and semi rigid boats.

The Australian company Western Boat Builders makes Special Forces vessels of various types. The Special Covert Operations and Insertion boat is an aluminium vessel designed especially for the Australian Special Air Service Regiment. Designed with reliability, speed and agility in mind, this boat has already proven its strength in trials. Of three manufacturers who supplied prototypes, this boat was the only one to complete the exhaustive 79 days of trials and tests by the army. The others lasted 12 and 18 days respectively and were not considered for the finale of a gruelling coastline voyage from Melbourne to Sydney.

Capable of being parachuted from aircraft into action these are a highly reliable and cost-effective option for Special Forces covert operations. Powered by a Styre engine and utilising Hamilton water jet propulsion this craft has a range of some 200 kilometers. Especially, designed for elite forces it is extremely strong and seaworthy. Military standards demand high quality and high performance, this boat meets such demands with an expected working life far in excess of other vessels of this type.

Meanwhile, US boat-maker Safe Boats International along with Raytheon Naval & Maritime Integrated Systems are currently carrying out a US $30 million contract to make assault boats to transport US Marine Corps' Special Forces in shallow waters. The first three test boats were shipped to Camp Lejeune, North Carolina, for evaluation. Once the test boats are evaluated, the contract will cover 25 to 30 additional boats. The 36-foot-long boats can transport up to 20 people—two Special Forces teams and a crew—at speeds over 40 knots. Equipped with a water-jet-propulsion system, made by HamiltonJet of Seattle, they can manoeuvre in the shallow waters of rivers and shorelines. Safe Boats supplies vessels to law enforcement agencies and the Coast Guard.

Landing Vessels and Vehicles

Numerous variations of the basic landing vessels/vehicles were produced to perform all manner of roles in the mission of landing troops ashore in big scale amphibious operations. Highly adaptable was the American amphibious wheeled DUKW or "duck", which carried a useful load and could drive on land without adjustment after swimming ashore, as too could the American Amtrac assault vehicles which were propelled through the water by their tracks and served as light tanks or armoured personnel carriers once ashore. These both the ducks and Amtracs, early versions thereof, have been deployed by the French in support of counter-insurgency and Special Forces operations against Vietminh insurgents during the earlier part of the Indo-China war.

Hovercraft Assault

The hovercraft was once judged by several forces, including the Royal Navy, as too noisy, too thirsty for fuel and too unreliable for all-weather military operations. The same problems also plagued hovercraft operations of US Forces during the Vietnam conflict. However, with improvements in technology, the air cushion craft or hovercraft has now been accepted by most navies as it allows for high-speed over-the-horizon assaults and can operate over swamps and shoals. These come in various sizes, from the small British Griffon series to larger vessels in the form of the Textron Marine & Land Systems-made Landing Craft Air Cushion or LCAC (in service with the US Navy and Japan's Maritime Self-Defence Force) and the Russian-built Project 12061 Murena LCAC.

Appendix D

Arm and Hand Signals

Jungle operations may demand working in complete silence. Hence, a very elaborate set of arm and hand signals have been developed to convey instructions silently. I am giving some of them here.

Listen or I Hear

Watch or I See

Cover This Area

Go Here or Move Up

Dog

Cell Leader

Column Formation
File Formation
Line Abreast Formation
Pistol
Rifle
Shotgun
I Understand
I Don't Understand
Crouch or Go Prone

Wedge Formation

Rally Point

Ammunition

Vehicle

Breach(er)

Gas

Door
Window
Point of Entry
ASSEMBLE
RIGHT (LEFT) FLANK MOVE
ECHELON RIGHT (LEFT)
FORM COLUMN
LINE FORMATION; DEPLOY INTO LINE ABREAST
"V" FORMATION
FORWARD
OPEN UP; EXTEND
CLOSED "V" FORMATION; CLOSE THE "V"
HALT; STOP
CLOSE UP
OPEN "V" FORMATION; OPEN THE "V"

A Select Bibliography

Adams, James, *Secret Armies*, Hutchinson, 1987.

Aircraft Armament, Systems and Components, US Army Weapons Command, Rock Island, December 1971.

Aircraft Weaponisation, Sub-system Photographs and Descriptions, US Army Weapons Command, Rock Island, September 1970.

Al Baker, Commander B Co, 4/9 Inf, RVN '67 - '68

Alan AD Hamilton, *The Boondocks and the Zoo*, Wargames Illustrated 22, June 1989.

Alspach, R., et al. *New and Improved: T-Ration and MRE Development*. Quartermaster Professional Bulletin. December 1988.

Armadilhas, Minas, E. (Tr)., *Mines and Booby-traps*, US Army Foreign Service and Technology Center, Department of the Army, 1969.

Armies of the Vietnam War 1962-75, Men-At-Arms Series 104, P Katcher & M Chappel, Osprey.

Army Special Operations Forces Unconventional Warfare, FM 3-05.130, US Army, 2008.

Army Special Operations Forces Unconventional Warfare, FM 3-05.130, US Army, 2008.

Army Special Operations Forces, FM 3-05, US Army, 2006.

Asher, Michael, *Shoot to Kill: A Soldier's Journey Through Violence*, Cassell Military Paperbacks, 1990.

Ballinger, Adam, *The Quiet Soldier: On Selection With 21 SAS*, Orion Paperbacks, 2004.

Barber, Noel, *The War of the Running Dogs: How Malaya Defeated the Communist Guerrillas*, 1948-60, Collins, 1971.

Barber, Noel, *The War of the Running Dogs: Malaya, 1948-1960*, New York: Weybright and Tulley, 1971.

Baudrier, Michael, *Love & Terror in Malaya*, Trafford Publishing, 2005.

Billiere, Peter de la, *Looking for Trouble: SAS to Gulf Command – The Autobiography*, Harper Collins, 1995.

Boot, Max. *The Savage Wars of Peace: Small Wars and the Rise of American Power*. Basic Books, 2002.

British Commandos, Special Series No. 1, MID 461, Military Intelligence Service, War Department, USA, 1942.

Callwell, Charles E Small, *Wars: Their Principles and Practice*. Lincoln, NE: University of Nebraska.

Camouflage, Concealment and Decoys, FM 20-3, US Army, 1999.

Camouflage, FM 5-20, US Army, 1968.

Cash, John A; Albright, John; and Sandstrum, Allan W., *Seven Firefights in Vietnam: Convoy Ambush On Highway 1, 21 November 1966*, US Army, Command and General Staff College, Combined Arms Research Library, US Army, Center for Military History: Vietnam Studies, 1985.

CFP 302(4) Part Two – *A Soldier's Guide to the Jungle*, Chief of Defence Staff, Canada.

Chant, Christopher, *Fighting Helicopters of the 20th Century (20th Century Military Series)*. Graham Beehag Books, 1996.

Chapman, Spencer, *The Jungle is Neutral*, Lyons Press, 2003.

Chiarelli, Peter W and Patrick R Michaelis, *Winning the Peace: The Requirement for Full-Spectrum Operations*, Military Review 85, 4 (July-Aug 2005), 4—17.

Chynoweth, John, *Hunting Terrorists in the Jungle*, The History Press, 2007.

Coffee, Hugh L, *Ditch Medicine: Advanced Field Procedures for Emergencies*, Paladin Press, 1993.

Collins, Michael; Collins, Patrick; Cummings, Charles; and Tyler, Hay, *Reliability of Load Bearing Systems*, Worcester Polytechnic Institute, 2010.

Combat Skills of the Soldier, FM-21-75, US Army, 1984.

Commander's Tactical Handbook, MCRP 3-11.1A, US Marine Corps, 1988.

Conventional Warfare: Ballistic, Blast and Burn Injuries, US Army Medical Department, Borden Institute.

Counter-ambush Techniques, Chapter 5, Seabee Combat Handbook Part 2, Naval Education and Training.

Counter IED Smart Book (Iraq), GTA 90-10-046, USA, 2008.

Counter Improvised Explosive Device, International Security Assistance Force, Smart Book.

Counter-guerrilla Operations, FM 90-8/MCRP 3-33A, US Marine Corps, 1986.

Counter-insurgency Lessons Learned #60, US Army, 10th September 1966.

Counter-insurgency, FM 3-24, US Army, 2006.

Crawford, Steve, *The SAS at Close Quarters: Great Battles of the SAS*, Pan MacMillan, 1993.

Crew-Served Machineguns, 5.56 mm and 7.62 mm, FM 3-22.68, US Army, 2003.

Cross, JP, *Jungle Warfare: Experiences and Encounters*, Arms & Armour Press, 1989.

Cummings & Del Beccaro: *Antibiotics to Prevent Infection of Simple Wounds: A Meta-Analysis of Randomized Studies*, Am J of Emerg Med, Vol. 13, No. 4, July 95.

Darman, Peter, *A-Z of the SAS*, Sidgwick & Jackson, 1993.

Darman, Peter, *SAS: The World's Best*, Sidgwick & Jackson, 1994.

Darman, Peter, *Weapons and Equipment of the SAS*, Stackpole Books, 1997.

de B Taillon, J Paul (2000). *The Evolution of Special Forces in Counter-Terrorism*, The British and American Experiences. Greenwood.

Debay, Yves, *Combat Helicopters*, Histoire & Collections, 1996.

Dickens, Peter, *SAS: The Jungle Frontier-22nd Specal Air Service regiment in The Borneo Campaign (1963-1966)*, Arms & Armour Press, 1983.

Doleman, Edgar D Tools of War, *The Vietnam Experience*. Boston Publishing, 1984.

Drendel, Lou, *Gunslingers in Action*, Squadron/Signal Publications, 1974.

Drendel, Lou. Huey, Squadron/Signal Publications, 1983.

Dunnigan, James F, *The Perfect Soldier: Special Operations*, Citadel Press, 2003.

Eden, Paul, ed. *Bell UH-1 Iroquois. Encyclopedia of Modern Military Aircraft*. Amber Books, 2004.

Ehrhart, WD, *Vietnam-Perkasie: A Combat Marine Memoir, with contrib*. H Bruce Franklin, University of Massachusetts Press (1995).

Ellis, John. *From the Barrel of a Gun: A History of Guerrilla, Revolutionary, and Counter-insurgency Warfare from the Romans to the Present*. Greenhill, 1995.

Emergency Bleeding Control, St John Ambulance Western Australia.

Ergonomic Load Bearing Systems: Final Technical Report, (Under The Funding of US Department of Justice), Blackhawk Products Group, Virginia, 2010.

Field Rations, Olive-Drab.com.

Fitness Programme, Air Force Instruction 10-248, US Air Force, 2006.

Fleet Marine Force Reference Publication (FMFRP) 12-40, *Professional Knowledge Gained from Operational Experience in Vietnam*, 1965-1966.

Fleet Marine Force Reference Publication (FMFRP) 12-41, *Professional Knowledge Gained from Operational Experience in Vietnam*, 1967.

Follows, Roy, *The Jungle Beat: Fighting Terrorists in Malaya*, Eye Books Direct, 1999.

Foot Marches, FM 21-18, US Army, 1971.

For Special Forces, FM 31-20-5, US Army, 1990.

Francillon, René J, *Vietnam: The War in the Air*. Arch Cape Press, 1987.

Fremont-Barnes, Gregory (2009). *Who Dares Wins – The SAS and the Iranian Embassy Siege 1980*. Osprey Publishing.

Galula, David, *Counter-insurgency Warfare – Theory and Practice*. Praeger, 1964.

Geraghty, Tony, *Inside The SAS*, Ballantine Books, 1980.

Gilbert, Marc Jason, *Why The North Won The Vietnam War*, Palgrave Macmillan, 2002.

Glade, Bill, *Caring for Wounds in the Field*, Backwoods Home Magazine, March 05, 2012.

Guilmartin, John Francis and Michael O'Leary. *The Illustrated History of The Vietnam War*, Volume 11: Helicopters. Bantam Books, 1988.

Hall, Peter, *Jungle Jim*, Publ. privately by Louis Scully.

Hammes, *TX The Sling and the Stone: On War in the 21st Century*, Zenith Press, 2004.

Harris, Dave, *Military History: The SAS – Jungle Warriors*

Hay, Jr, John H Hay, *Tactical and Materiel Innovations*, US Army, Vietnam Studies, 1989.

Helicopter Losses During the Vietnam War, Vietnam Helicopter Pilots Association.

Helicopter Rope Suspension Techniques (HRST) Operations, MCRP 3-11.4A, US Marine Corps, 2003.

Henderson, Charles, *Marine Sniper: 93 Confirmed Kills*, Berkely, 1988.

Herbert, Anthony B, *Soldier's Handbook*, Cloverleaf Press, 1979.

History of Military Nutrition in The United States, Wikipedia.

History of Military Nutrition, Military-Nutrition.com.

Horne, Alistair, *A Savage War of Peace*. New York: Viking, 1977.

Horner, David, *Phantoms of the Jungle: History of The Australian SAS*, Allen & Unwin, 1989.

Hunter-Killer Squadron, Matthew Brennan, Pocket Books.

ILBE Improved Load Bearing Equipment, Olive-Drab.com.

In The 'Stan IEDs Come From Above, US Naval Institute, citing *USA Today*, Jan 26, 2009.

Indian National Snakebite Protocols 2007, Indian National Snakebite Protocol Consultation Meeting, Delhi, 2007.

Infantry Ambush and Counter-Ambush, B-GL-392-008/FP-001, Chief of Land Staff, Canada, 2001.

Infantry in Vietnam: Small Unit Actions in the Early Days 1965-66, edited by LTC Albert N. Garland, USA (Ret)., The Battery Press, 1982 Edition.

Infantry Rifle Platoon and Squad, FM 7-8, US Army, 1992.

Inside the VC and the NVA, Michael Lee Lanning & Dan Cragg, Ivy Books 1994.

Institute of Medicine (US), Committee on Optimization of Nutrient Composition of Military Rations for Short-Term, High-Stress Situations, Nutrient composition of rations for short-term, high-intensity combat operations.

Interagency Helicopter Rappel Guide, Rappel Guide Task Group, National Interagency Rappel Working Group,

Jungle Operations, FM 90-5, US Army, !982.

Jungle Operations, FM 90-5, US Marine Corps, 1982.

Kearny, Cresson H (Maj), *Jungle Snafus...And Remedies*, Oregon Institute (1996).

Kennedy, Michael Paul, *Soldier 'I' SAS*, Bloomsbury, 1990.

Kilcullen, David. *Twenty-Eight Articles: Fundamentals of Company-level Counter-insurgency*. Military Review 86, 3 (May-Jun 2006), 103—108.

Kragh JF, Walters TJ, Baer DG, Fox CJ, Wade CE, Salinas J, Holcomb, JB, *Practical Use of Emergency Tourniquets to Stop Bleeding in Major Limb Trauma, J Trauma 64* (2 Suppl): S38–49, February 2008.

Krepinevich Jr, Andrew F, *The Army and Vietnam*, Johns Hopkins University Press, 1986.

Larteguy, Jean. *The Centurions*. New York: Dutton, 1962.

Linn, Brian McAllister. *The Philippine War*, 1899—1902. Lawrence, KS: University Press of Kansas, 2002.

Lookout Training Handbook, NAVEDTRA 12968-B, 2005.

Low Level Hell, Hugh L Mills, Dell Books.

Macdonald, Peter, *The SAS in Action*, Sidgwick & Jackson, 1990.

Maitland, Terrence, *A Contagion of War: The Vietnam Experience Series*, Boston Publishing Company, 1983.

Mao Zedong. *On Guerrilla Warfare*. London: Cassell, 1965.

Maraniss, David, *They Marched Into Sunlight*, Simon & Schuster, 2004.

Marine Corps Common Skills Handbook, Book 1B All Marines, Individual Training Standards, US Marine Corps, 2001.

Marine Corps Physical Fitness Programme, MCO 6100.13, US Marine Corps, 2008.

Marine Corps Physical Fitness Test and Body Composition Programme Manual, MCO P6100.12, US Marine Corps, 2002.

Marine Physical Readiness for Combat, MCRP 3-02A, Marine Corps Combat Development Command, US Marine Corps, 1988.

Martinage, Robert, Center for Strategic and Budgetary Assessments, *Special Operations Forces: Challenges and Opportunities, Testimony Before the US House of Representatives*, House Committee on Armed Services,

Subcommittee on Terrorism, Unconventional Threats and Capabilities, 2009.

McAllion, Harry, *Killing Zone*, Blloomsbury, 1996.

McBreen, BB, *War Stories: Infantry Techniques I*, Project Leatherneck, US Marine Corps, 1995.

McCuen, John J *The Art of Counter-Revolutionary War*, St Petersburg, FL: Hailer Publishing, 2005.

McKenna, Tech. Sgt. Pat (1998-04-01). *Lean, Mean Fighting Cuisine*. Airman Magazine (Air Force News Agency). http://www.af.mil/news/airman/0498/mre2.htm.

Mcnab, Andy, *Bravo Two-Zero: The true Story of an SAS Patrol Behind Enemy Lines in Iraq*, Corgi, 1994.

McNab, Andy, *Immediate Action*, Corgi, 1996.

McNab, Chris, *The SAS Training Manual*, Zenith Imprint, 2002.

Medication Appendix, FMST Student Manual, Field Medical Training Battalion, United States Marine Corps.

Mesko, Jim. *Airmobile: The Helicopter War in Vietnam*. Squadron/Signal Publications, 1984.

Miglietta, Maurizio A., *Trauma and Gunshot wounds: What You Need to Know to Save a Life*, NYU Physician, Vol. 58, No. 1, Fall 2006.

Mikesh, Robert C, *Flying Dragons: The South Vietnamese Air Force*. Osprey Publishing, 1988.

Military Nutrition Division Brochure. USARIEM. 2008.

Military Operations; Vietnam Primer - Dept of the Army, 1967 by Brig Gen SLA Marshall (Ret) & Lt Col David Hackworth (Ret)

MK 19, 40 mm Grenade Machinegun, Mod 3, FM 3-22.27, US Army, 2003.

Modern Military Nutrition Research (1986–present), Military Nutrition.com.

Modular Lightweight Load Carrying Equipment (MOLLE), Olive-Drab.com.

Moreman, Tim, Chindit (1942-45) Warrior, Osprey Publishing, 2009.

Mountain Operations, FM 31-72, US Army, 1959.

Moynahan, Bryan, *Jungle Soldier: The True Story of Freddy Spnecer Chapman*, Quercus, 2009.

Mutza, Wayne, *UH-1 Huey in Action*. Squadron/Signal Publications, 1986.

Nagl, John A, *Learning to Eat Soup with a Knife: Counter-insurgency Lessons from Malaya and Vietnam*, Chicago: University of Chicago Press, 2005.

Nbk, American & NVA Weapons & Tactics in Vietnam, eBook.

Night Warrior Handbook: A Guide to Individual Training for Night Combat in the Infantry Company, 2nd Battalion, 5th Marines, Camp Pendleton, California, 2000.

Non-Operative Field Wound Care, Col Cliff Coonan, Vice Chair, Dept of Military and Emergency Medicine USU

O'Neill, Bard E, *Insurgency and Terrorism: From Revolution to Apocalypse.* Dulles, VA: Potomac Press, 1996.

Opposing Force Organisation Guide, FM 7-100.4, US Army, 2007.

Page, Tim and Pimlott, John (Eds)., *'Nam, The Vietnam Experience*, Orbis Publishing Ltd, 1987.

Peavey, Robert E, *Praying for Slack: A Marine Corps Tank Commander in Vietnam*, Zenith Imprint Press (2004).

Petraeus, David. *Learning Counter-insurgency: Observations from Soldiering in Iraq*. Military Review 86, 1 (Jan-Feb 2006), 2—12.

Philip, Craig; and Taylor, Alex, Bloomsbury, 1994.

Physical Fitness Training, FM 21-20, US Army, 1998.

Physical Security, FM 3-19.30, US Army, 2001.

Pike, Douglas, *PAVN: Peoples Army of Vietnam*, Presidio, 1996.

Plaster, John L, *SOG: The Secret Wars of America's Commandos in Vietnam*, Onyx, 1998.

Pribbenow, Merle, (Tr)., *Victory in Vietnam. The Official History of the People's Army of Vietnam*, University Press of Kansas, 2002

Price, Major David H., *The Army Aviation Story Part XI: The Mid-1960*, US Army Aviation Digest, July 1976.

Professional Development and Technology Center, USA, 1996.

Professional Knowledge Gained From Operational Experience in Vietnam, 1968, FMFRP 12-42, US Marine Corps, 1989.

Ramsay, Jack, *SAS: The Soldier's Story*, Pan Books, 1997.

RAND Corp, *Insurgent Organisation and Operations: A Case Study of the Viet Cong in the Delta, 1964-1966*, (Santa Monica: August 1967).

Ranger Handbook, SH 21-76, Ranger Training Brigade, United States Army Infantry School, 2006.

Ranger Unit Operations, FM 7-85, US Army, 1987.

Rappelling Techniques and Procedures, B-GL-392-003/FP-001, Chief of Land Staff, Canada, 2002.

Rappelling, TC 21-24, US Army, 2008.

Ryan, Chris, *The One That Got Away*, Arrow, 2008.

Ryan, Chris, *Who Dares Wins*, Century, 2009.

Ryan, *The Evolution of the Modern Military Backpack*, Military Surplus, 2010.

Scholey, Pete; Forsyth, Frederick (2008). *Who Dares Wins: Special Forces Heroes of the SAS*. Osprey Publishing.

Scouting and Patrolling, MCWP 3-11.3, US Marine Corps, 2000.

Secrets of the Viet Cong, J W McCoy, Hippocrene Books 1992,

Self-care in the Field, Sydney Vail, Director of Trauma & Trauma Critical Care, Carilion Roanoke Memorial Hospital, Roanoke, Virginia, Adjunct Instructor Heckler & Koch International Training Division, Tactical Emergency Medicine Courses, Medical Director Tactical EMS Support for Emergency Response Team, Salem, Virginia

Sepp, Kalev I, *Best Practices in Counter-insurgency.* Military Review 85, 3 (May-Jun 2005), 8 – 12.

Small Wars Manual, US Marine Corps. Washington, D.C.: Government Printing Office, 1987.

Sniper Sustainment Training, US Army Snipers.

Sniper Training, FM 23-10, US Army, 1994.

Special Forces Operational Techniques, FM 31-20, US Army, 1971.

Special Forces Operations, FM 3-05.20, US Army, 2001.

Special Forces Operations, ST 31-201, John F Kennedy Special Warfare Center, US Army, 1978.

Special Forces Sniper Training and Employment, FM 3-05.222, US Army, 2003.

Special Reconnaissance Tactics, Techniques, and Procedures

Specific Operations Vol. 4, Part One, *Jungle Operations,* B-OG-302-004/FP-001 (CFP 30214), Part One), Chief of Defence Staff, Canada, 1978.

Stevens, Gordon (2005). *The Originals – The Secret History of the Birth of the SAS in their Own Words.* Ebury Press.

Survival and Austere Medicine: An Introduction Second edition, Written and Edited by The Remote, Austere, Wilderness and Third World Medicine Discussion Board Moderators, April 2005

Survival, Evasion, and Recovery: Multiservice Procedures for Survival, Evasion, and Recovery, FM 21-76-1, MCRP 3-02H, NWP 3-50.3, and AFTTP(I) 3-2.26, US Army, Marine Corps, Navy, Air Force, 1999.

Survival, FM 3-05.70, US Army, 2002.

Taber, Robert. *War of the Flea: The Classic Study of Guerrilla Warfare.* Dulles, VA: Potomac Books, 2002.

Tactical Combat Casualty Care, US Army Institute of Surgical Research, Feb. 2010

Tactics in Counter-insurgency, FM 3-24.2, US Army, 2009.

The Guerrilla and How to Fight Him, FMFRP 12-25, Fleet Marine Force Reference Publication, US Marine Corps, 1990.

The Infantry Battalion, FM 3-21.20, US Army, 2006.

The Infantryman's Combat Load, Globalsecurity.org, 1985.

The Soviet Army: Specialised Warfare and Rear Area Support, FM 100-2-2, US Army, 1984.

The Special Air Service Regiment, The Defence Reserves Yearbook 2004-05.

The US Army in Vietnam, Leroy Thompson, David & Charles Publishers,

Thompson, Leroy (1994). *SAS: Great Britain's Elite Special Air Service*. Zenith Imprint.

Thompson, Leroy, *SAS: Great Britain's Elite Special Air Service*, Motorbooks International, 1994.

Trinquier, Roger. *Modern Warfare – A French View of Counter-insurgency*. New York: Praeger, 1964.

Unit Defense Checklist, Appendix H, FM 6-50, US Army, 1990.

United States Marine Corps. Tactics (Marine Corps Doctrinal Publications MCDP 1.3). New York: Wildside, 2005.

US Army Military Assistance Advisory Group Vietnam (MAAG) - *Lessons Learned No. 25* Search Techniques (December 1962).

US Army Military Assistance Advisory Group Vietnam (MAAG) - *Lessons Learned No. 71 Counter-measures Against Standoff Attacks* (March 1969).

US Army Military Assistance Advisory Group, Vietnam (MAAG), *Lessons Learned No. 56 Operations Against Tunnel Complexes*, April 1966.

US Army Special Forces Medical Handbook, ST 31-91B, US Army Institute for Medical Assistance, *Tactical Combat Casualty Care and Wound Treatment, Sub-course MD0554*, US Army Medical Department Center and School, Fort Sam Houston, Texas.

US Army Special Operations Target Interdiction Course, *Sniper Training and Employment*.

Vietcong Mine Warfare, US Marine Corps Base, Quantico, Department of the Navy, 1966.

Vietnam Lessons Learned No. 39: Ambush Operations. US Army Military Assistance Advisory Group Vietnam (MAAG), March 1964.

Vietnam Lessons Learned No. 77: Fire Support Coordination in the Republic of Vietnam. United States Military Assistance Command, Vietnam, 20th May 1970.

Vietnam Weapons Handbook, David Rosser-Owen, Patrick Stephens Limited, 1986,

Vietnam, Handbook: What A Platoon Leader Should Know about the Enemy's Jungle Tactics, US Army Combined Intelligence Center, 1967.

Walters, Thomas J, and Mabry, Robert L, *Issues Related to the Use of Tourniquets on the Battlefield*, United States Army Institute of Surgical Research Combat Casualty Care Research Programme.

Weapons and Tactics of the Soviet Army, David C Isby, Janes Publishing,

Wells, Robert, ed, *The Invisible Enemy: Booby-traps in Vietnam*, Miami, FL: J Flores Publications, 1992.

Westheider, James E, *The Vietnam War*, Greenwood Publishing Group (2007).

Westmoreland, WC, *Report On Operations in South Vietnam*, January 1964-June 1968, in "Report On The War in Vietnam [As of 30 June 1968]', By

United States Pacific Command, Government Printing Office, Washington, DC, 1969.

Westrate, Edwin V, *Forward Observer*, New York: Stratford Press, 1944

White, Terry, *The Making of the SAS and the World's Elite Forces*, Greenhill Books, 1994.

White, Terry, *The SAS Fighting Techniques Handbook*, Globe Pequot Press (2007).

Willbanks, James H, *Abandoning Vietnam: How America Left and South Vietnam Lost Its War*, University Press of Kansas, 2004.

Wilson, Clay, *Improvised Explosive Devices (IEDs) in Iraq and Afghanistan: Effects and Counter-measures*, CRS Report for Congress, September 25, 2006.

Wilson, Clay, *Improvised Explosive Devices in Iraq: Effects and Counter-measures*, CRS Report for Congress, November 23, 2005.

Wiseman, Jose, *The SAS Survival Handbook*, Harvill, Harper Collins, 1986.

Index